# A Certain Magical Index

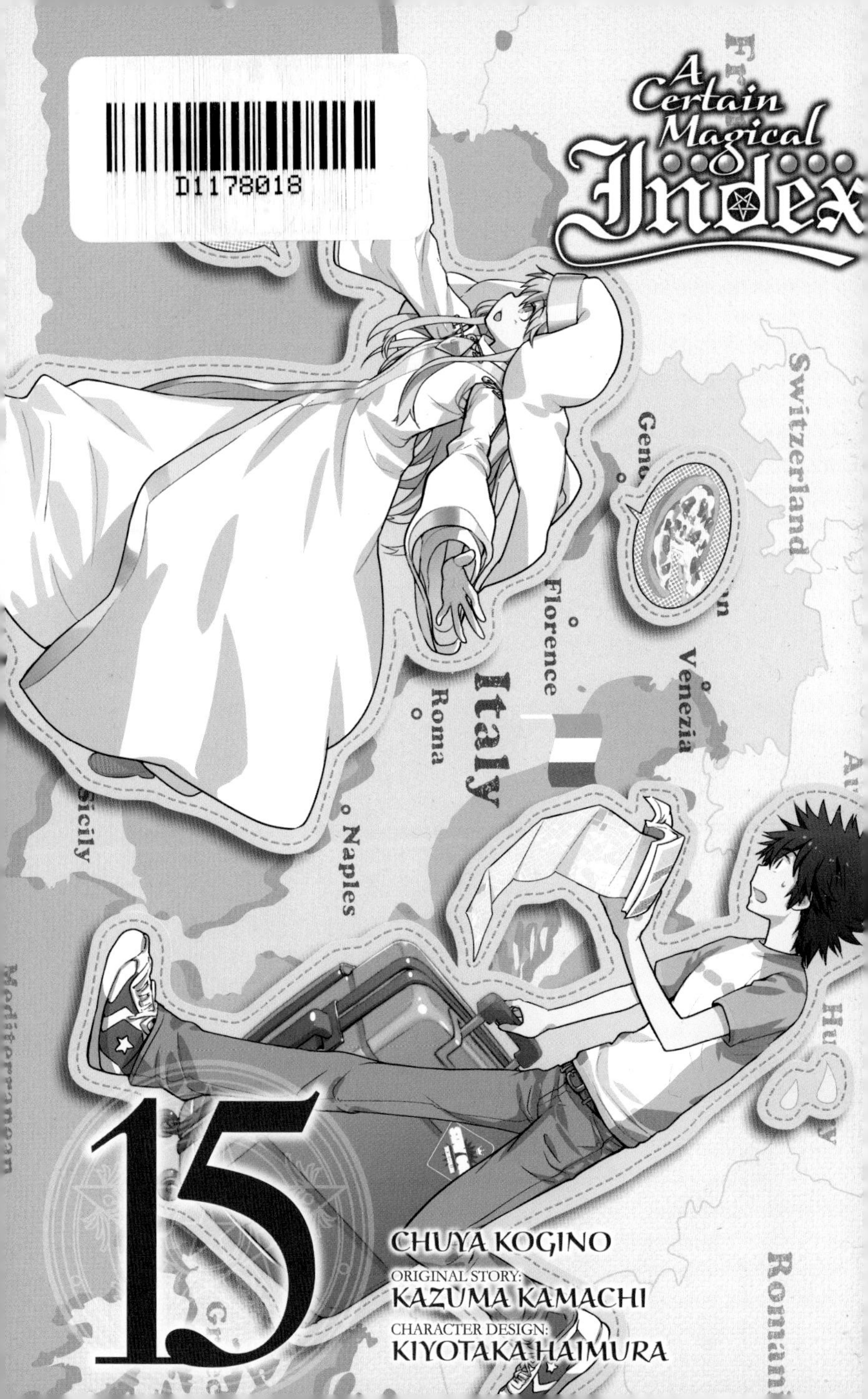
Switzerland
Florence
Venezia
Italy
Roma
Naples
Sicily

15

CHUYA KOGINO

ORIGINAL STORY:
KAZUMA KAMACHI

CHARACTER DESIGN:
KIYOTAKA HAIMURA

A CERTAIN MAGICAL INDEX ⑮ TABLE OF CONTENTS

Index Librorum Prohibitorum



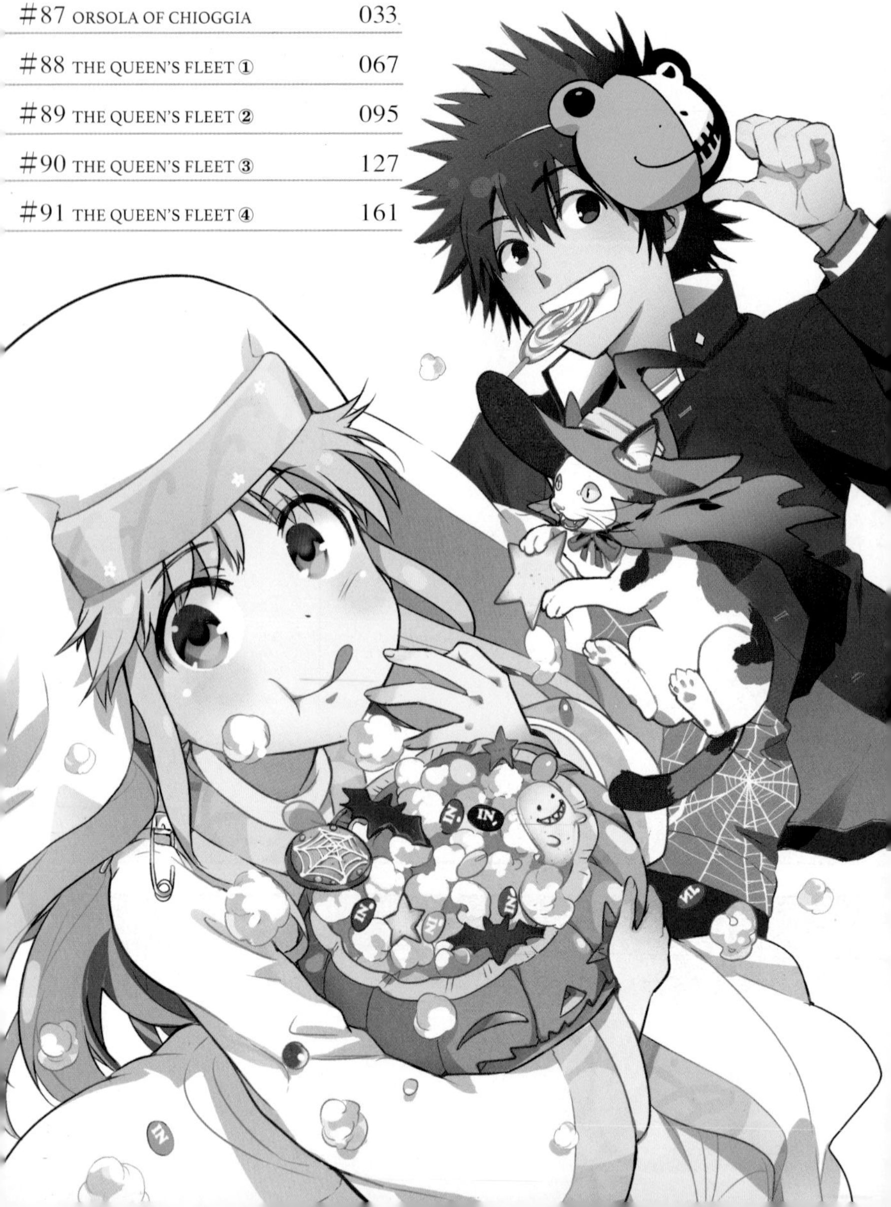

SIGN: FIVE NIGHTS, SEVEN DAYS / TRIP FOR TWO

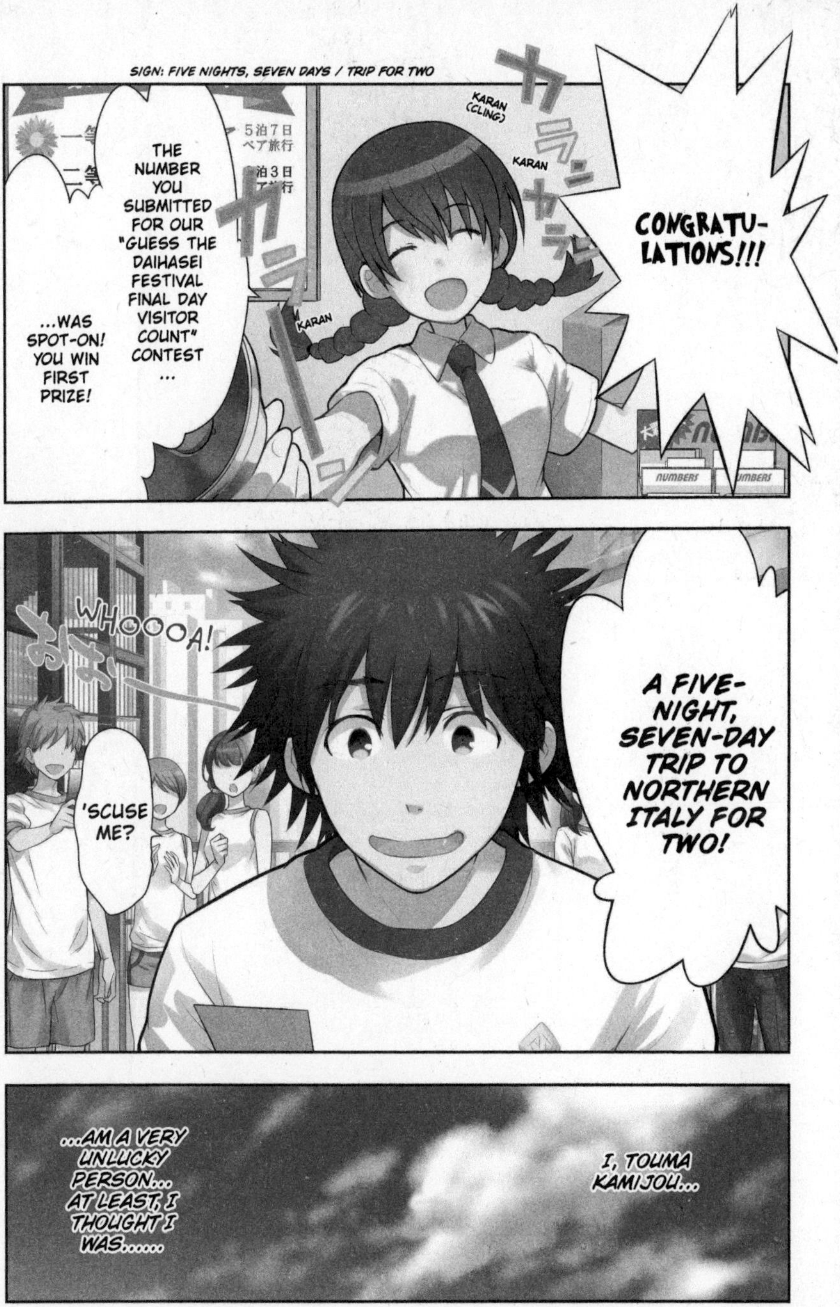
KARAN (CLING)
KARAN
CONGRATULATIONS!!!
KARAN
5泊7日 ペア旅行
THE NUMBER YOU SUBMITTED FOR OUR "GUESS THE DAIHASEI FESTIVAL FINAL DAY VISITOR COUNT" CONTEST...
...WAS SPOT-ON! YOU WIN FIRST PRIZE!
NUMBERS
NUMBERS
A FIVE-NIGHT, SEVEN-DAY TRIP TO NORTHERN ITALY FOR TWO!
WHOOOOA!
'SCUSE ME?
I, TOUMA KAMIJOU...
...AM A VERY UNLUCKY PERSON... AT LEAST, I THOUGHT I WAS......

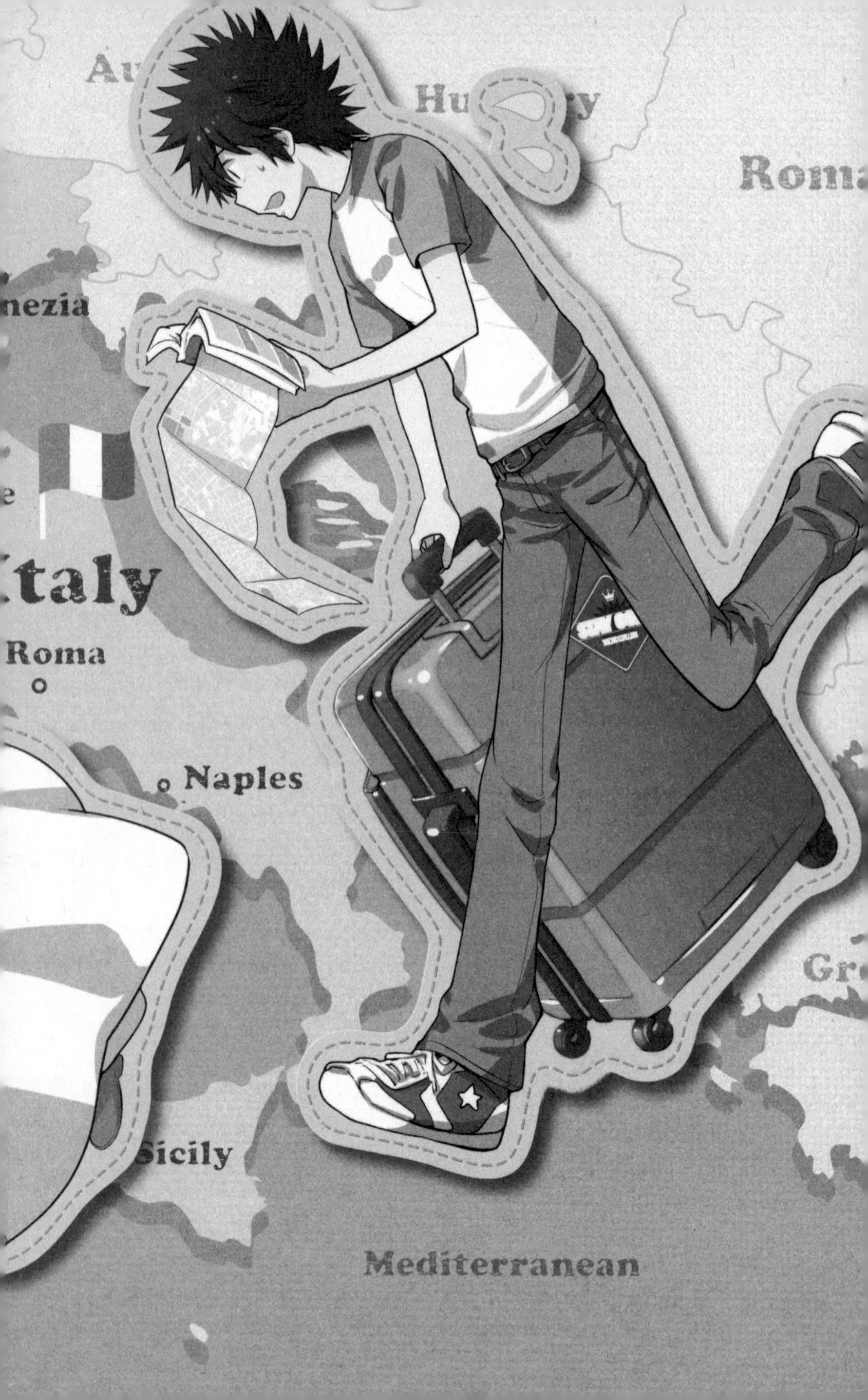
Au
Hu ry
Roma
nezia
e
Italy
Roma
Naples
Gr
Sicily
Mediterranean

# #86 LET'S GO ON A TRIP TO ITALY!

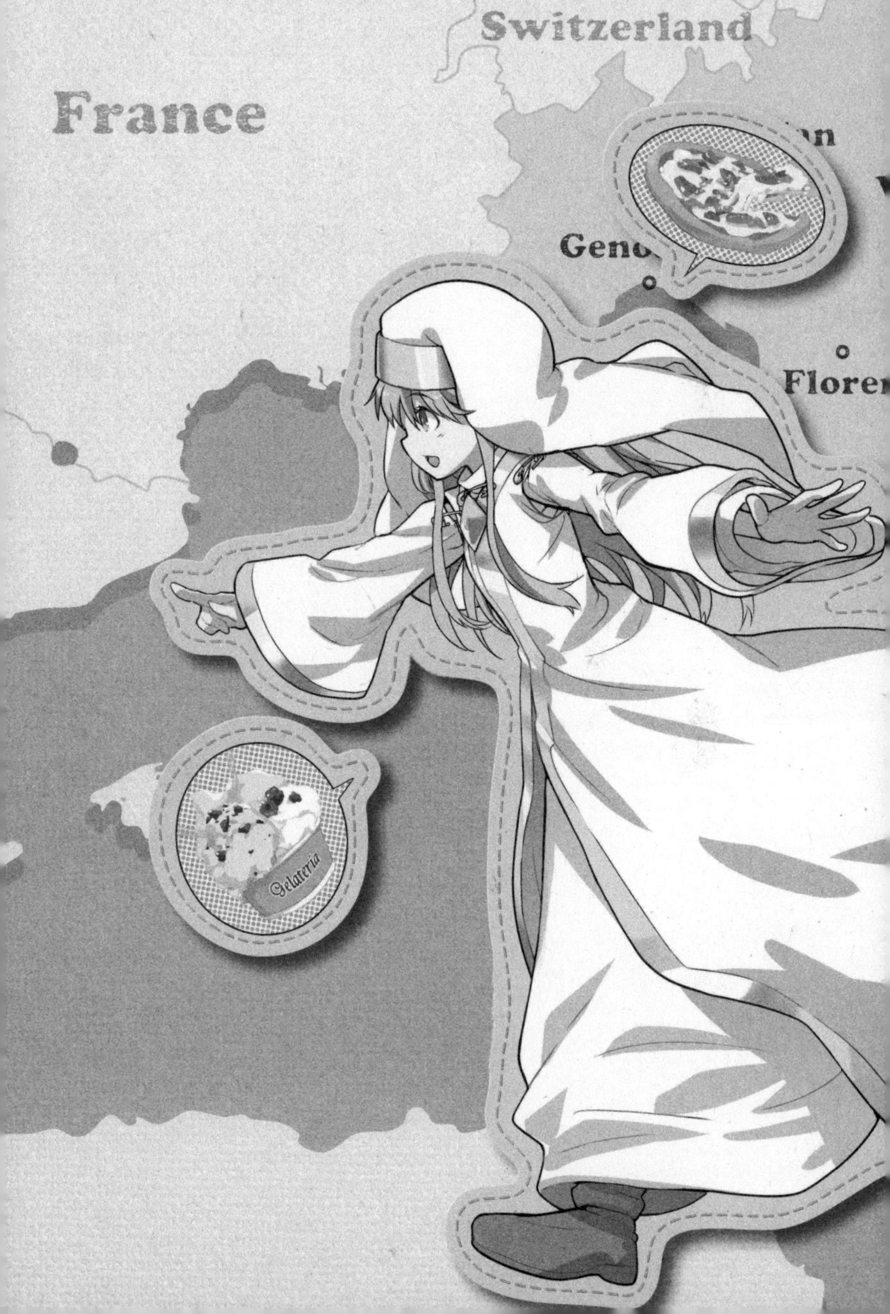
Switzerland
France
Gelateria

# A Certain Magical Index

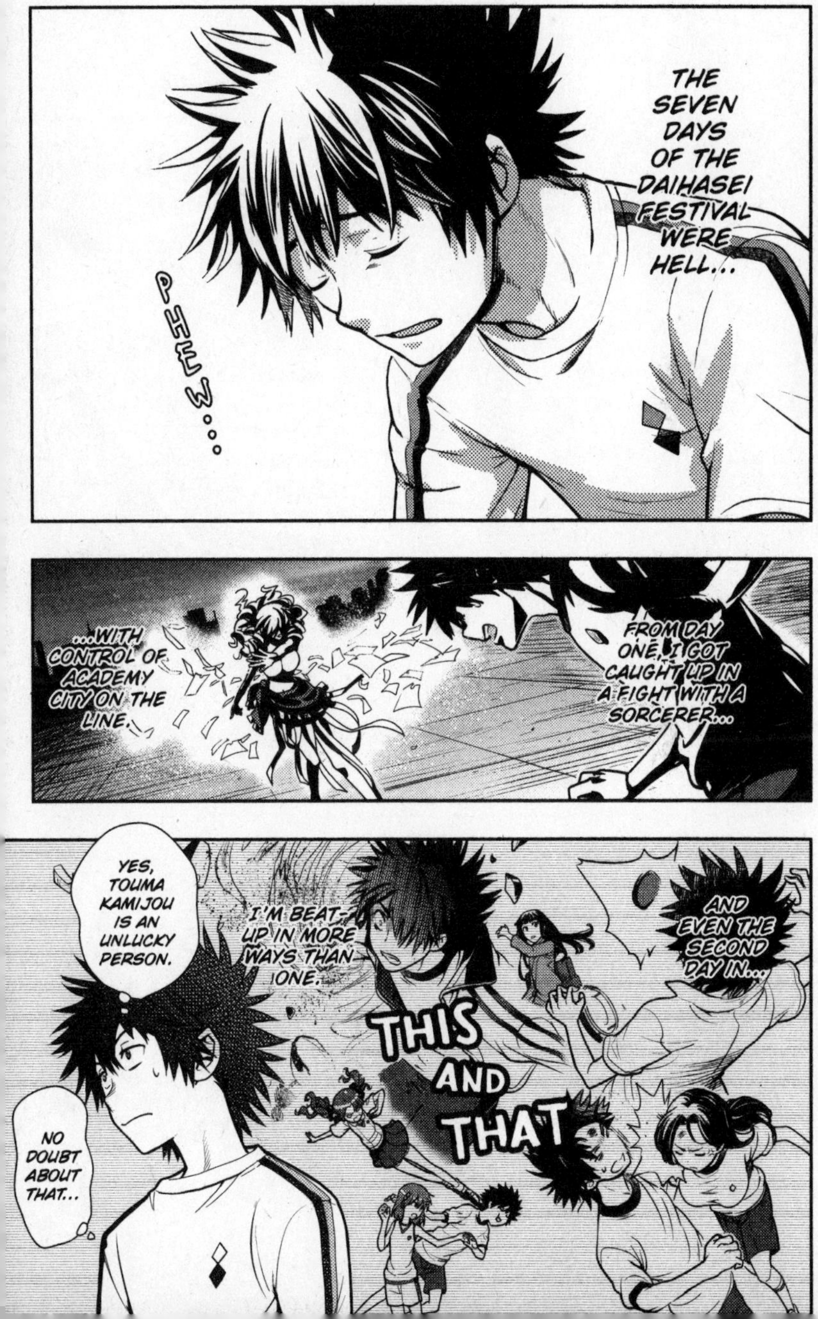
THE SEVEN DAYS OF THE DAIHASEI FESTIVAL WERE HELL...
PHEW...
FROM DAY ONE, I GOT CAUGHT UP IN A FIGHT WITH A SORCERER...
...WITH CONTROL OF ACADEMY CITY ON THE LINE.
AND EVEN THE SECOND DAY IN...
I'M BEAT-UP IN MORE WAYS THAN ONE.
THIS AND THAT
YES, TOUMA KAMIJOU IS AN UNLUCKY PERSON.
NO DOUBT ABOUT THAT...

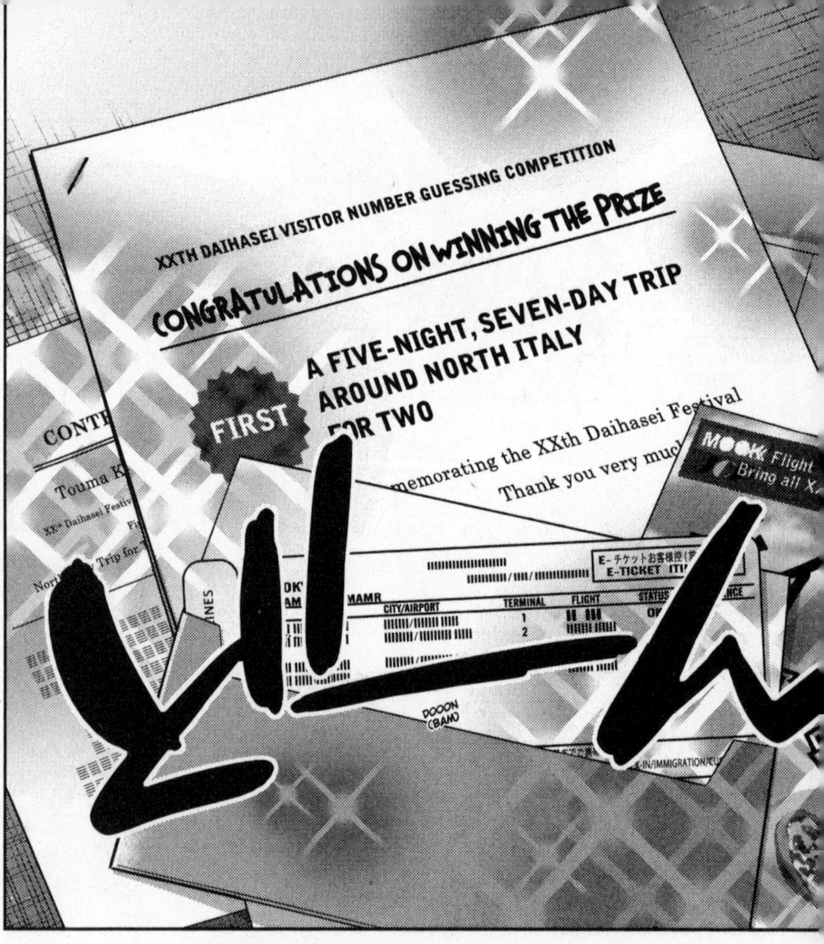
XXTH DAIHASEI VISITOR NUMBER GUESSING COMPETITION
CONGRATULATIONS ON WINNING THE PRIZE
FIRST
A FIVE-NIGHT, SEVEN-DAY TRIP AROUND NORTH ITALY FOR TWO
memorating the XXth Daihasei Festival
Thank you very muc
E-TICKET ITI
CITY/AIRPORT
TERMINAL
FLIGHT
STATUS
DOOON (BAM)
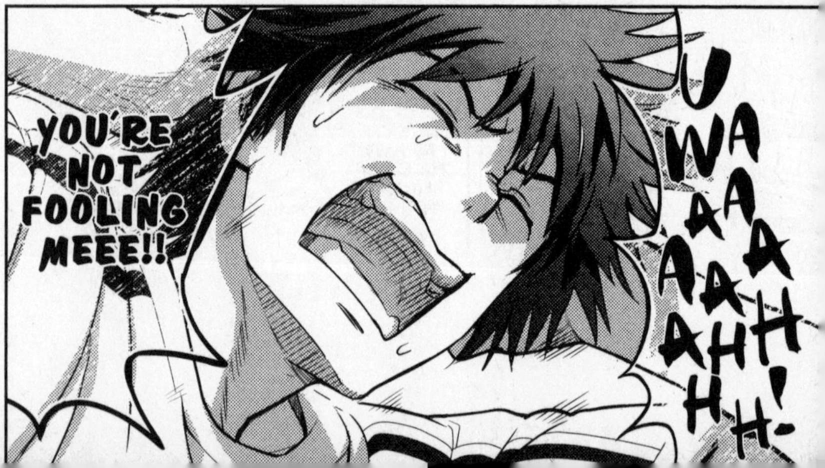
YOU'RE NOT FOOLING MEEE!!
UWAAAAAAAHHHH!!

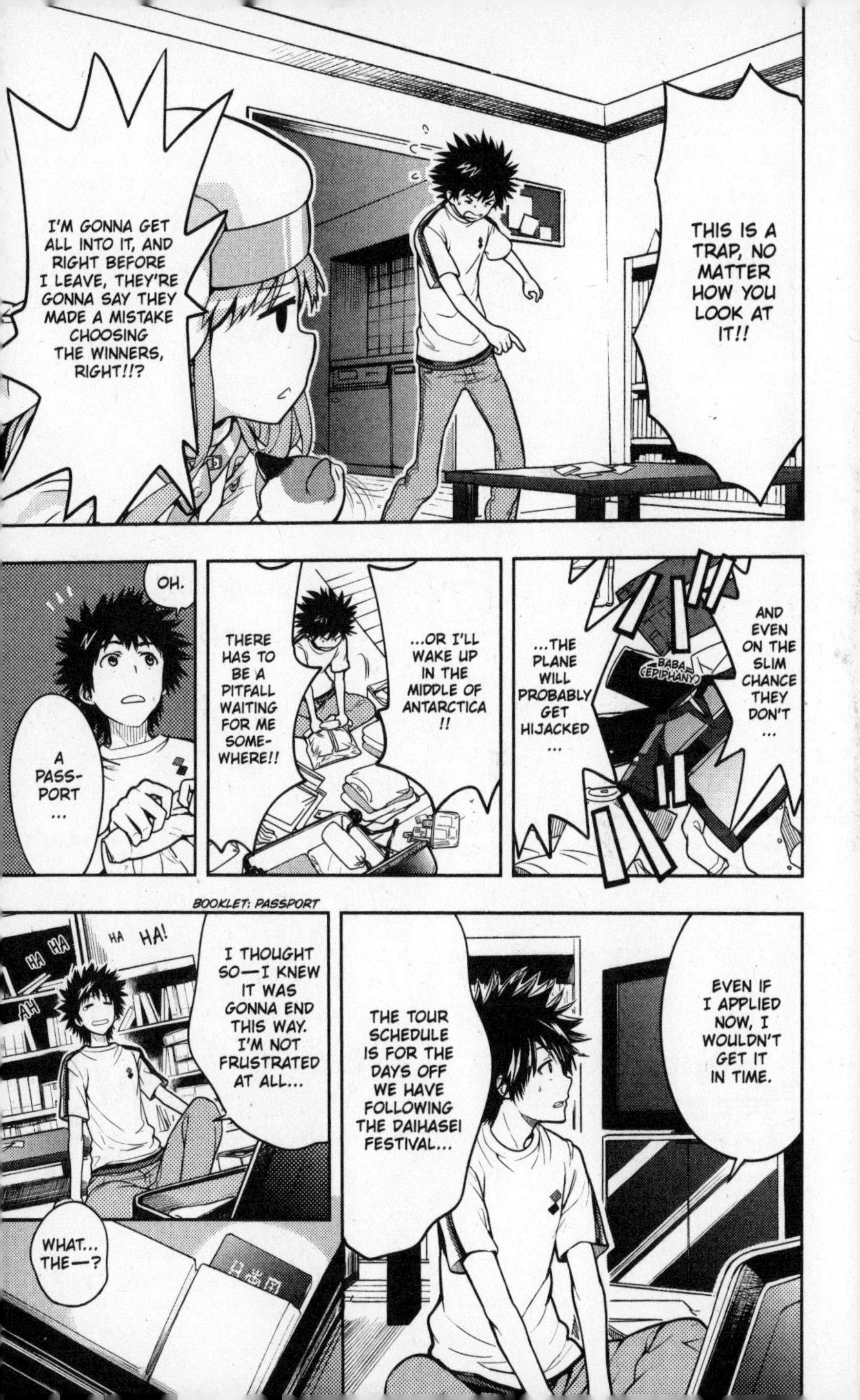
THIS IS A TRAP, NO MATTER HOW YOU LOOK AT IT!!
I'M GONNA GET ALL INTO IT, AND RIGHT BEFORE I LEAVE, THEY'RE GONNA SAY THEY MADE A MISTAKE CHOOSING THE WINNERS, RIGHT!!?
AND EVEN ON THE SLIM CHANCE THEY DON'T...
BABA (EPIPHANY)
...THE PLANE WILL PROBABLY GET HIJACKED...
...OR I'LL WAKE UP IN THE MIDDLE OF ANTARCTICA!!
THERE HAS TO BE A PITFALL WAITING FOR ME SOMEWHERE!!
OH.
A PASSPORT...
EVEN IF I APPLIED NOW, I WOULDN'T GET IT IN TIME.
THE TOUR SCHEDULE IS FOR THE DAYS OFF WE HAVE FOLLOWING THE DAIHASEI FESTIVAL...
BOOKLET: PASSPORT
I THOUGHT SO—I KNEW IT WAS GONNA END THIS WAY. I'M NOT FRUSTRATED AT ALL...
HA HA
HA HA!
AH
WHAT... THE—?

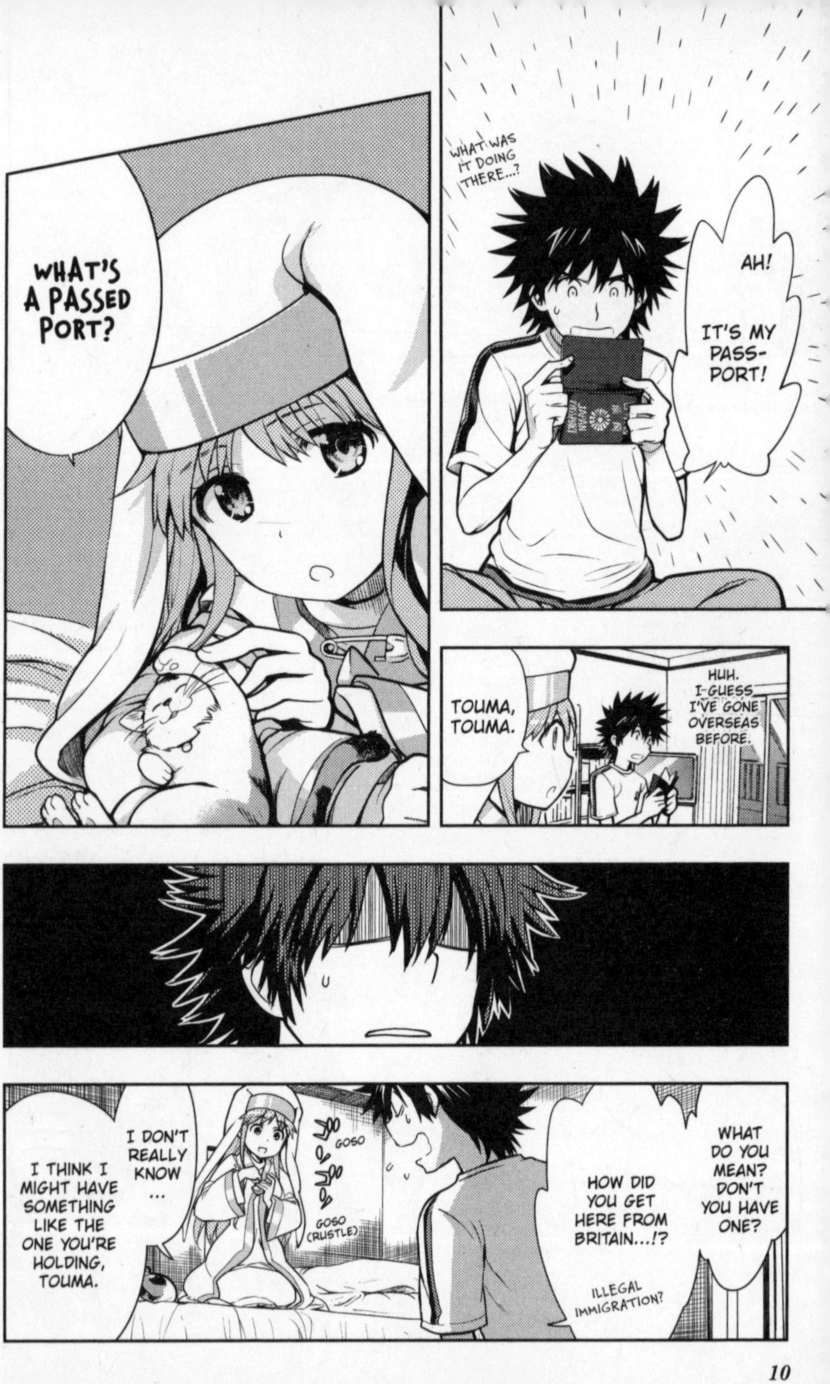
WHAT WAS IT DOING THERE...?
AH!
IT'S MY PASS-PORT!
HUH. I GUESS I'VE GONE OVERSEAS BEFORE.
TOUMA, TOUMA.
WHAT'S A PASSED PORT?
WHAT DO YOU MEAN? DON'T YOU HAVE ONE?
HOW DID YOU GET HERE FROM BRITAIN...!?
ILLEGAL IMMIGRATION?
GOSO
GOSO (RUSTLE)
I DON'T REALLY KNOW...
I THINK I MIGHT HAVE SOMETHING LIKE THE ONE YOU'RE HOLDING, TOUMA.

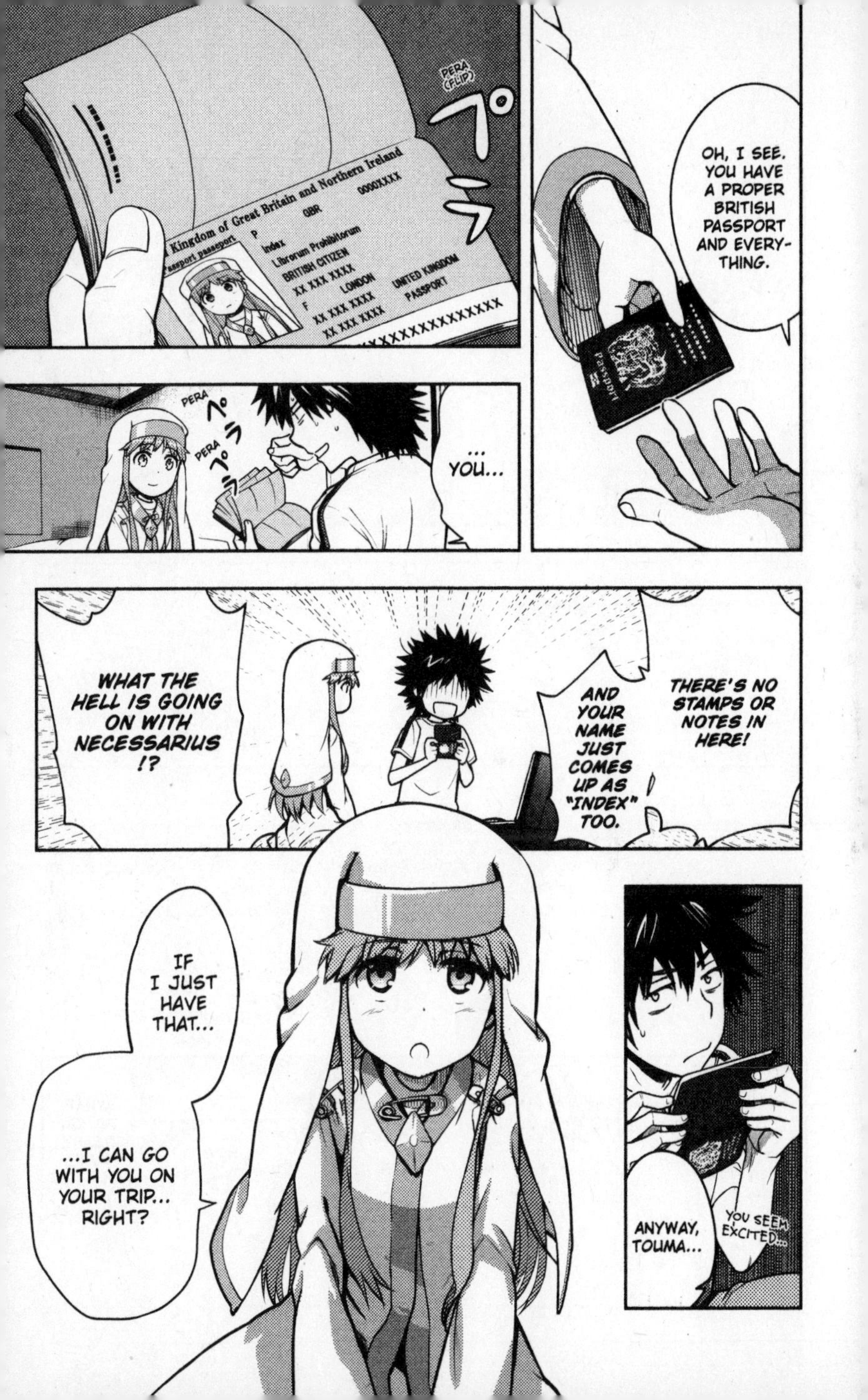
OH, I SEE. YOU HAVE A PROPER BRITISH PASSPORT AND EVERYTHING.
Passport
PERA (FLIP)
Kingdom of Great Britain and Northern Ireland
Passport passeport
P
GBR
000XXXX
Index
Librorum Prohibitorum
BRITISH CITIZEN
XX XXX XXXX
F
LONDON
XX XXX XXXX
UNITED KINGDOM PASSPORT
XX XXX XXXX
PERA
PERA
... YOU...
THERE'S NO STAMPS OR NOTES IN HERE!
AND YOUR NAME JUST COMES UP AS "INDEX" TOO.
WHAT THE HELL IS GOING ON WITH NECESSARIUS !?
YOU SEEM EXCITED...
ANYWAY, TOUMA...
IF I JUST HAVE THAT...
...I CAN GO WITH YOU ON YOUR TRIP... RIGHT?

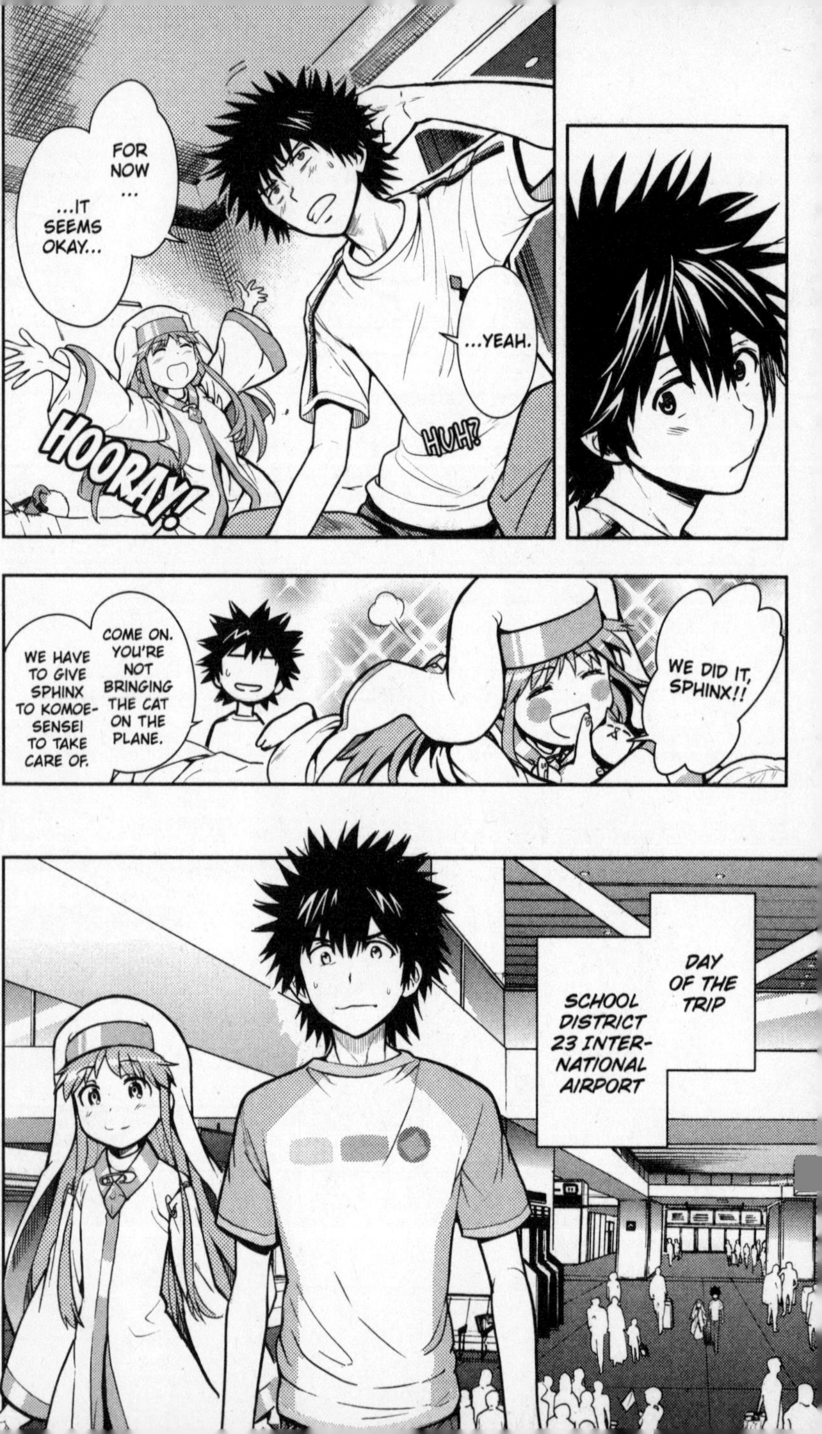
FOR NOW ... ...IT SEEMS OKAY...
...YEAH.
HUH?
HOORAY!!
WE DID IT, SPHINX!!
COME ON. YOU'RE NOT BRINGING THE CAT ON THE PLANE.
WE HAVE TO GIVE SPHINX TO KOMOE-SENSEI TO TAKE CARE OF.
DAY OF THE TRIP
SCHOOL DISTRICT 23 INTER-NATIONAL AIRPORT

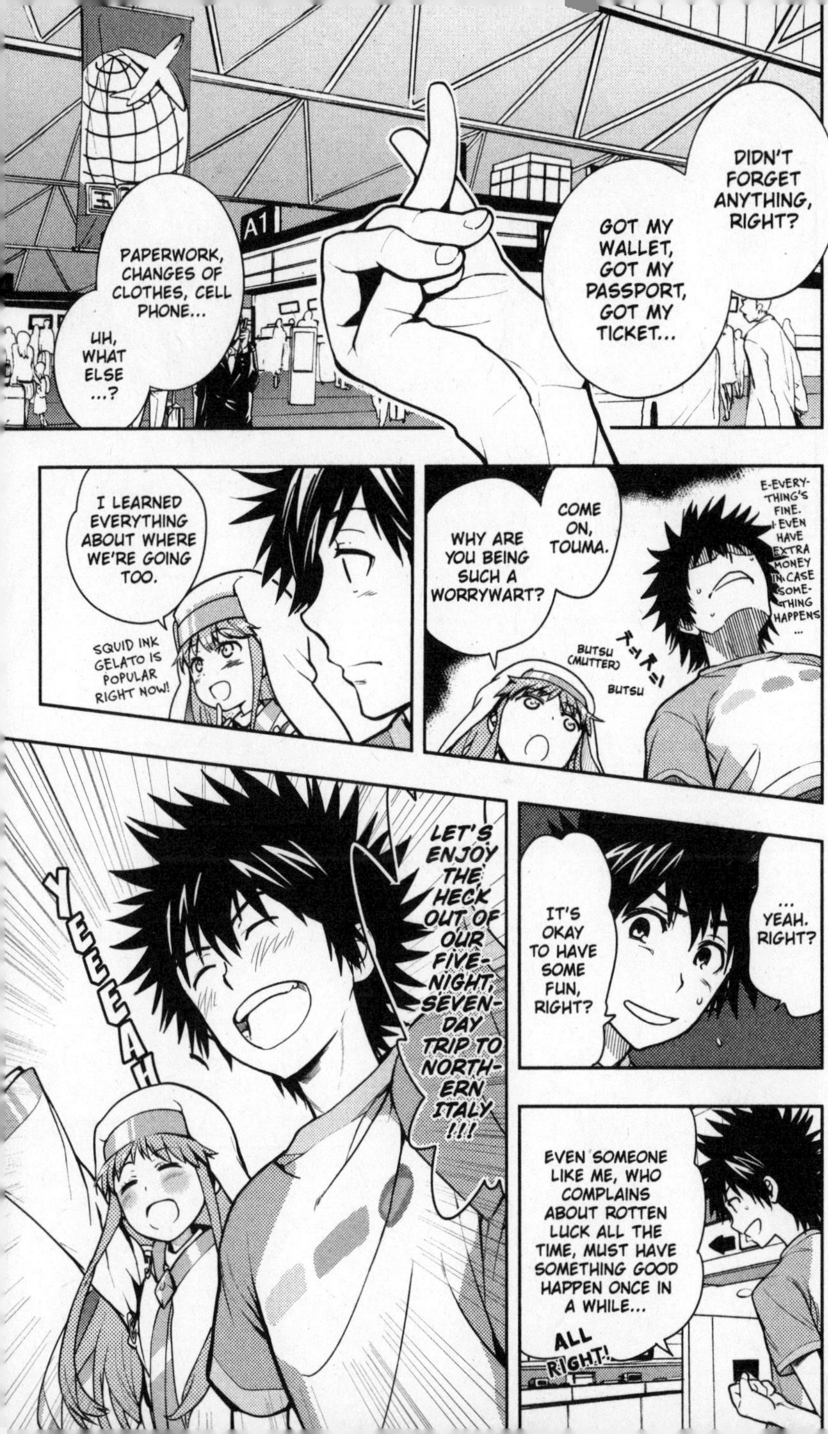
DIDN'T FORGET ANYTHING, RIGHT?
GOT MY WALLET, GOT MY PASSPORT, GOT MY TICKET...
PAPERWORK, CHANGES OF CLOTHES, CELL PHONE...
UH, WHAT ELSE ...?
E-EVERYTHING'S FINE. I EVEN HAVE EXTRA MONEY IN CASE SOMETHING HAPPENS...
COME ON, TOUMA.
WHY ARE YOU BEING SUCH A WORRYWART?
BUTSU (MUTTER)
BUTSU
I LEARNED EVERYTHING ABOUT WHERE WE'RE GOING TOO.
SQUID INK GELATO IS POPULAR RIGHT NOW!
... YEAH. RIGHT?
IT'S OKAY TO HAVE SOME FUN, RIGHT?
EVEN SOMEONE LIKE ME, WHO COMPLAINS ABOUT ROTTEN LUCK ALL THE TIME, MUST HAVE SOMETHING GOOD HAPPEN ONCE IN A WHILE...
ALL RIGHT!
LET'S ENJOY THE HECK OUT OF OUR FIVE-NIGHT, SEVEN-DAY TRIP TO NORTHERN ITALY!!!
YEEEEAH

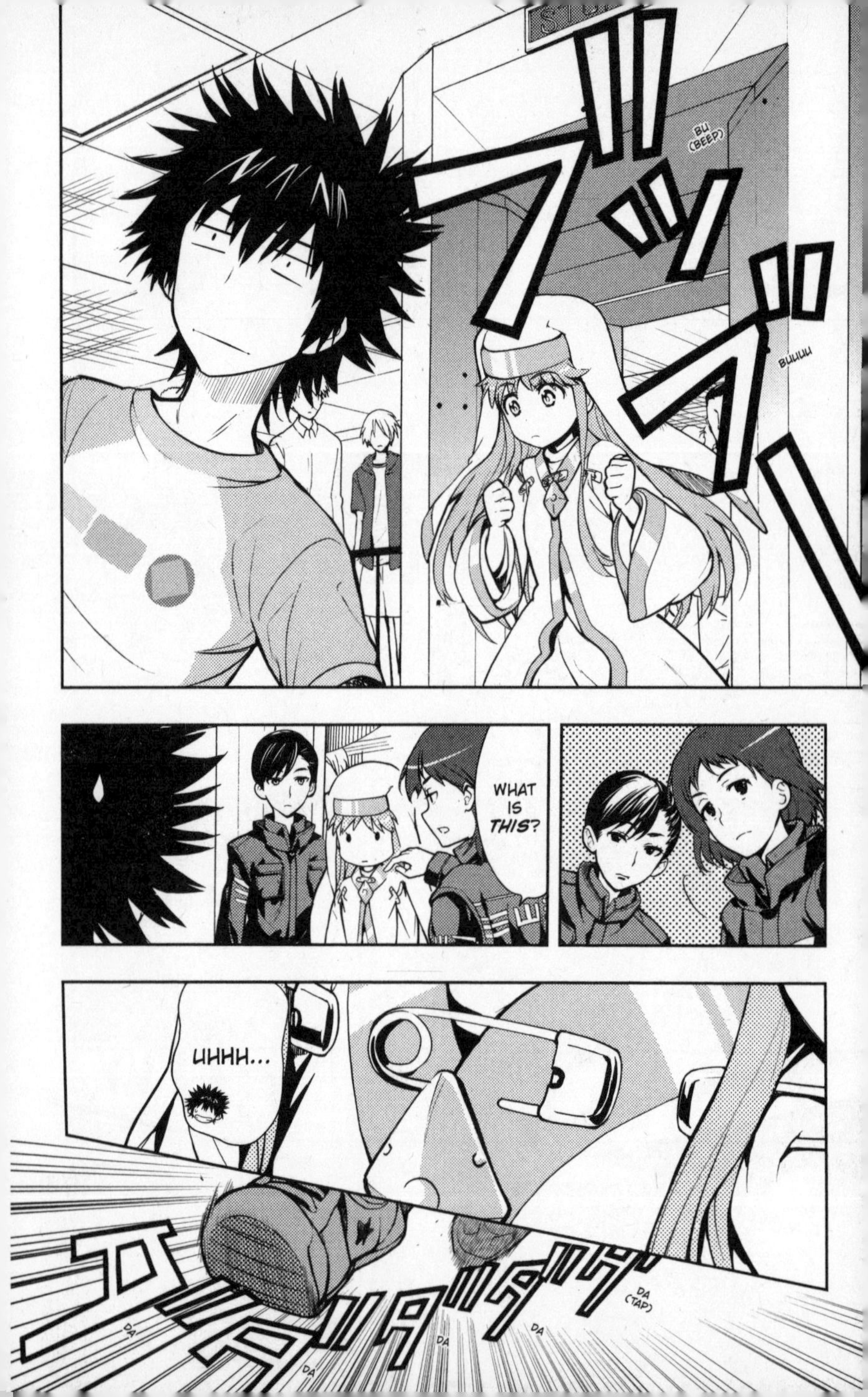

BU (BEEP)
BUUUU
WHAT IS THIS?
UHHH...
DA (TAP)
DA
DA
DA
DA
DA

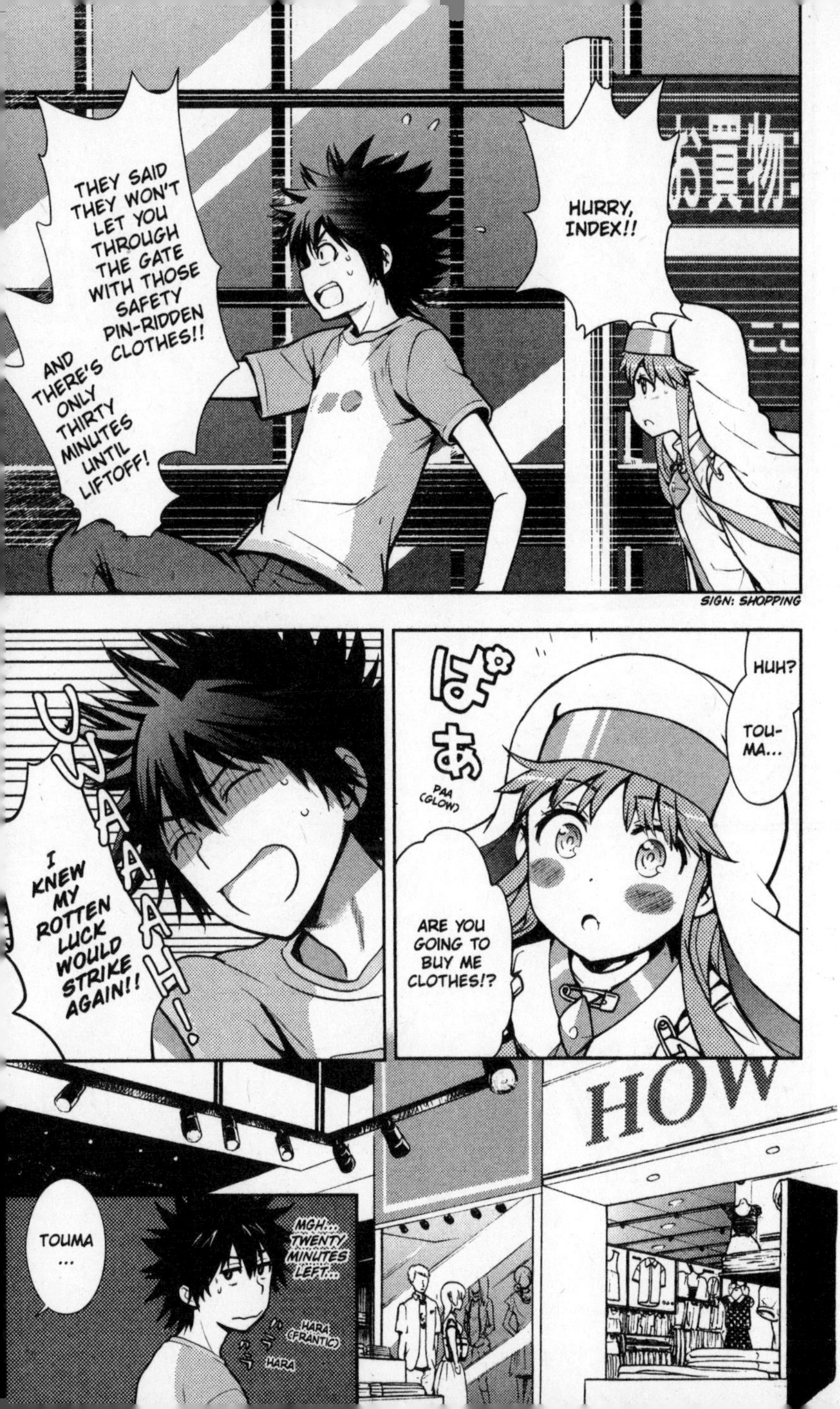
HURRY, INDEX!!
お買物
THEY SAID THEY WON'T LET YOU THROUGH THE GATE WITH THOSE SAFETY PIN-RIDDEN CLOTHES!!
AND THERE'S ONLY THIRTY MINUTES UNTIL LIFTOFF!
SIGN: SHOPPING
HUH?
TOU-MA...
ぱあ
PAA (GLOW)
ARE YOU GOING TO BUY ME CLOTHES!?
UWAAAAH!
I KNEW MY ROTTEN LUCK WOULD STRIKE AGAIN!!
HOW
MGH... TWENTY MINUTES LEFT...
HARA (FRANTIC)
HARA
TOUMA ...

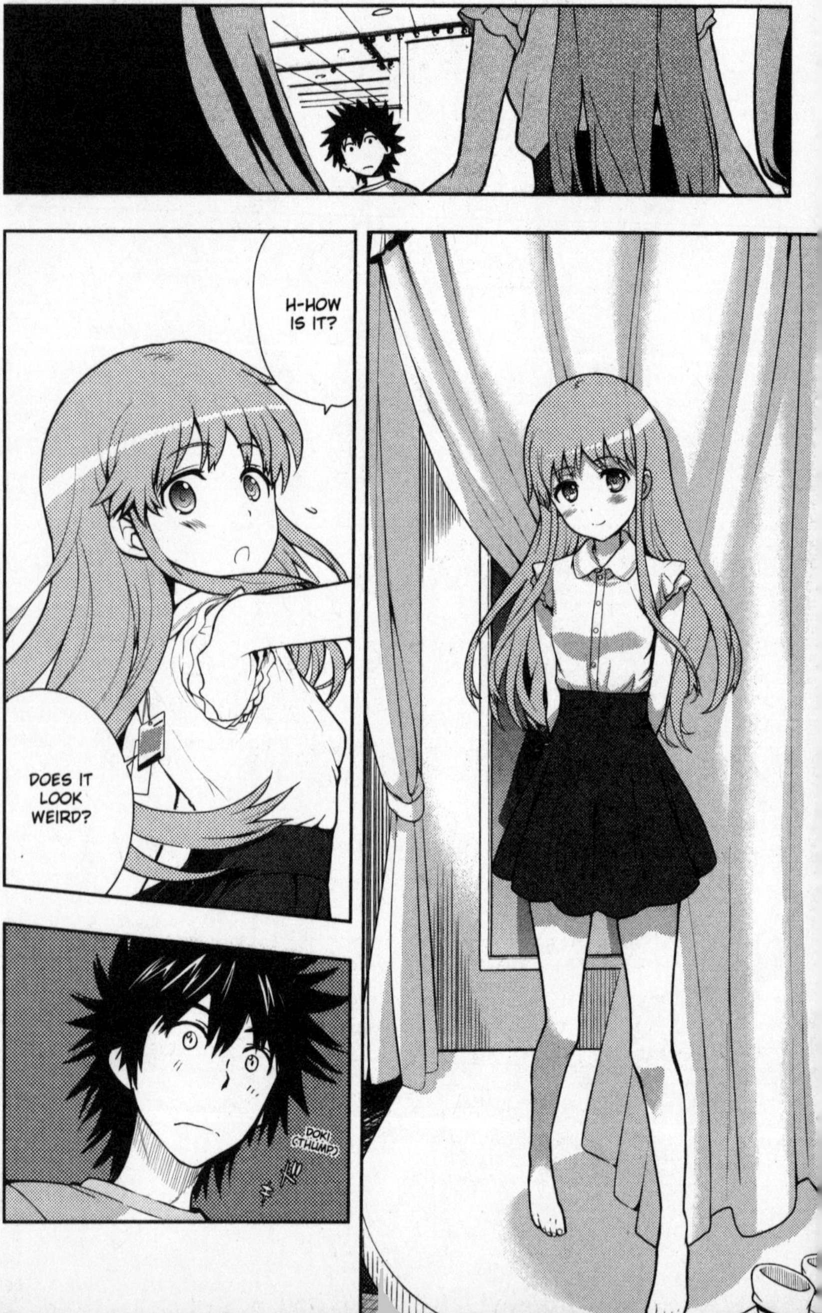
H-HOW IS IT?
DOES IT LOOK WEIRD?
DOKI (THUMP)

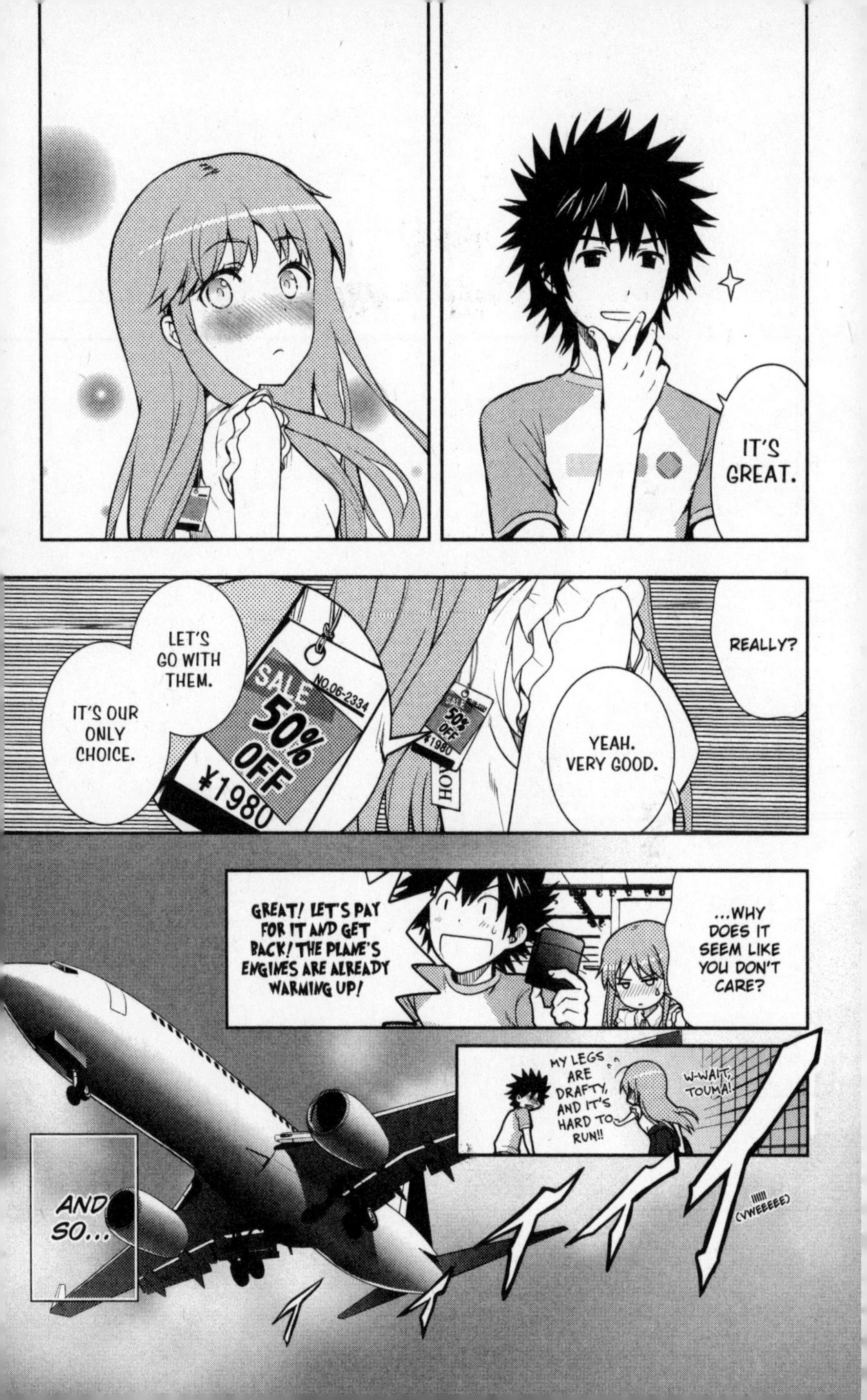
IT'S GREAT.
REALLY?
YEAH. VERY GOOD.
NO.06-2334
SALE 50% OFF ¥1980
LET'S GO WITH THEM.
IT'S OUR ONLY CHOICE.
...WHY DOES IT SEEM LIKE YOU DON'T CARE?
GREAT! LET'S PAY FOR IT AND GET BACK! THE PLANE'S ENGINES ARE ALREADY WARMING UP!
W-WAIT, TOUMA!
MY LEGS ARE DRAFTY, AND IT'S HARD TO RUN!!
(VWEEEEE)
AND SO...

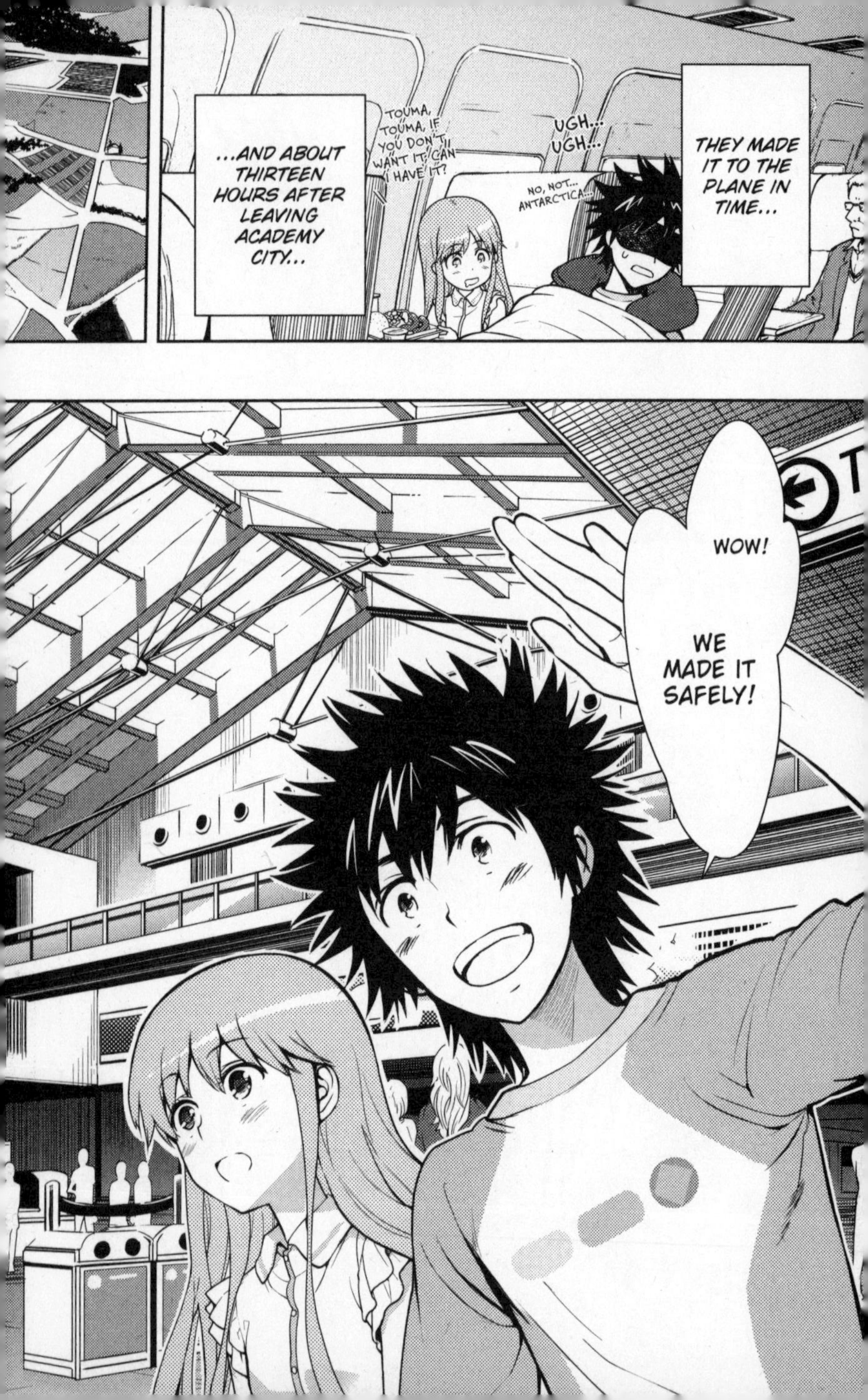
THEY MADE IT TO THE PLANE IN TIME...
UGH... UGH...
NO, NOT... ANTARCTICA...
TOUMA, TOUMA, IF YOU DON'T WANT IT, CAN I HAVE IT?
...AND ABOUT THIRTEEN HOURS AFTER LEAVING ACADEMY CITY...
WOW!
WE MADE IT SAFELY!

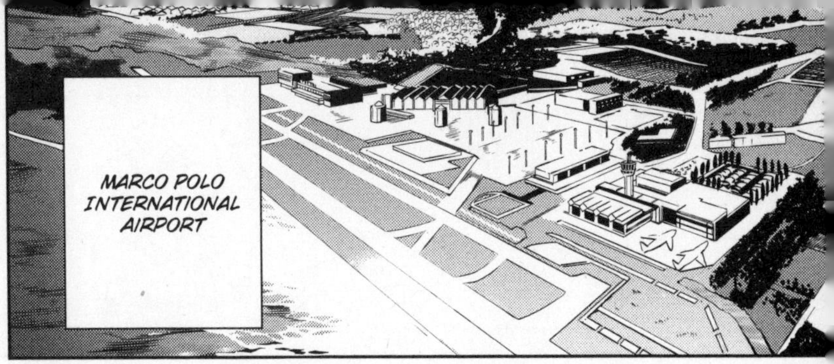
MARCO POLO INTERNATIONAL AIRPORT

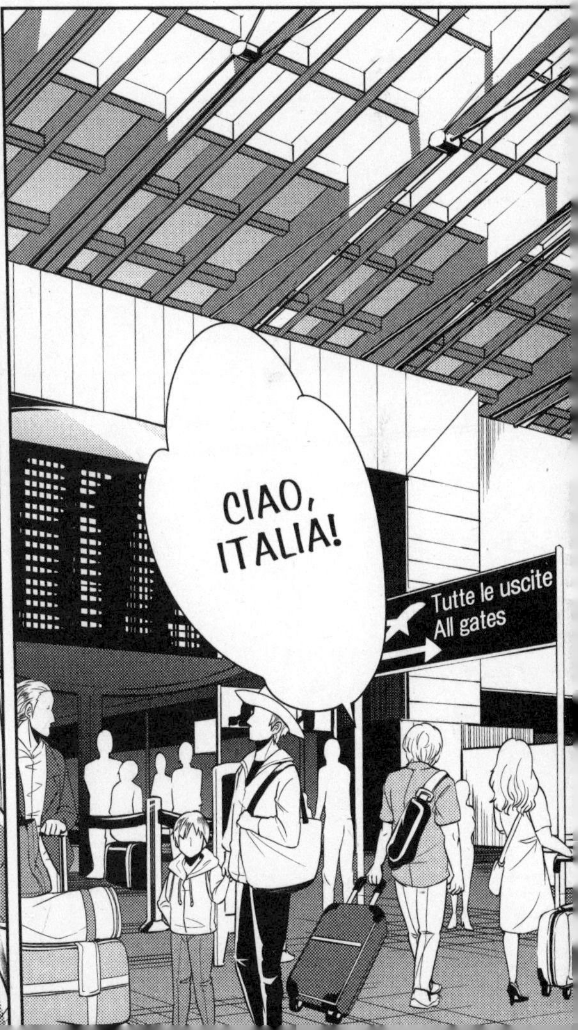
CIAO, ITALIA!
Tutte le uscite
All gates

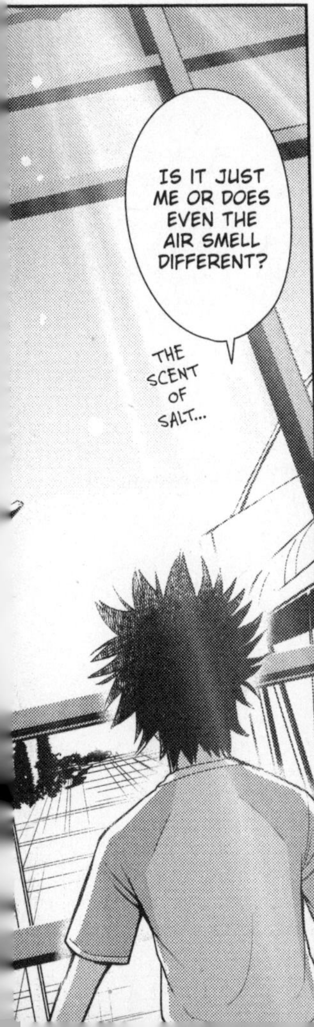
IS IT JUST ME OR DOES EVEN THE AIR SMELL DIFFERENT?
THE SCENT OF SALT...

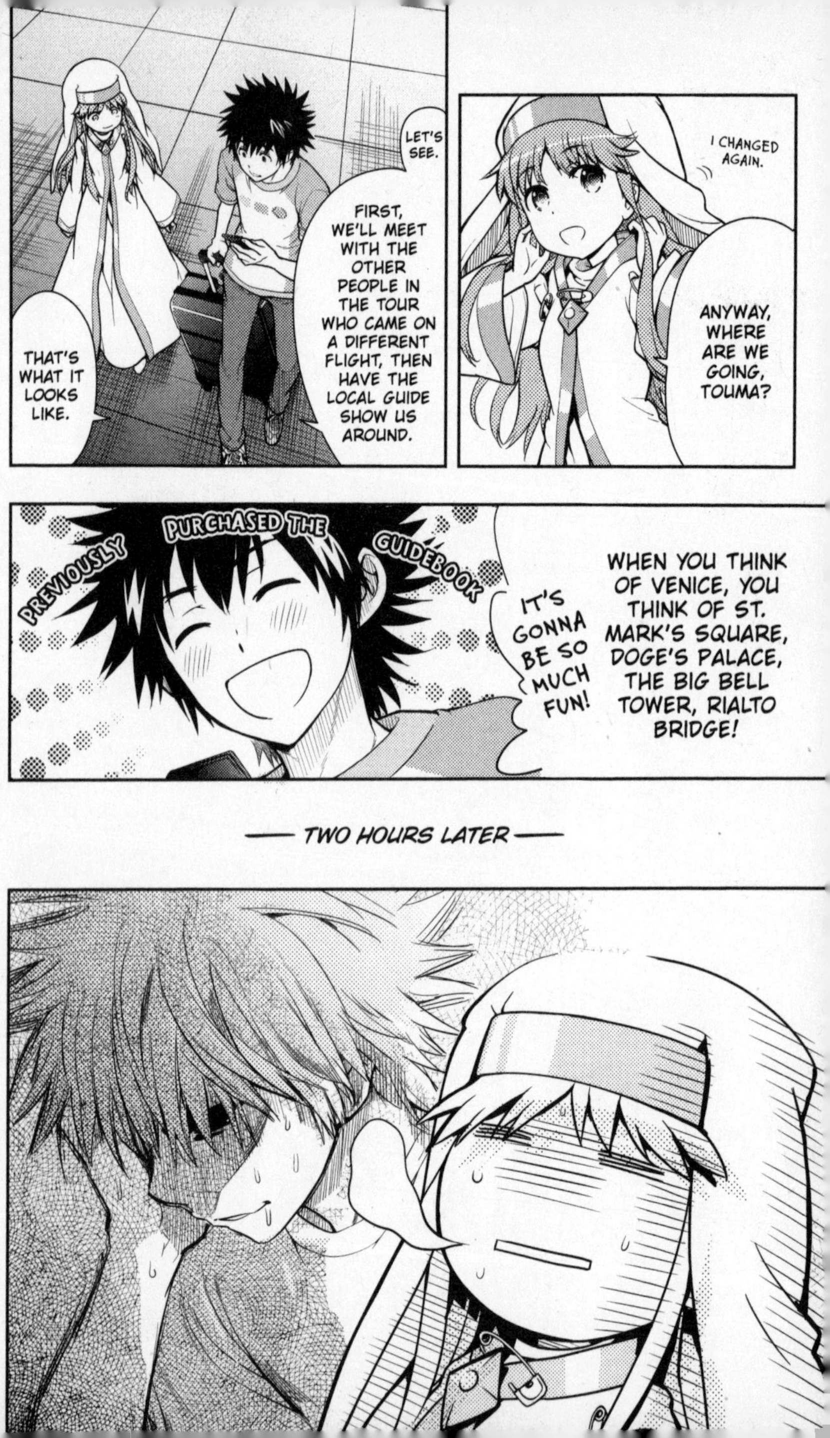
I CHANGED AGAIN.
ANYWAY, WHERE ARE WE GOING, TOUMA?
LET'S SEE.
FIRST, WE'LL MEET WITH THE OTHER PEOPLE IN THE TOUR WHO CAME ON A DIFFERENT FLIGHT, THEN HAVE THE LOCAL GUIDE SHOW US AROUND.
THAT'S WHAT IT LOOKS LIKE.
WHEN YOU THINK OF VENICE, YOU THINK OF ST. MARK'S SQUARE, DOGE'S PALACE, THE BIG BELL TOWER, RIALTO BRIDGE!
IT'S GONNA BE SO MUCH FUN!
PREVIOUSLY PURCHASED THE GUIDEBOOK
—TWO HOURS LATER—

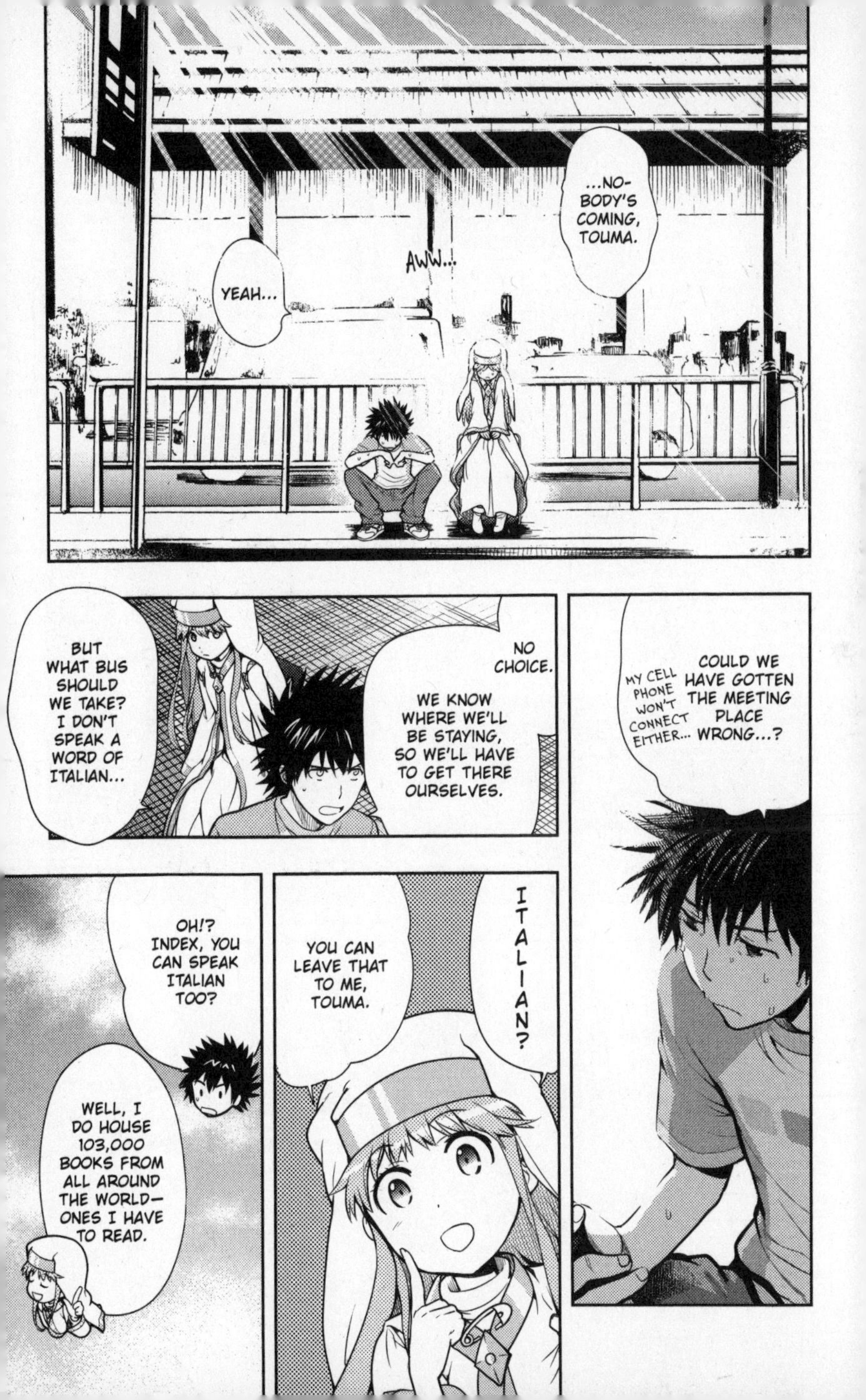
...NO-BODY'S COMING, TOUMA.
AWW...
YEAH...
COULD WE HAVE GOTTEN THE MEETING PLACE WRONG...?
MY CELL PHONE WON'T CONNECT EITHER...
NO CHOICE.
WE KNOW WHERE WE'LL BE STAYING, SO WE'LL HAVE TO GET THERE OURSELVES.
BUT WHAT BUS SHOULD WE TAKE? I DON'T SPEAK A WORD OF ITALIAN...
ITALIAN?
YOU CAN LEAVE THAT TO ME, TOUMA.
OH!? INDEX, YOU CAN SPEAK ITALIAN TOO?
WELL, I DO HOUSE 103,000 BOOKS FROM ALL AROUND THE WORLD—ONES I HAVE TO READ.

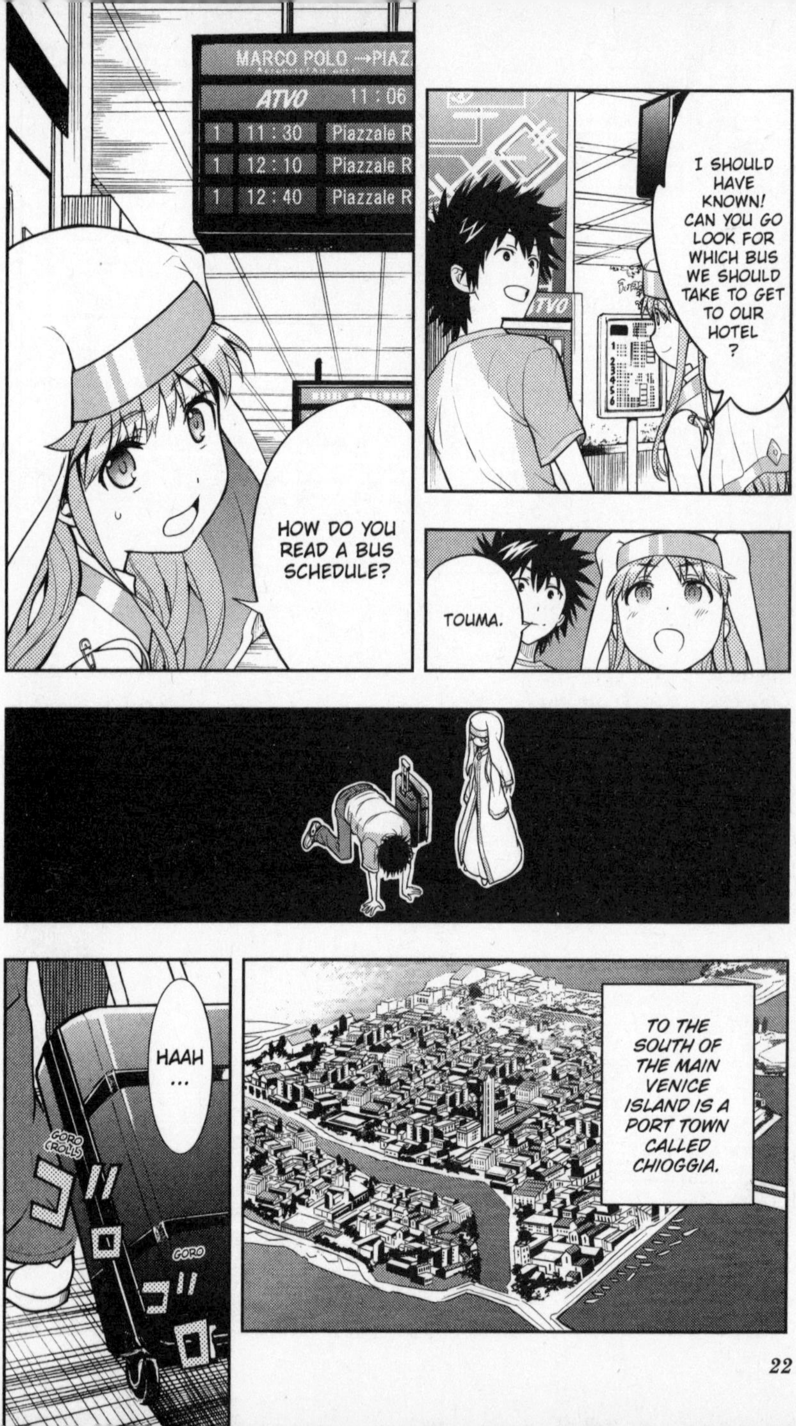
I SHOULD HAVE KNOWN! CAN YOU GO LOOK FOR WHICH BUS WE SHOULD TAKE TO GET TO OUR HOTEL ?
TOUMA.
MARCO POLO →PIAZ
ATVO 11:06
1 11:30 Piazzale R
1 12:10 Piazzale R
1 12:40 Piazzale R
HOW DO YOU READ A BUS SCHEDULE?
TO THE SOUTH OF THE MAIN VENICE ISLAND IS A PORT TOWN CALLED CHIOGGIA.
HAAH ...
GORO (ROLL)
GORO

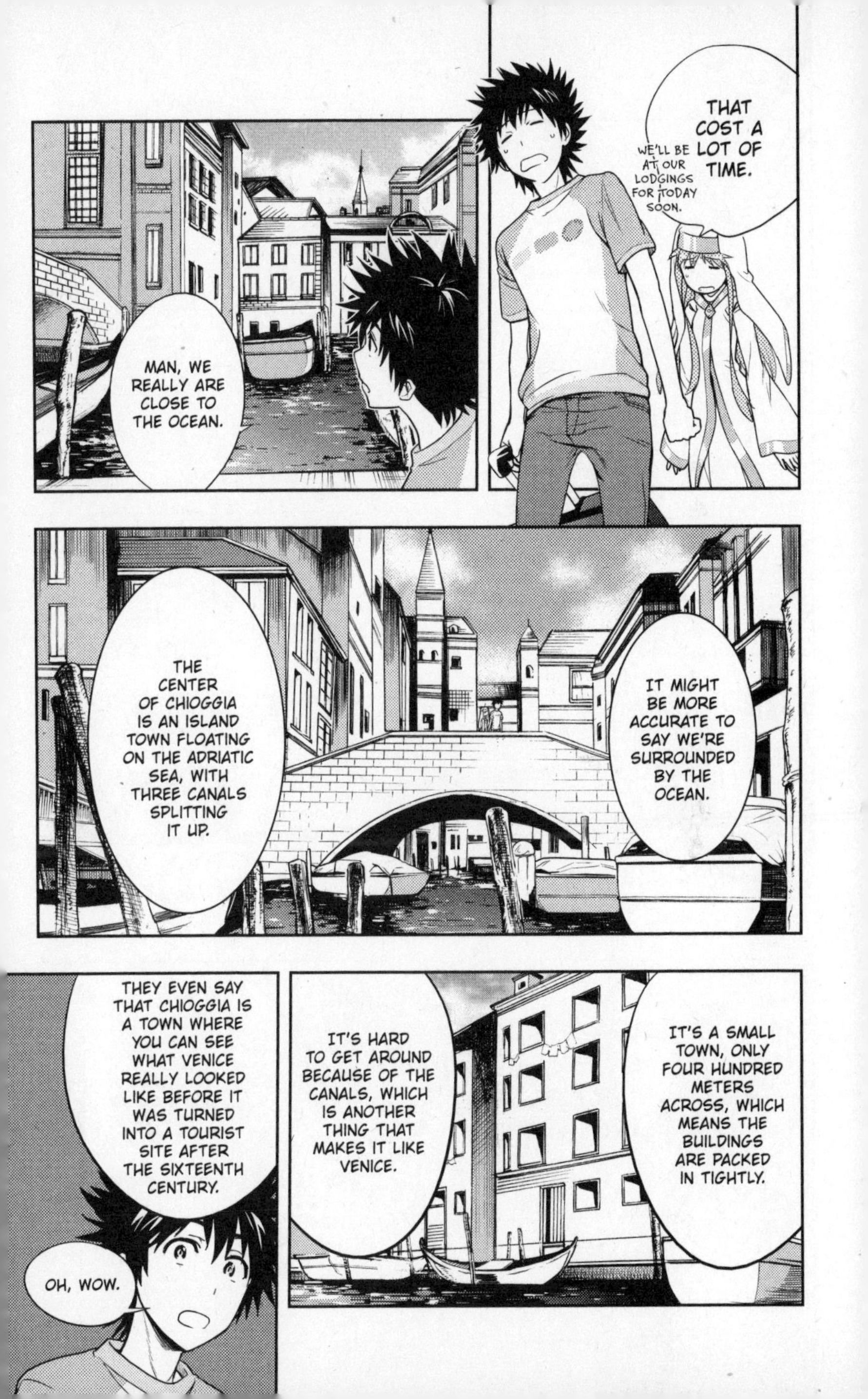
THAT COST A LOT OF TIME.
WE'LL BE AT OUR LODGINGS FOR TODAY SOON.
MAN, WE REALLY ARE CLOSE TO THE OCEAN.
IT MIGHT BE MORE ACCURATE TO SAY WE'RE SURROUNDED BY THE OCEAN.
THE CENTER OF CHIOGGIA IS AN ISLAND TOWN FLOATING ON THE ADRIATIC SEA, WITH THREE CANALS SPLITTING IT UP.
IT'S A SMALL TOWN, ONLY FOUR HUNDRED METERS ACROSS, WHICH MEANS THE BUILDINGS ARE PACKED IN TIGHTLY.
IT'S HARD TO GET AROUND BECAUSE OF THE CANALS, WHICH IS ANOTHER THING THAT MAKES IT LIKE VENICE.
THEY EVEN SAY THAT CHIOGGIA IS A TOWN WHERE YOU CAN SEE WHAT VENICE REALLY LOOKED LIKE BEFORE IT WAS TURNED INTO A TOURIST SITE AFTER THE SIXTEENTH CENTURY.
OH, WOW.

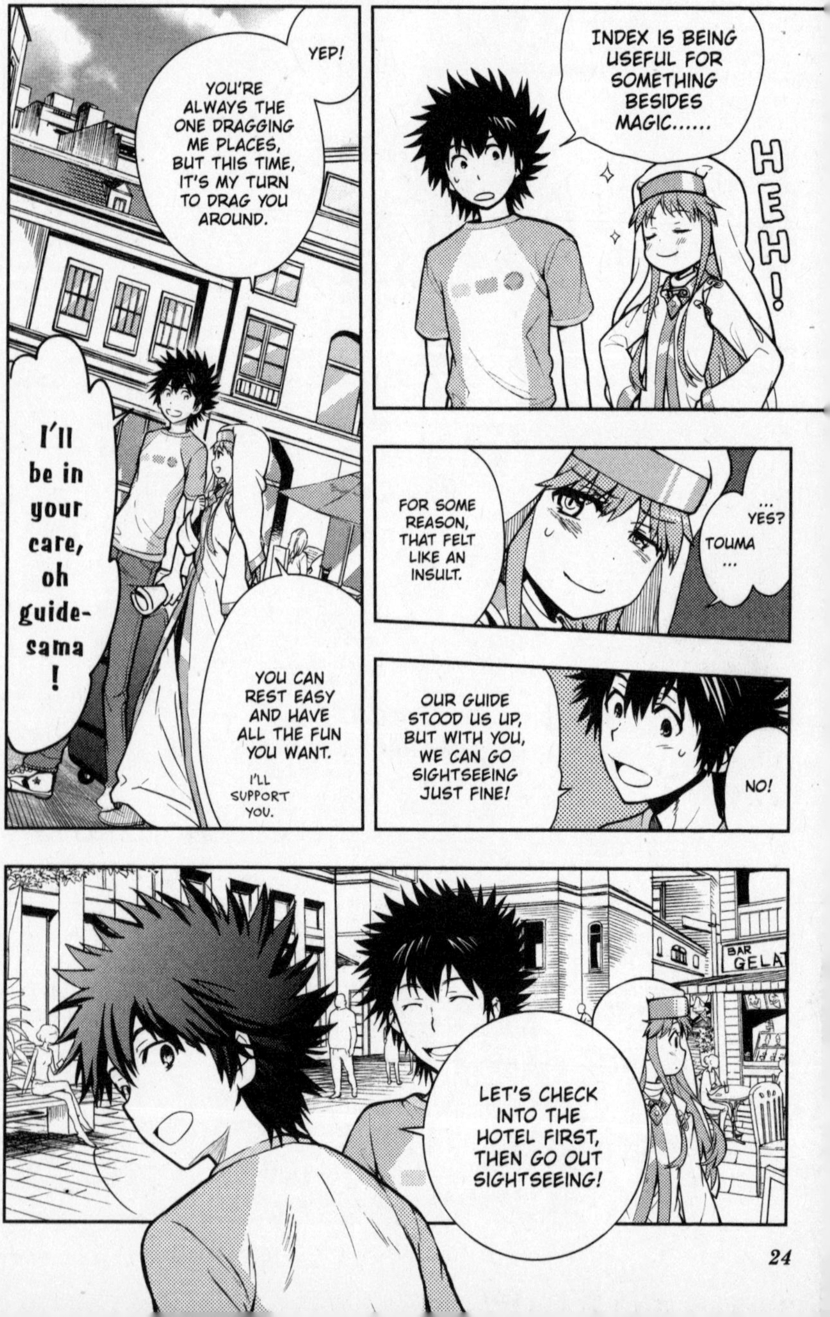
INDEX IS BEING USEFUL FOR SOMETHING BESIDES MAGIC......
HEH!
... YES?
TOUMA ...
FOR SOME REASON, THAT FELT LIKE AN INSULT.
OUR GUIDE STOOD US UP, BUT WITH YOU, WE CAN GO SIGHTSEEING JUST FINE!
NO!
YEP!
YOU'RE ALWAYS THE ONE DRAGGING ME PLACES, BUT THIS TIME, IT'S MY TURN TO DRAG YOU AROUND.
I'll be in your care, oh guide-sama!
YOU CAN REST EASY AND HAVE ALL THE FUN YOU WANT.
I'LL SUPPORT YOU.
BAR GELAT
LET'S CHECK INTO THE HOTEL FIRST, THEN GO OUT SIGHTSEEING!

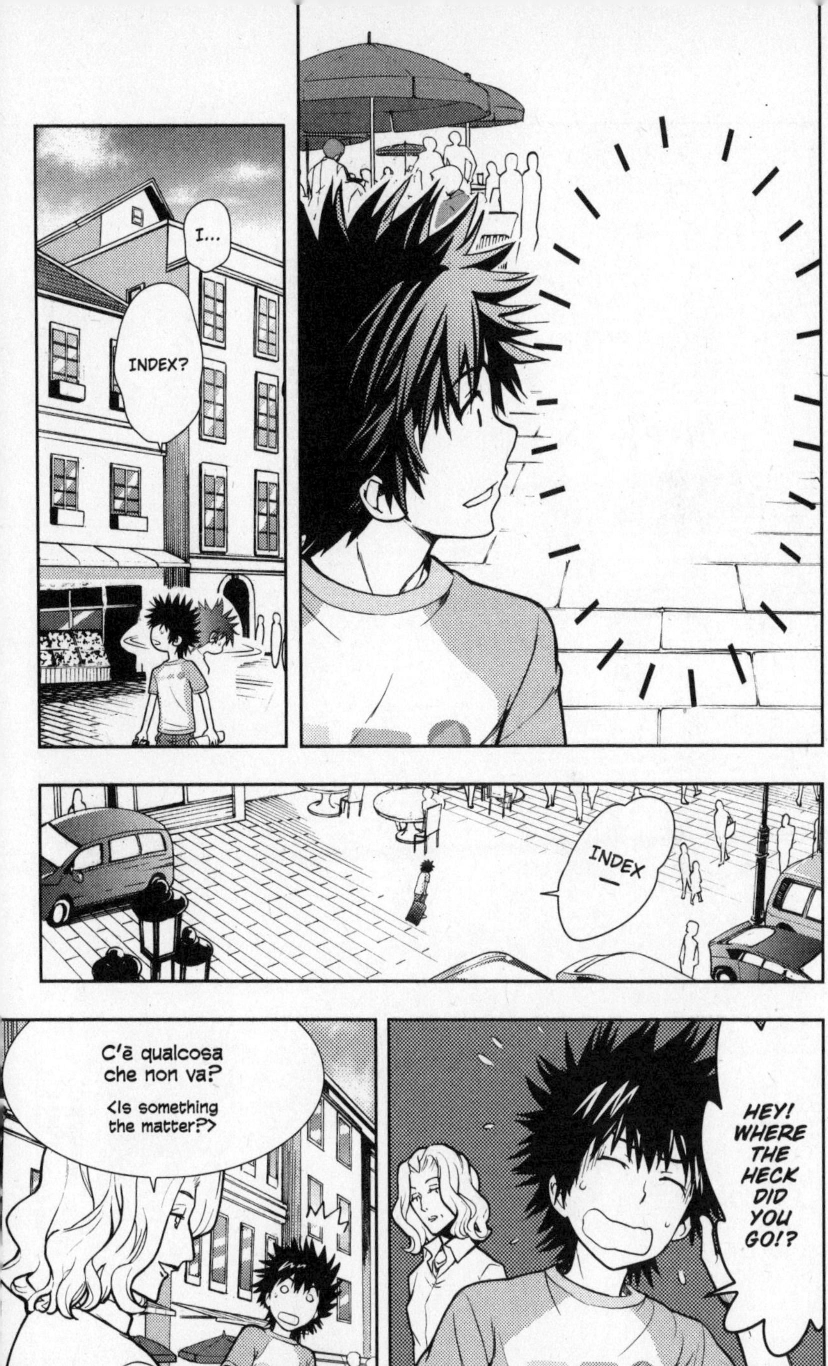
I...
INDEX?
INDEX—
HEY! WHERE THE HECK DID YOU GO!?
C'è qualcosa che non va?
<Is something the matter?>

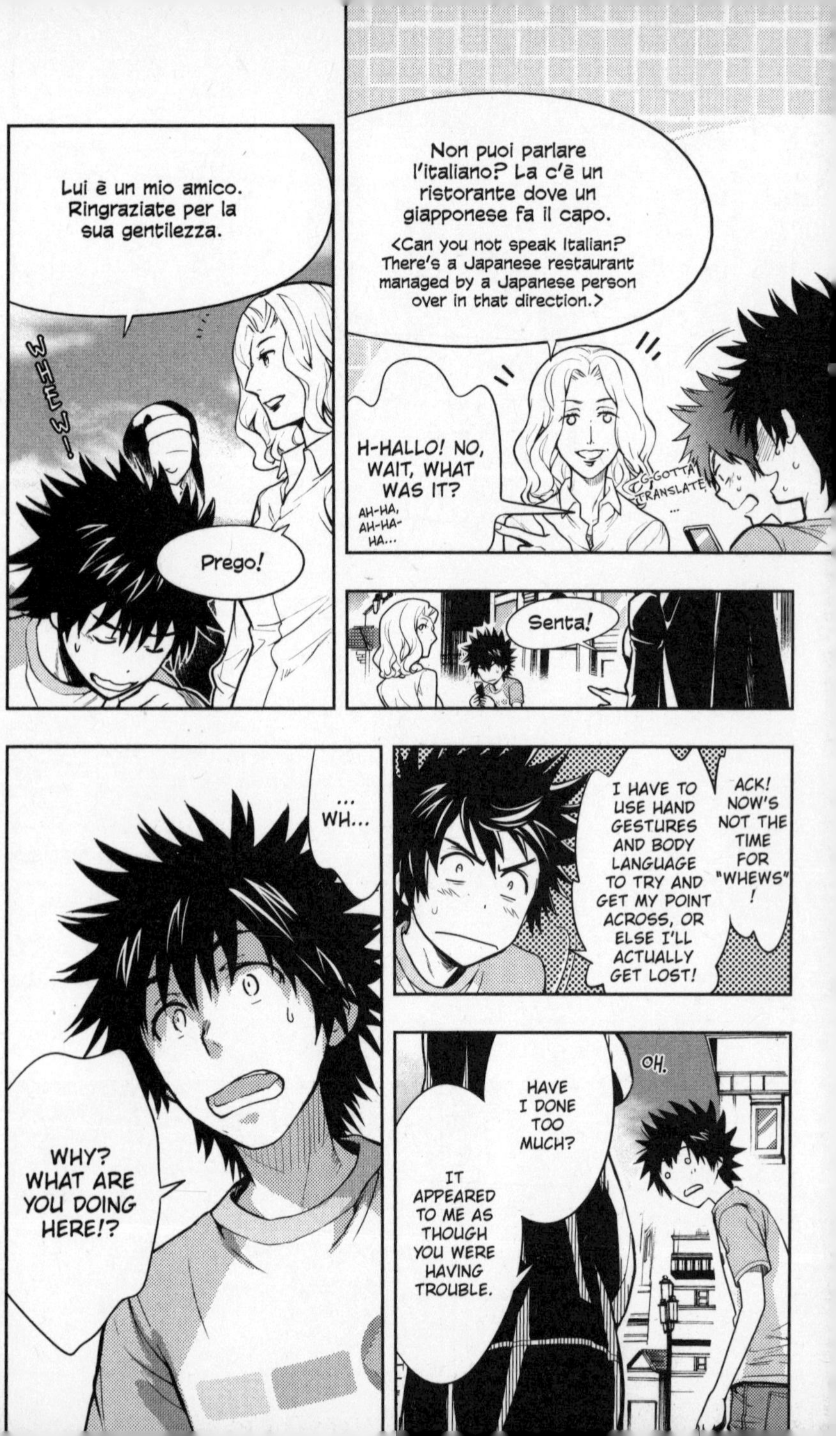
Non puoi parlare l'italiano? La c'è un ristorante dove un giapponese fa il capo.
<Can you not speak Italian? There's a Japanese restaurant managed by a Japanese person over in that direction.>
G-GOTTA TRANSLATE...
H-HALLO! NO, WAIT, WHAT WAS IT?
AH-HA, AH-HA-HA...
Senta!
Lui è un mio amico. Ringraziate per la sua gentilezza.
WHEW!
Prego!
ACK! NOW'S NOT THE TIME FOR "WHEWS"!
I HAVE TO USE HAND GESTURES AND BODY LANGUAGE TO TRY AND GET MY POINT ACROSS, OR ELSE I'LL ACTUALLY GET LOST!
OH.
HAVE I DONE TOO MUCH?
IT APPEARED TO ME AS THOUGH YOU WERE HAVING TROUBLE.
...WH...
WHY? WHAT ARE YOU DOING HERE!?

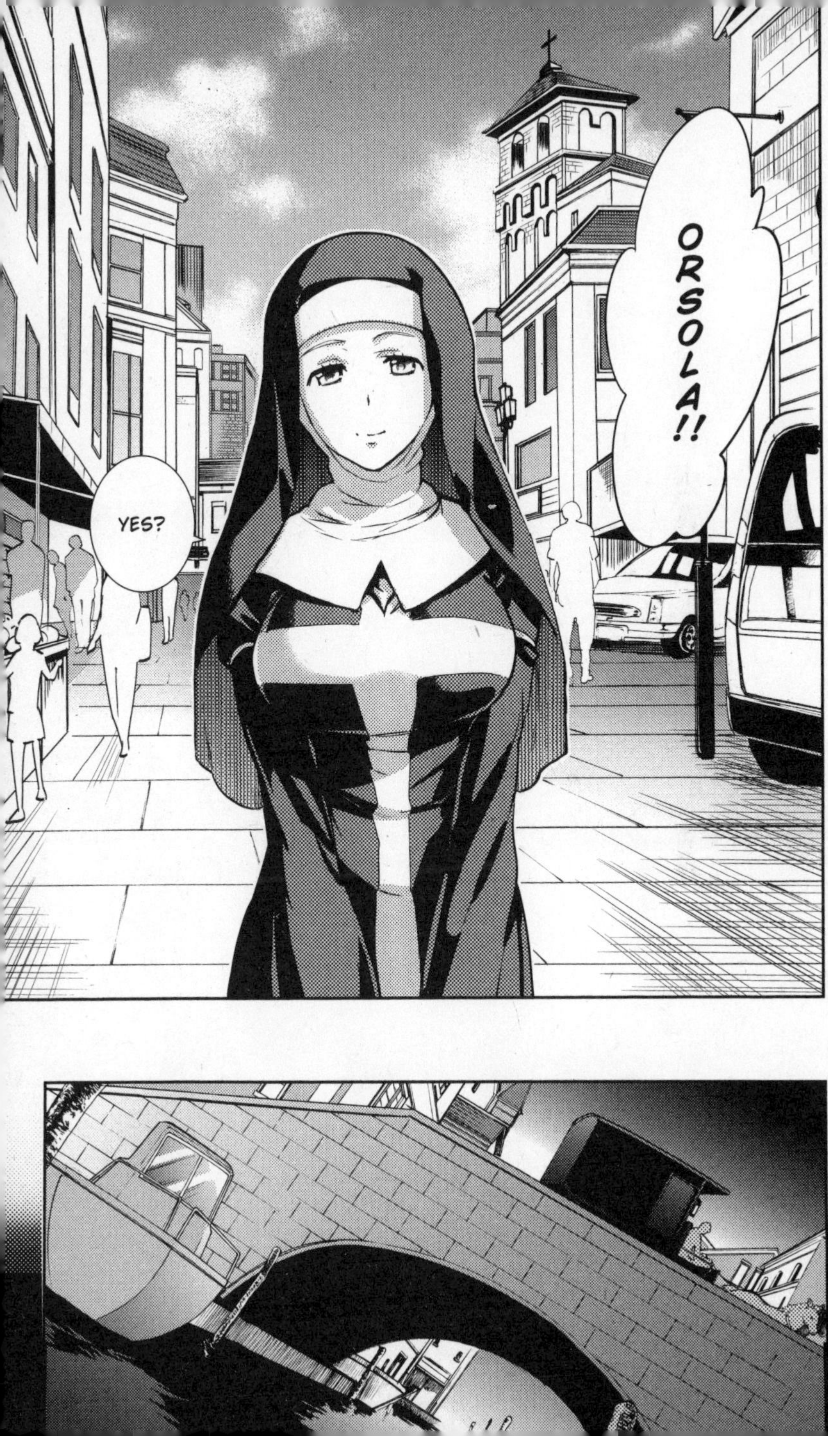
ORSOLA!!
YES?

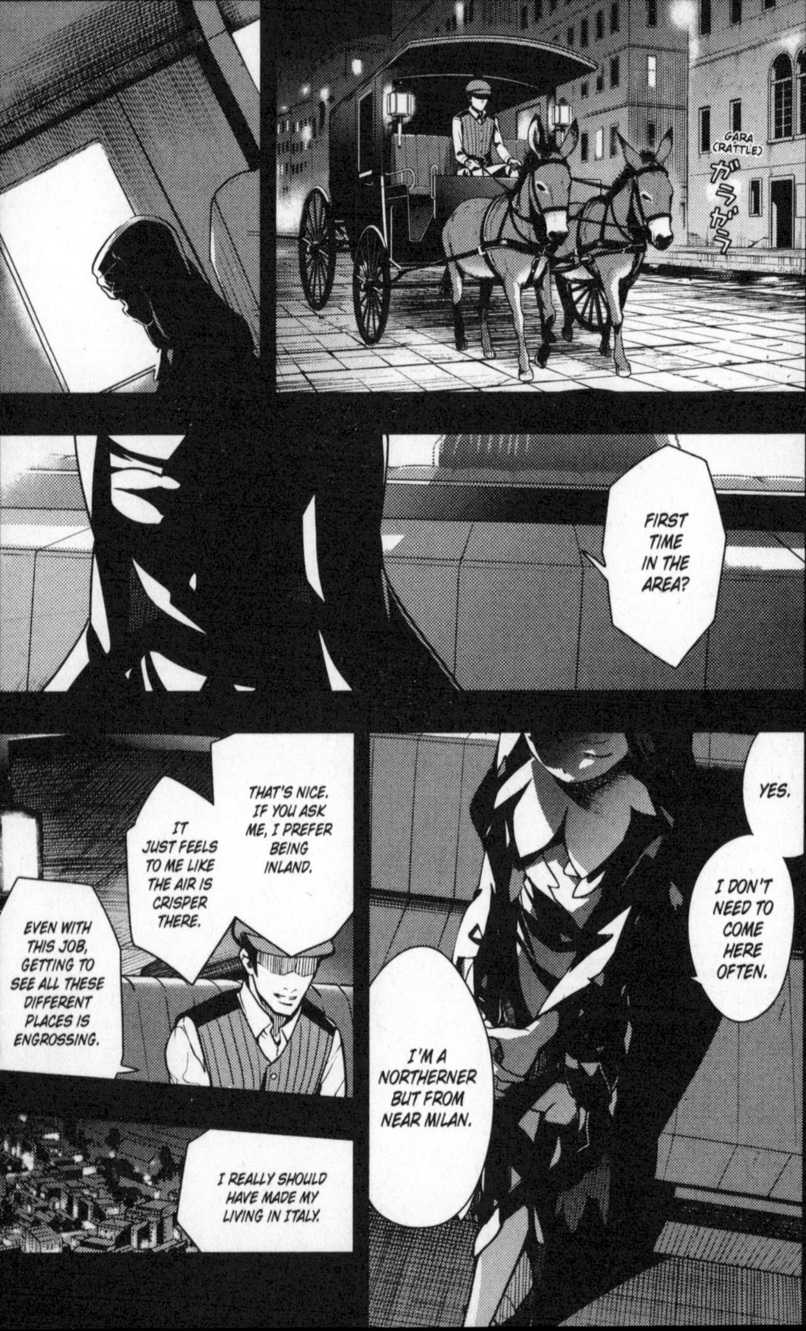
GARA (RATTLE)
ガラガラ
FIRST TIME IN THE AREA?
YES.
I DON'T NEED TO COME HERE OFTEN.
I'M A NORTHERNER BUT FROM NEAR MILAN.
THAT'S NICE. IF YOU ASK ME, I PREFER BEING INLAND.
IT JUST FEELS TO ME LIKE THE AIR IS CRISPER THERE.
EVEN WITH THIS JOB, GETTING TO SEE ALL THESE DIFFERENT PLACES IS ENGROSSING.
I REALLY SHOULD HAVE MADE MY LIVING IN ITALY.

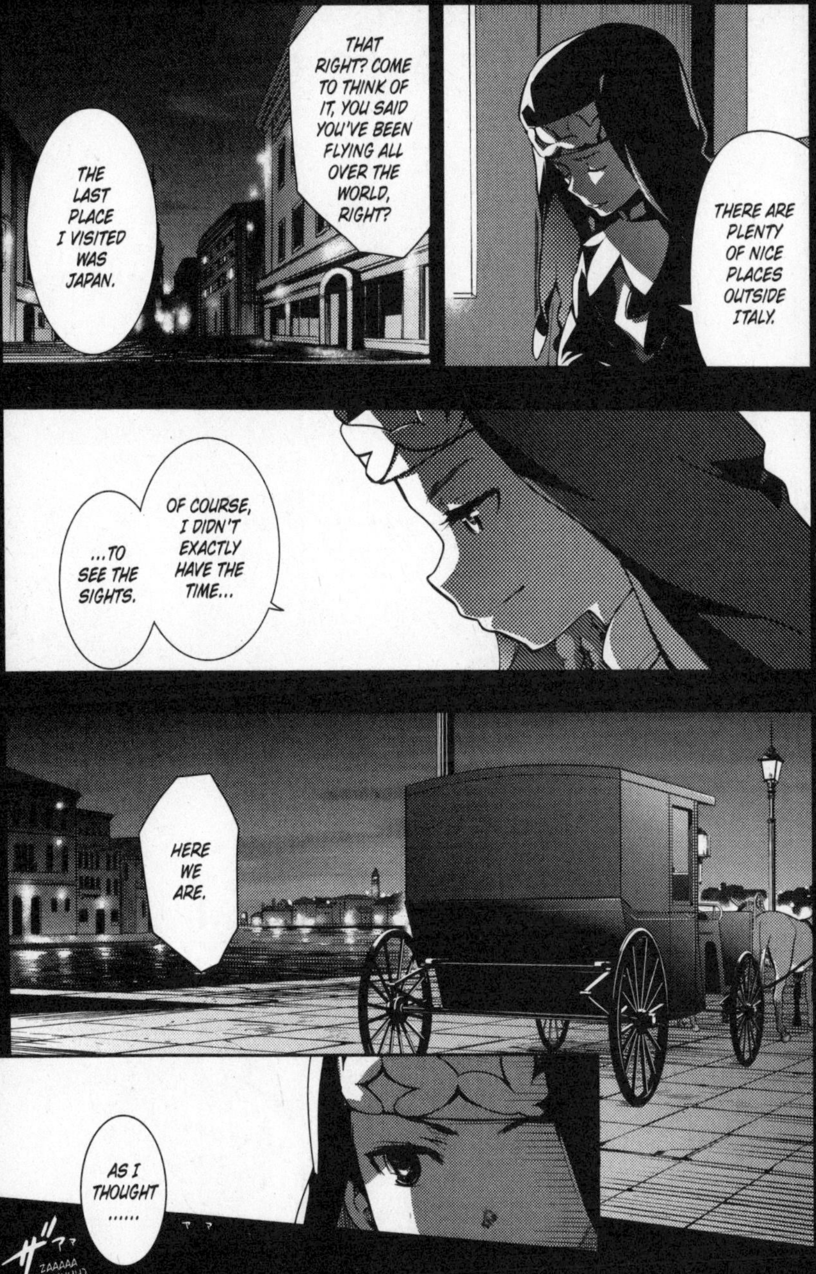
THERE ARE PLENTY OF NICE PLACES OUTSIDE ITALY.
THAT RIGHT? COME TO THINK OF IT, YOU SAID YOU'VE BEEN FLYING ALL OVER THE WORLD, RIGHT?
THE LAST PLACE I VISITED WAS JAPAN.
OF COURSE, I DIDN'T EXACTLY HAVE THE TIME...
...TO SEE THE SIGHTS.
HERE WE ARE.
AS I THOUGHT ......
ZAAAAA (SHHHHH)

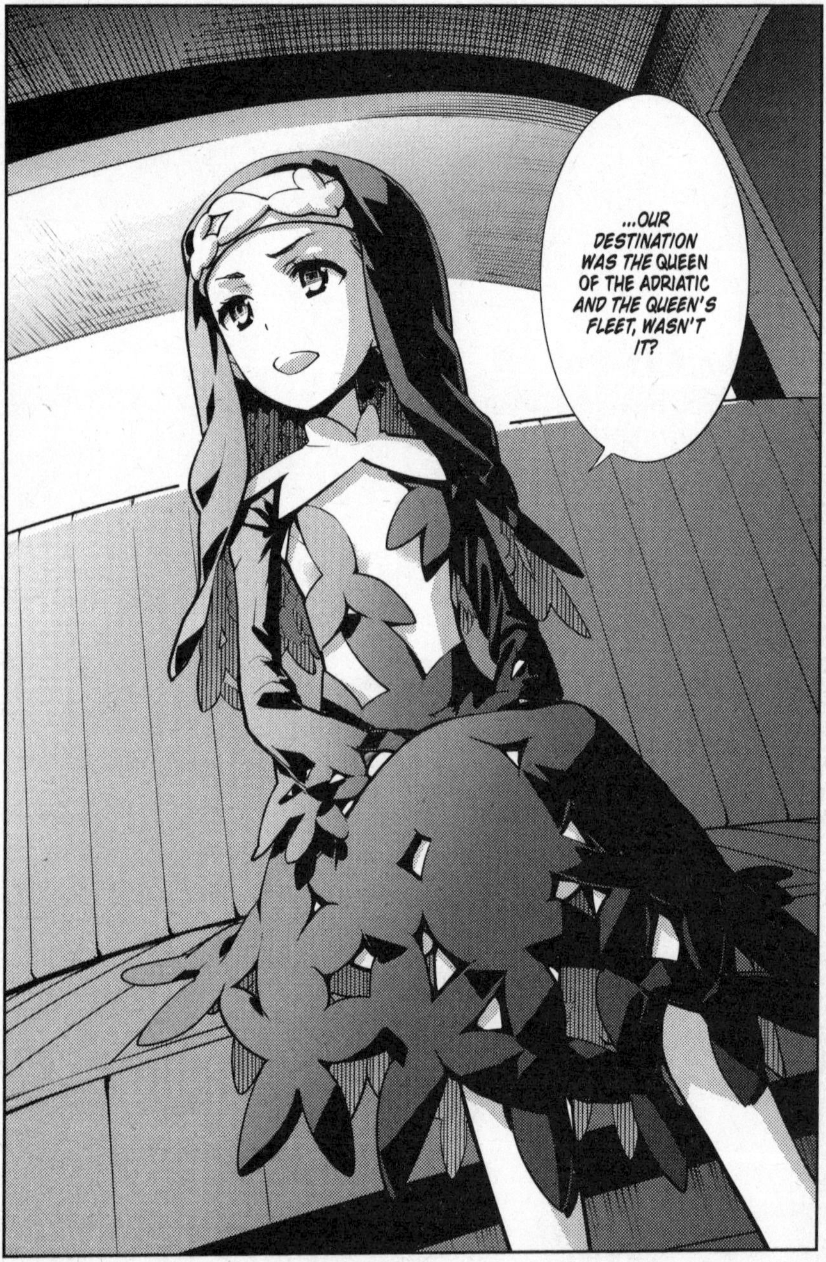
...OUR DESTINATION WAS THE QUEEN OF THE ADRIATIC AND THE QUEEN'S FLEET, WASN'T IT?

A Certain Magical Index

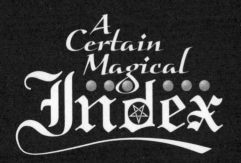

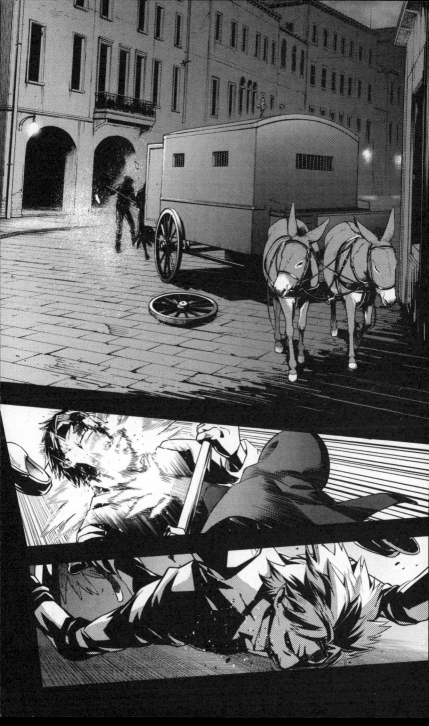

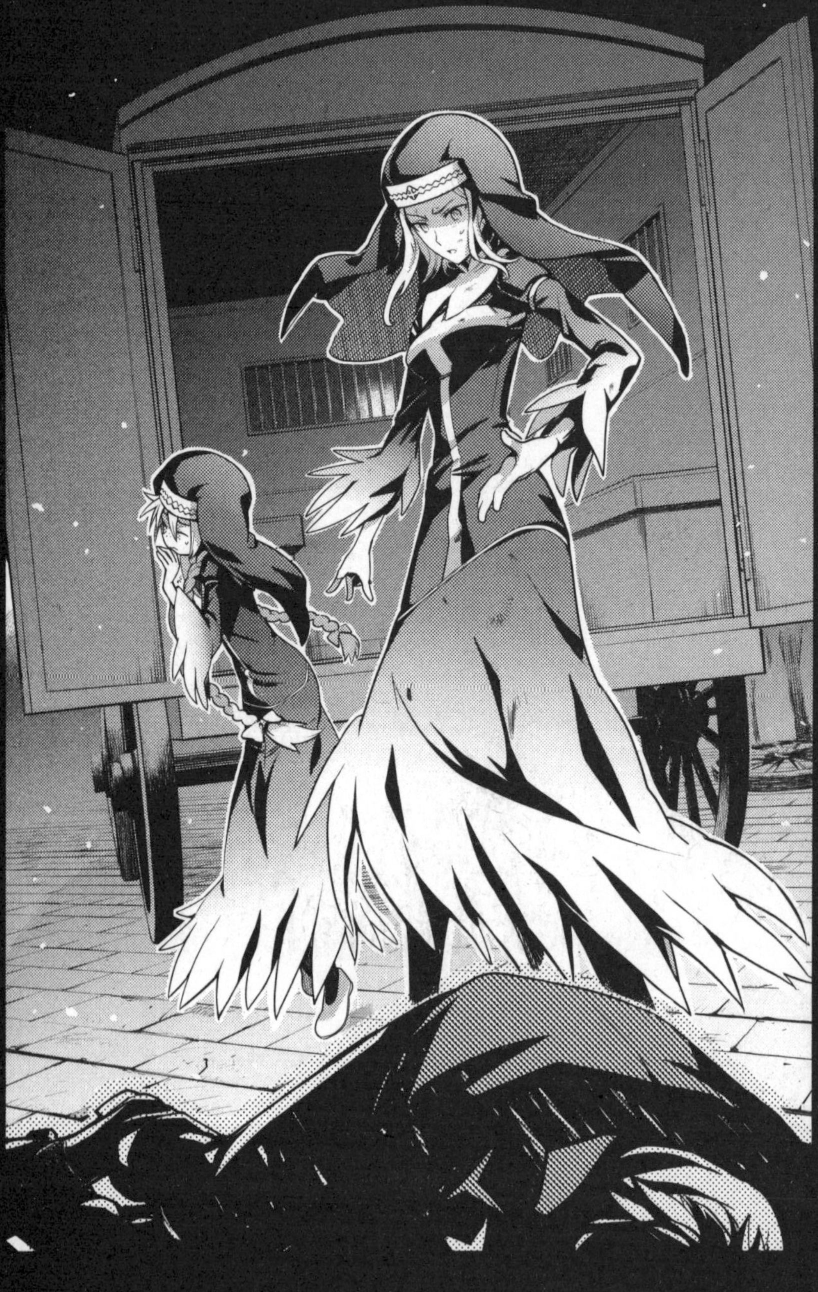

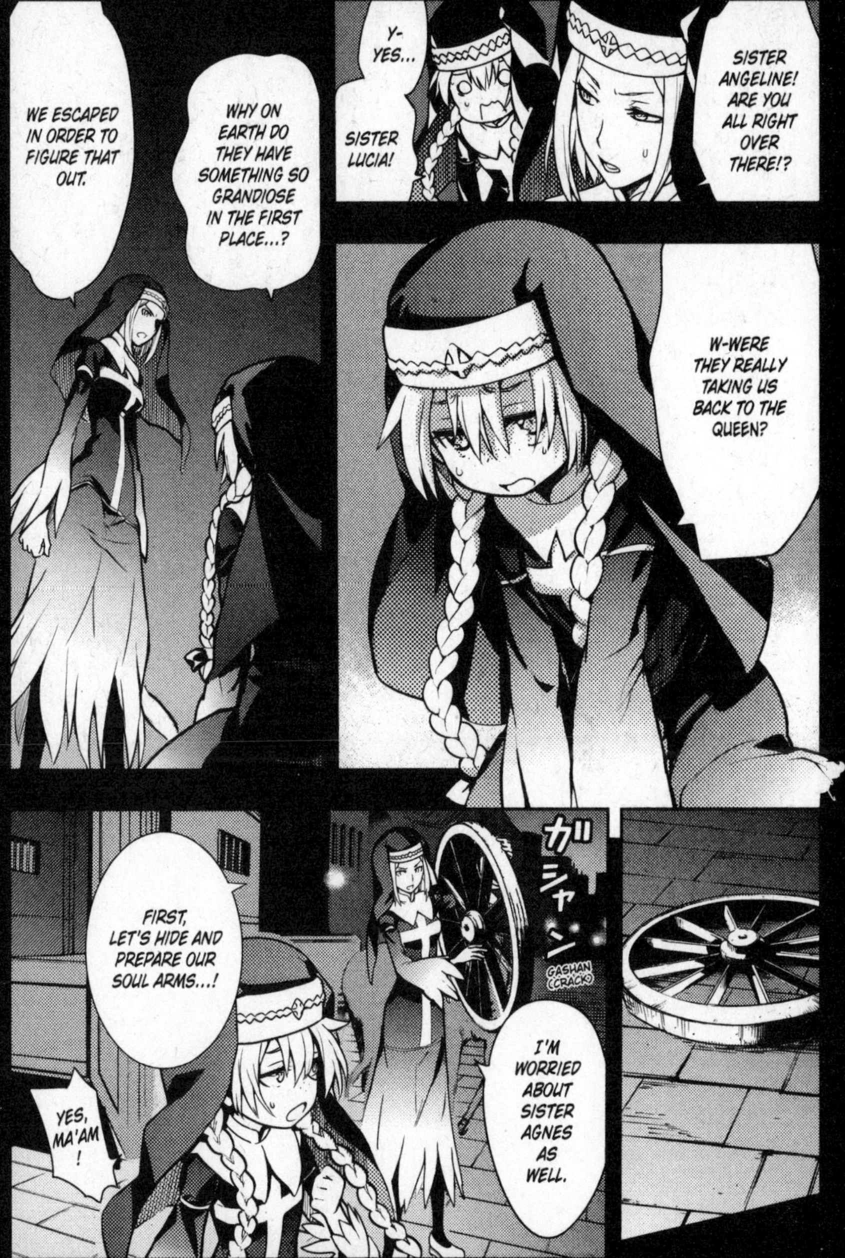

SISTER ANGELINE! ARE YOU ALL RIGHT OVER THERE!?
Y- YES... SISTER LUCIA!
W-WERE THEY REALLY TAKING US BACK TO THE QUEEN?
WHY ON EARTH DO THEY HAVE SOMETHING SO GRANDIOSE IN THE FIRST PLACE...?
WE ESCAPED IN ORDER TO FIGURE THAT OUT.
ガシャン
GASHAN (CRACK)
I'M WORRIED ABOUT SISTER AGNES AS WELL.
FIRST, LET'S HIDE AND PREPARE OUR SOUL ARMS...!
YES, MA'AM!

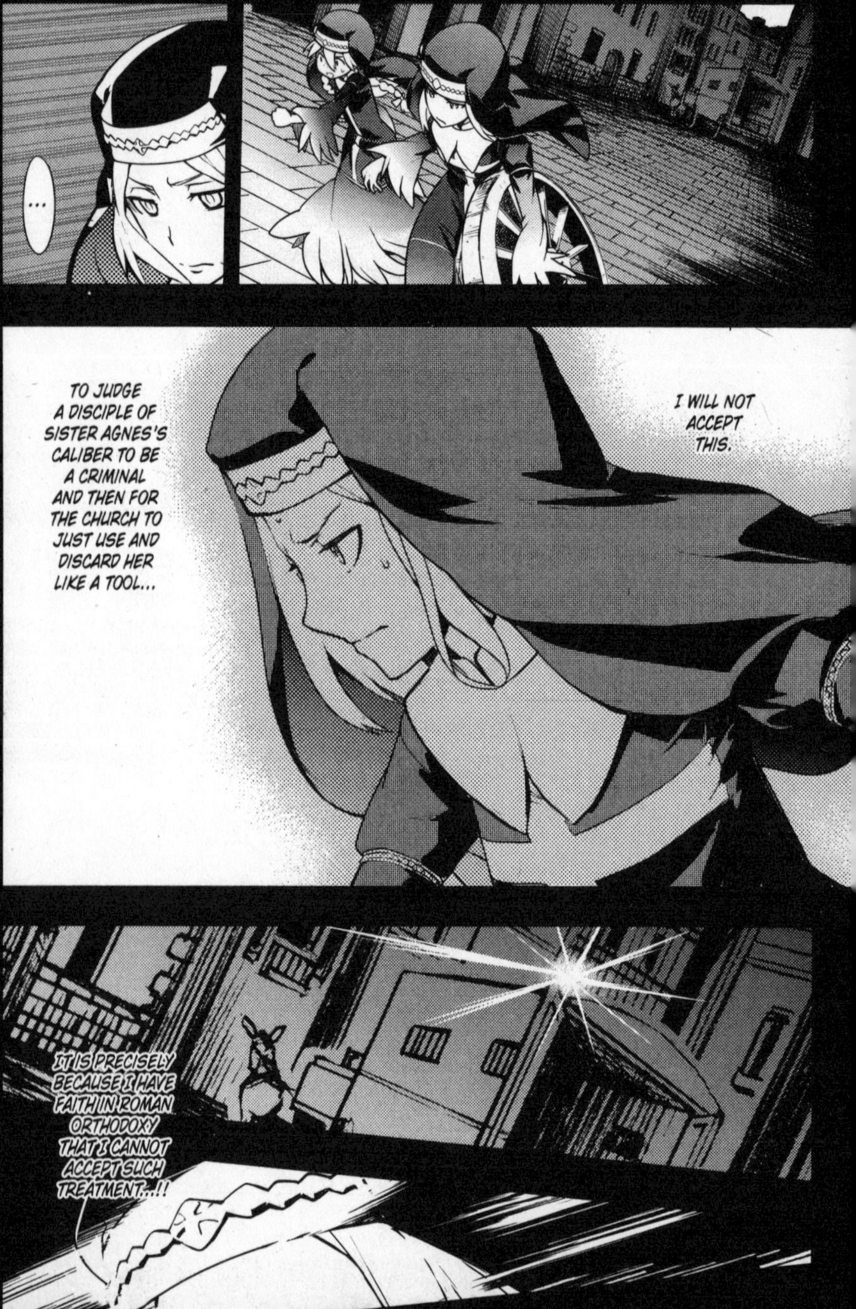
...
I WILL NOT ACCEPT THIS.
TO JUDGE A DISCIPLE OF SISTER AGNES'S CALIBER TO BE A CRIMINAL AND THEN FOR THE CHURCH TO JUST USE AND DISCARD HER LIKE A TOOL...
IT IS PRECISELY BECAUSE I HAVE FAITH IN ROMAN ORTHODOXY THAT I CANNOT ACCEPT SUCH TREATMENT...!!

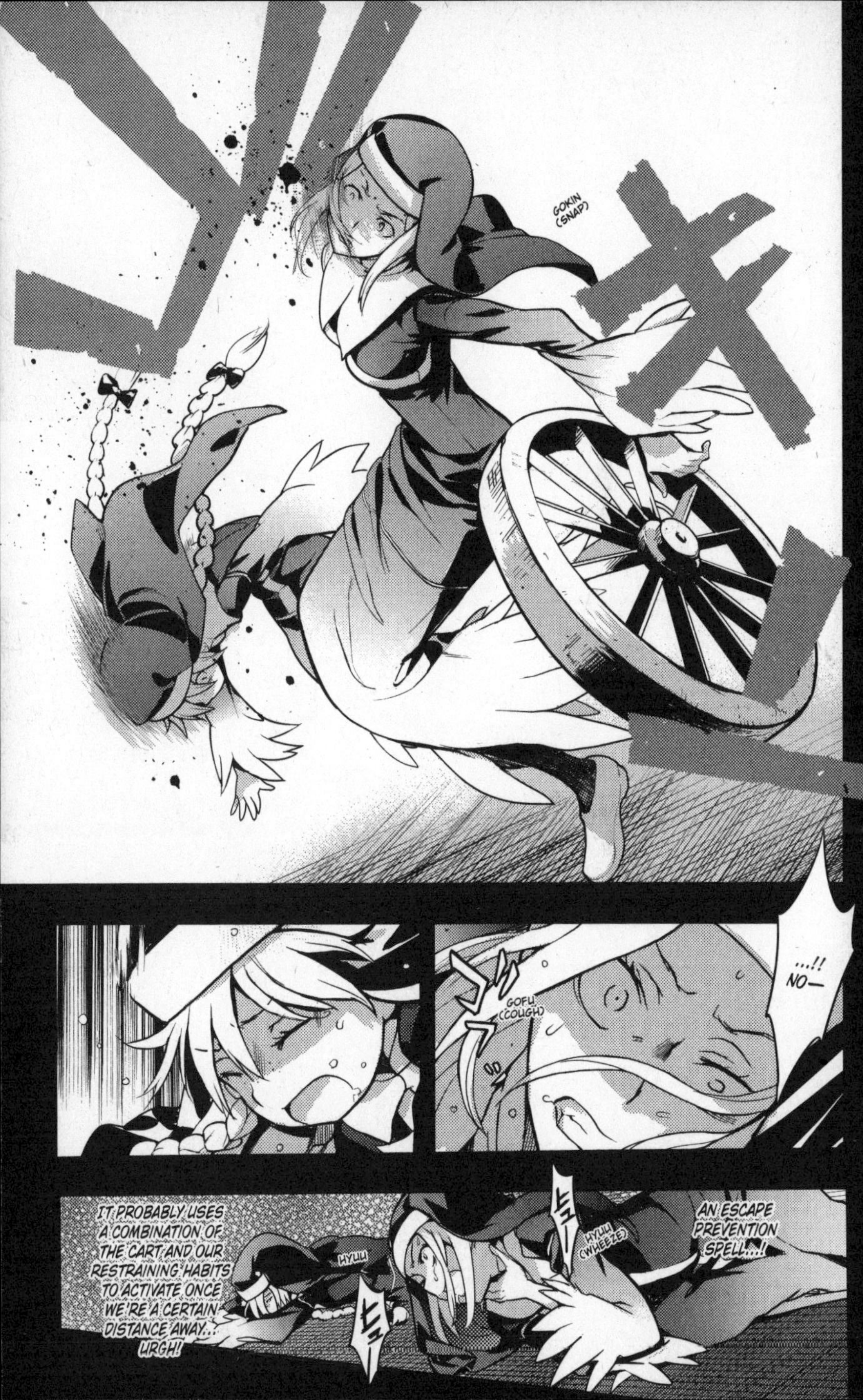
GOKIN (SNAP)
...!! NO—
GOFU (COUGH)
AN ESCAPE PREVENTION SPELL...!
HYUU (WHEEZE)
HYUU
IT PROBABLY USES A COMBINATION OF THE CART AND OUR RESTRAINING HABITS TO ACTIVATE ONCE WE'RE A CERTAIN DISTANCE AWAY... URGH!

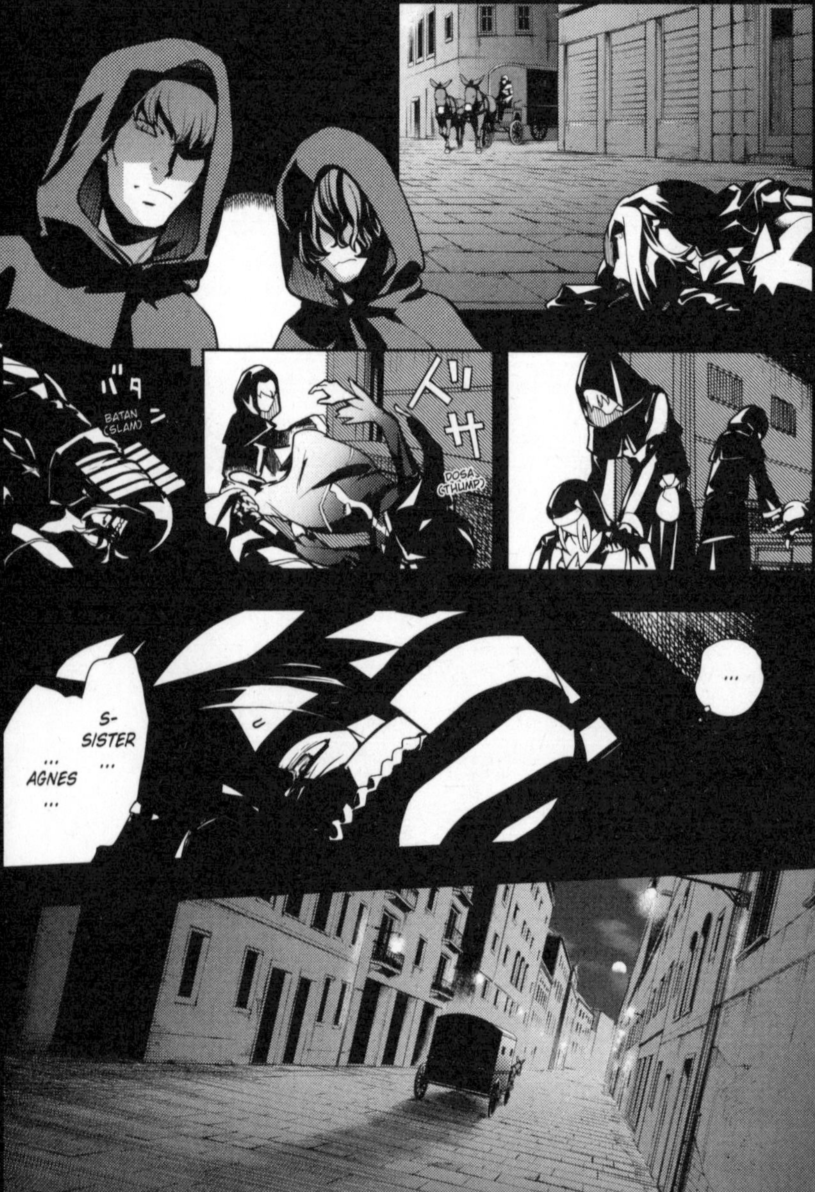
ドサ
DOSA (THUMP)
バタン
BATAN (SLAM)
...
S-SISTER ... AGNES ...

# #87 ORSOLA OF CHIOGGIA

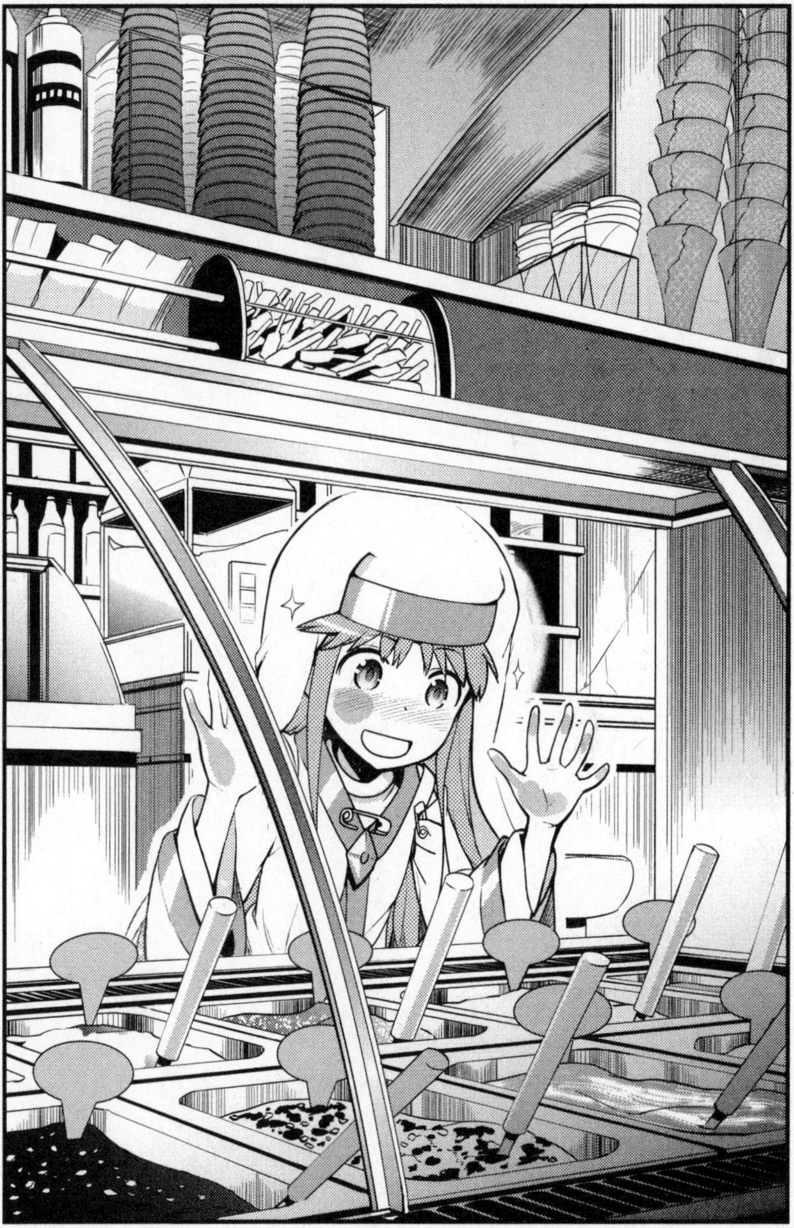

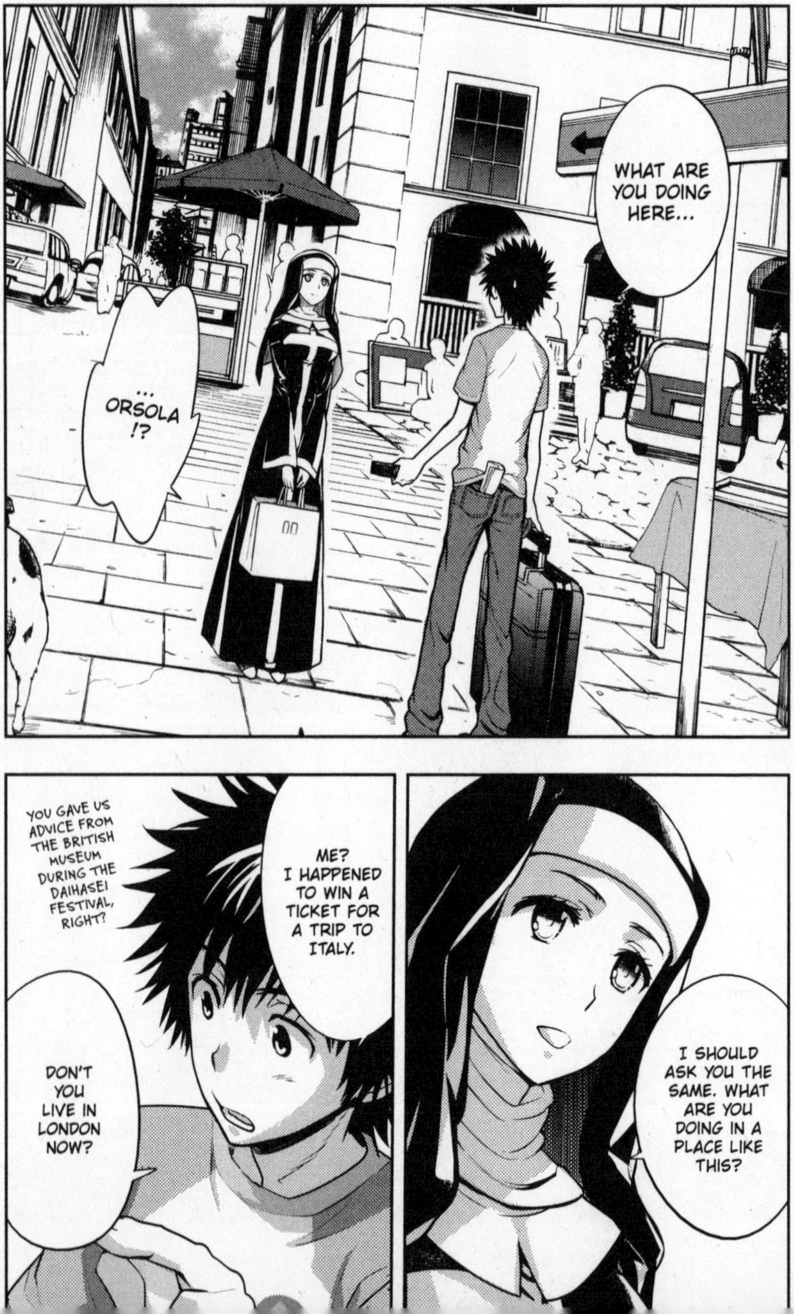
WHAT ARE YOU DOING HERE...
... ORSOLA !?
I SHOULD ASK YOU THE SAME. WHAT ARE YOU DOING IN A PLACE LIKE THIS?
ME? I HAPPENED TO WIN A TICKET FOR A TRIP TO ITALY.
YOU GAVE US ADVICE FROM THE BRITISH MUSEUM DURING THE DAIHASEI FESTIVAL, RIGHT?
DON'T YOU LIVE IN LONDON NOW?

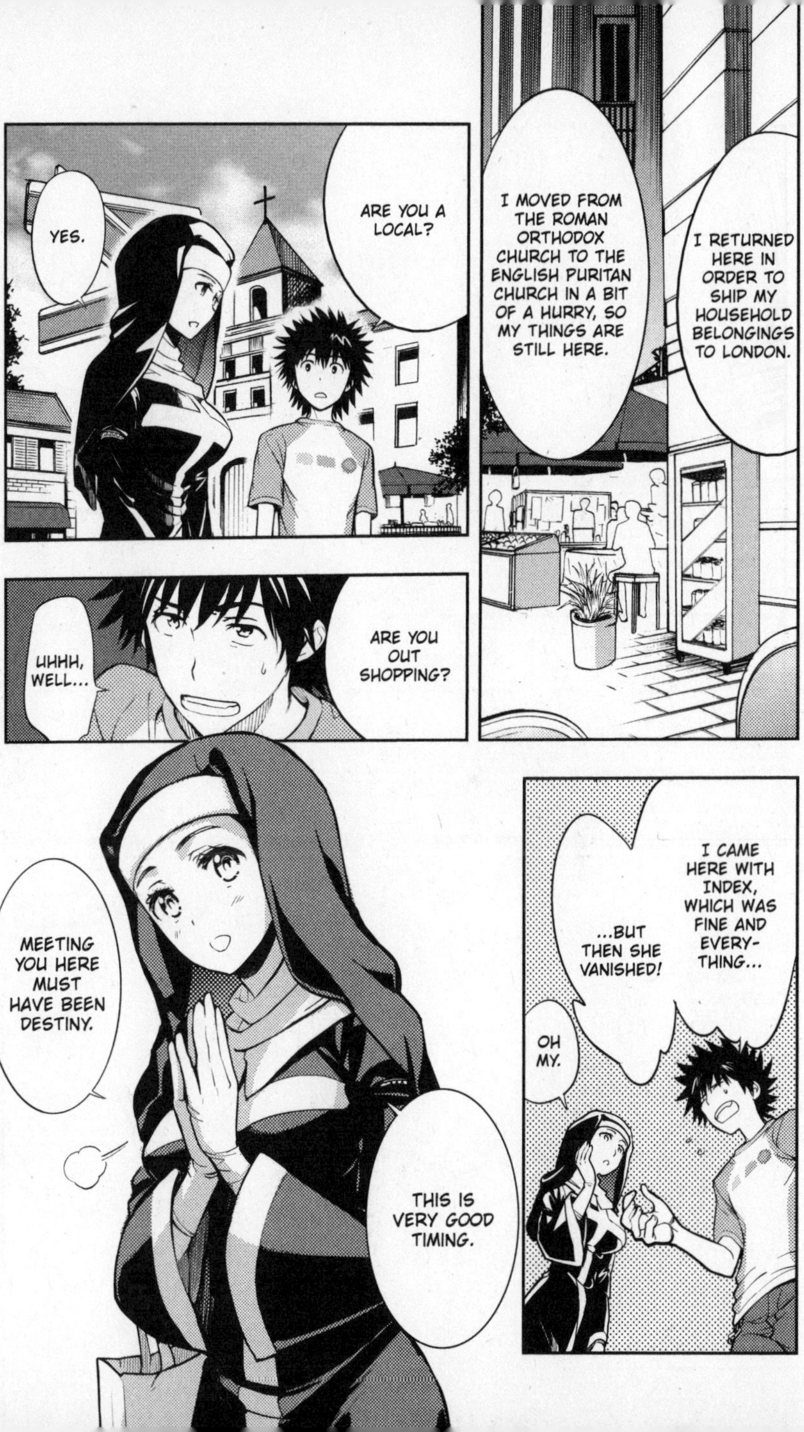
I RETURNED HERE IN ORDER TO SHIP MY HOUSEHOLD BELONGINGS TO LONDON.
I MOVED FROM THE ROMAN ORTHODOX CHURCH TO THE ENGLISH PURITAN CHURCH IN A BIT OF A HURRY, SO MY THINGS ARE STILL HERE.
ARE YOU A LOCAL?
YES.
ARE YOU OUT SHOPPING?
UHHH, WELL...
I CAME HERE WITH INDEX, WHICH WAS FINE AND EVERY-THING...
...BUT THEN SHE VANISHED!
OH MY.
MEETING YOU HERE MUST HAVE BEEN DESTINY.
THIS IS VERY GOOD TIMING.

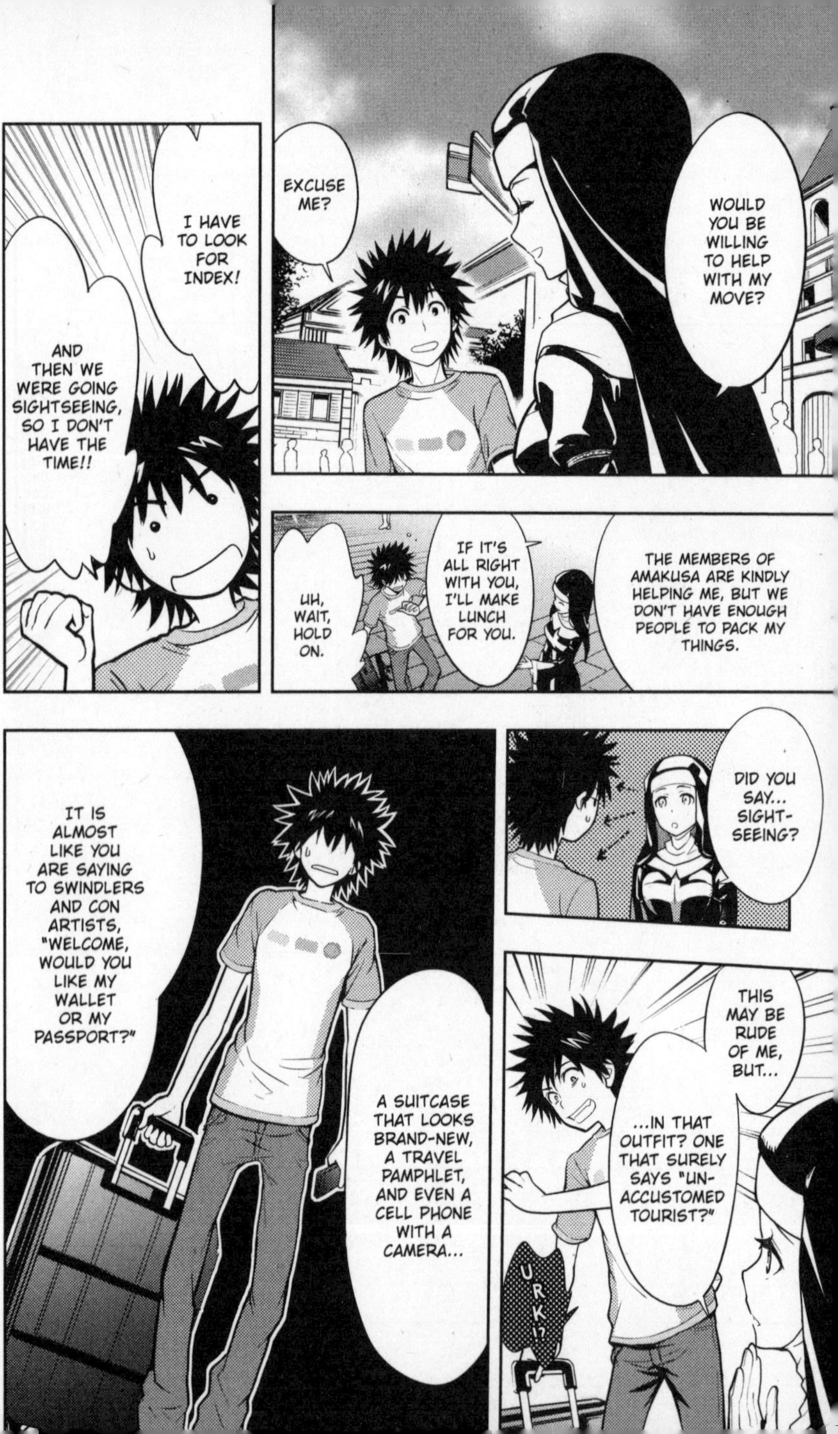
WOULD YOU BE WILLING TO HELP WITH MY MOVE?
EXCUSE ME?
THE MEMBERS OF AMAKUSA ARE KINDLY HELPING ME, BUT WE DON'T HAVE ENOUGH PEOPLE TO PACK MY THINGS.
IF IT'S ALL RIGHT WITH YOU, I'LL MAKE LUNCH FOR YOU.
UH, WAIT, HOLD ON.
I HAVE TO LOOK FOR INDEX!
AND THEN WE WERE GOING SIGHTSEEING, SO I DON'T HAVE THE TIME!!
DID YOU SAY... SIGHT-SEEING?
THIS MAY BE RUDE OF ME, BUT...
...IN THAT OUTFIT? ONE THAT SURELY SAYS "UN-ACCUSTOMED TOURIST?"
URK!?
A SUITCASE THAT LOOKS BRAND-NEW, A TRAVEL PAMPHLET, AND EVEN A CELL PHONE WITH A CAMERA...
IT IS ALMOST LIKE YOU ARE SAYING TO SWINDLERS AND CON ARTISTS, "WELCOME, WOULD YOU LIKE MY WALLET OR MY PASSPORT?"

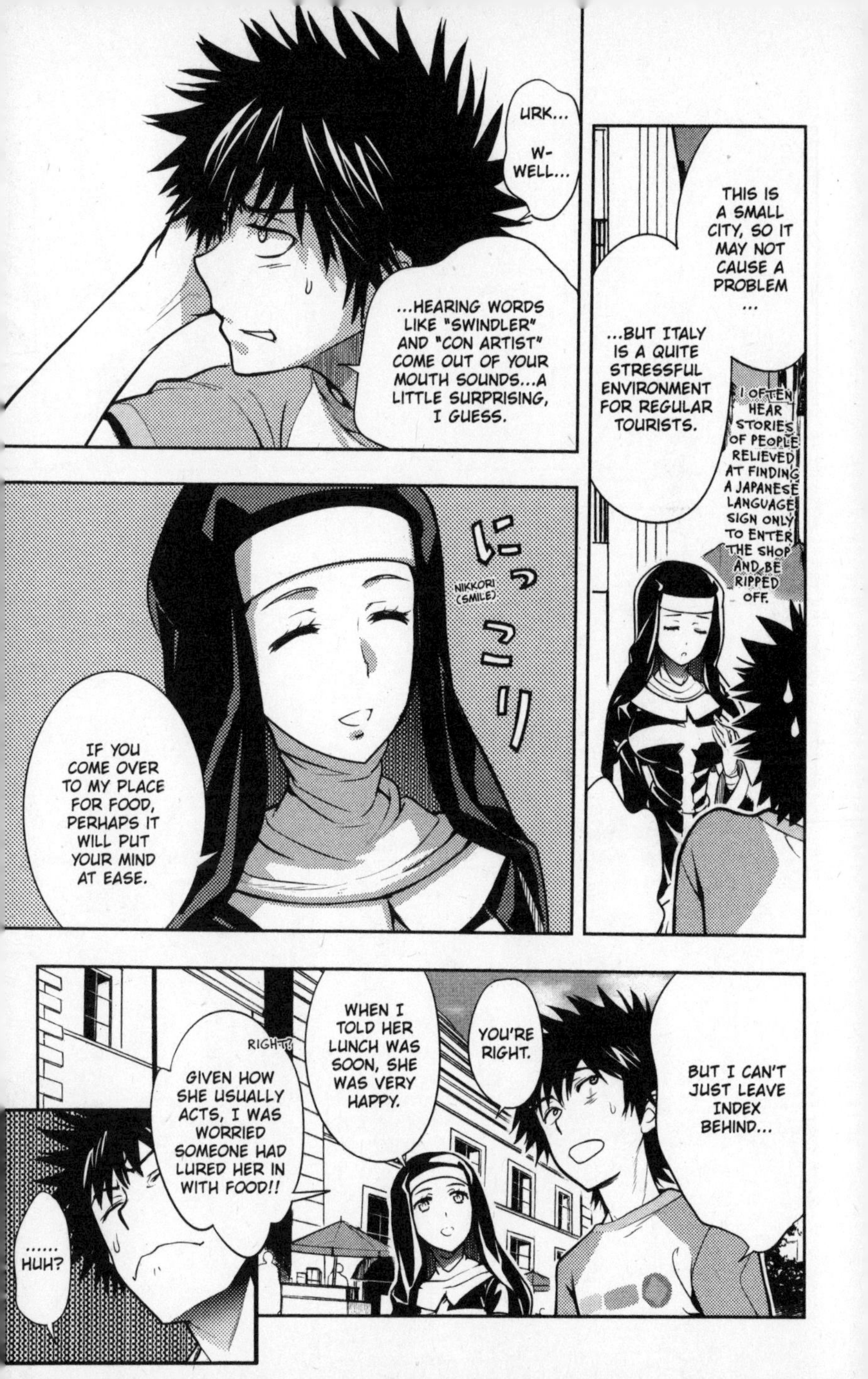
THIS IS A SMALL CITY, SO IT MAY NOT CAUSE A PROBLEM ...
...BUT ITALY IS A QUITE STRESSFUL ENVIRONMENT FOR REGULAR TOURISTS.
I OFTEN HEAR STORIES OF PEOPLE RELIEVED AT FINDING A JAPANESE LANGUAGE SIGN ONLY TO ENTER THE SHOP AND BE RIPPED OFF.
URK...
W-WELL...
...HEARING WORDS LIKE "SWINDLER" AND "CON ARTIST" COME OUT OF YOUR MOUTH SOUNDS...A LITTLE SURPRISING, I GUESS.
にっこーり
NIKKORI (SMILE)
IF YOU COME OVER TO MY PLACE FOR FOOD, PERHAPS IT WILL PUT YOUR MIND AT EASE.
BUT I CAN'T JUST LEAVE INDEX BEHIND...
YOU'RE RIGHT.
WHEN I TOLD HER LUNCH WAS SOON, SHE WAS VERY HAPPY.
GIVEN HOW SHE USUALLY ACTS, I WAS WORRIED SOMEONE HAD LURED HER IN WITH FOOD!!
RIGHT?
......HUH?

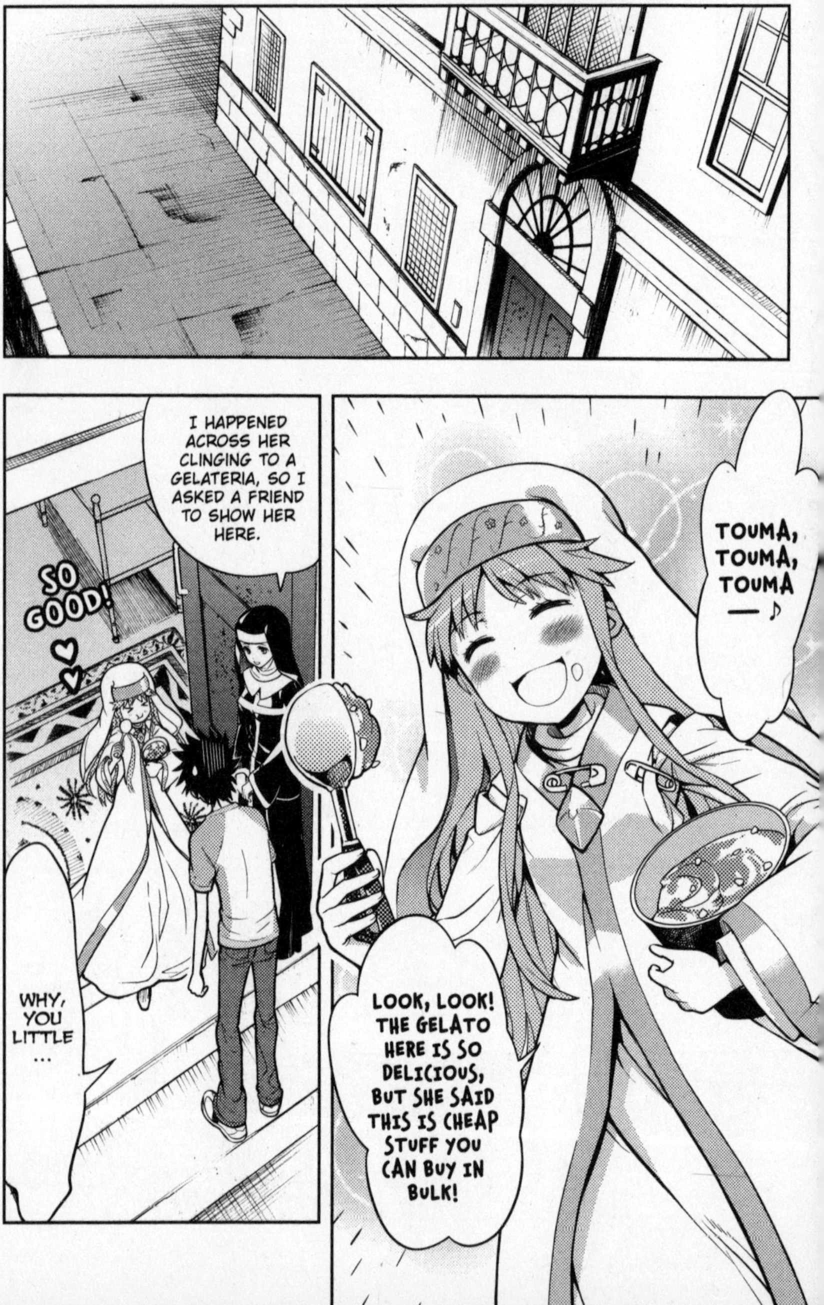
TOUMA, TOUMA, TOUMA—♪
LOOK, LOOK! THE GELATO HERE IS SO DELICIOUS, BUT SHE SAID THIS IS CHEAP STUFF YOU CAN BUY IN BULK!
I HAPPENED ACROSS HER CLINGING TO A GELATERIA, SO I ASKED A FRIEND TO SHOW HER HERE.
SO GOOD! ♥
WHY, YOU LITTLE ...

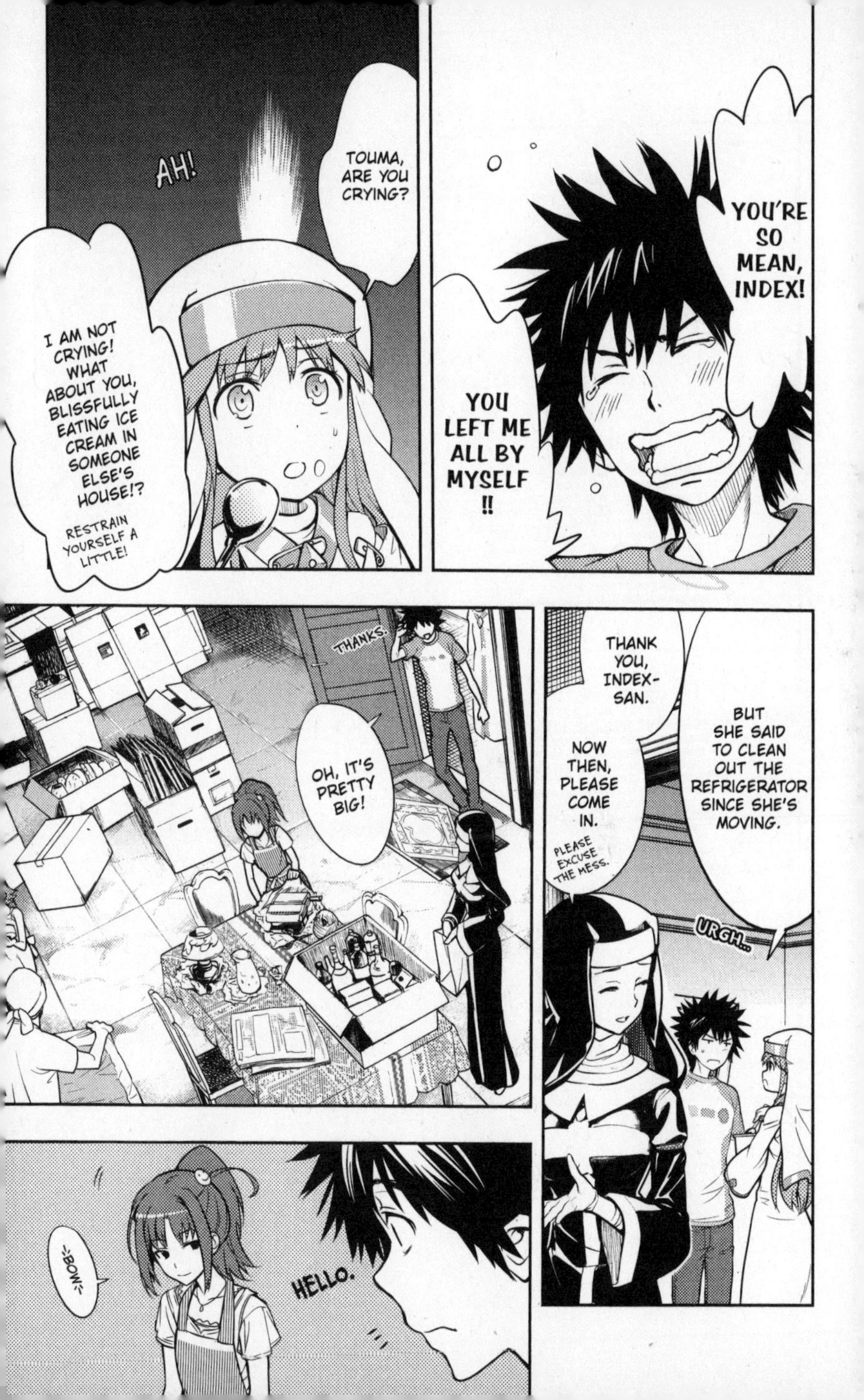
YOU'RE SO MEAN, INDEX!
YOU LEFT ME ALL BY MYSELF !!
AH!
TOUMA, ARE YOU CRYING?
I AM NOT CRYING! WHAT ABOUT YOU, BLISSFULLY EATING ICE CREAM IN SOMEONE ELSE'S HOUSE!?
RESTRAIN YOURSELF A LITTLE!
BUT SHE SAID TO CLEAN OUT THE REFRIGERATOR SINCE SHE'S MOVING.
URGH...
THANK YOU, INDEX-SAN.
NOW THEN, PLEASE COME IN.
PLEASE EXCUSE THE MESS.
THANKS.
OH, IT'S PRETTY BIG!
HELLO.
-BOW-

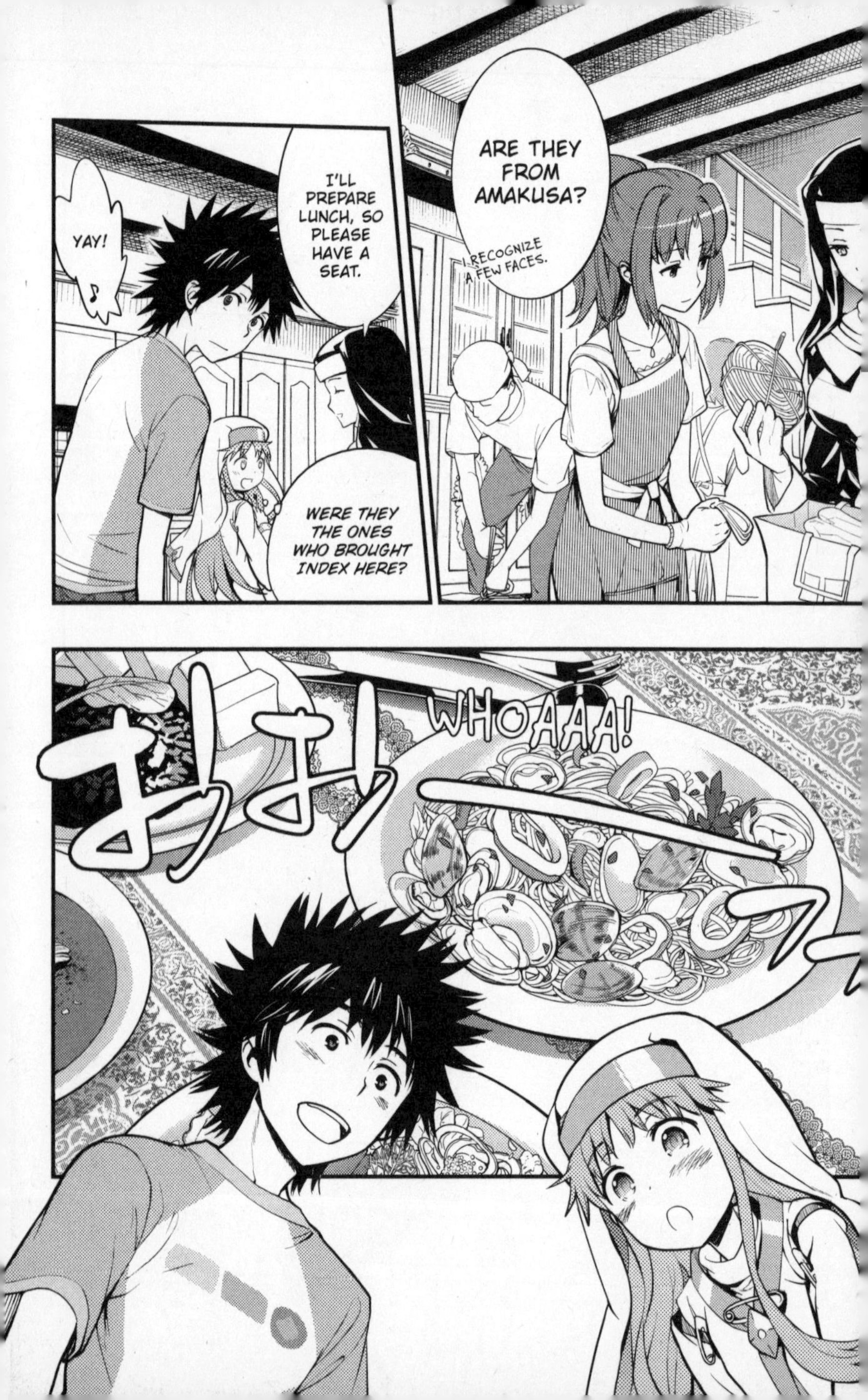
ARE THEY FROM AMAKUSA?
I RECOGNIZE A FEW FACES.
I'LL PREPARE LUNCH, SO PLEASE HAVE A SEAT.
YAY!
WERE THEY THE ONES WHO BROUGHT INDEX HERE?
WHOAAA!

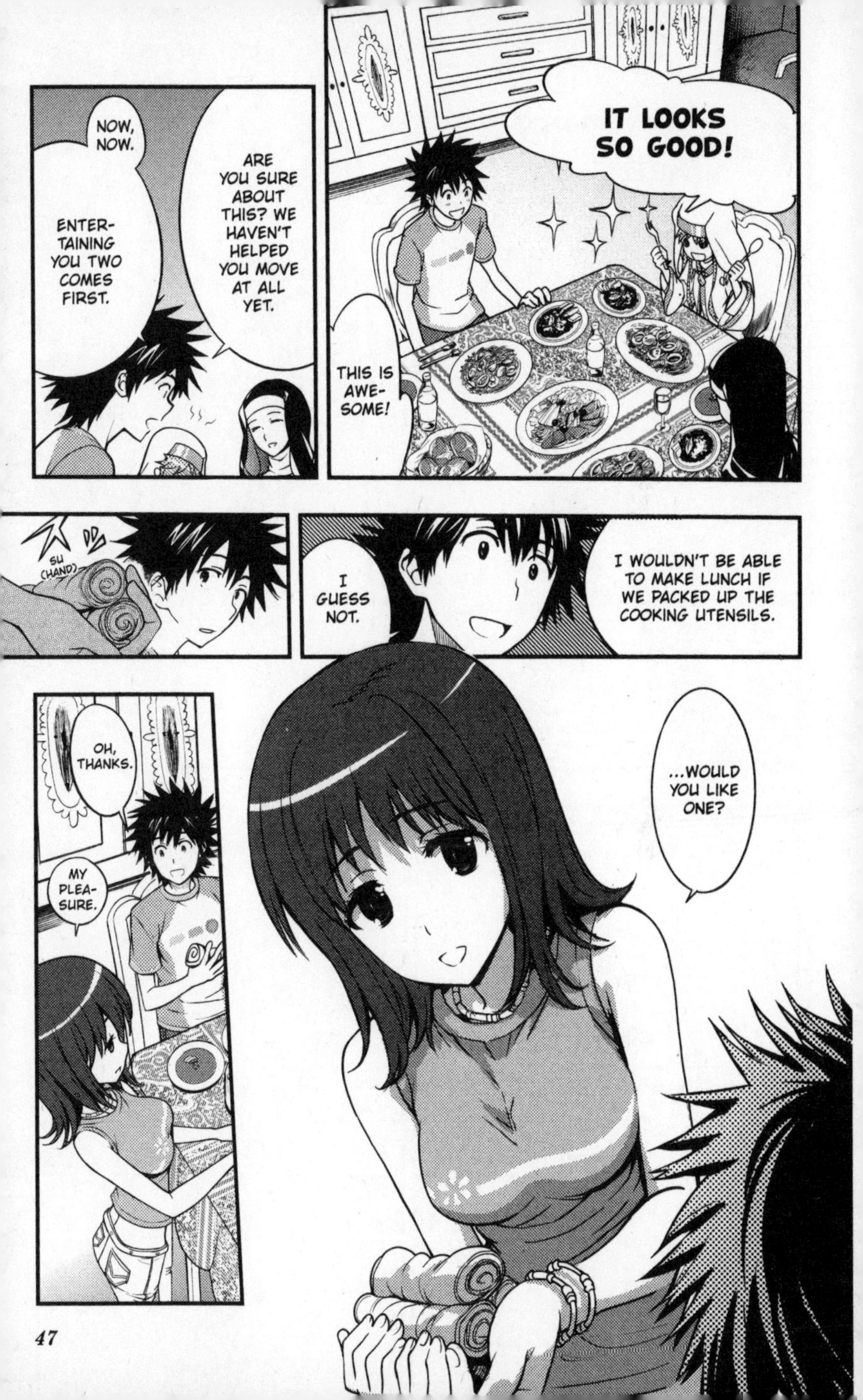
IT LOOKS SO GOOD!
THIS IS AWESOME!
ARE YOU SURE ABOUT THIS? WE HAVEN'T HELPED YOU MOVE AT ALL YET.
NOW, NOW.
ENTER-TAINING YOU TWO COMES FIRST.
I WOULDN'T BE ABLE TO MAKE LUNCH IF WE PACKED UP THE COOKING UTENSILS.
I GUESS NOT.
SU (HAND)
...WOULD YOU LIKE ONE?
OH, THANKS.
MY PLEA-SURE.

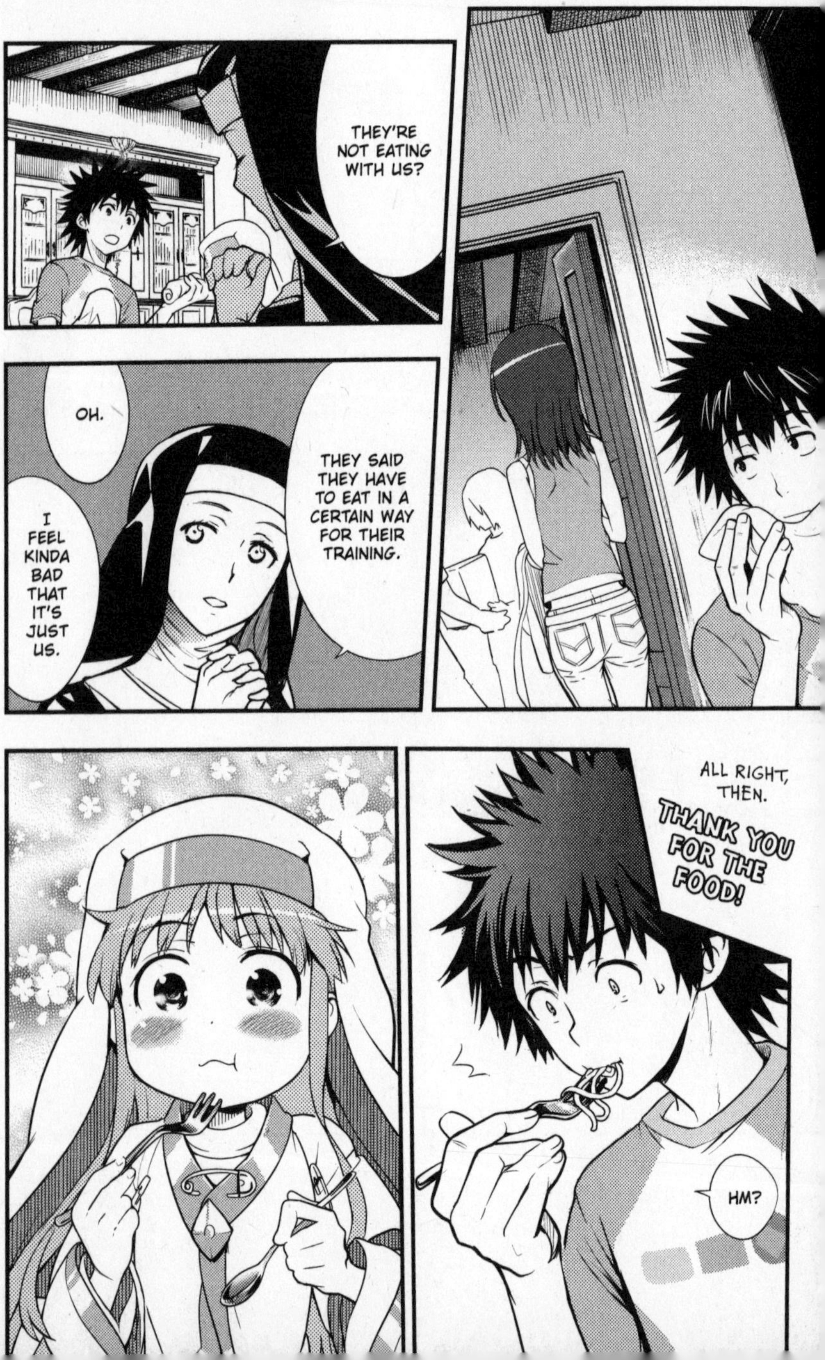
THEY'RE NOT EATING WITH US?
THEY SAID THEY HAVE TO EAT IN A CERTAIN WAY FOR THEIR TRAINING.
OH.
I FEEL KINDA BAD THAT IT'S JUST US.
ALL RIGHT, THEN.
THANK YOU FOR THE FOOD!
HM?

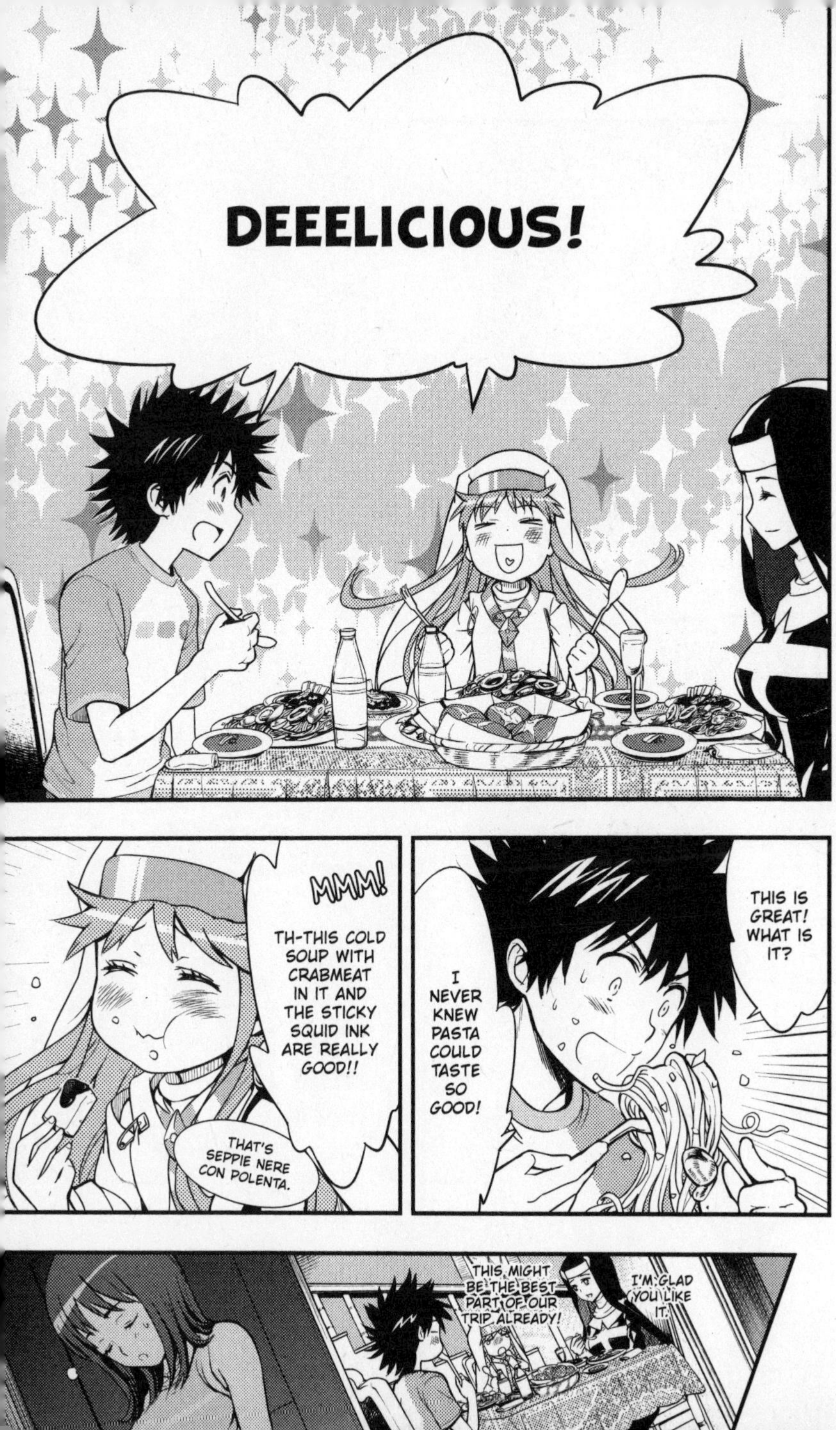
DEEELICIOUS!
THIS IS GREAT! WHAT IS IT?
I NEVER KNEW PASTA COULD TASTE SO GOOD!
MMM!
TH-THIS COLD SOUP WITH CRABMEAT IN IT AND THE STICKY SQUID INK ARE REALLY GOOD!!
THAT'S SEPPIE NERE CON POLENTA.
I'M GLAD YOU LIKE IT.
THIS MIGHT BE THE BEST PART OF OUR TRIP ALREADY!

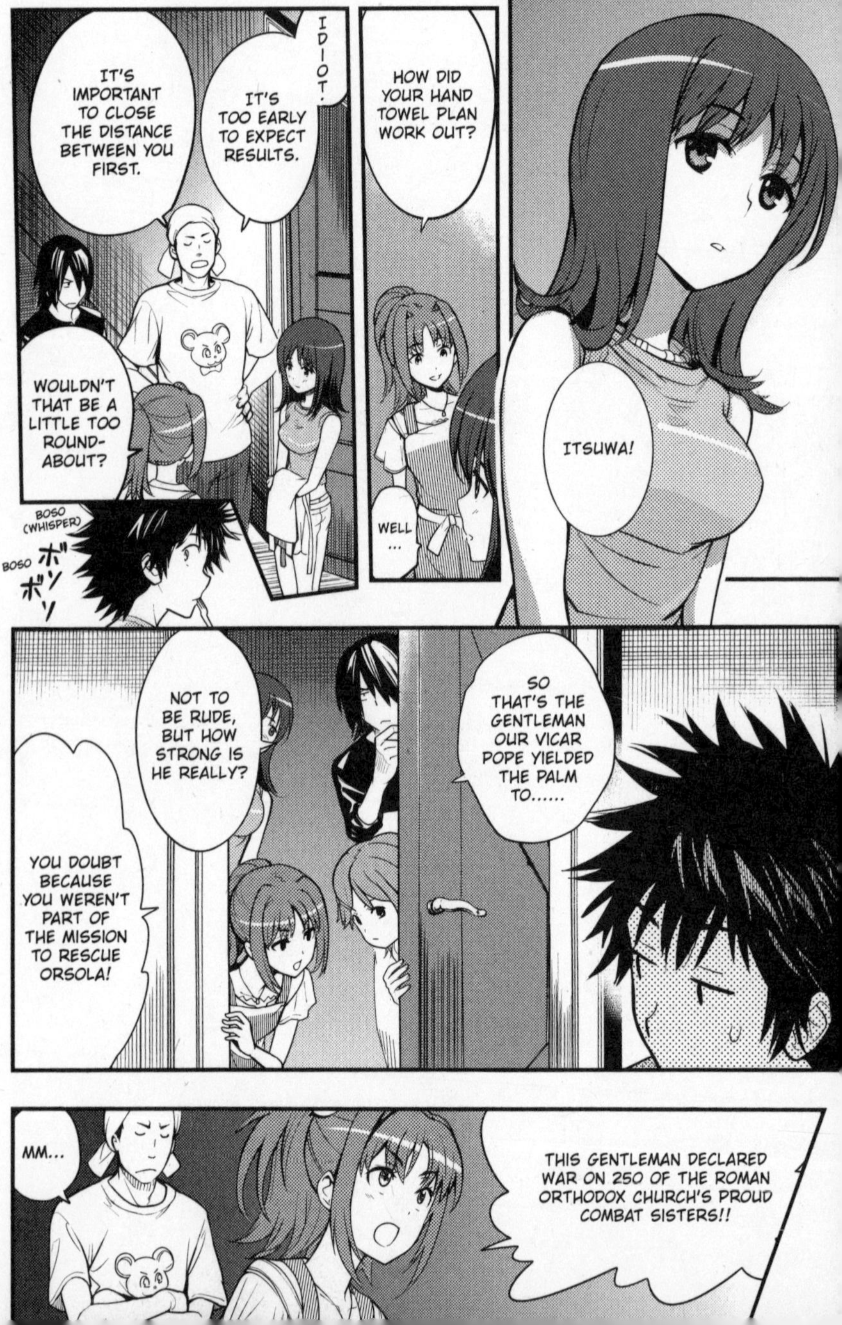
ITSUWA!
HOW DID YOUR HAND TOWEL PLAN WORK OUT?
WELL ...
IDIOT.
IT'S TOO EARLY TO EXPECT RESULTS.
IT'S IMPORTANT TO CLOSE THE DISTANCE BETWEEN YOU FIRST.
WOULDN'T THAT BE A LITTLE TOO ROUND-ABOUT?
BOSO (WHISPER)
BOSO
ボソ ボソ
SO THAT'S THE GENTLEMAN OUR VICAR POPE YIELDED THE PALM TO......
NOT TO BE RUDE, BUT HOW STRONG IS HE REALLY?
YOU DOUBT BECAUSE YOU WEREN'T PART OF THE MISSION TO RESCUE ORSOLA!
THIS GENTLEMAN DECLARED WAR ON 250 OF THE ROMAN ORTHODOX CHURCH'S PROUD COMBAT SISTERS!!
MM...

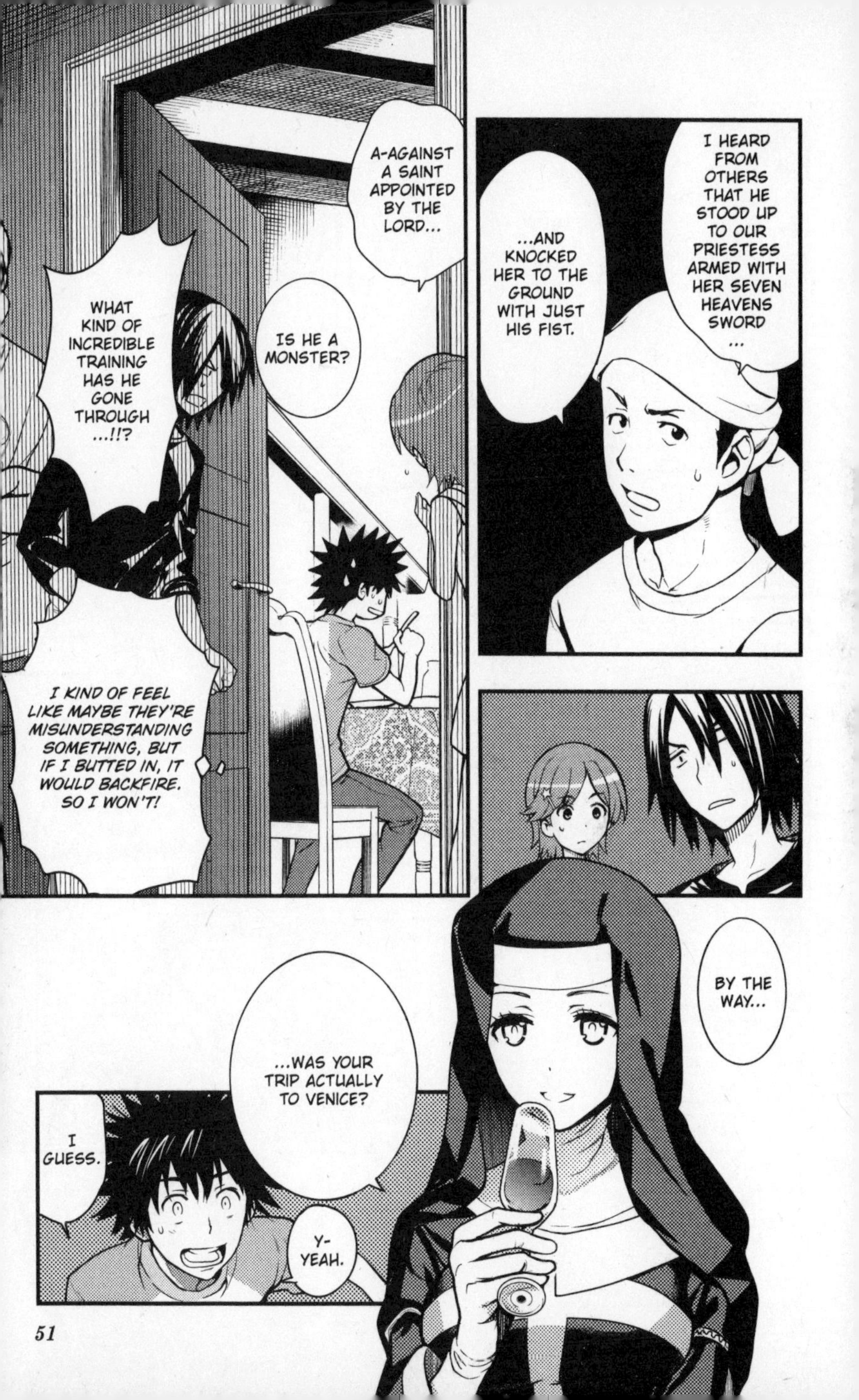
I HEARD FROM OTHERS THAT HE STOOD UP TO OUR PRIESTESS ARMED WITH HER SEVEN HEAVENS SWORD...
...AND KNOCKED HER TO THE GROUND WITH JUST HIS FIST.
A-AGAINST A SAINT APPOINTED BY THE LORD...
IS HE A MONSTER?
WHAT KIND OF INCREDIBLE TRAINING HAS HE GONE THROUGH...!!?
I KIND OF FEEL LIKE MAYBE THEY'RE MISUNDERSTANDING SOMETHING, BUT IF I BUTTED IN, IT WOULD BACKFIRE. SO I WON'T!
BY THE WAY...
...WAS YOUR TRIP ACTUALLY TO VENICE?
Y-YEAH.
I GUESS.

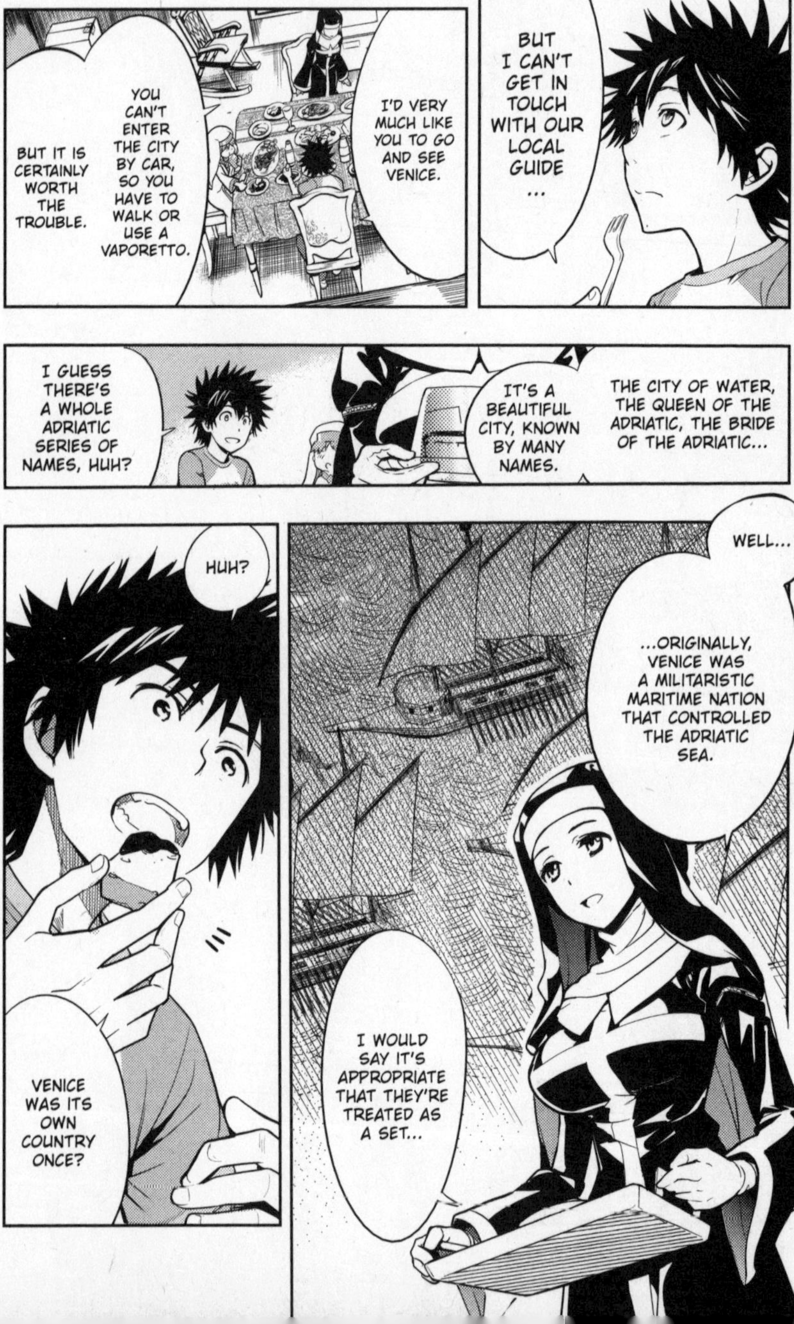
BUT I CAN'T GET IN TOUCH WITH OUR LOCAL GUIDE ...
I'D VERY MUCH LIKE YOU TO GO AND SEE VENICE.
YOU CAN'T ENTER THE CITY BY CAR, SO YOU HAVE TO WALK OR USE A VAPORETTO.
BUT IT IS CERTAINLY WORTH THE TROUBLE.
THE CITY OF WATER, THE QUEEN OF THE ADRIATIC, THE BRIDE OF THE ADRIATIC...
IT'S A BEAUTIFUL CITY, KNOWN BY MANY NAMES.
I GUESS THERE'S A WHOLE ADRIATIC SERIES OF NAMES, HUH?
WELL...
...ORIGINALLY, VENICE WAS A MILITARISTIC MARITIME NATION THAT CONTROLLED THE ADRIATIC SEA.
I WOULD SAY IT'S APPROPRIATE THAT THEY'RE TREATED AS A SET...
HUH?
VENICE WAS ITS OWN COUNTRY ONCE?

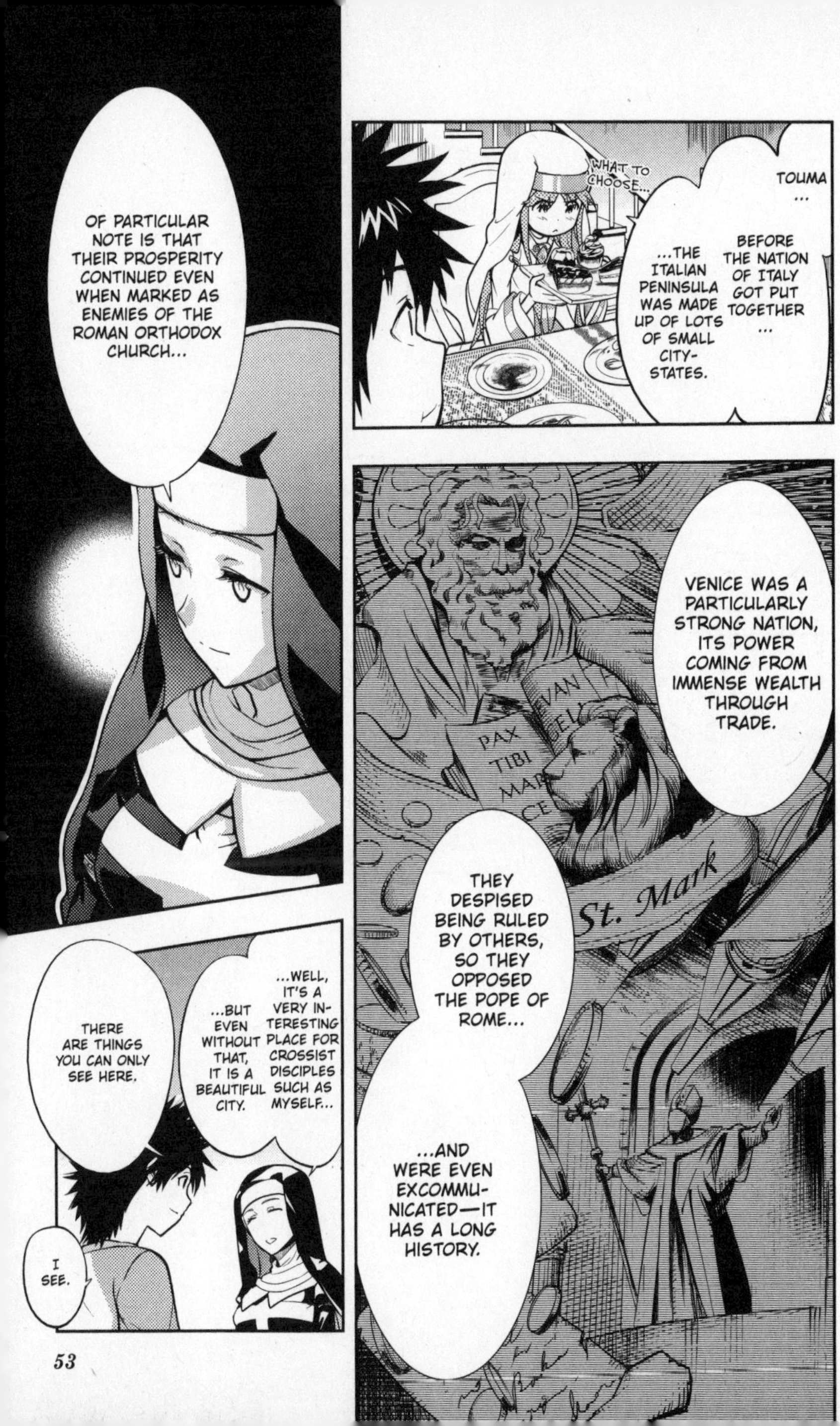
TOUMA...
BEFORE THE NATION OF ITALY GOT PUT TOGETHER...
...THE ITALIAN PENINSULA WAS MADE UP OF LOTS OF SMALL CITY-STATES.
WHAT TO CHOOSE...
VENICE WAS A PARTICULARLY STRONG NATION, ITS POWER COMING FROM IMMENSE WEALTH THROUGH TRADE.
PAX TIBI MAR
VAN EL
St. Mark
THEY DESPISED BEING RULED BY OTHERS, SO THEY OPPOSED THE POPE OF ROME...
...AND WERE EVEN EXCOMMUNICATED—IT HAS A LONG HISTORY.
OF PARTICULAR NOTE IS THAT THEIR PROSPERITY CONTINUED EVEN WHEN MARKED AS ENEMIES OF THE ROMAN ORTHODOX CHURCH...
...WELL, IT'S A VERY INTERESTING PLACE FOR CROSSIST DISCIPLES SUCH AS MYSELF...
...BUT EVEN WITHOUT THAT, IT IS A BEAUTIFUL CITY.
THERE ARE THINGS YOU CAN ONLY SEE HERE.
I SEE.

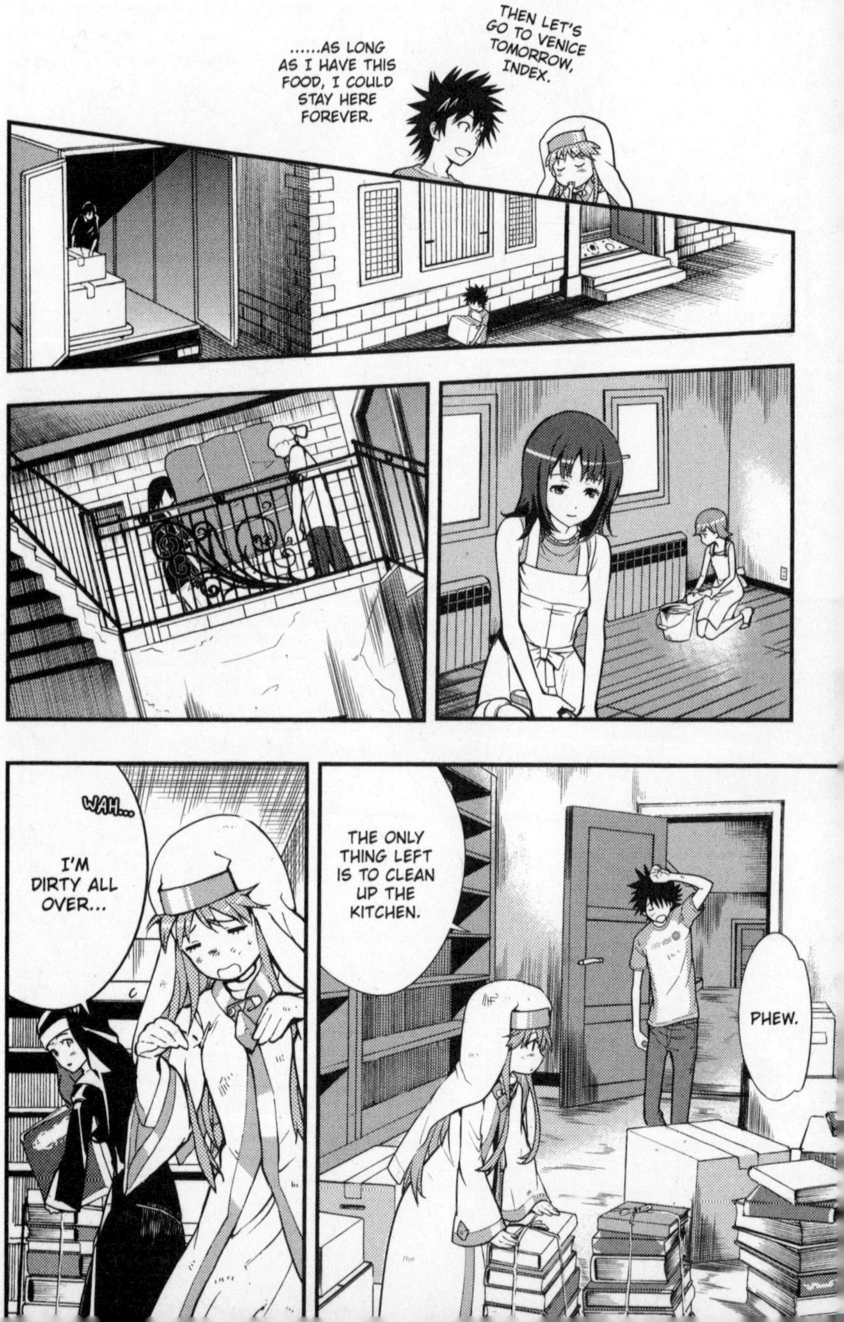
THEN LET'S GO TO VENICE TOMORROW, INDEX.
......AS LONG AS I HAVE THIS FOOD, I COULD STAY HERE FOREVER.
PHEW.
THE ONLY THING LEFT IS TO CLEAN UP THE KITCHEN.
WAH...
I'M DIRTY ALL OVER...

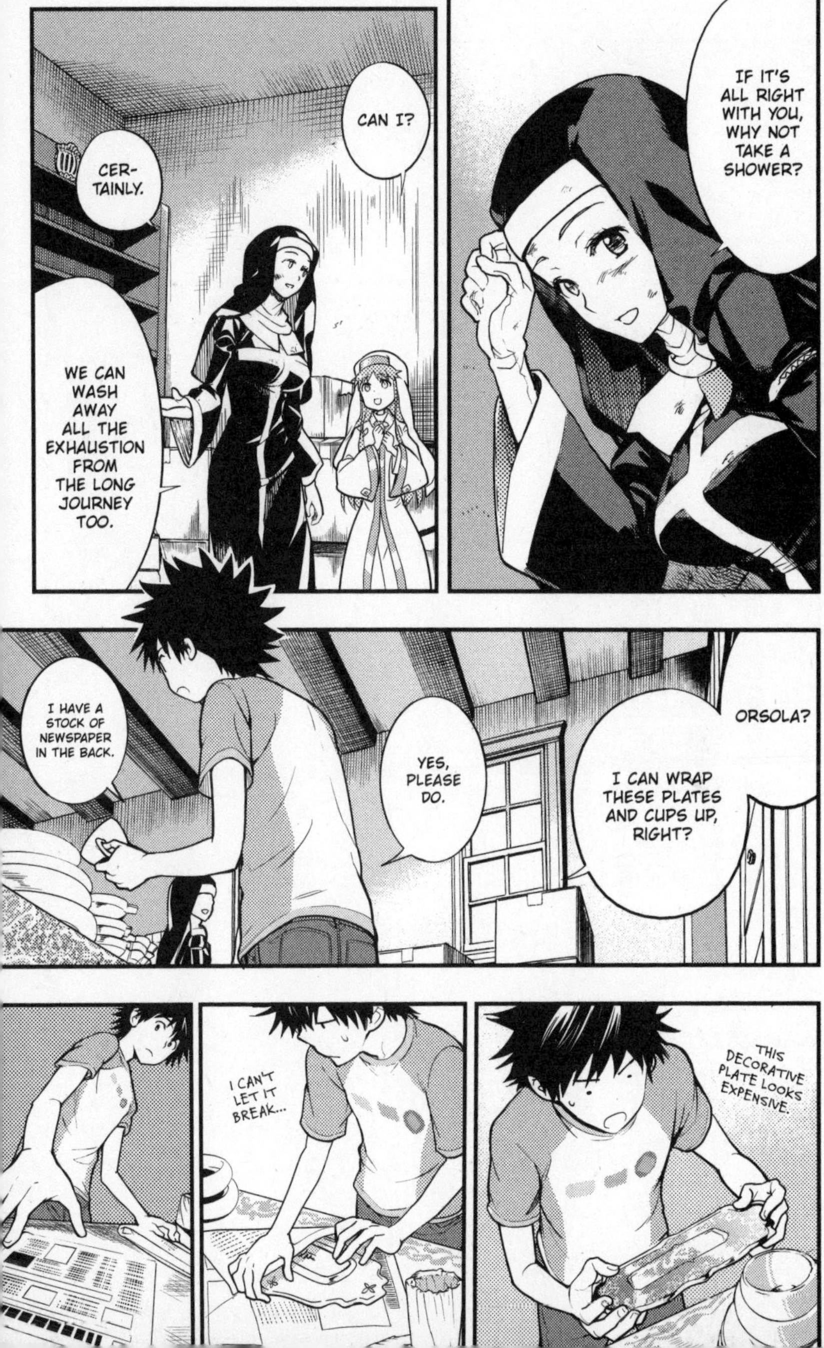
IF IT'S ALL RIGHT WITH YOU, WHY NOT TAKE A SHOWER?
CAN I?
CER-TAINLY.
WE CAN WASH AWAY ALL THE EXHAUSTION FROM THE LONG JOURNEY TOO.
ORSOLA?
I CAN WRAP THESE PLATES AND CUPS UP, RIGHT?
YES, PLEASE DO.
I HAVE A STOCK OF NEWSPAPER IN THE BACK.
THIS DECORATIVE PLATE LOOKS EXPENSIVE.
I CAN'T LET IT BREAK...

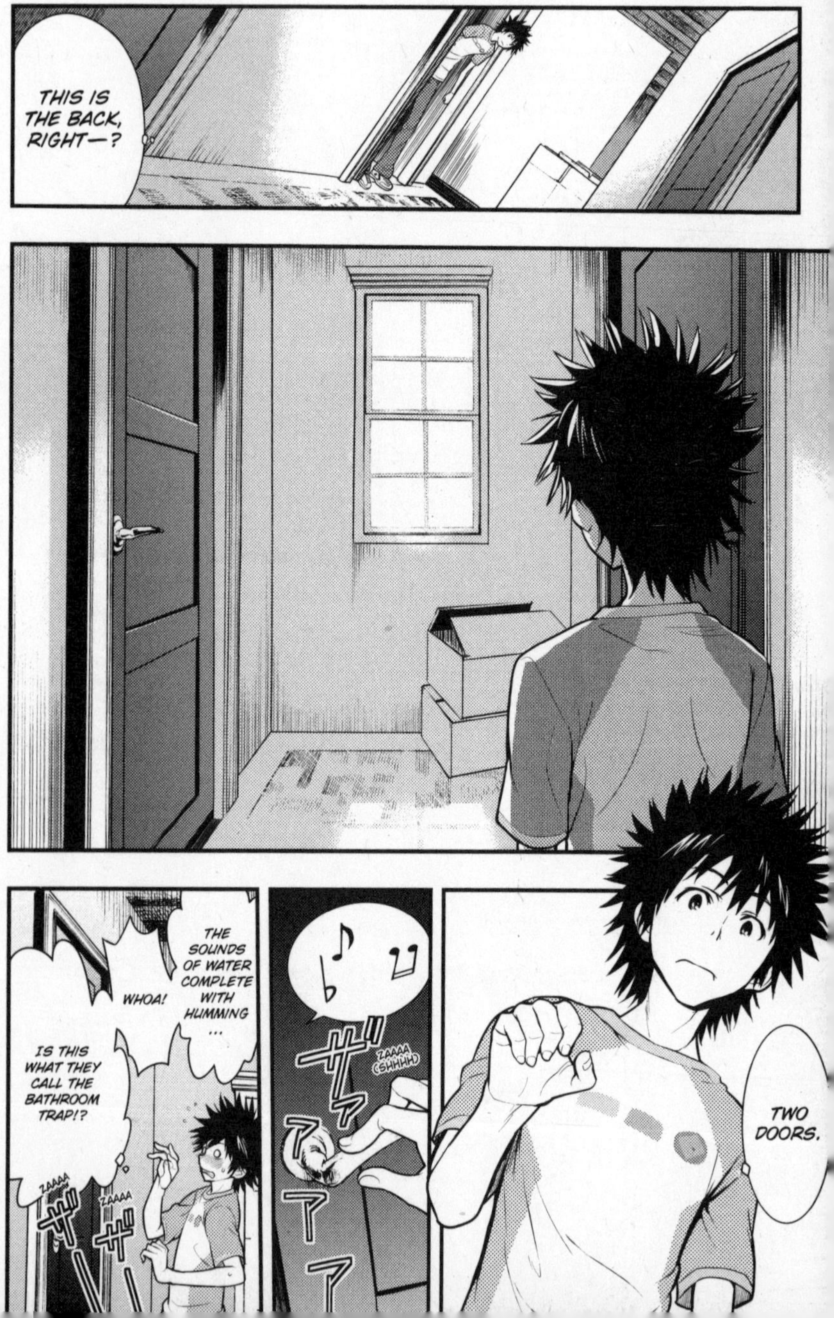
THIS IS THE BACK, RIGHT—?
TWO DOORS.
ZAAAA (SHHHH)
THE SOUNDS OF WATER COMPLETE WITH HUMMING...
WHOA!
IS THIS WHAT THEY CALL THE BATHROOM TRAP!?
ZAAAA
ZAAAA

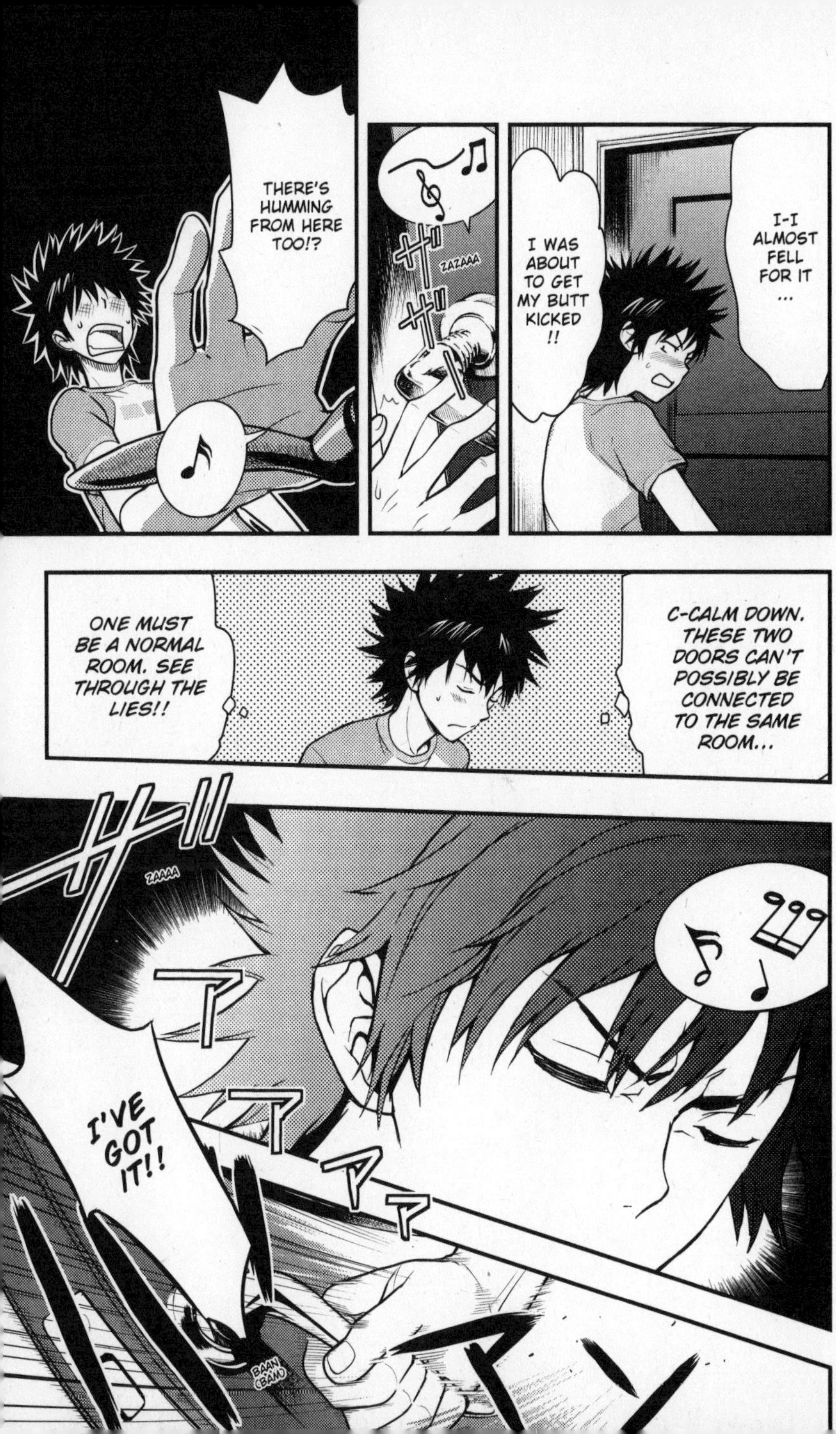
I-I ALMOST FELL FOR IT ...
I WAS ABOUT TO GET MY BUTT KICKED !!
ZAZAAA
THERE'S HUMMING FROM HERE TOO!?
C-CALM DOWN. THESE TWO DOORS CAN'T POSSIBLY BE CONNECTED TO THE SAME ROOM...
ONE MUST BE A NORMAL ROOM. SEE THROUGH THE LIES!!
ZAAAA
I'VE GOT IT!!
BAAN (BAM)

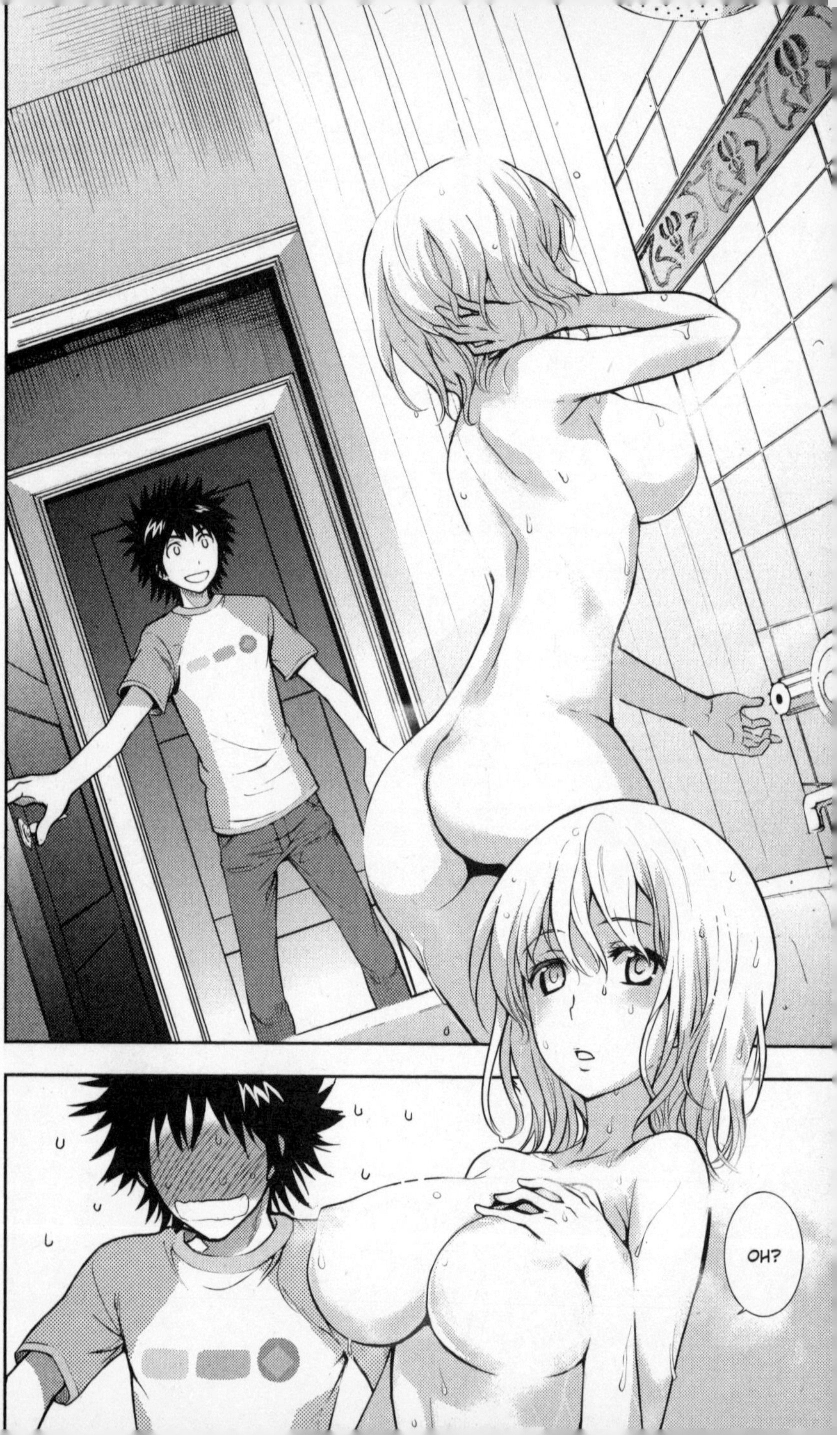
OH?

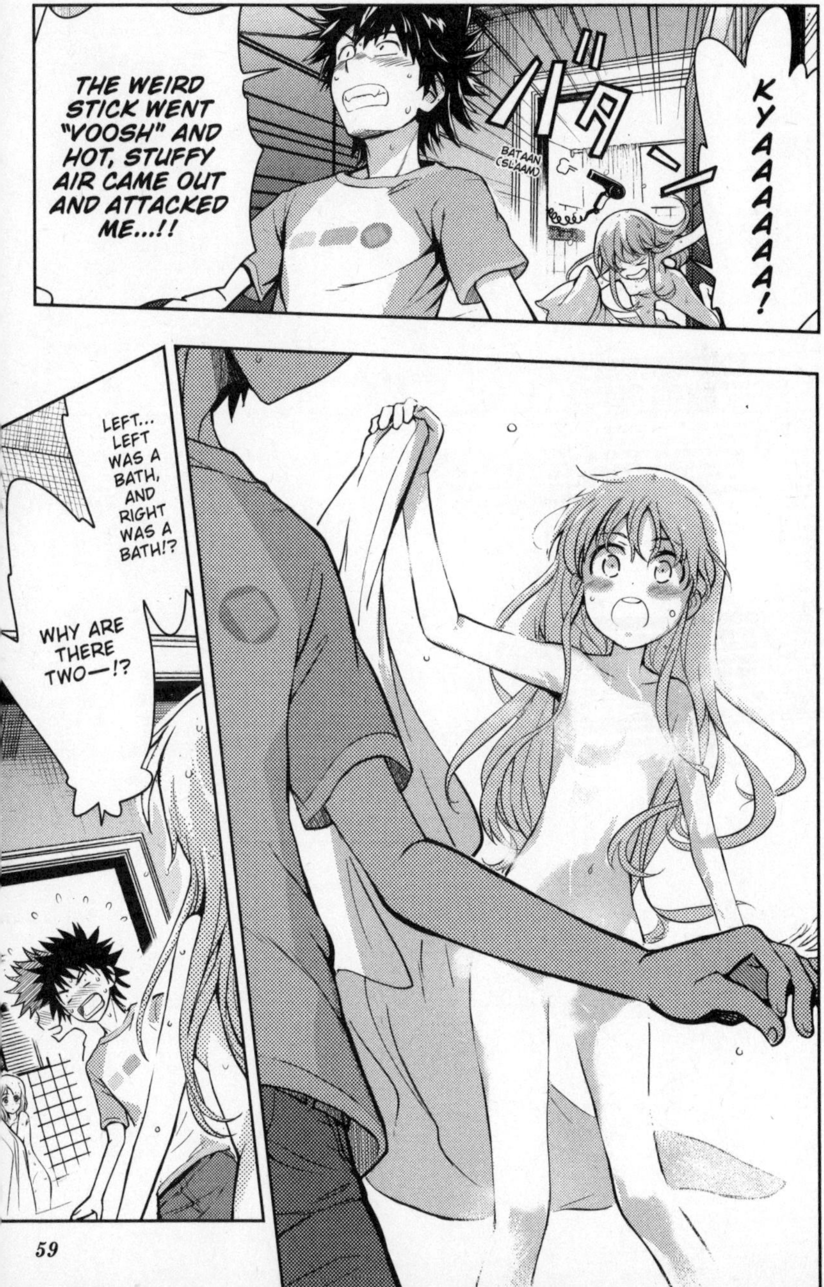
KYAAAAAAA!
BATAAN (SLAAM)
THE WEIRD STICK WENT "VOOSH" AND HOT, STUFFY AIR CAME OUT AND ATTACKED ME...!!
LEFT... LEFT WAS A BATH, AND RIGHT WAS A BATH!?
WHY ARE THERE TWO—!?

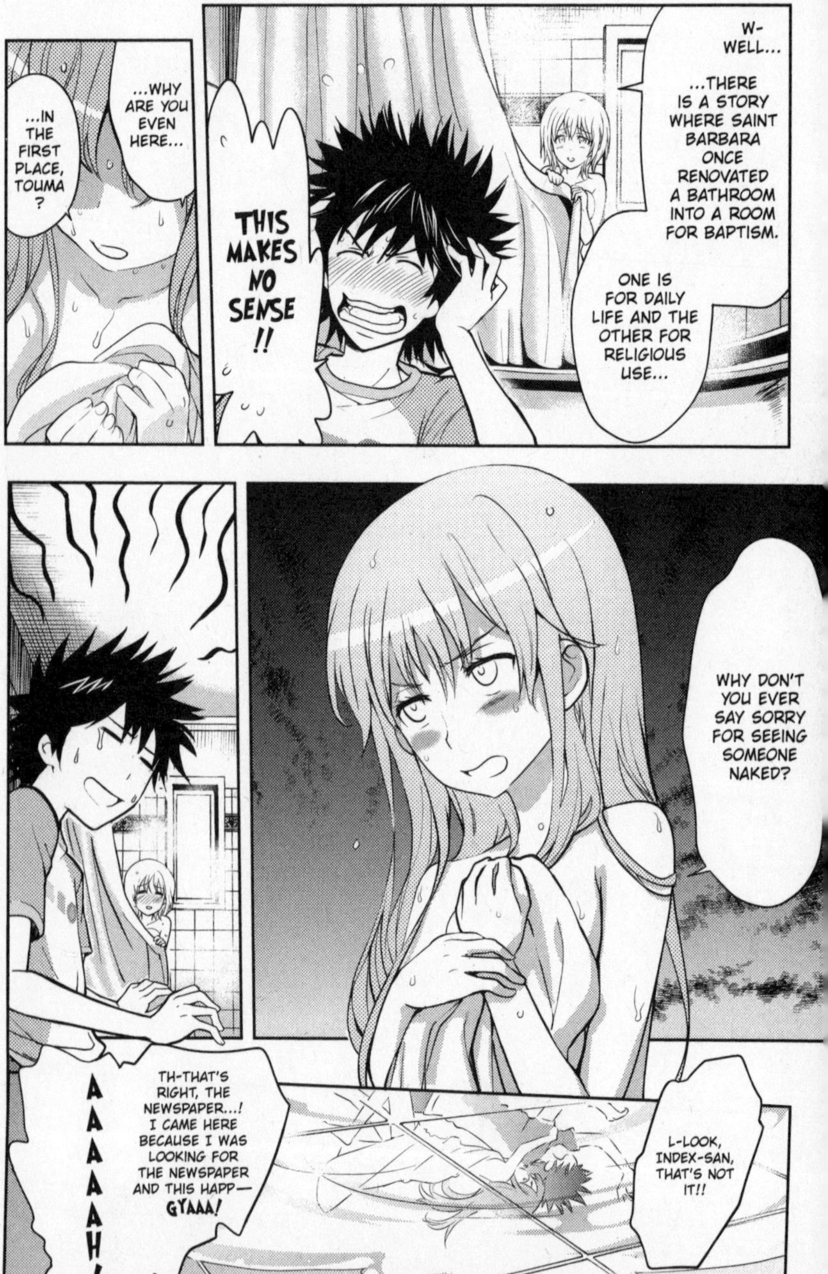
W-WELL...
...THERE IS A STORY WHERE SAINT BARBARA ONCE RENOVATED A BATHROOM INTO A ROOM FOR BAPTISM.
ONE IS FOR DAILY LIFE AND THE OTHER FOR RELIGIOUS USE...
THIS MAKES NO SENSE!!
...WHY ARE YOU EVEN HERE...
...IN THE FIRST PLACE, TOUMA?
WHY DON'T YOU EVER SAY SORRY FOR SEEING SOMEONE NAKED?
L-LOOK, INDEX-SAN, THAT'S NOT IT!!
TH-THAT'S RIGHT, THE NEWSPAPER...! I CAME HERE BECAUSE I WAS LOOKING FOR THE NEWSPAPER AND THIS HAPP— GYAAA!
AAAAAAH!

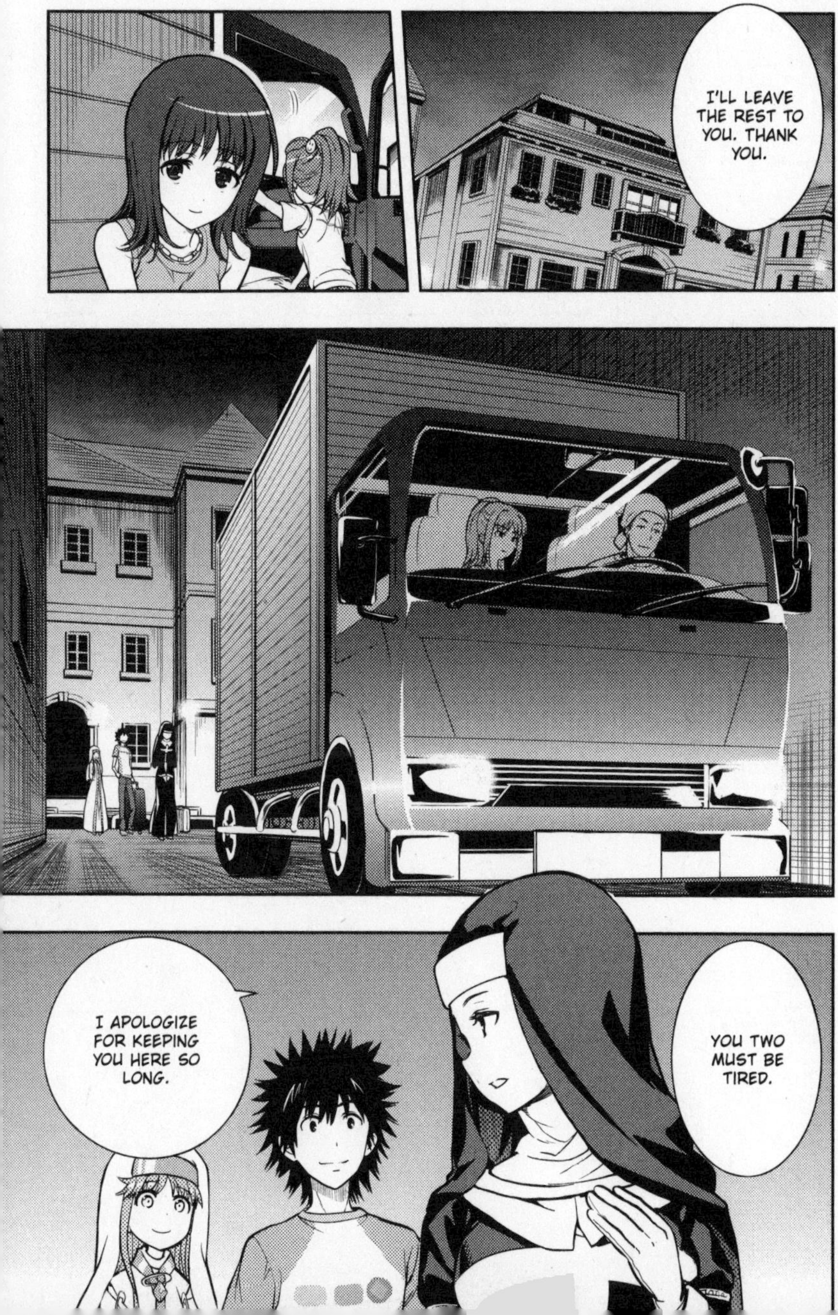
I'LL LEAVE THE REST TO YOU. THANK YOU.
YOU TWO MUST BE TIRED.
I APOLOGIZE FOR KEEPING YOU HERE SO LONG.

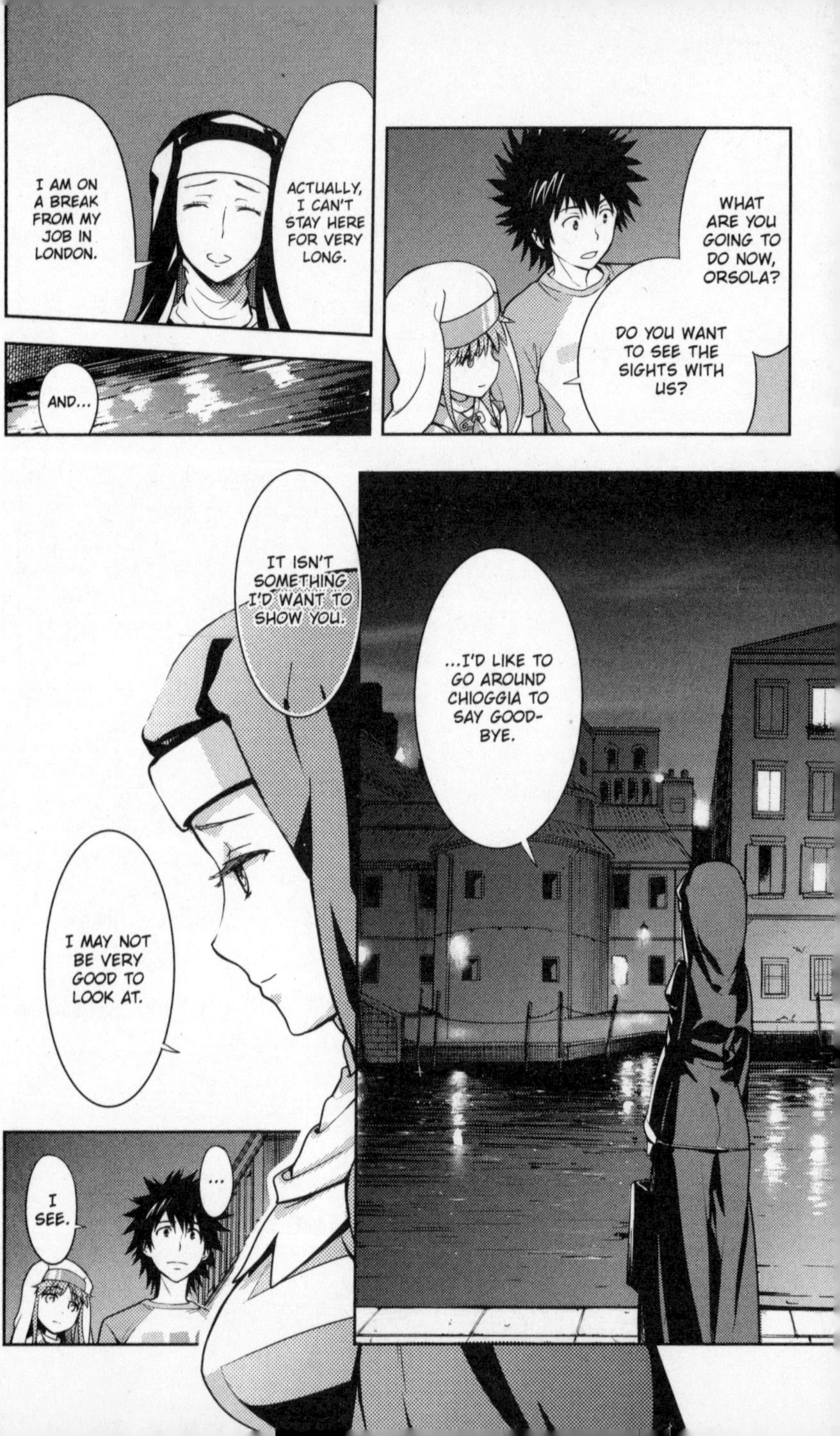
WHAT ARE YOU GOING TO DO NOW, ORSOLA?
DO YOU WANT TO SEE THE SIGHTS WITH US?
ACTUALLY, I CAN'T STAY HERE FOR VERY LONG.
I AM ON A BREAK FROM MY JOB IN LONDON.
AND...
...I'D LIKE TO GO AROUND CHIOGGIA TO SAY GOOD-BYE.
IT ISN'T SOMETHING I'D WANT TO SHOW YOU.
I MAY NOT BE VERY GOOD TO LOOK AT.
...
I SEE.

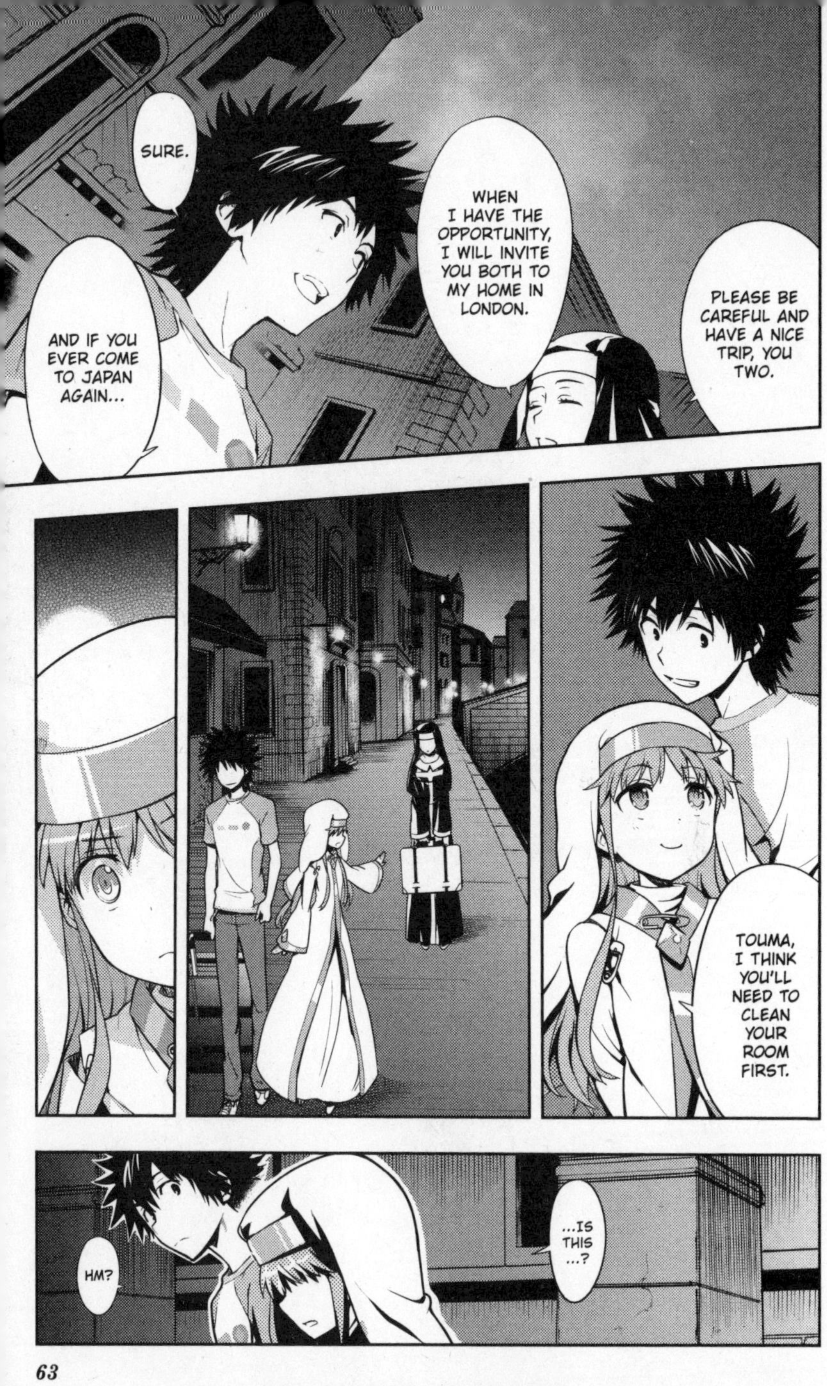
PLEASE BE CAREFUL AND HAVE A NICE TRIP, YOU TWO.
WHEN I HAVE THE OPPORTUNITY, I WILL INVITE YOU BOTH TO MY HOME IN LONDON.
SURE.
AND IF YOU EVER COME TO JAPAN AGAIN...
TOUMA, I THINK YOU'LL NEED TO CLEAN YOUR ROOM FIRST.
...IS THIS ...?
HM?

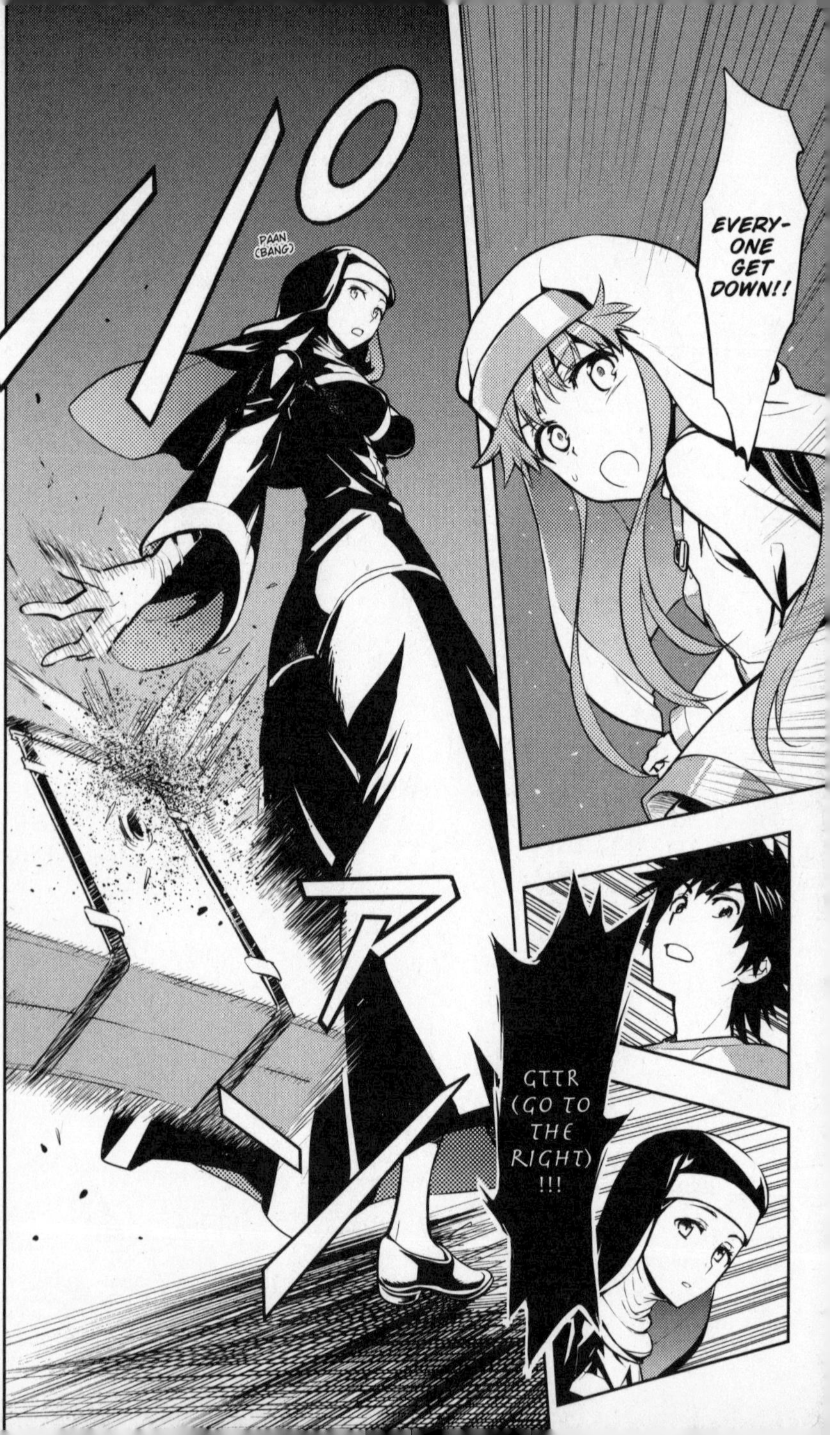
EVERY-ONE GET DOWN!!
PAAN (BANG)
GTTR (GO TO THE RIGHT) !!!

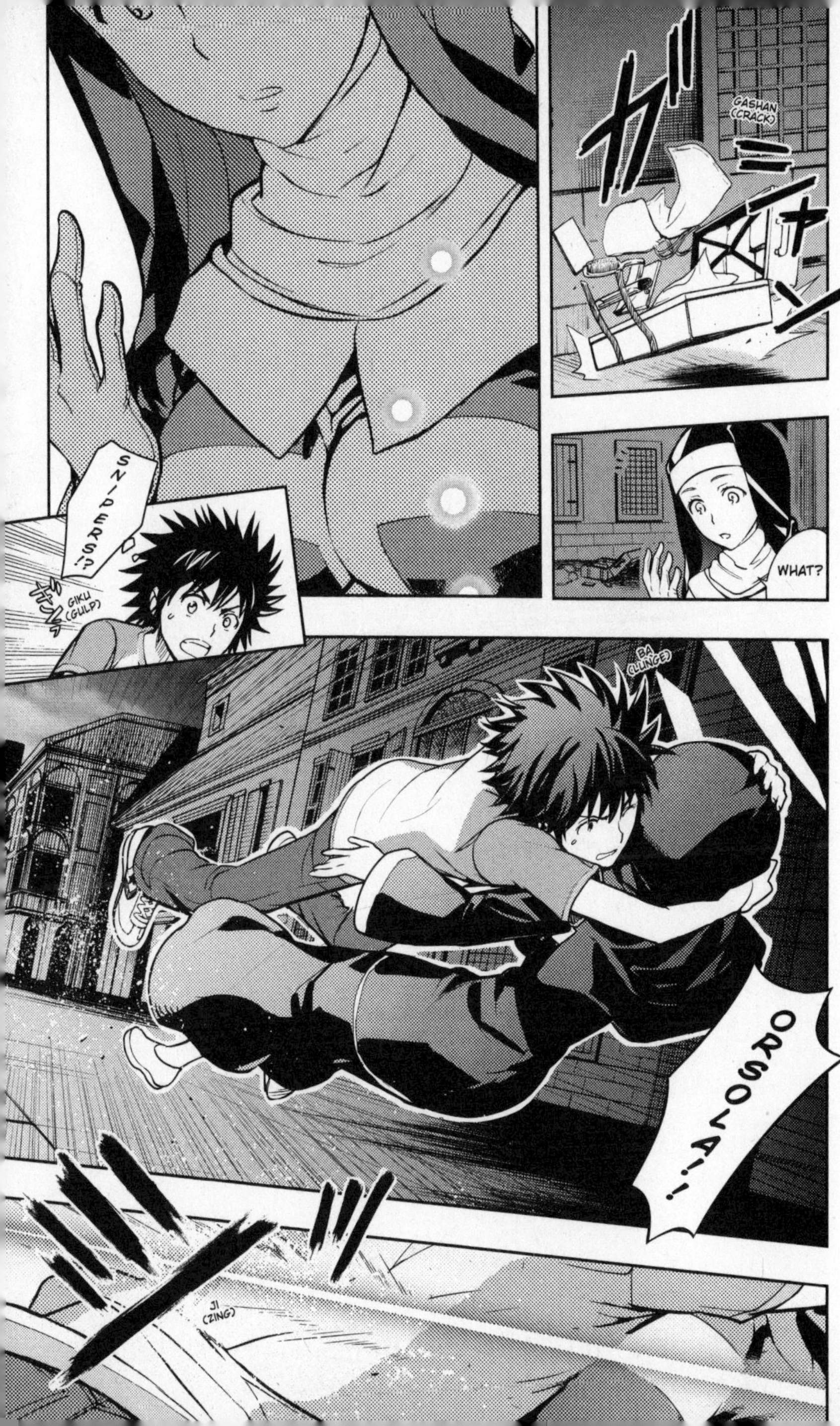
GASHAN (CRACK)
SNIPERS!?
GIKU (GULP)
WHAT?
BA (LUNGE)
ORSOLA!!
JI (ZING)

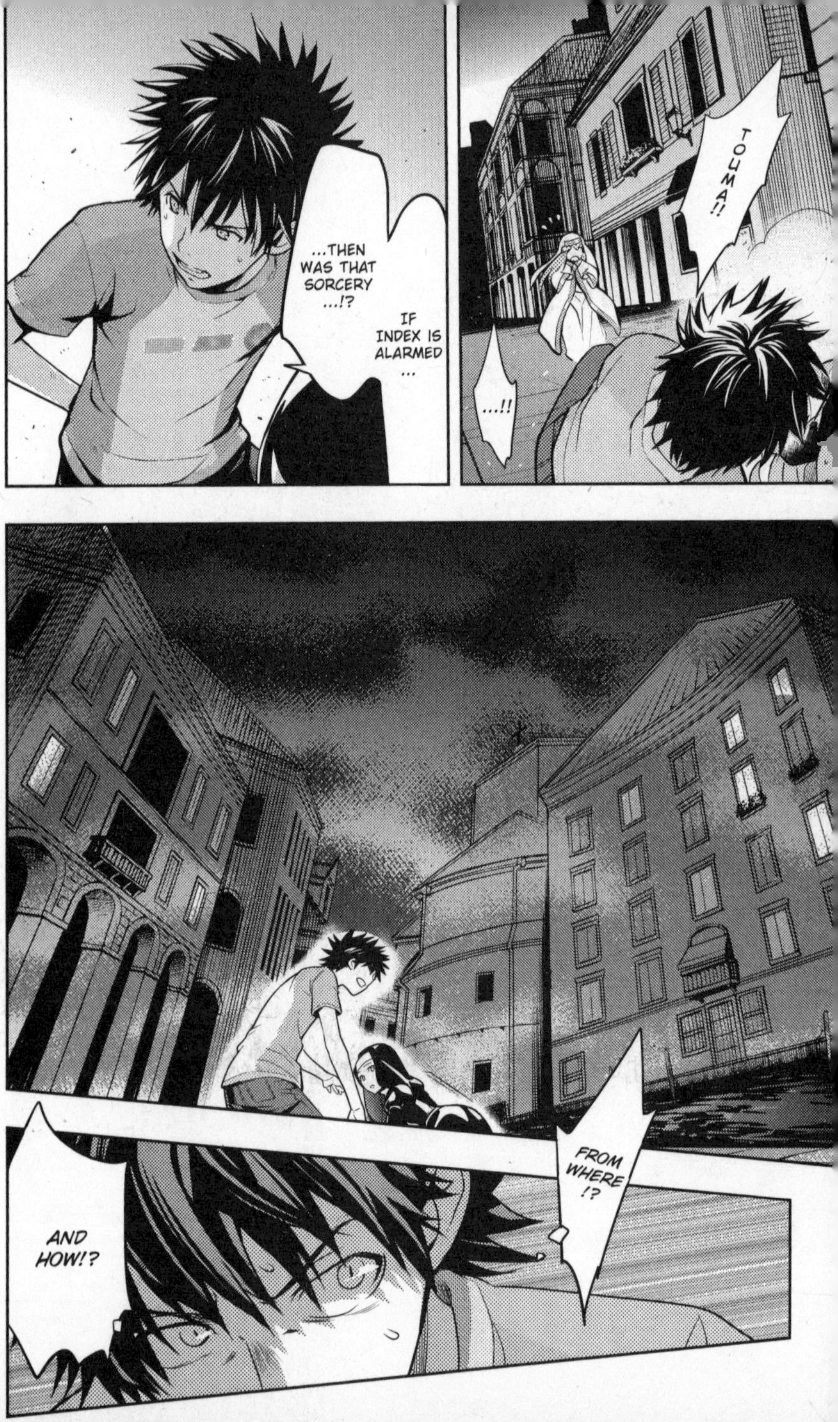
TOUMA!!
...!!
...THEN WAS THAT SORCERY ...!?
IF INDEX IS ALARMED ...
FROM WHERE !?
AND HOW!?

# #88 THE QUEEN'S FLEET ①

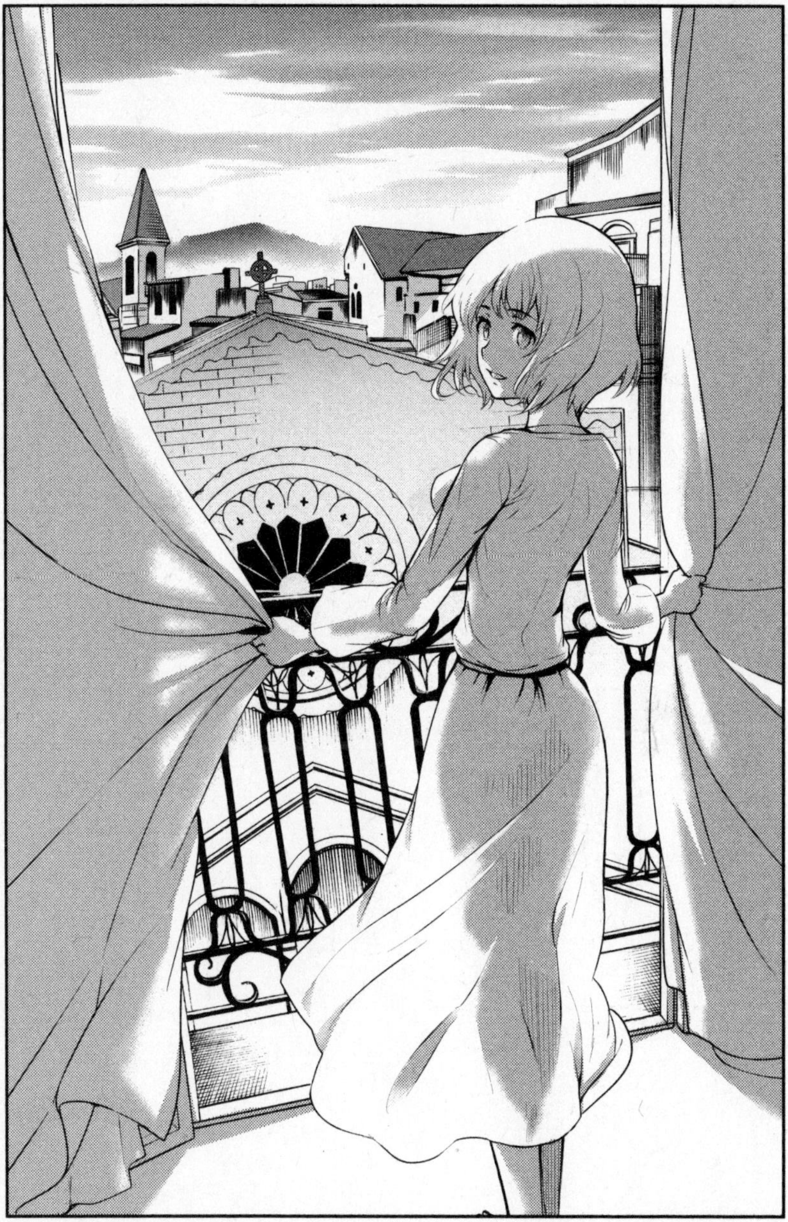

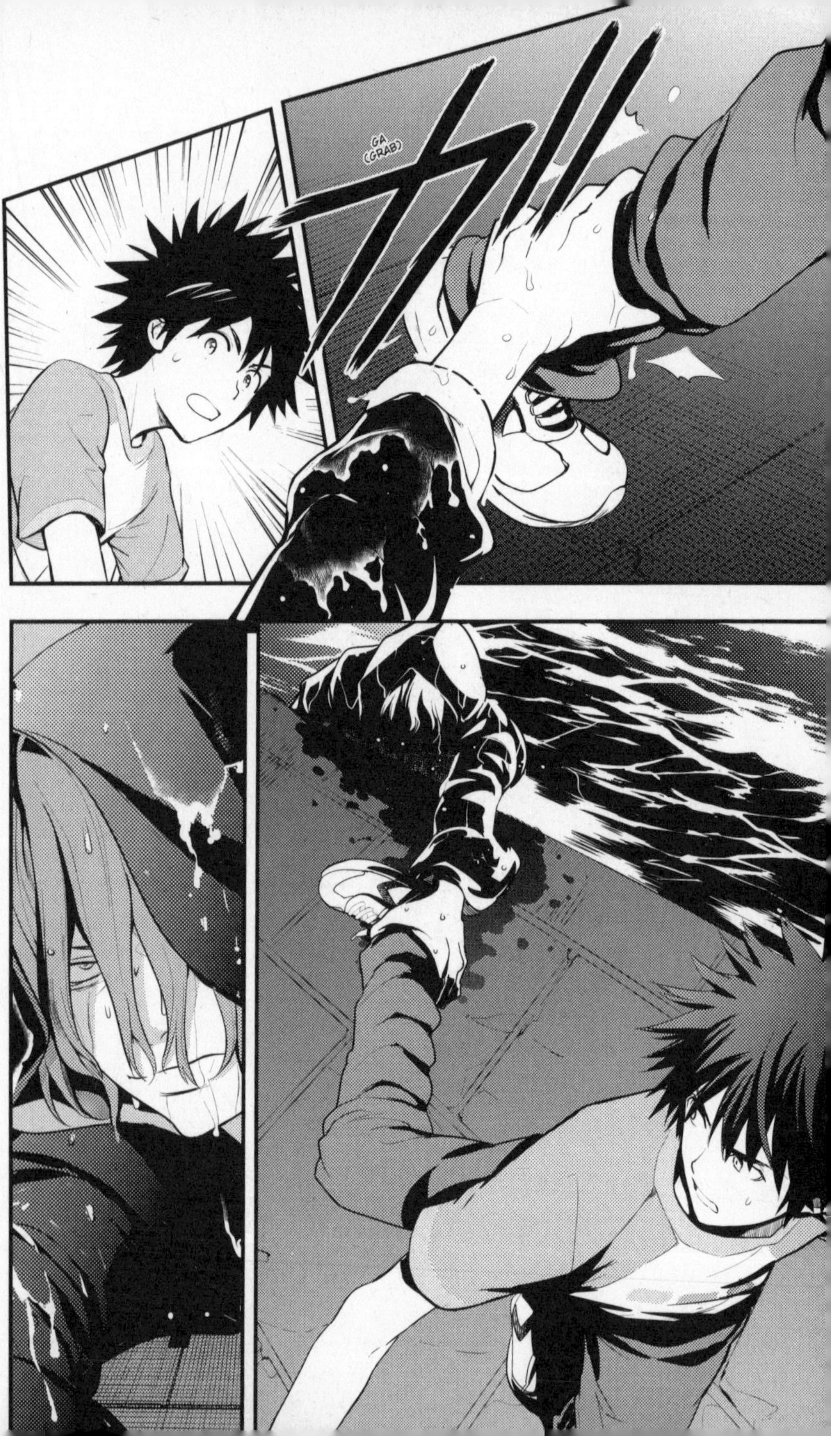
GA
(GRAB)

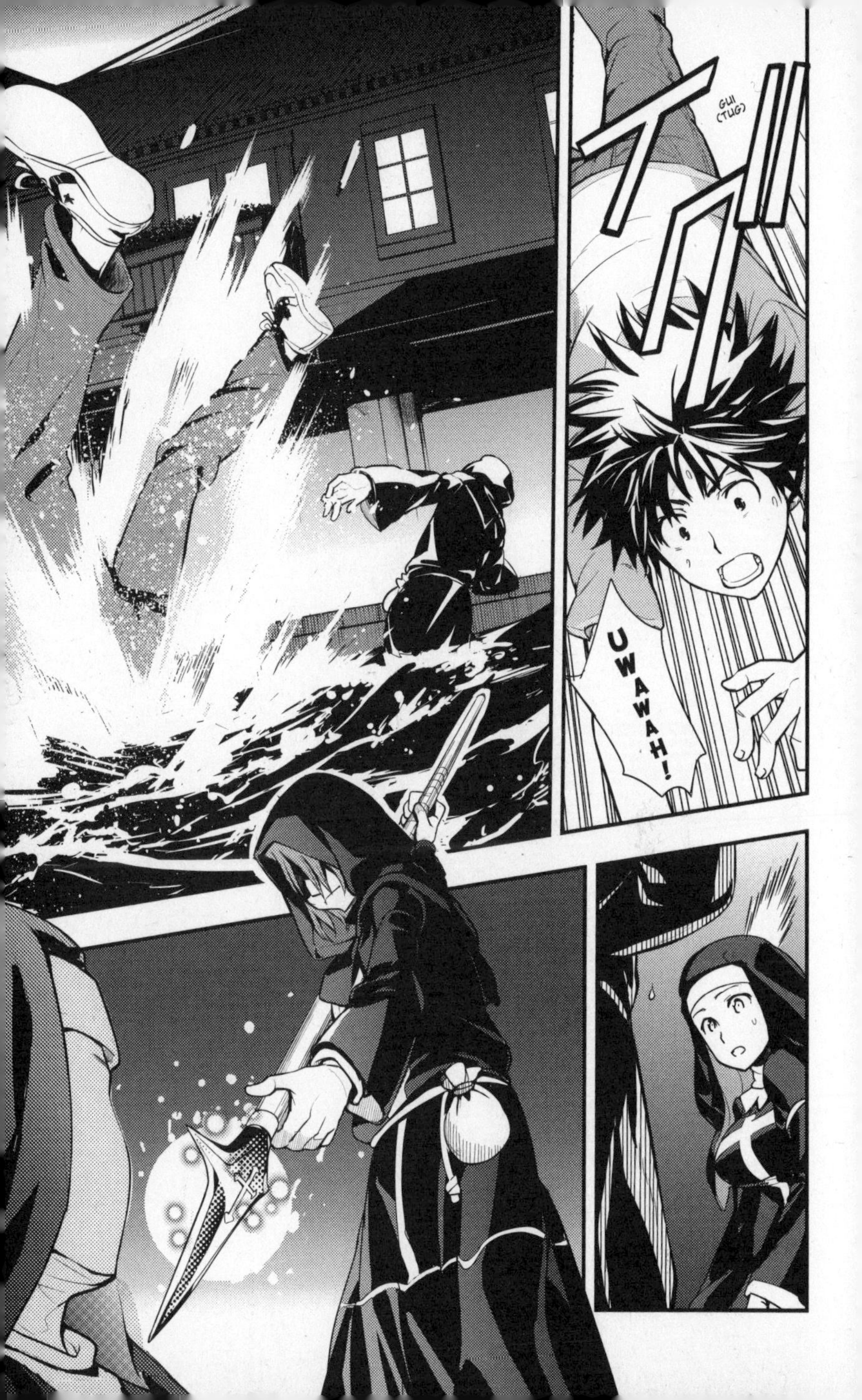
GUI (TUG)
UWAWAH!

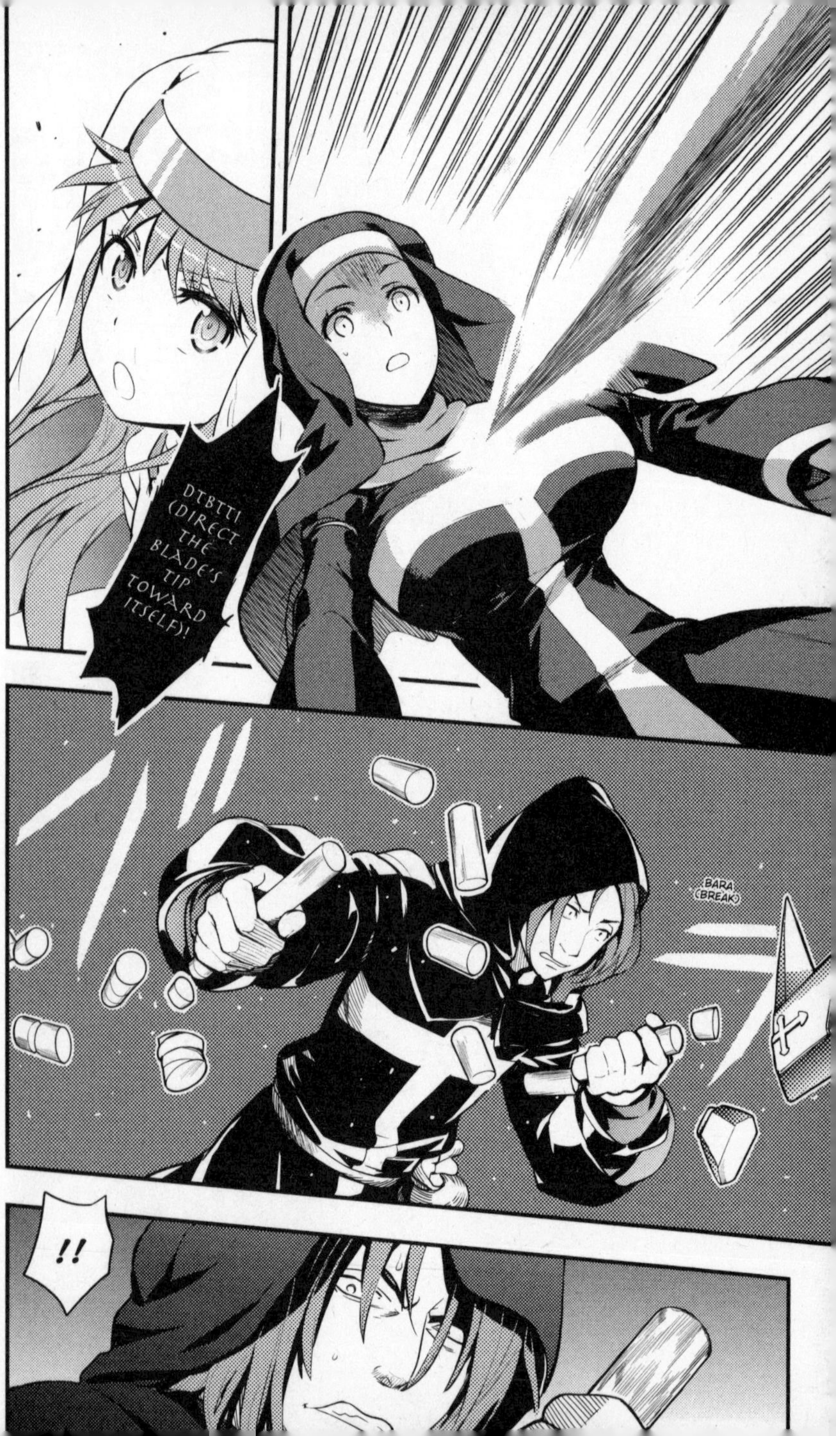
DTBTTI (DIRECT THE BLADE'S TIP TOWARD ITSELF)!
BARA (BREAK)
!!

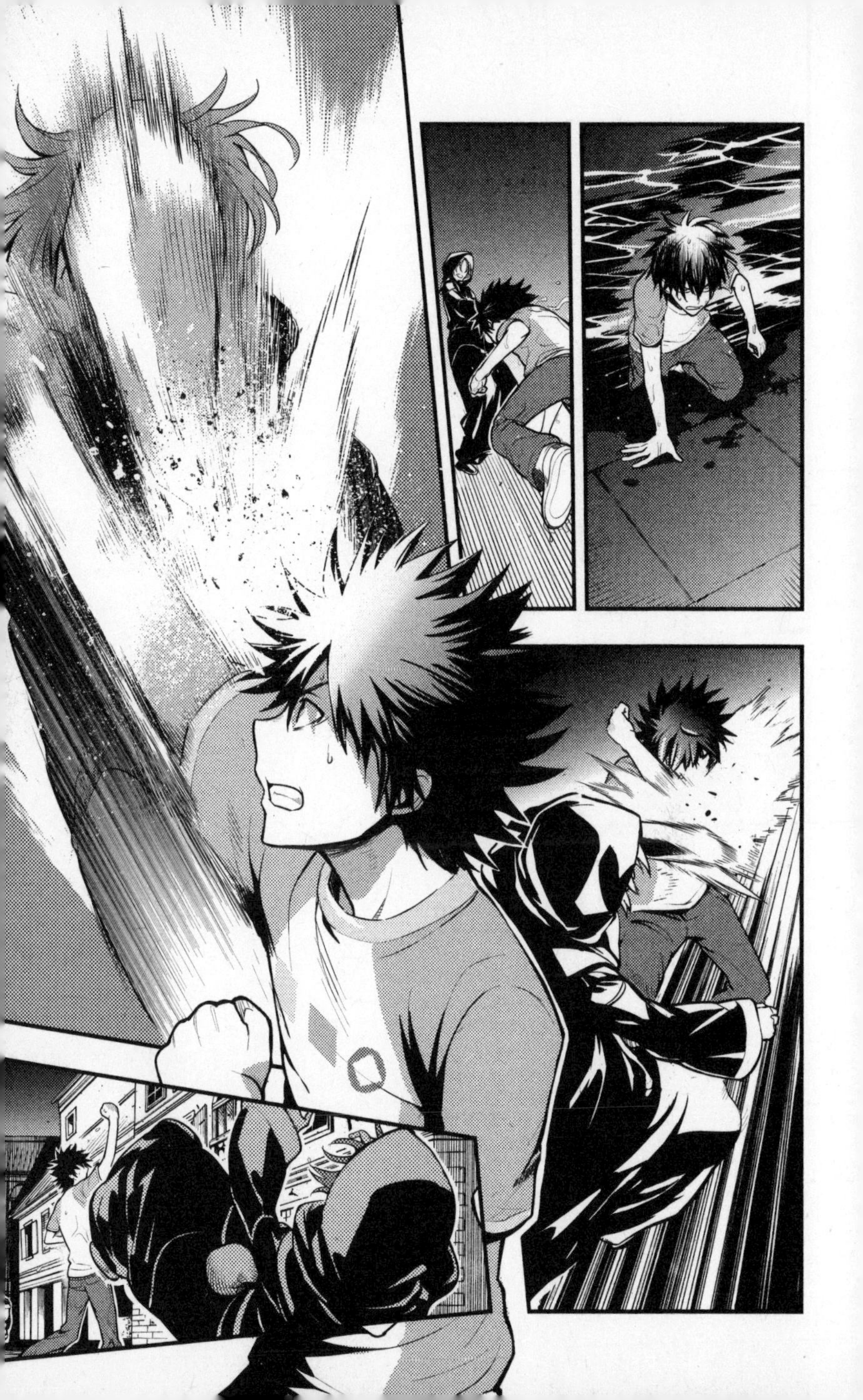

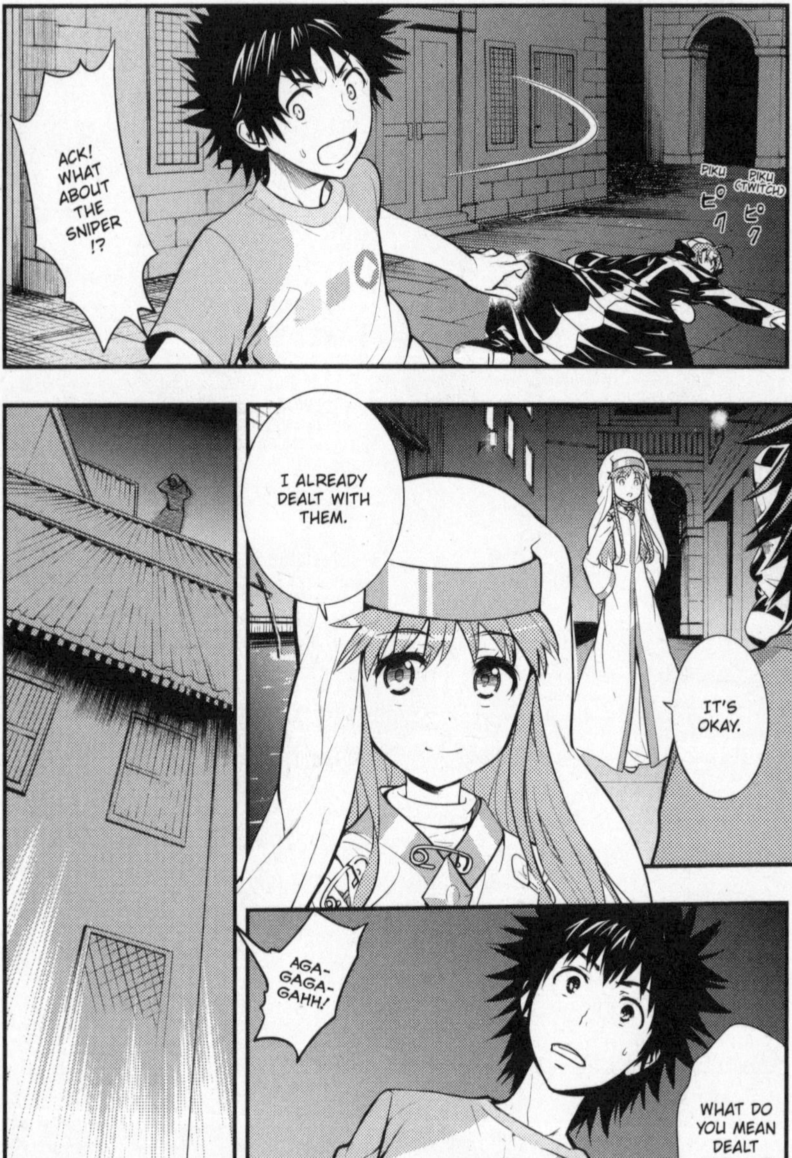
ピク ピク
PIKU PIKU (TWITCH)
ACK! WHAT ABOUT THE SNIPER !?
I ALREADY DEALT WITH THEM.
IT'S OKAY.
WHAT DO YOU MEAN DEALT WITH—?
AGA-GAGA-GAHH!

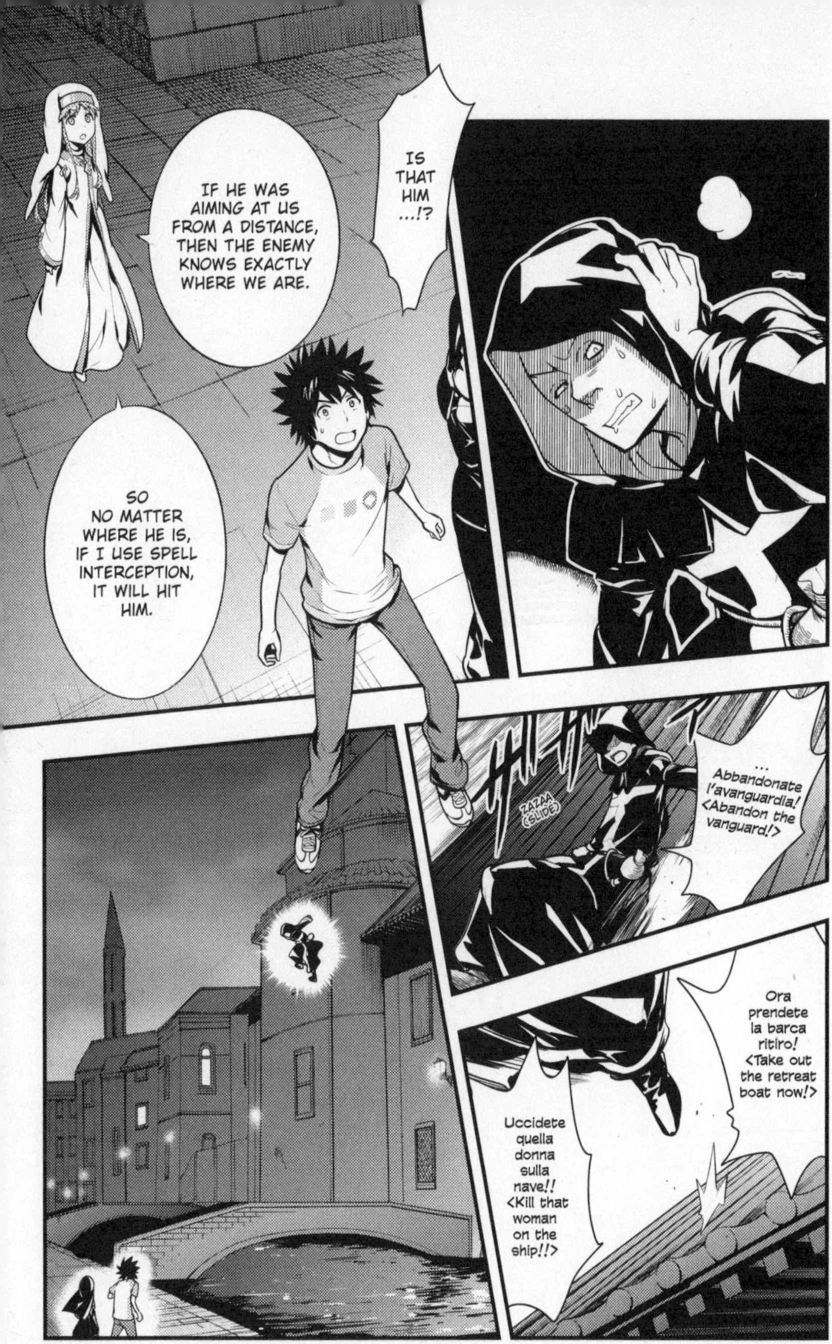
IS THAT HIM ...!?
IF HE WAS AIMING AT US FROM A DISTANCE, THEN THE ENEMY KNOWS EXACTLY WHERE WE ARE.
SO NO MATTER WHERE HE IS, IF I USE SPELL INTERCEPTION, IT WILL HIT HIM.
... Abbandonate l'avanguardia! <Abandon the vanguard!>
ZAZAA (SLIDE)
Ora prendete la barca ritiro! <Take out the retreat boat now!>
Uccidete quella donna sulla nave!! <Kill that woman on the ship!!>

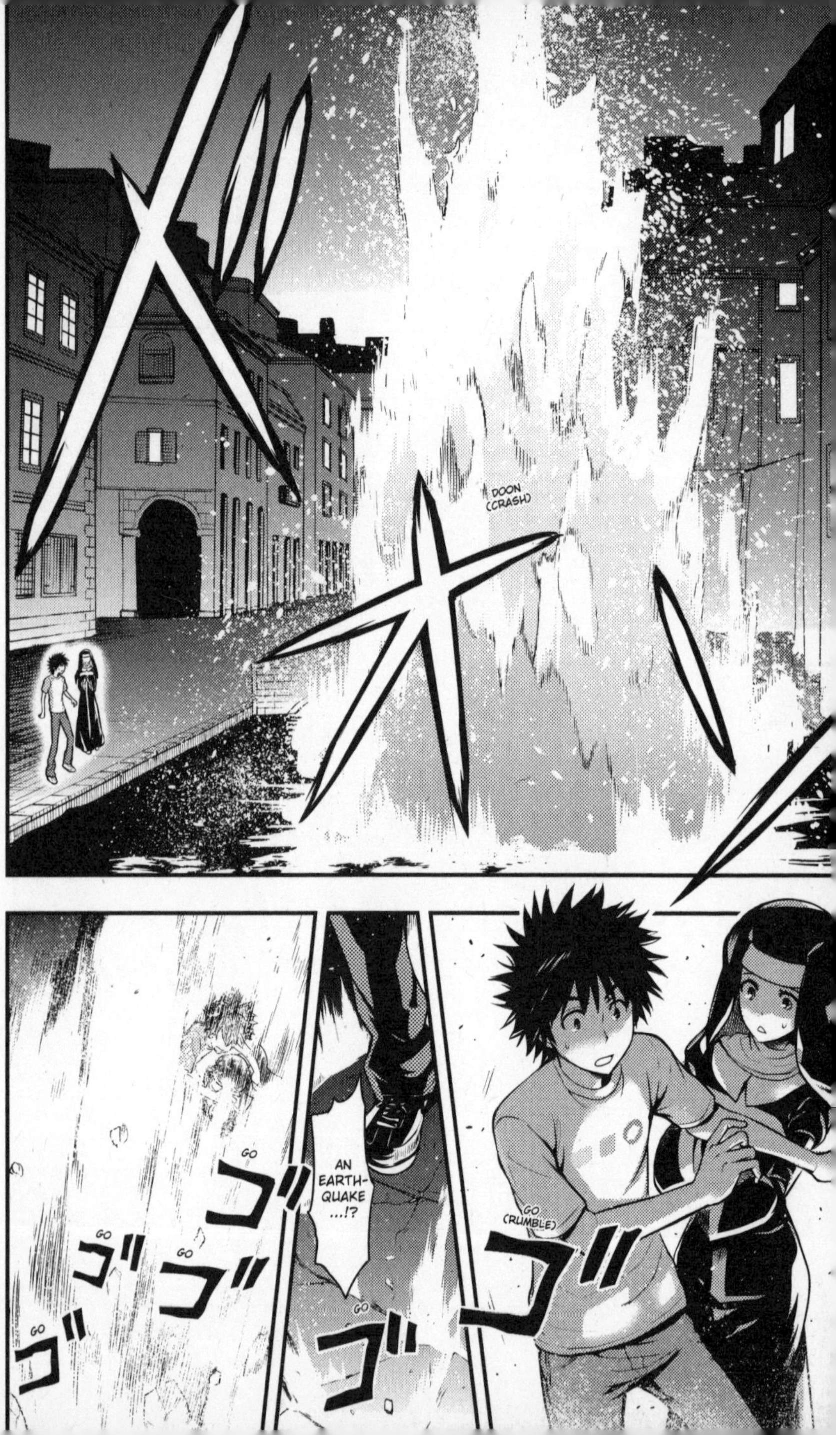
DOON (CRASH)
GO (RUMBLE)
ゴーゴ
AN EARTH-QUAKE ...!?
GO
ゴ
GO
ゴ
GO
ゴ
GO
ゴ
GO
ゴ

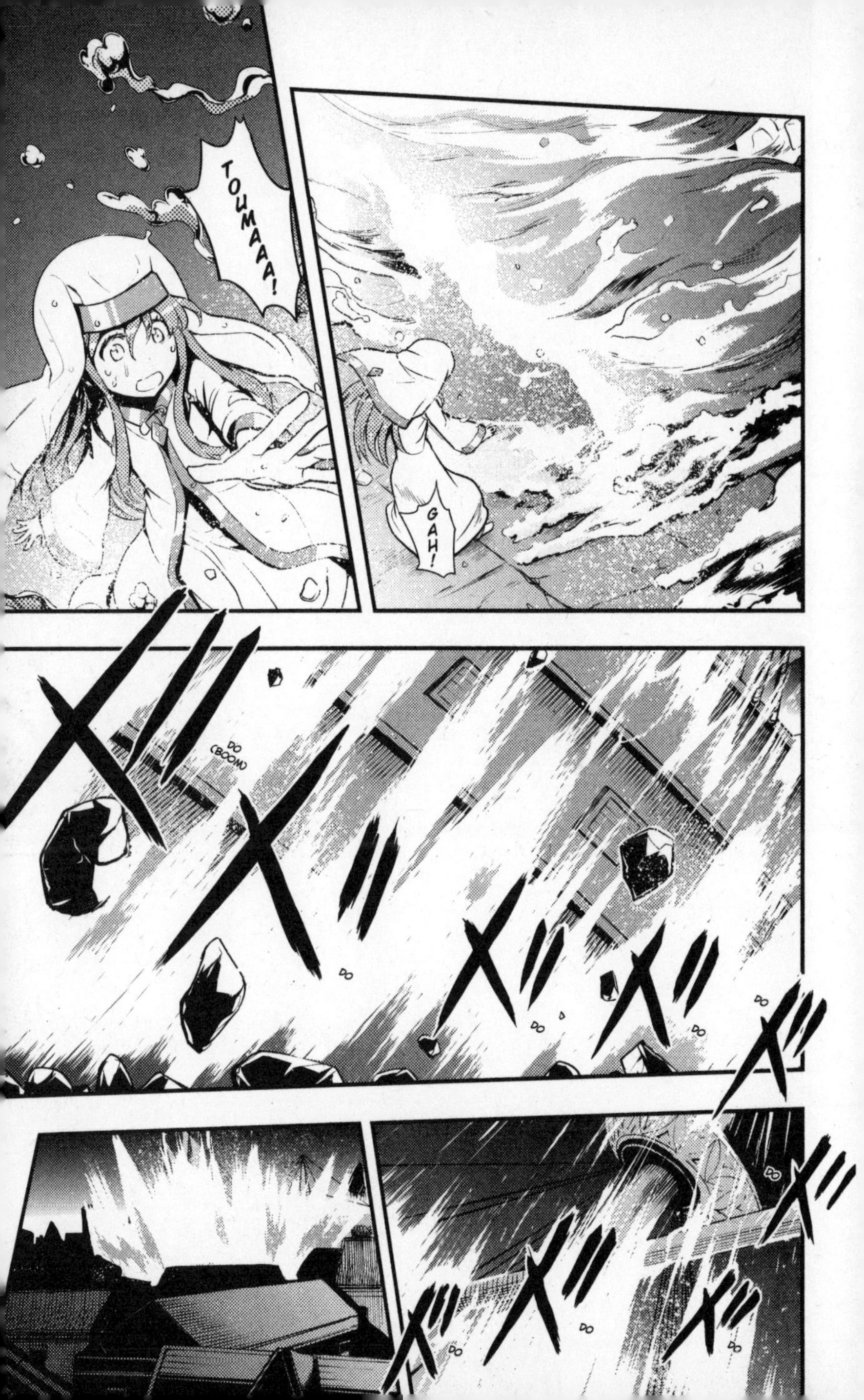
GAH!
TOUMAAA!
DO (BOOM)
DO
DO
DO
DO
DO
DO
DO
DO

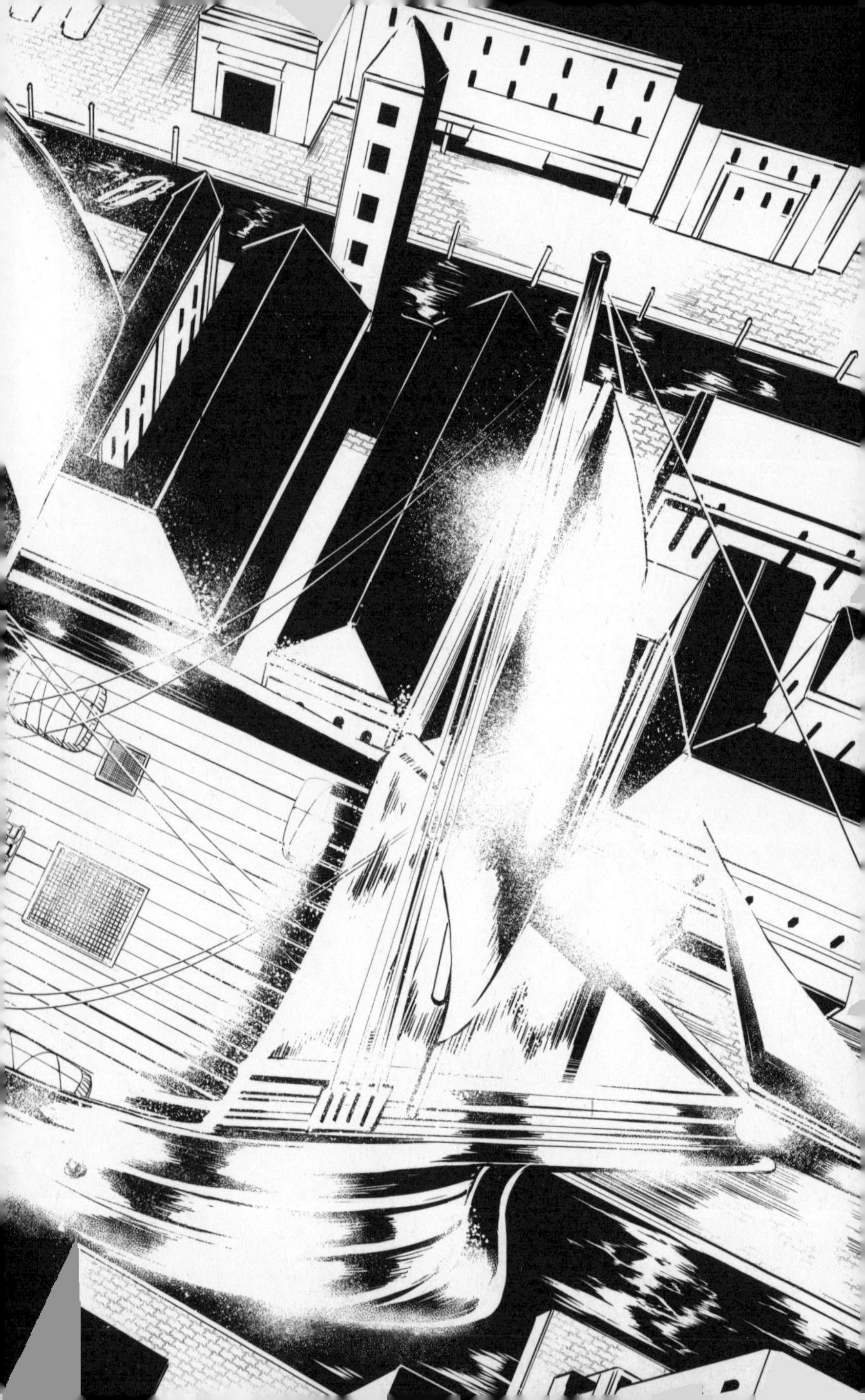

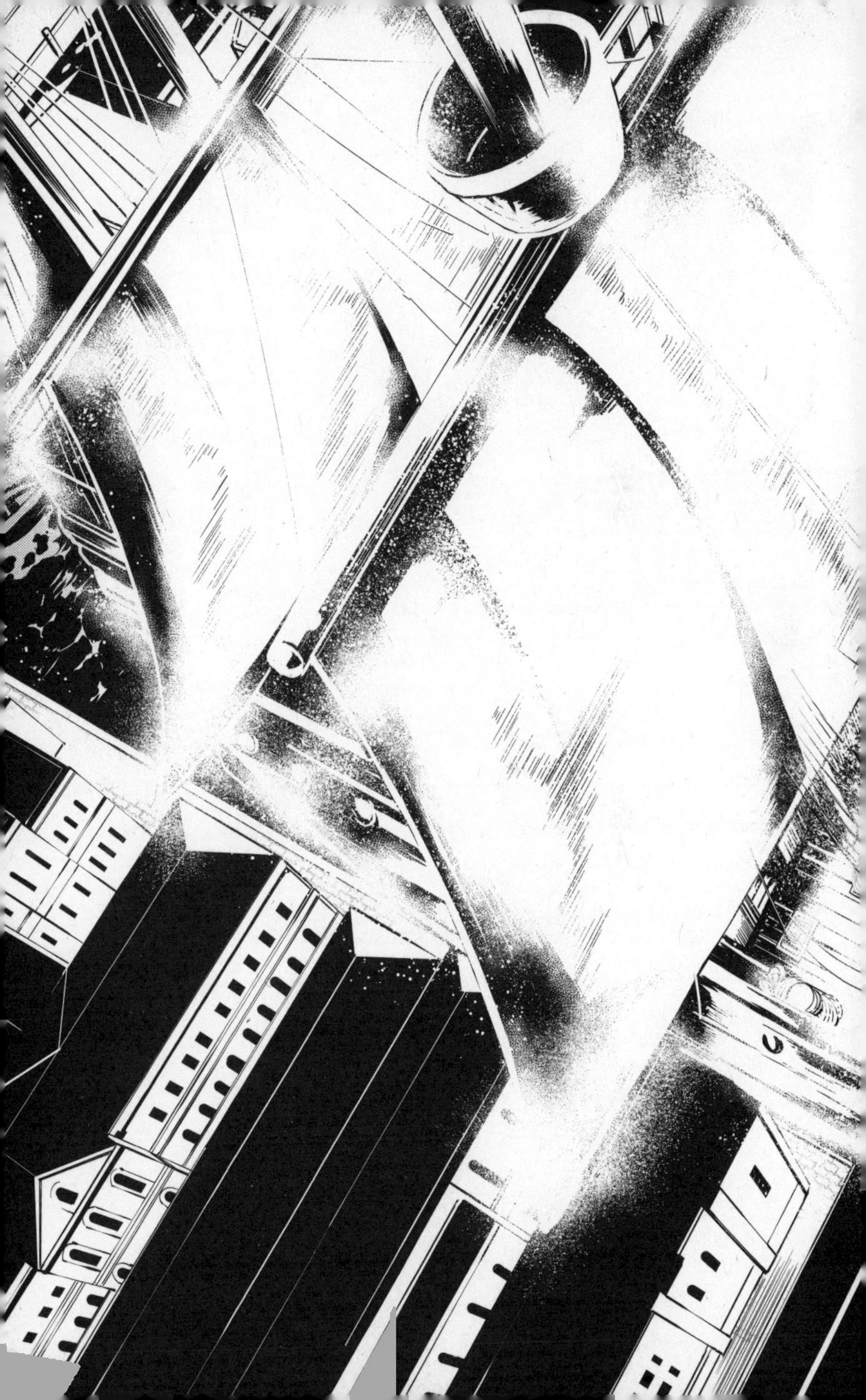

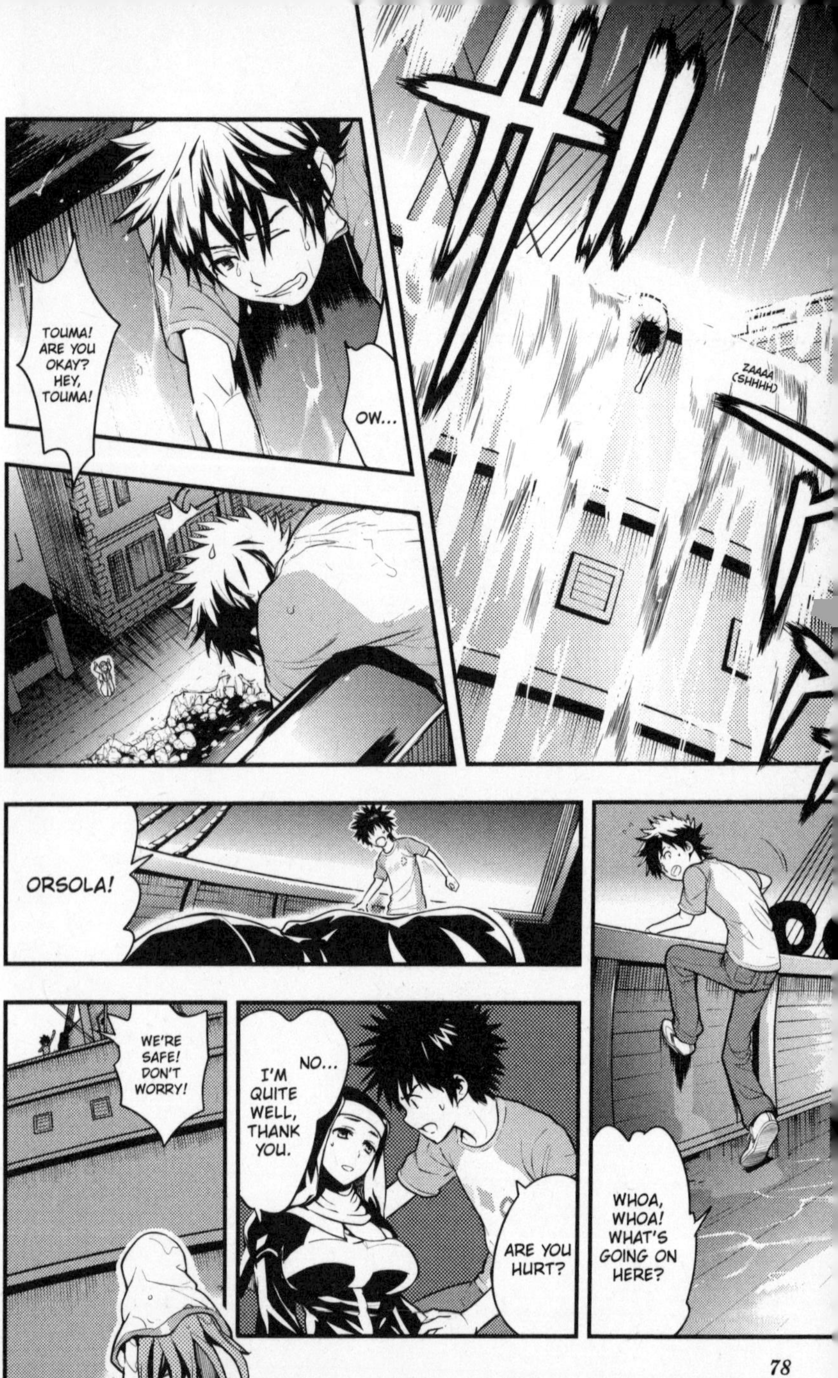
ZAAAA (SHHHH)
TOUMA! ARE YOU OKAY? HEY, TOUMA!
OW...
WHOA, WHOA! WHAT'S GOING ON HERE?
ORSOLA!
ARE YOU HURT?
NO... I'M QUITE WELL, THANK YOU.
WE'RE SAFE! DON'T WORRY!

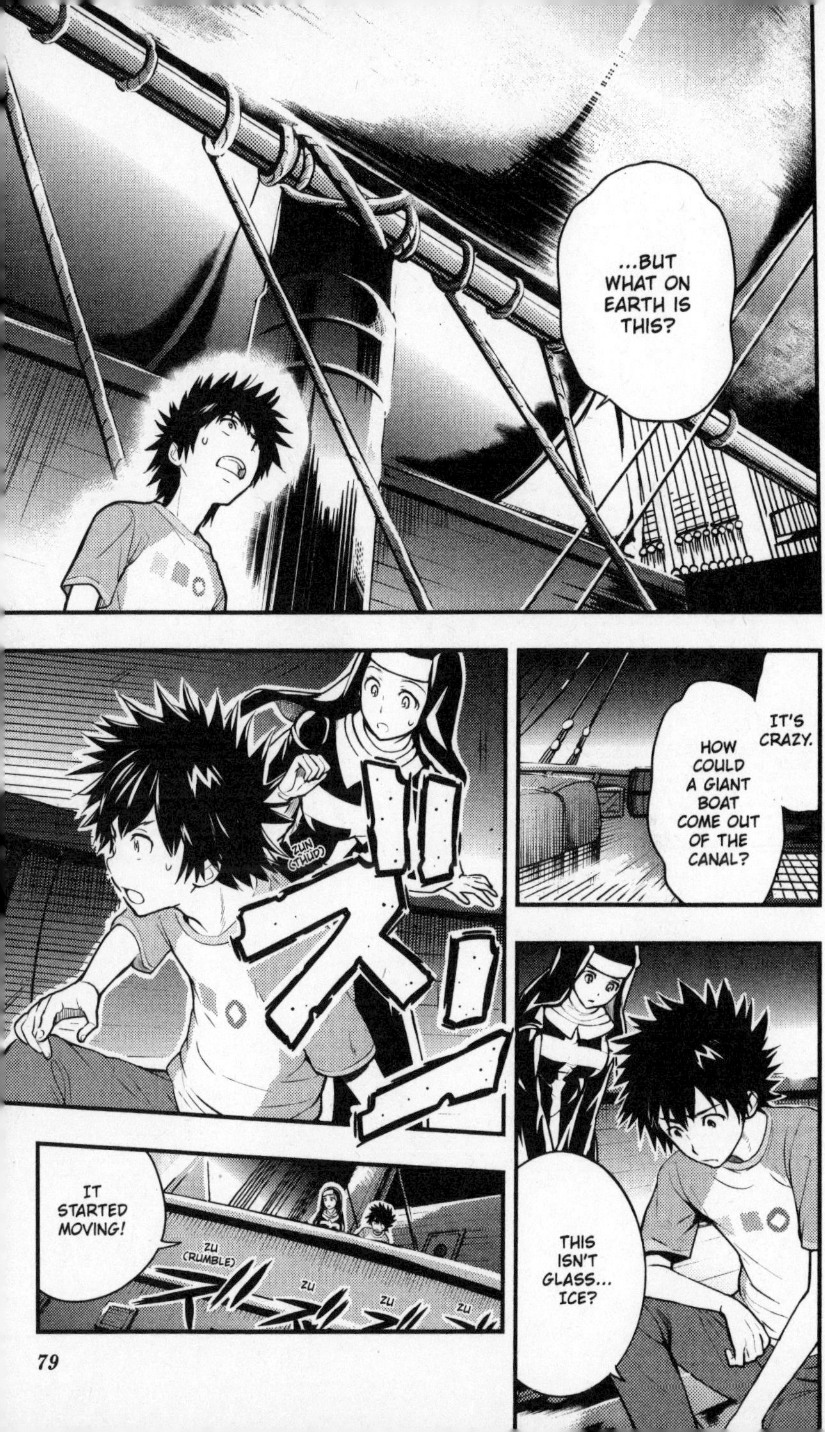
...BUT WHAT ON EARTH IS THIS?
IT'S CRAZY.
HOW COULD A GIANT BOAT COME OUT OF THE CANAL?
ZUN (THUD)
THIS ISN'T GLASS... ICE?
IT STARTED MOVING!
ZU (RUMBLE)
ZU
ZU
ZU

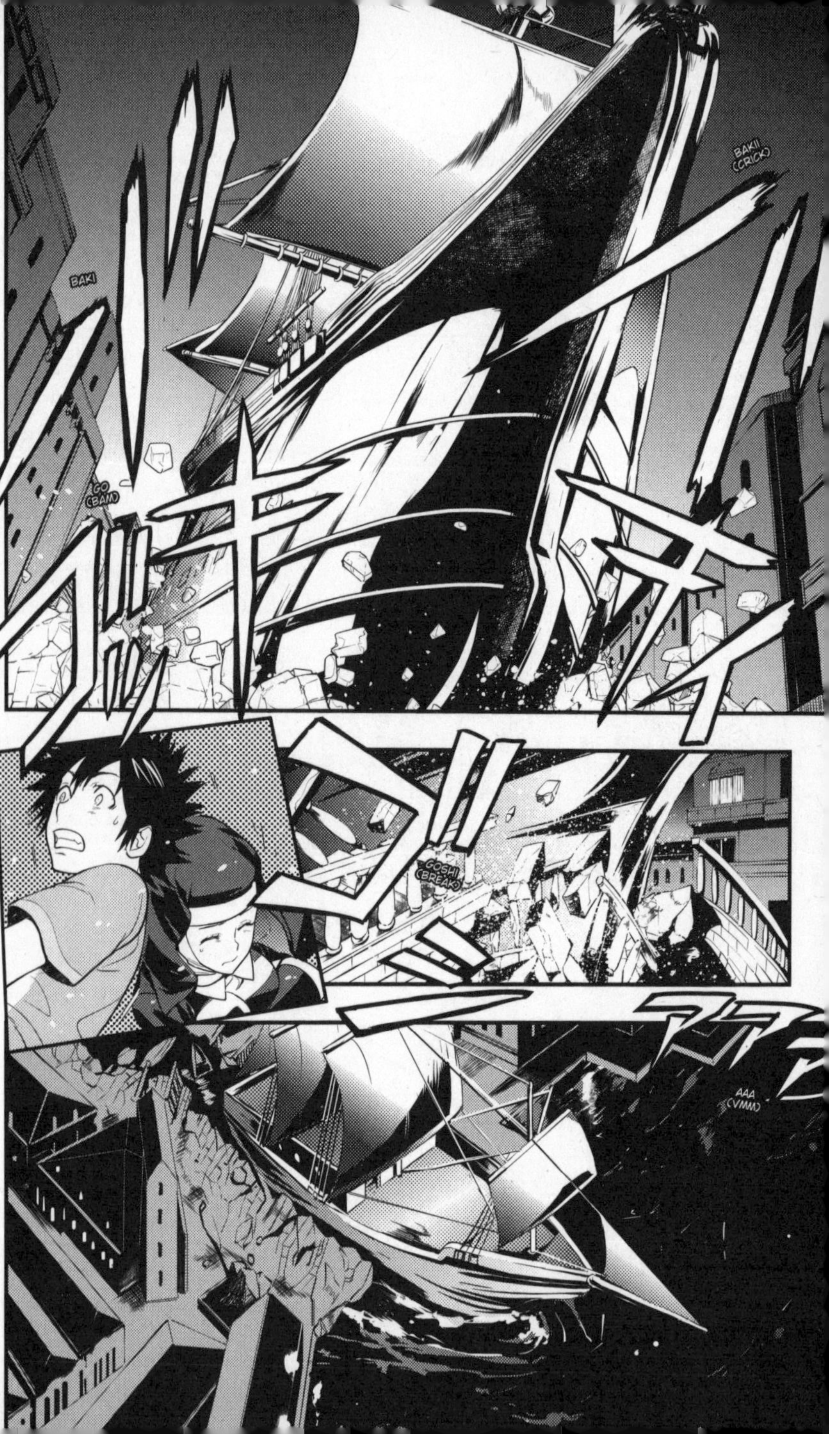
BAKII (CRICK)
BAKI
GO (BAM)
GOSHI (BREAK)
AAA (VMM)

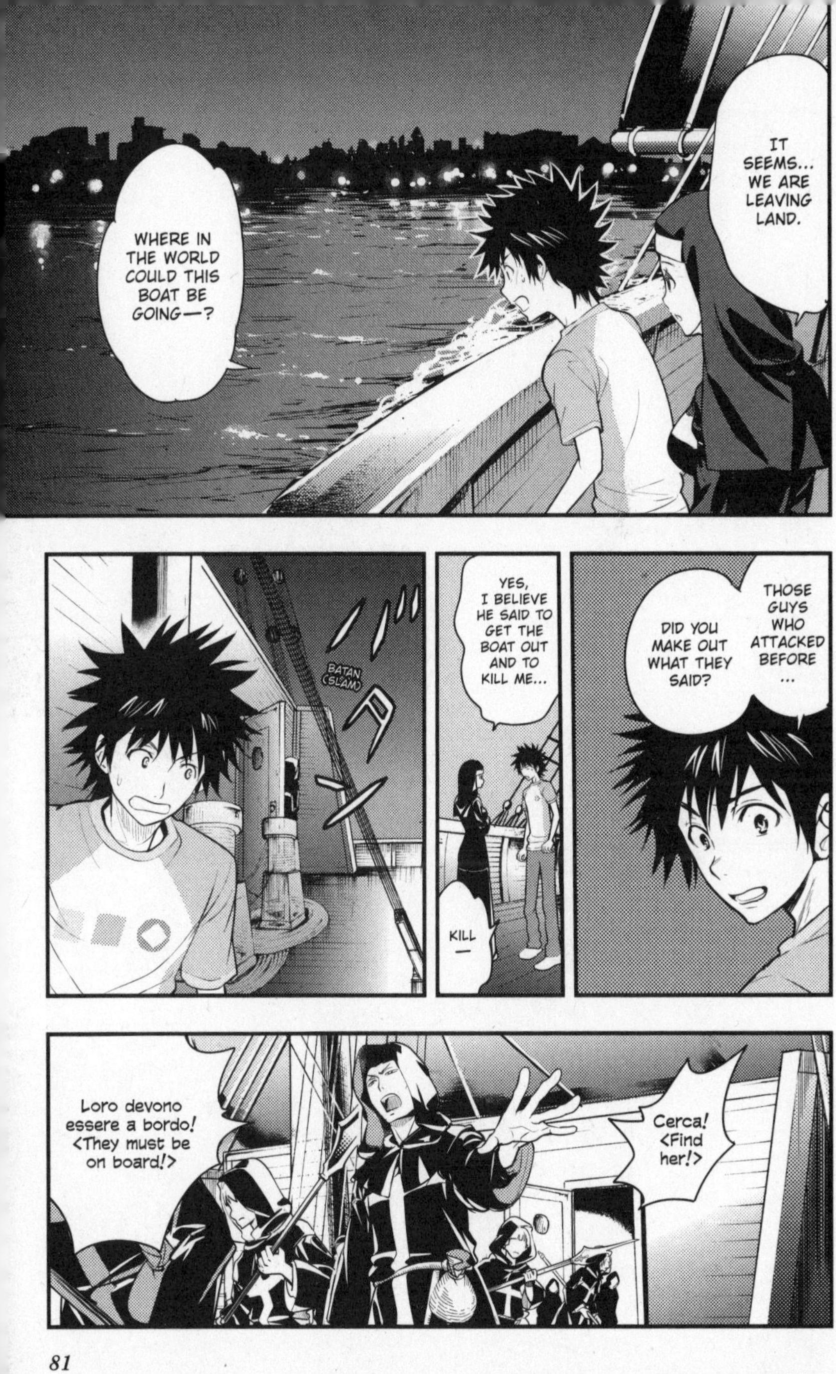
IT SEEMS... WE ARE LEAVING LAND.
WHERE IN THE WORLD COULD THIS BOAT BE GOING—?
THOSE GUYS WHO ATTACKED BEFORE...
DID YOU MAKE OUT WHAT THEY SAID?
YES, I BELIEVE HE SAID TO GET THE BOAT OUT AND TO KILL ME...
KILL—
BATAN (SLAM)
Cerca! <Find her!>
Loro devono essere a bordo! <They must be on board!>

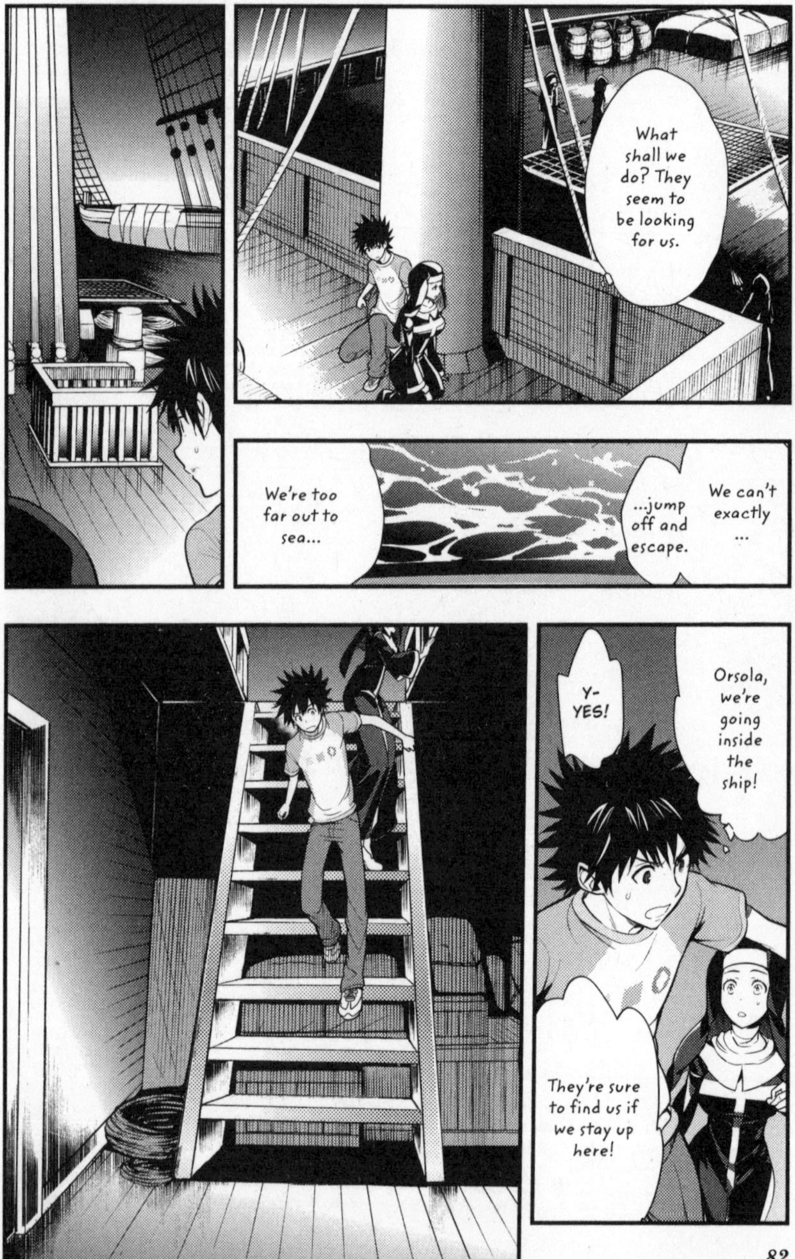
What shall we do? They seem to be looking for us.
We can't exactly ...
...jump off and escape.
We're too far out to sea...
Orsola, we're going inside the ship!
Y-YES!
They're sure to find us if we stay up here!

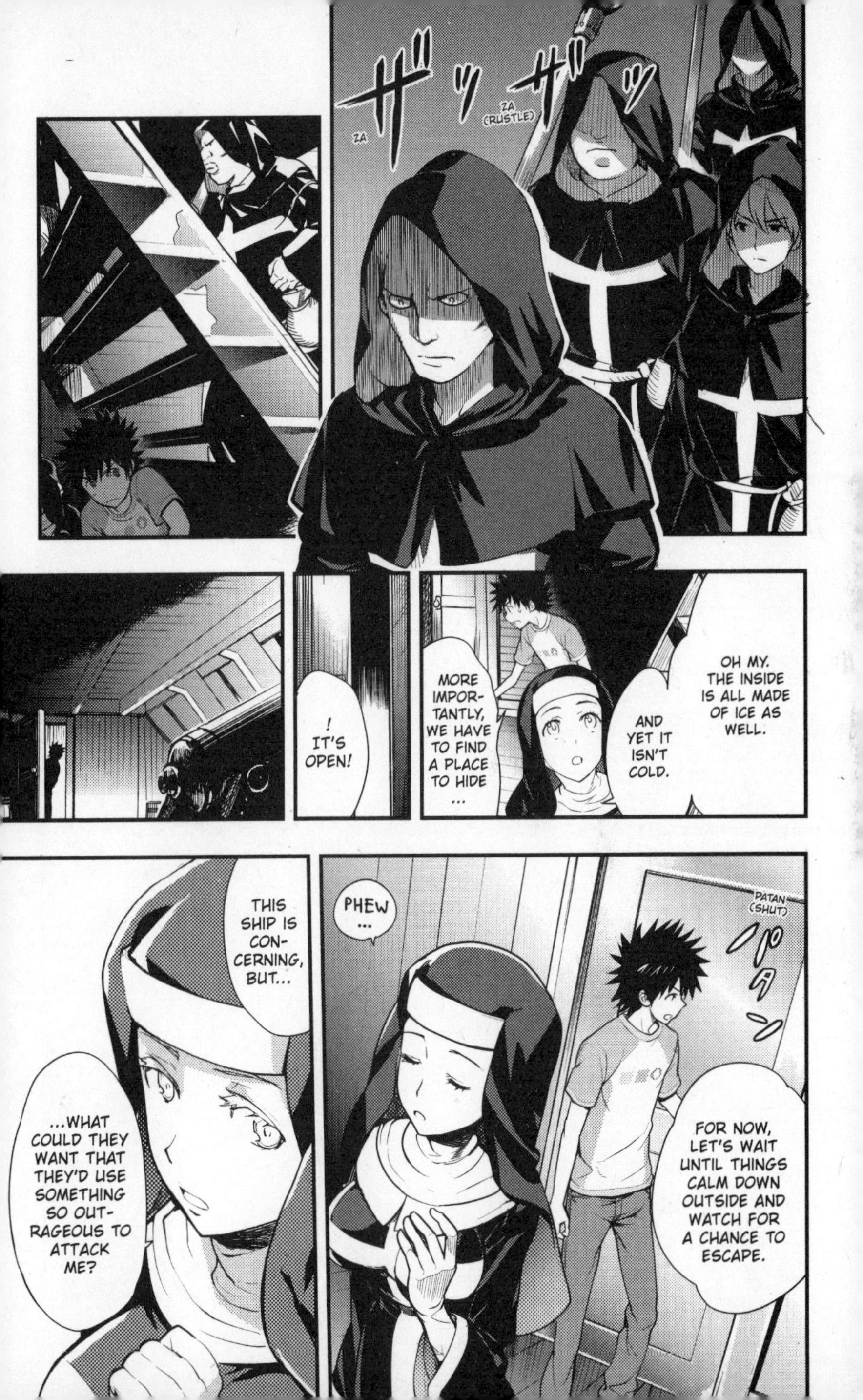
ZA (RUSTLE)
ZA
OH MY. THE INSIDE IS ALL MADE OF ICE AS WELL.
AND YET IT ISN'T COLD.
MORE IMPORTANTLY, WE HAVE TO FIND A PLACE TO HIDE ...
! IT'S OPEN!
PATAN (SHUT)
PHEW ...
FOR NOW, LET'S WAIT UNTIL THINGS CALM DOWN OUTSIDE AND WATCH FOR A CHANCE TO ESCAPE.
THIS SHIP IS CONCERNING, BUT...
...WHAT COULD THEY WANT THAT THEY'D USE SOMETHING SO OUTRAGEOUS TO ATTACK ME?

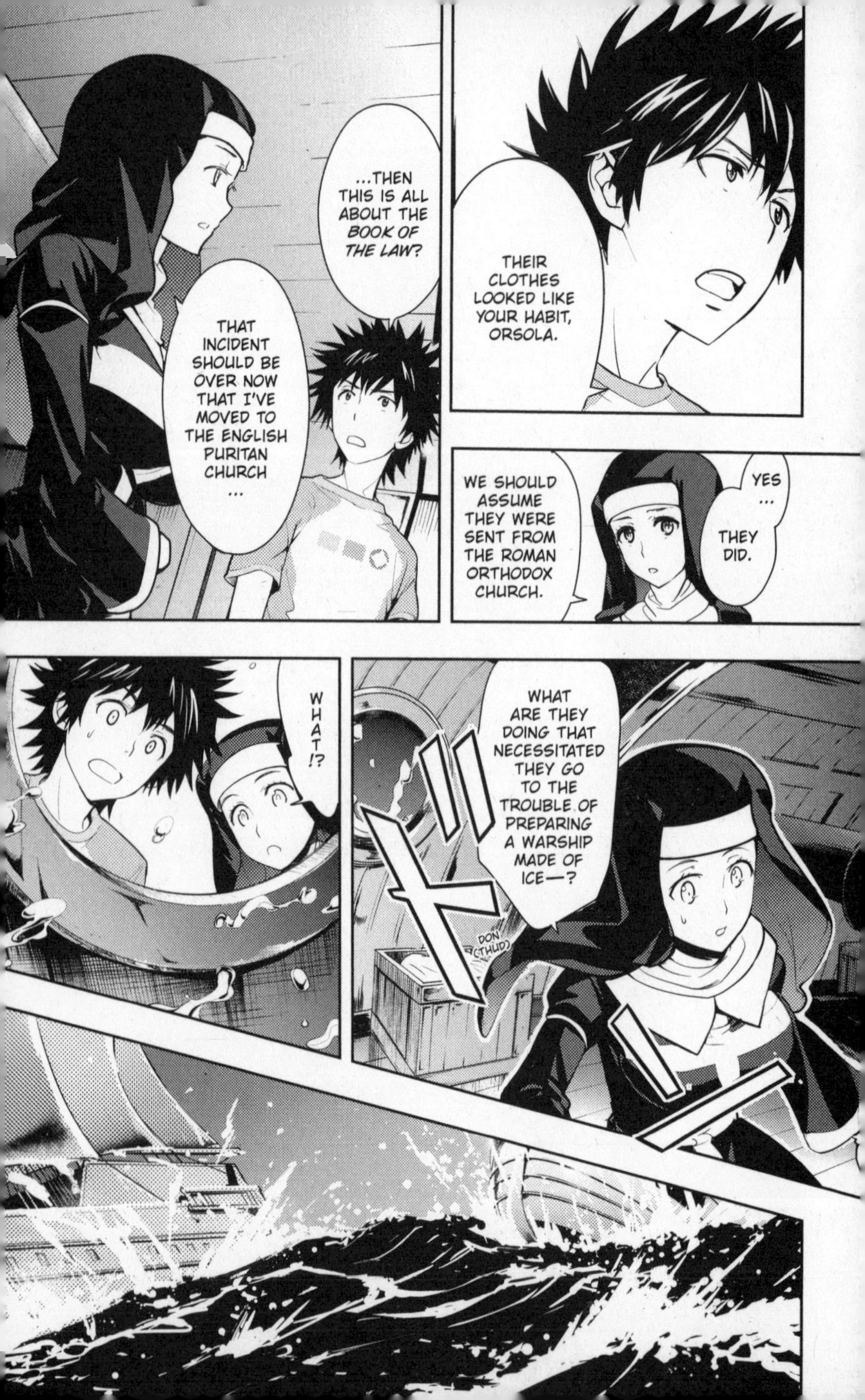
THEIR CLOTHES LOOKED LIKE YOUR HABIT, ORSOLA.
YES... THEY DID.
WE SHOULD ASSUME THEY WERE SENT FROM THE ROMAN ORTHODOX CHURCH.
...THEN THIS IS ALL ABOUT THE *BOOK OF THE LAW*?
THAT INCIDENT SHOULD BE OVER NOW THAT I'VE MOVED TO THE ENGLISH PURITAN CHURCH...
WHAT ARE THEY DOING THAT NECESSITATED THEY GO TO THE TROUBLE OF PREPARING A WARSHIP MADE OF ICE—?
DON (THUD)
WHAT!?

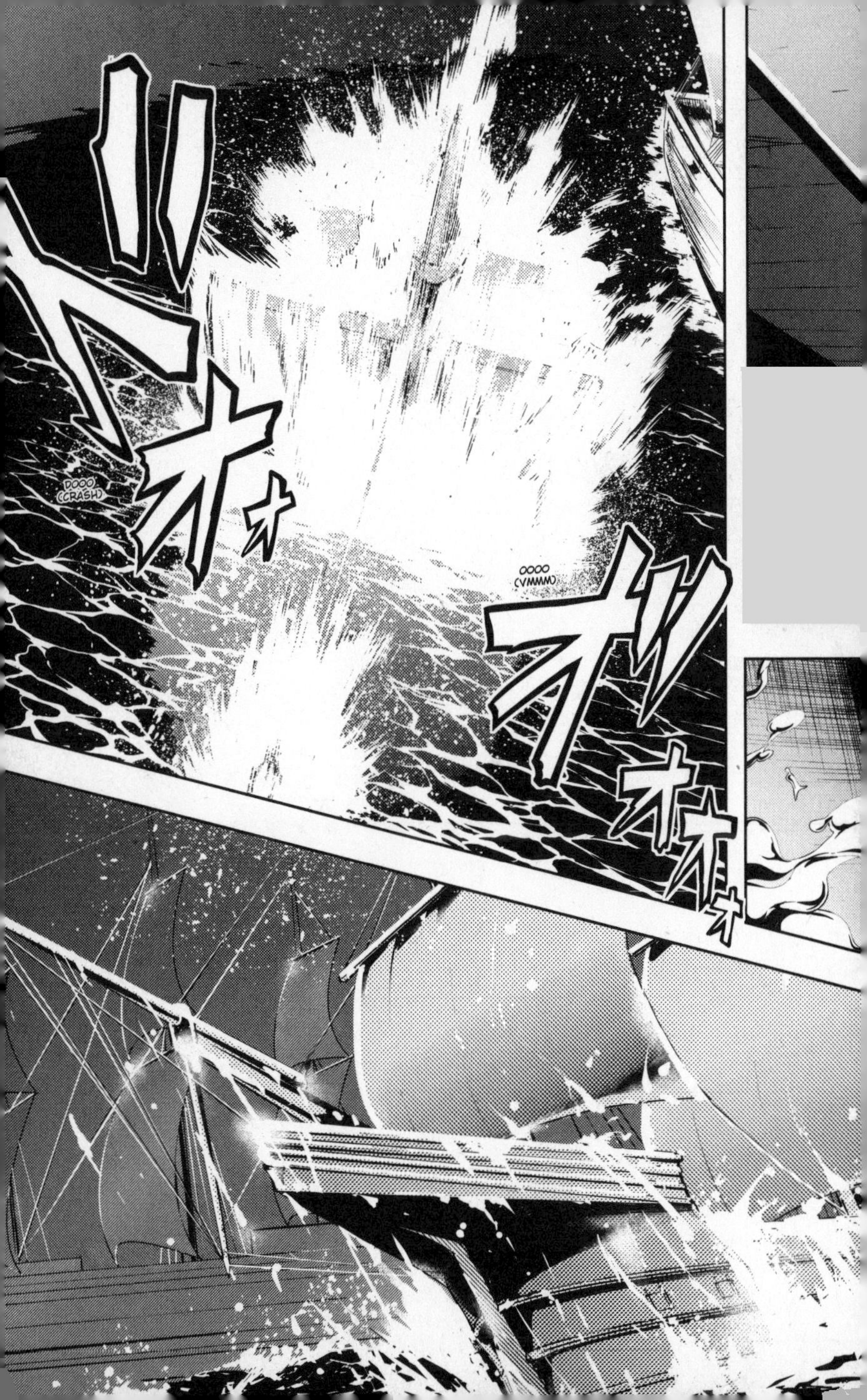
DOOO (CRASH)
OOOO (VMMM)

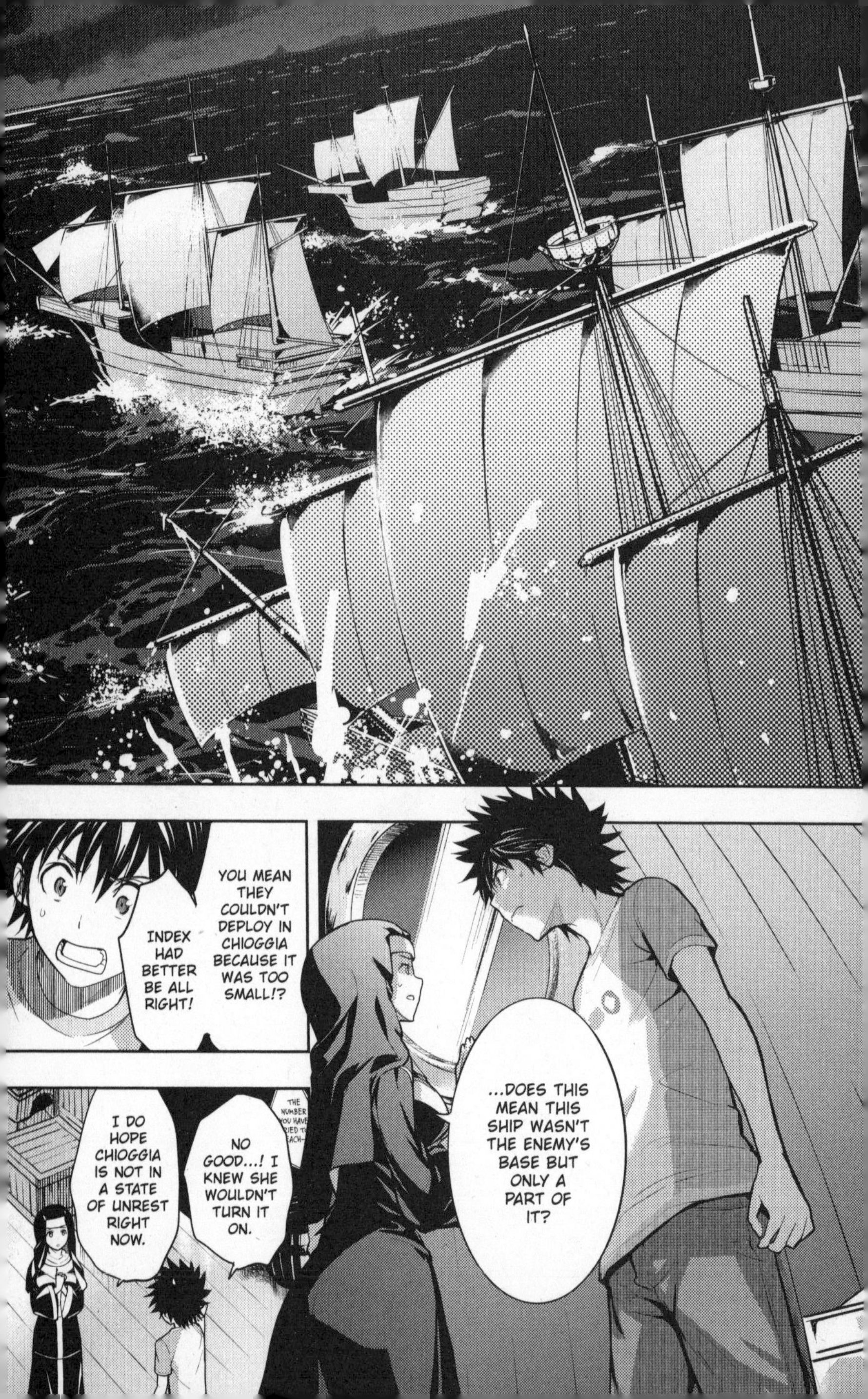
...DOES THIS MEAN THIS SHIP WASN'T THE ENEMY'S BASE BUT ONLY A PART OF IT?
YOU MEAN THEY COULDN'T DEPLOY IN CHIOGGIA BECAUSE IT WAS TOO SMALL!?
INDEX HAD BETTER BE ALL RIGHT!
THE NUMBER YOU HAVE
NO GOOD...! I KNEW SHE WOULDN'T TURN IT ON.
I DO HOPE CHIOGGIA IS NOT IN A STATE OF UNREST RIGHT NOW.

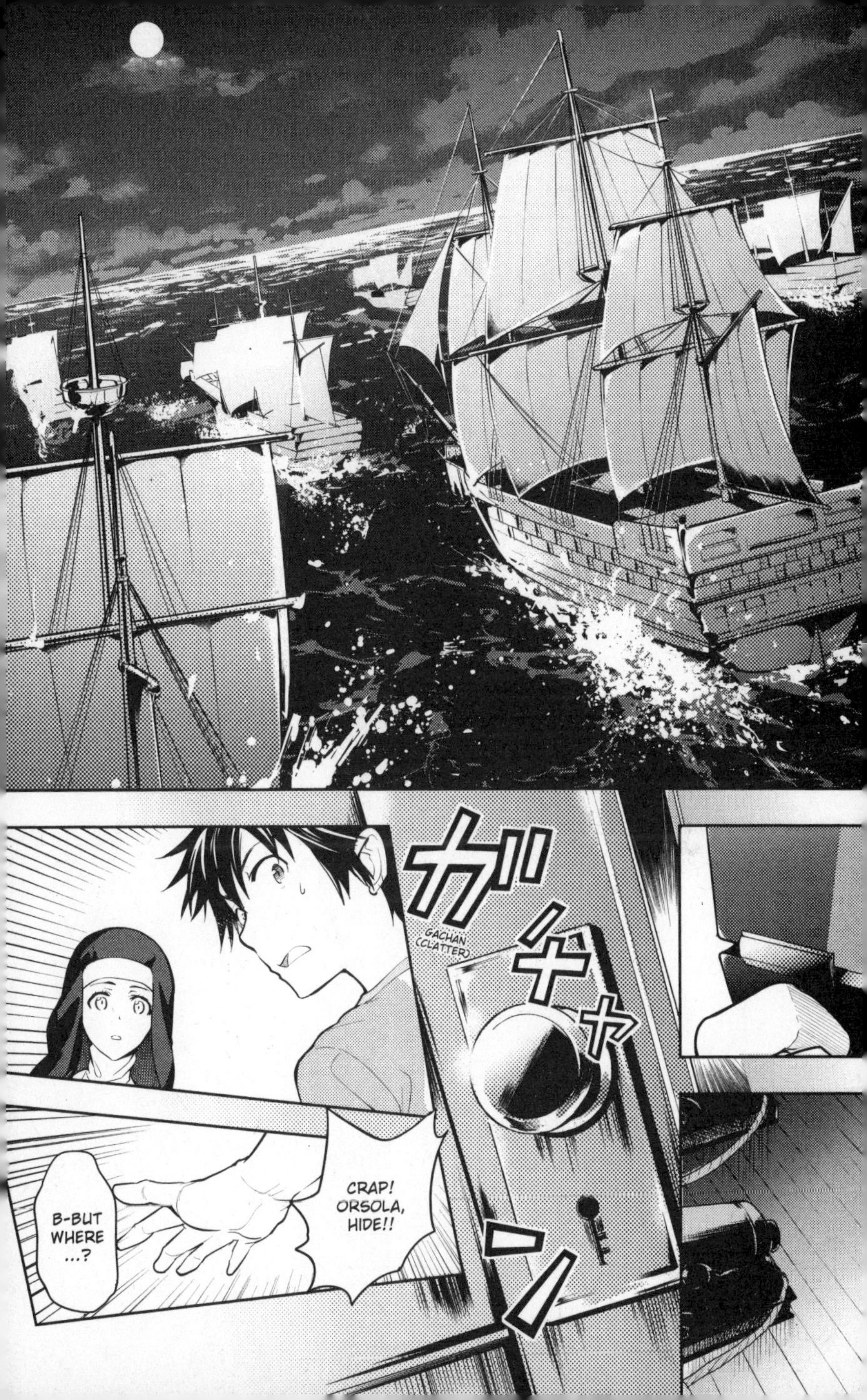

GACHAN (CLATTER)
CRAP! ORSOLA, HIDE!!
B-BUT WHERE ...?

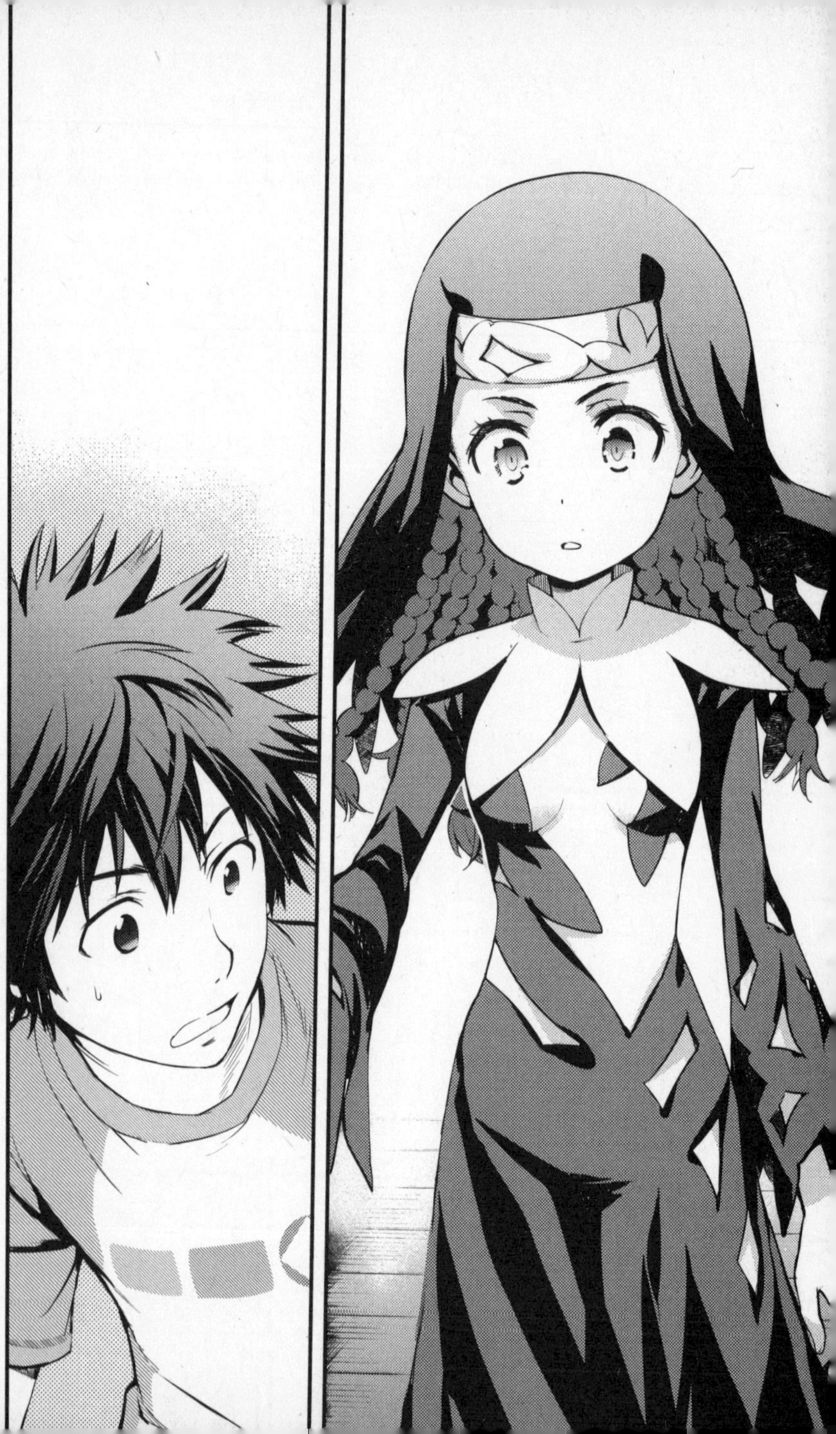

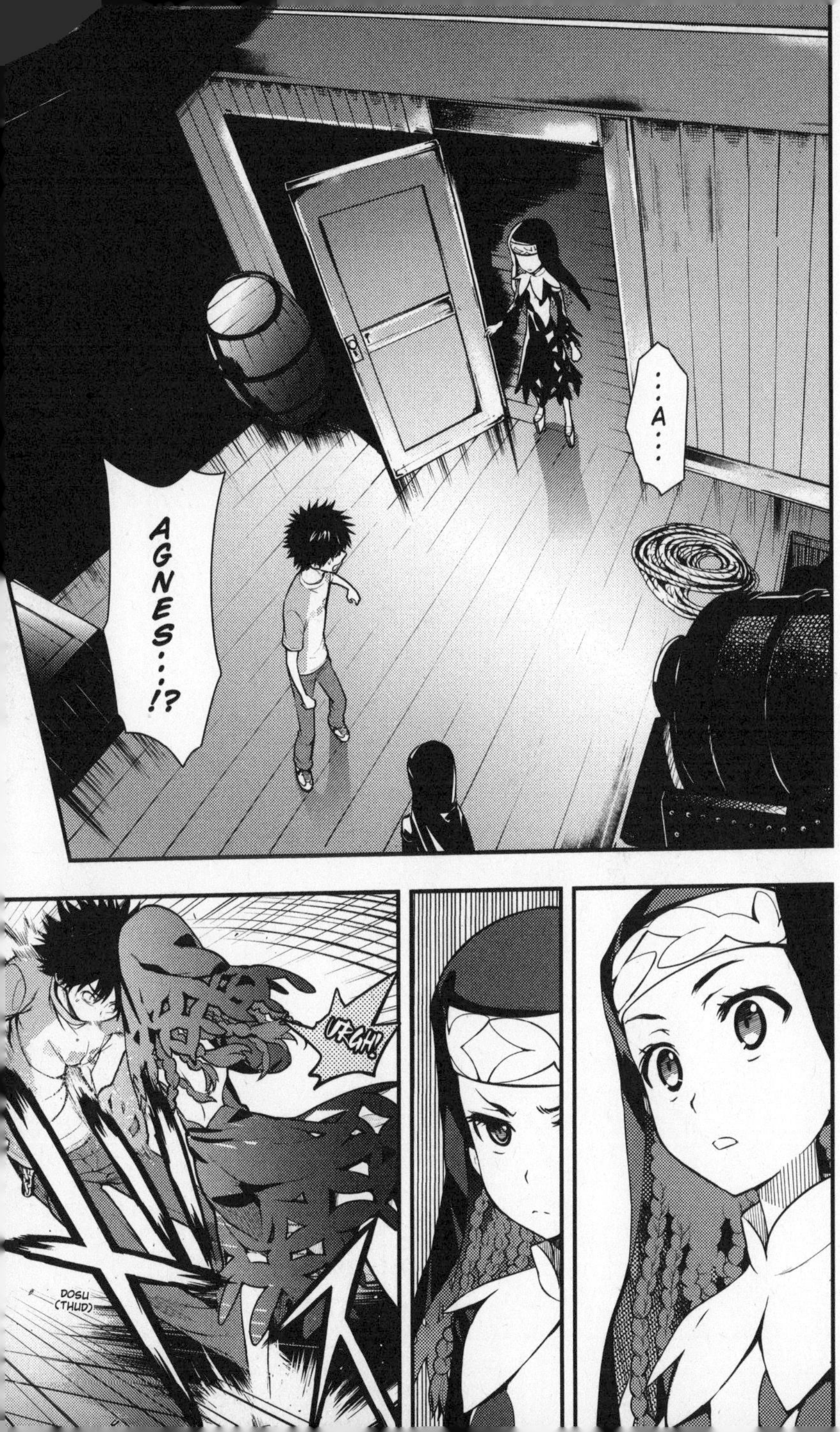
...A...
AGNES...!?
URGH!
DOSU
(THUD)

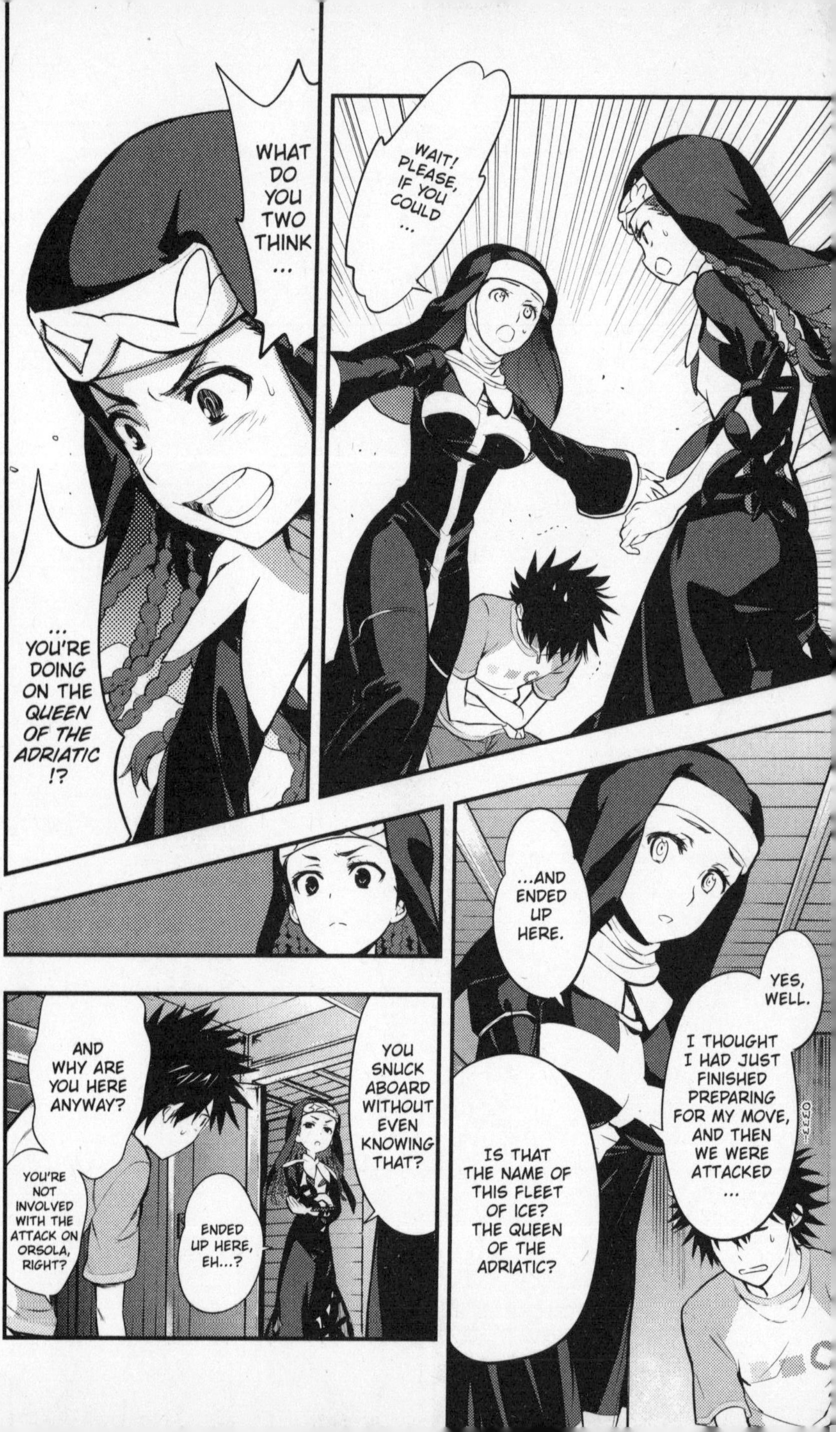
WAIT! PLEASE, IF YOU COULD ...
WHAT DO YOU TWO THINK ...
... YOU'RE DOING ON THE QUEEN OF THE ADRIATIC !?
YES, WELL.
I THOUGHT I HAD JUST FINISHED PREPARING FOR MY MOVE, AND THEN WE WERE ATTACKED ...
...AND ENDED UP HERE.
IS THAT THE NAME OF THIS FLEET OF ICE? THE QUEEN OF THE ADRIATIC?
YOU SNUCK ABOARD WITHOUT EVEN KNOWING THAT?
AND WHY ARE YOU HERE ANYWAY?
ENDED UP HERE, EH...?
YOU'RE NOT INVOLVED WITH THE ATTACK ON ORSOLA, RIGHT?

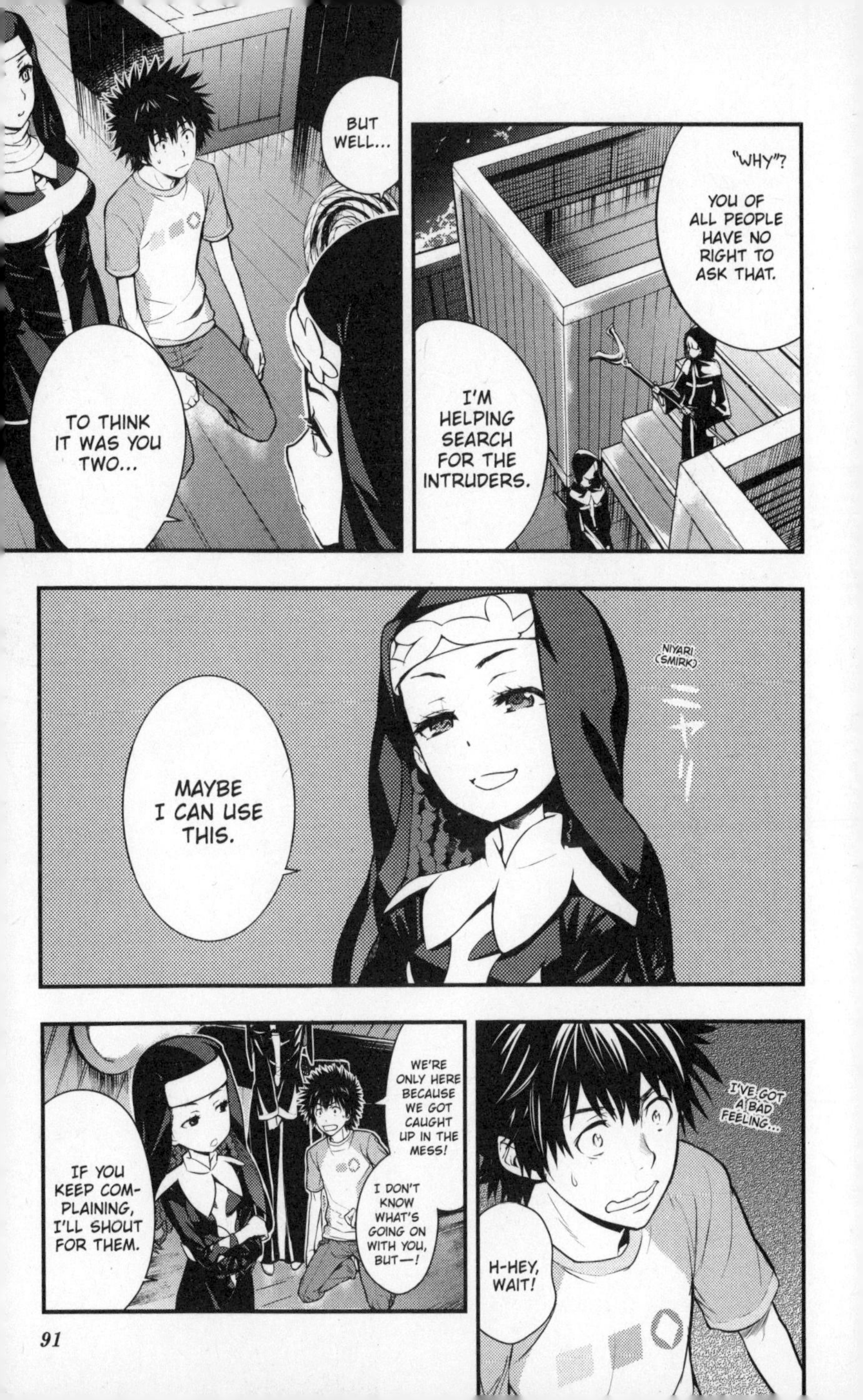
"WHY"?
YOU OF ALL PEOPLE HAVE NO RIGHT TO ASK THAT.
I'M HELPING SEARCH FOR THE INTRUDERS.
BUT WELL...
TO THINK IT WAS YOU TWO...
NIYARI (SMIRK)
ニヤリ
MAYBE I CAN USE THIS.
I'VE GOT A BAD FEELING...
H-HEY, WAIT!
WE'RE ONLY HERE BECAUSE WE GOT CAUGHT UP IN THE MESS!
I DON'T KNOW WHAT'S GOING ON WITH YOU, BUT—!
IF YOU KEEP COM-PLAINING, I'LL SHOUT FOR THEM.

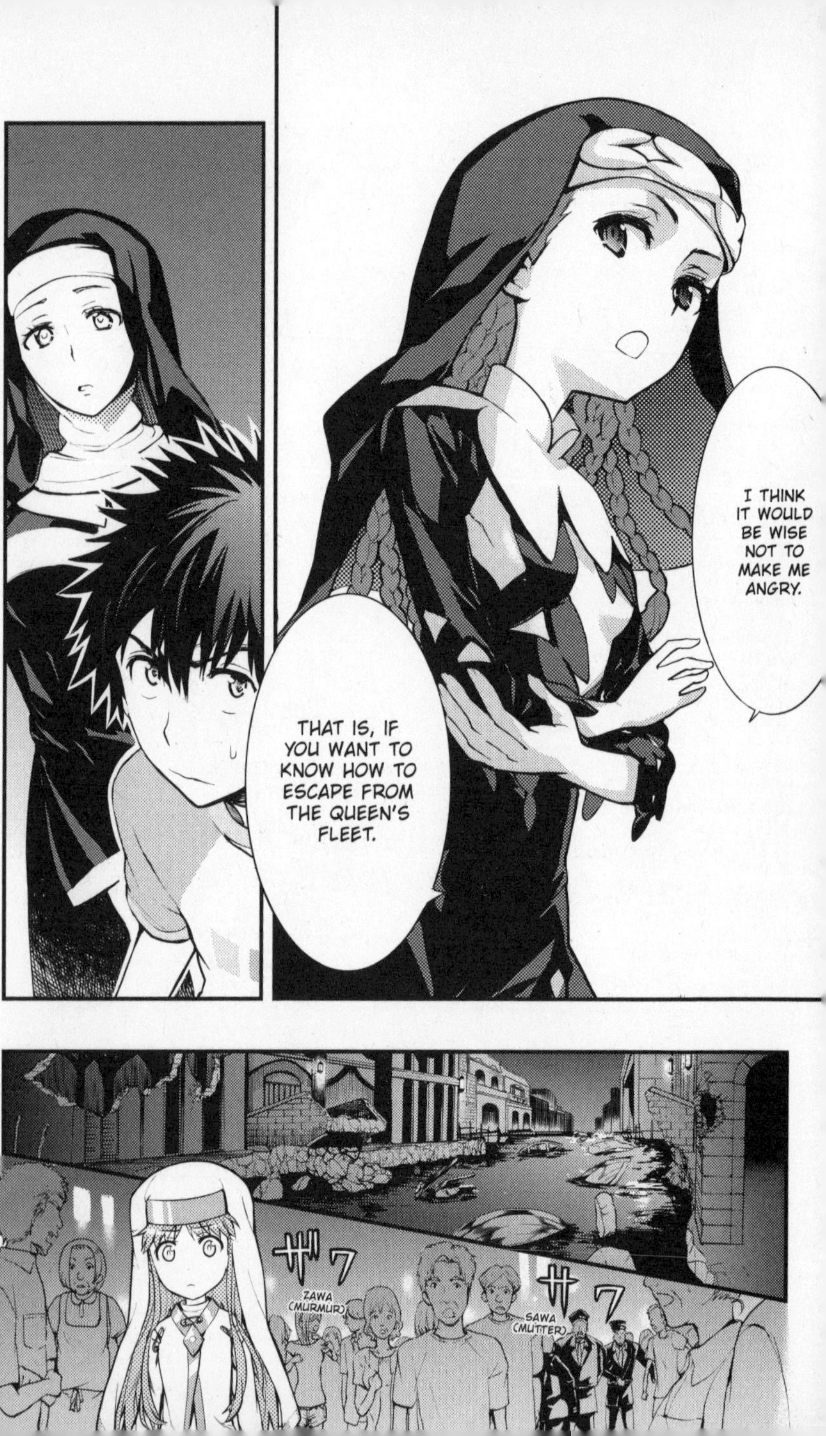
I THINK IT WOULD BE WISE NOT TO MAKE ME ANGRY.
THAT IS, IF YOU WANT TO KNOW HOW TO ESCAPE FROM THE QUEEN'S FLEET.
サワ
SAWA (MUTTER)
ザワ
ZAWA (MURMUR)

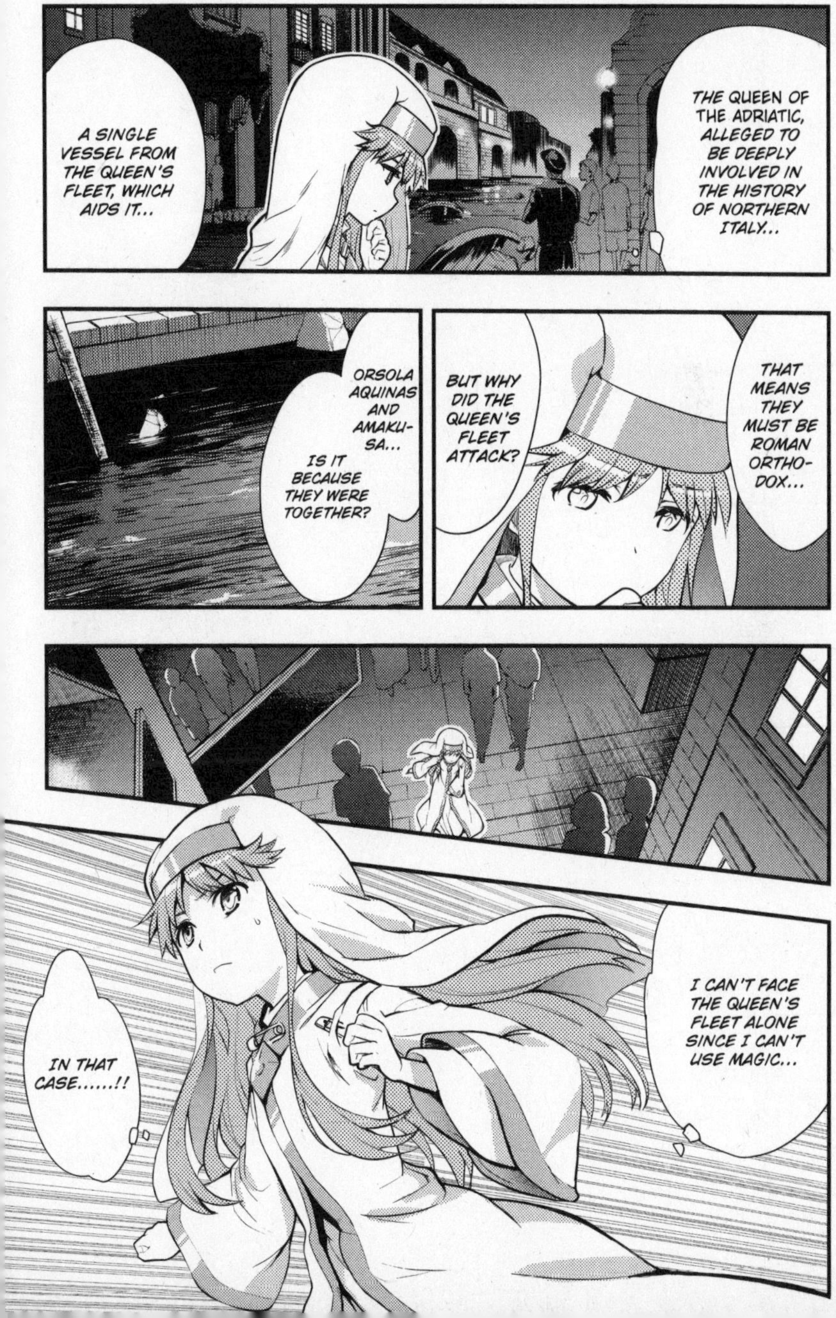
THE QUEEN OF THE ADRIATIC, ALLEGED TO BE DEEPLY INVOLVED IN THE HISTORY OF NORTHERN ITALY...
A SINGLE VESSEL FROM THE QUEEN'S FLEET, WHICH AIDS IT...
THAT MEANS THEY MUST BE ROMAN ORTHODOX...
BUT WHY DID THE QUEEN'S FLEET ATTACK?
ORSOLA AQUINAS AND AMAKUSA...
IS IT BECAUSE THEY WERE TOGETHER?
I CAN'T FACE THE QUEEN'S FLEET ALONE SINCE I CAN'T USE MAGIC...
IN THAT CASE......!!

A Certain Magical Index

# #89 THE QUEEN'S FLEET ②

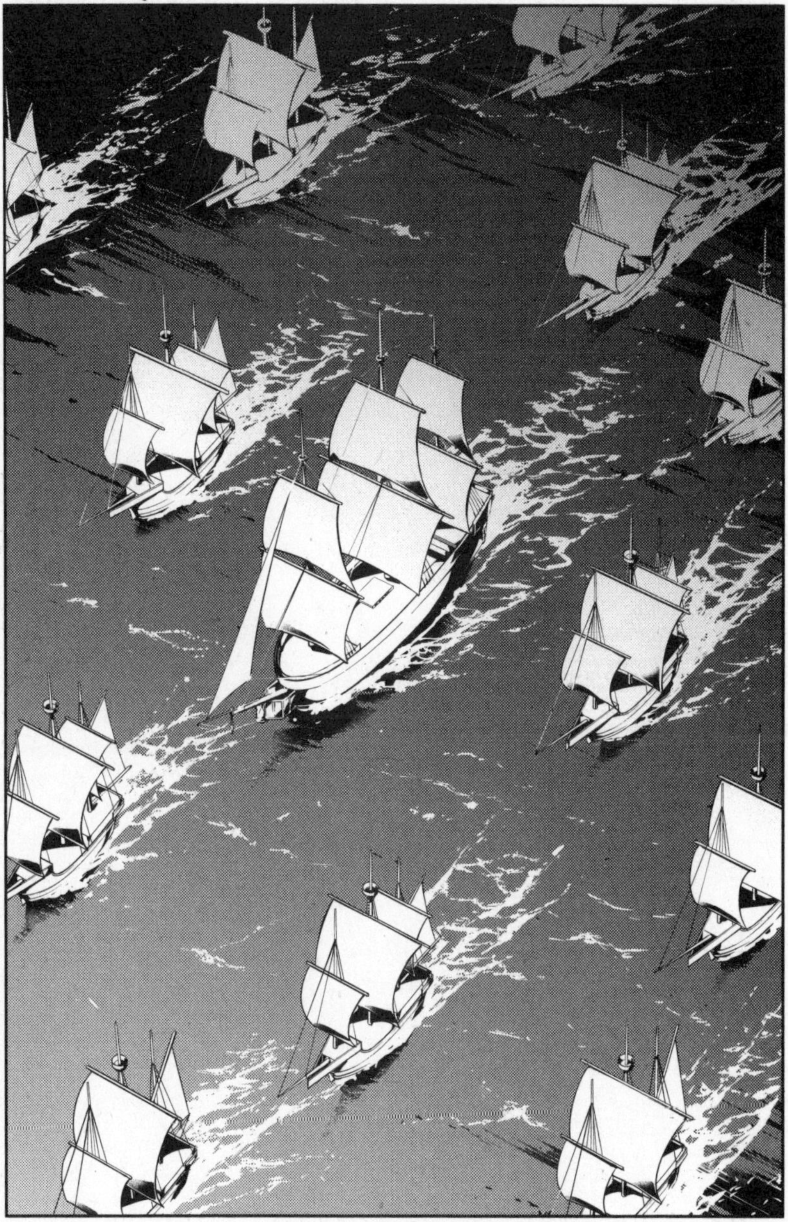

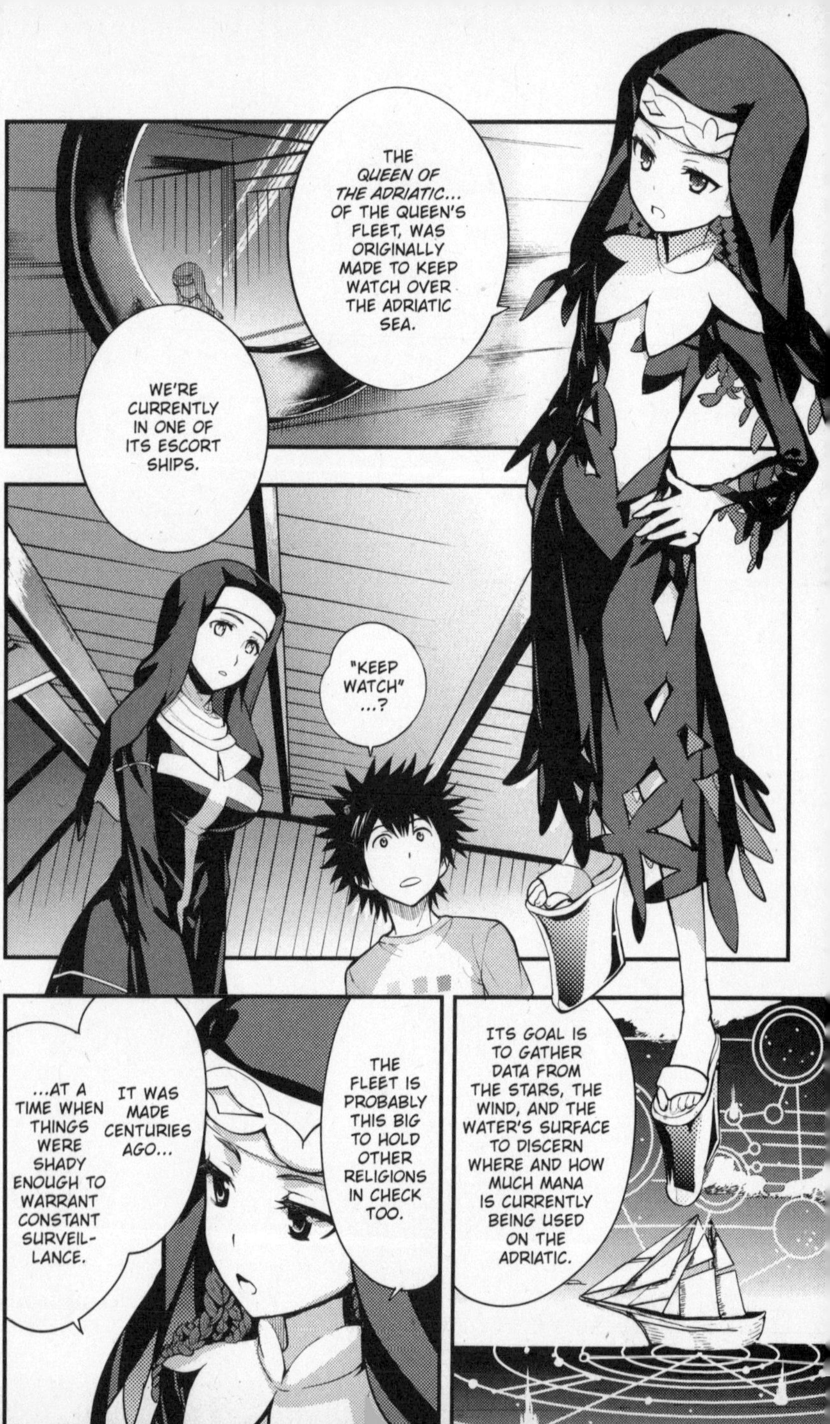

THE *QUEEN OF THE ADRIATIC*... OF THE QUEEN'S FLEET, WAS ORIGINALLY MADE TO KEEP WATCH OVER THE ADRIATIC SEA.
WE'RE CURRENTLY IN ONE OF ITS ESCORT SHIPS.
"KEEP WATCH" ...?
ITS GOAL IS TO GATHER DATA FROM THE STARS, THE WIND, AND THE WATER'S SURFACE TO DISCERN WHERE AND HOW MUCH MANA IS CURRENTLY BEING USED ON THE ADRIATIC.
THE FLEET IS PROBABLY THIS BIG TO HOLD OTHER RELIGIONS IN CHECK TOO.
IT WAS MADE CENTURIES AGO...
...AT A TIME WHEN THINGS WERE SHADY ENOUGH TO WARRANT CONSTANT SURVEIL-LANCE.

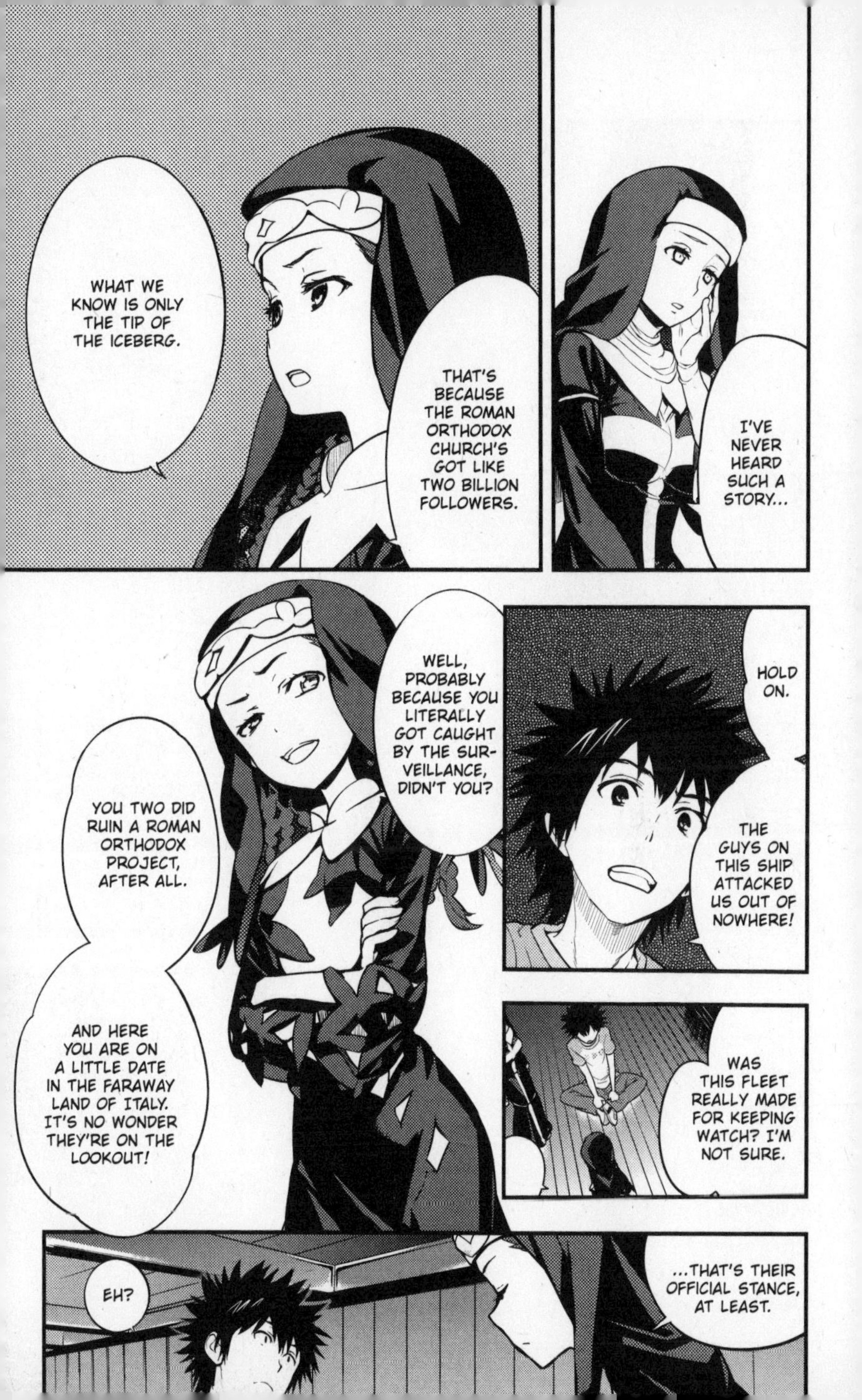
I'VE NEVER HEARD SUCH A STORY...
THAT'S BECAUSE THE ROMAN ORTHODOX CHURCH'S GOT LIKE TWO BILLION FOLLOWERS.
WHAT WE KNOW IS ONLY THE TIP OF THE ICEBERG.
HOLD ON.
THE GUYS ON THIS SHIP ATTACKED US OUT OF NOWHERE!
WAS THIS FLEET REALLY MADE FOR KEEPING WATCH? I'M NOT SURE.
WELL, PROBABLY BECAUSE YOU LITERALLY GOT CAUGHT BY THE SUR-VEILLANCE, DIDN'T YOU?
YOU TWO DID RUIN A ROMAN ORTHODOX PROJECT, AFTER ALL.
AND HERE YOU ARE ON A LITTLE DATE IN THE FARAWAY LAND OF ITALY. IT'S NO WONDER THEY'RE ON THE LOOKOUT!
...THAT'S THEIR OFFICIAL STANCE, AT LEAST.
EH?

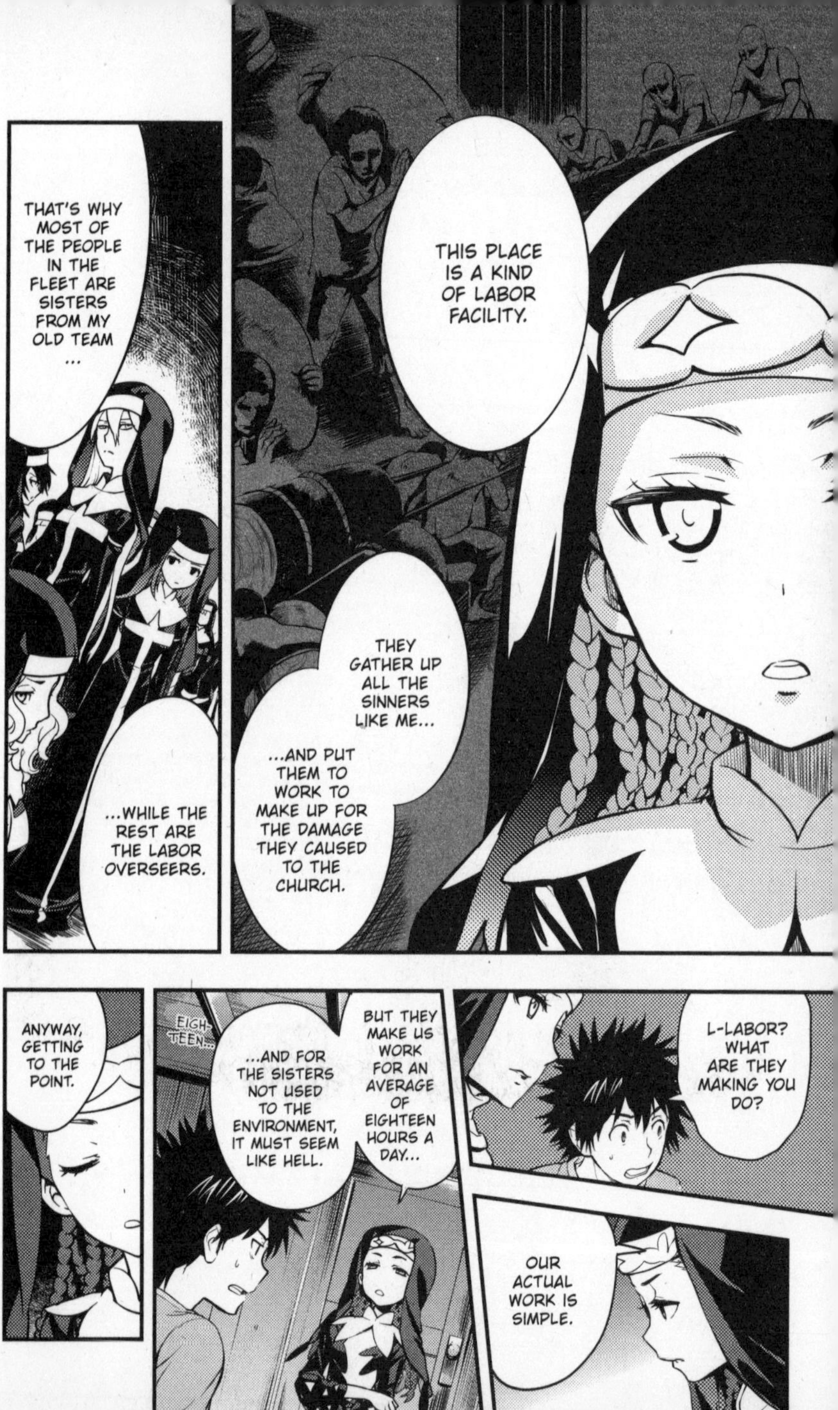
THIS PLACE IS A KIND OF LABOR FACILITY.
THEY GATHER UP ALL THE SINNERS LIKE ME...
...AND PUT THEM TO WORK TO MAKE UP FOR THE DAMAGE THEY CAUSED TO THE CHURCH.
THAT'S WHY MOST OF THE PEOPLE IN THE FLEET ARE SISTERS FROM MY OLD TEAM ...
...WHILE THE REST ARE THE LABOR OVERSEERS.
L-LABOR? WHAT ARE THEY MAKING YOU DO?
BUT THEY MAKE US WORK FOR AN AVERAGE OF EIGHTEEN HOURS A DAY...
EIGH-TEEN...
...AND FOR THE SISTERS NOT USED TO THE ENVIRONMENT, IT MUST SEEM LIKE HELL.
ANYWAY, GETTING TO THE POINT.
OUR ACTUAL WORK IS SIMPLE.

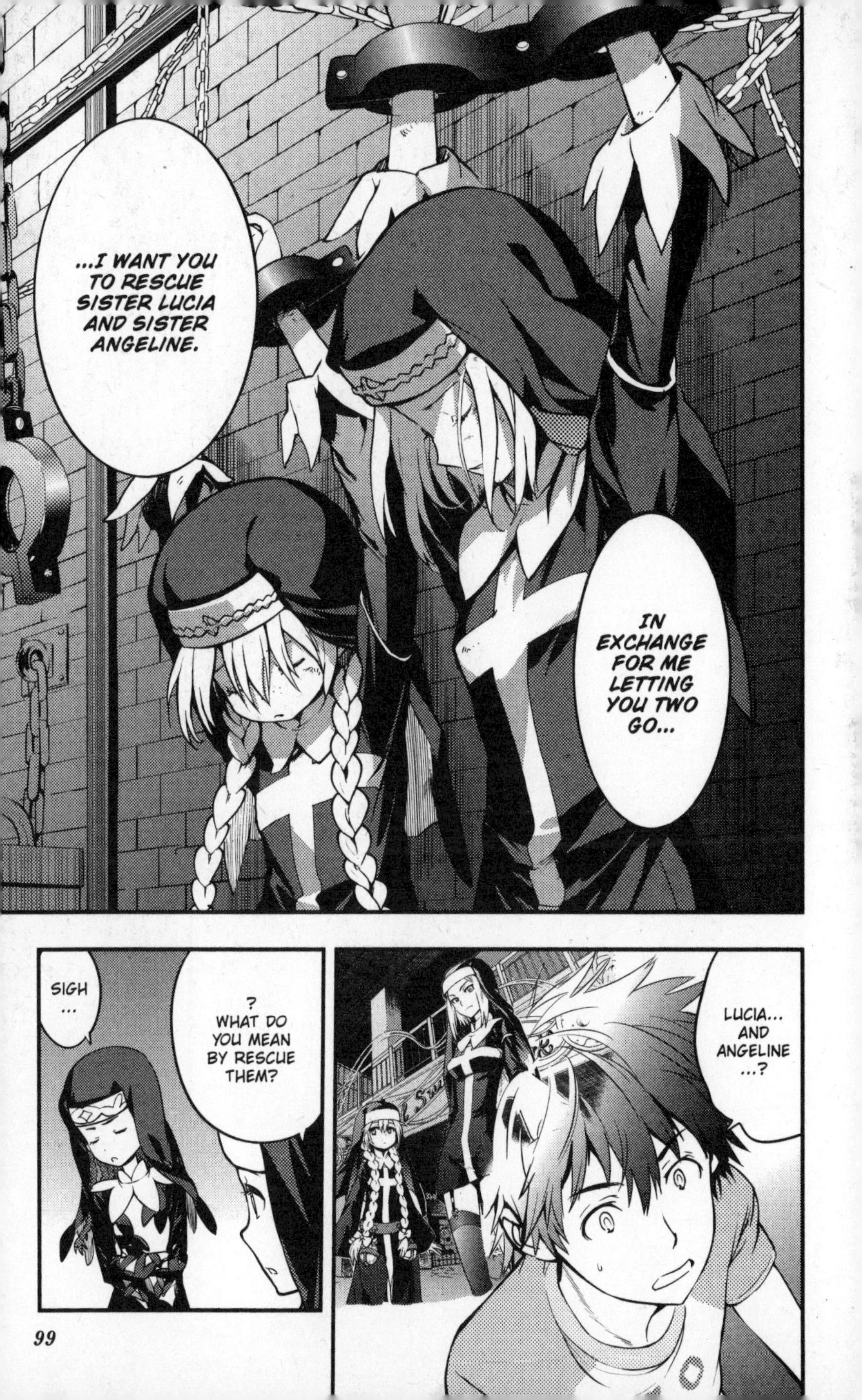
IN EXCHANGE FOR ME LETTING YOU TWO GO...
...I WANT YOU TO RESCUE SISTER LUCIA AND SISTER ANGELINE.
LUCIA... AND ANGELINE ...?
? WHAT DO YOU MEAN BY RESCUE THEM?
SIGH ...

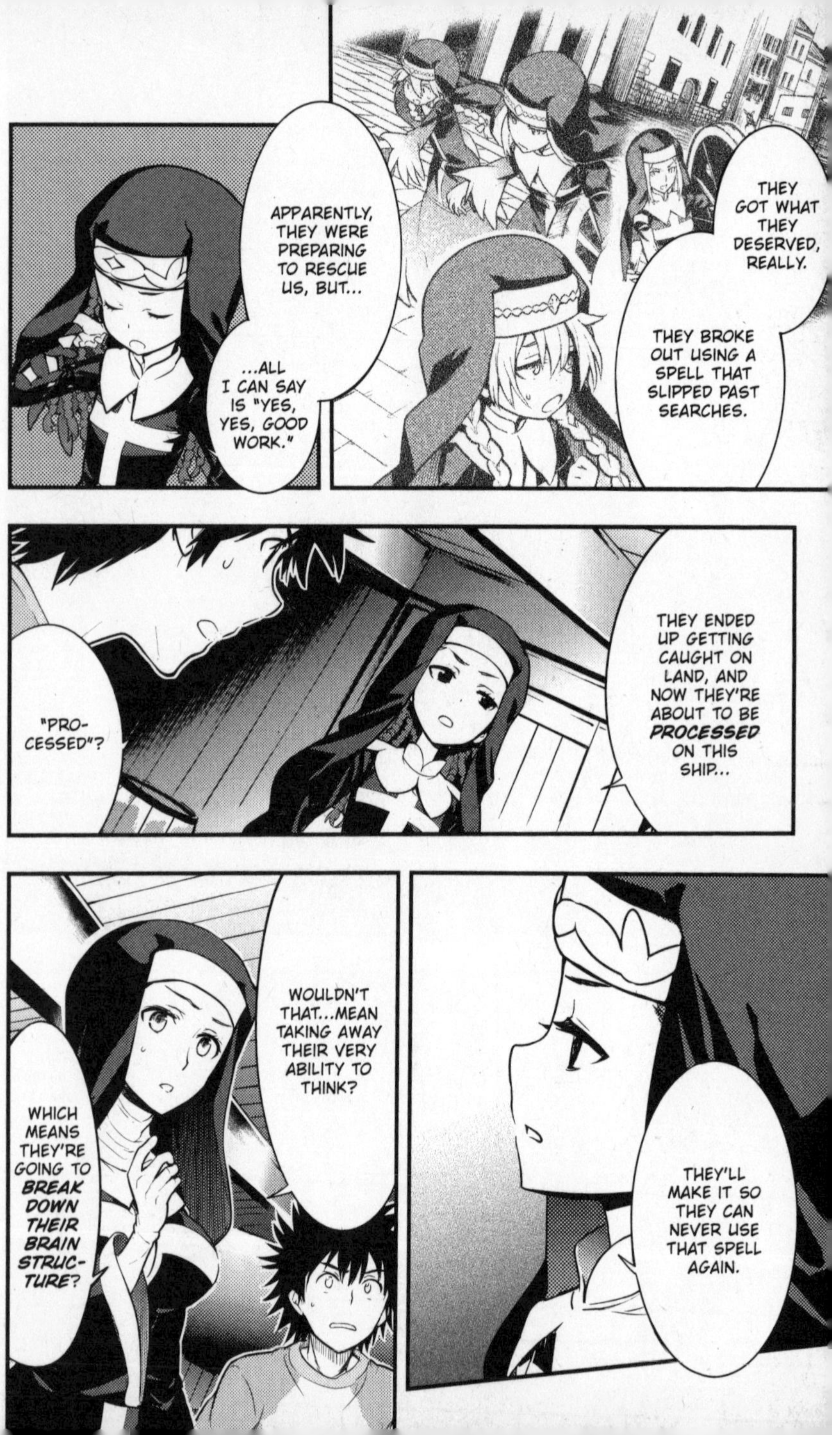
THEY GOT WHAT THEY DESERVED, REALLY.
THEY BROKE OUT USING A SPELL THAT SLIPPED PAST SEARCHES.
APPARENTLY, THEY WERE PREPARING TO RESCUE US, BUT...
...ALL I CAN SAY IS "YES, YES, GOOD WORK."
THEY ENDED UP GETTING CAUGHT ON LAND, AND NOW THEY'RE ABOUT TO BE ***PROCESSED*** ON THIS SHIP...
"PRO-CESSED"?
THEY'LL MAKE IT SO THEY CAN NEVER USE THAT SPELL AGAIN.
WOULDN'T THAT...MEAN TAKING AWAY THEIR VERY ABILITY TO THINK?
WHICH MEANS THEY'RE GOING TO ***BREAK DOWN THEIR BRAIN STRUCTURE?***

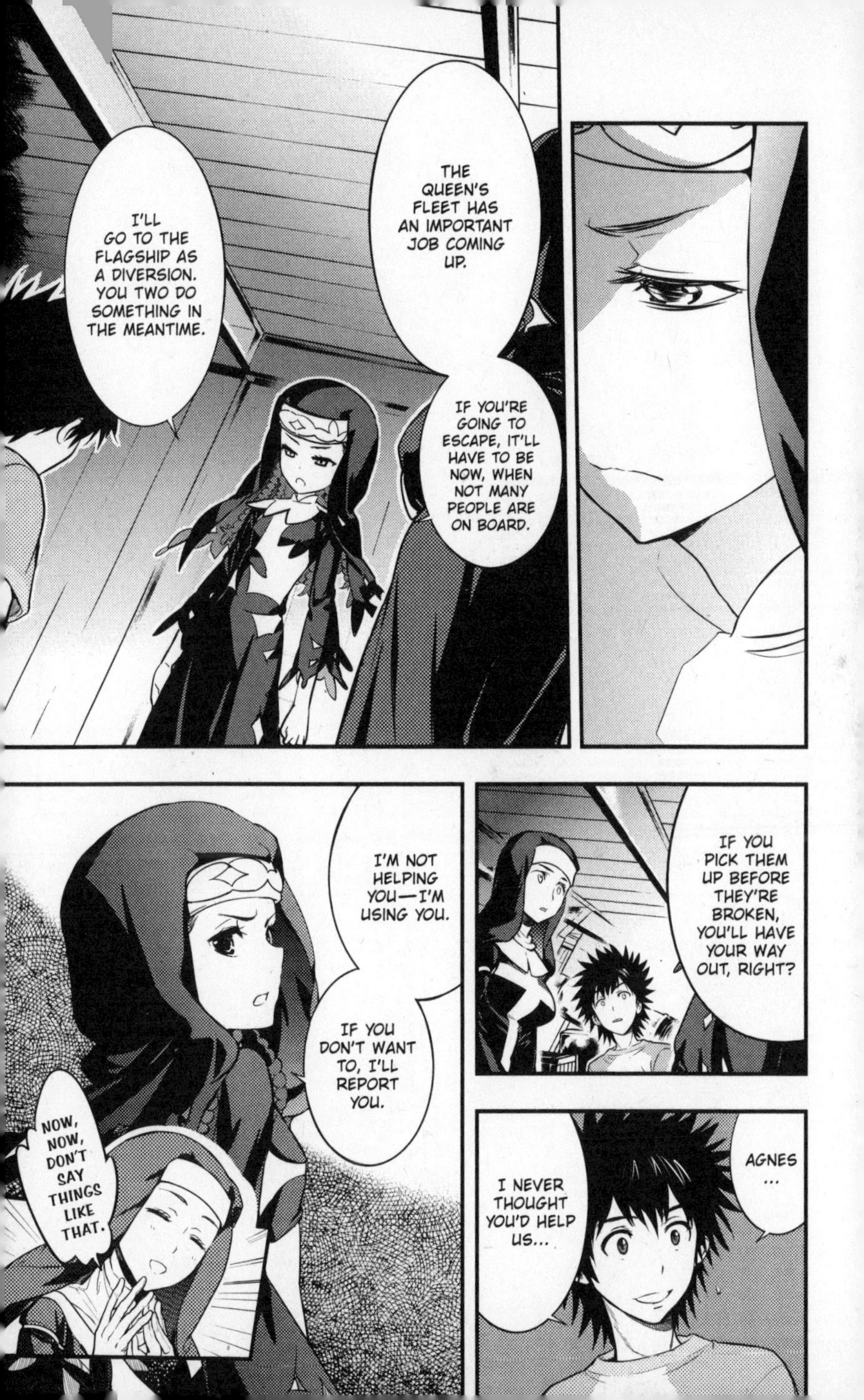
THE QUEEN'S FLEET HAS AN IMPORTANT JOB COMING UP.
IF YOU'RE GOING TO ESCAPE, IT'LL HAVE TO BE NOW, WHEN NOT MANY PEOPLE ARE ON BOARD.
I'LL GO TO THE FLAGSHIP AS A DIVERSION. YOU TWO DO SOMETHING IN THE MEANTIME.
IF YOU PICK THEM UP BEFORE THEY'RE BROKEN, YOU'LL HAVE YOUR WAY OUT, RIGHT?
AGNES...
I NEVER THOUGHT YOU'D HELP US...
I'M NOT HELPING YOU—I'M USING YOU.
IF YOU DON'T WANT TO, I'LL REPORT YOU.
NOW, NOW, DON'T SAY THINGS LIKE THAT.

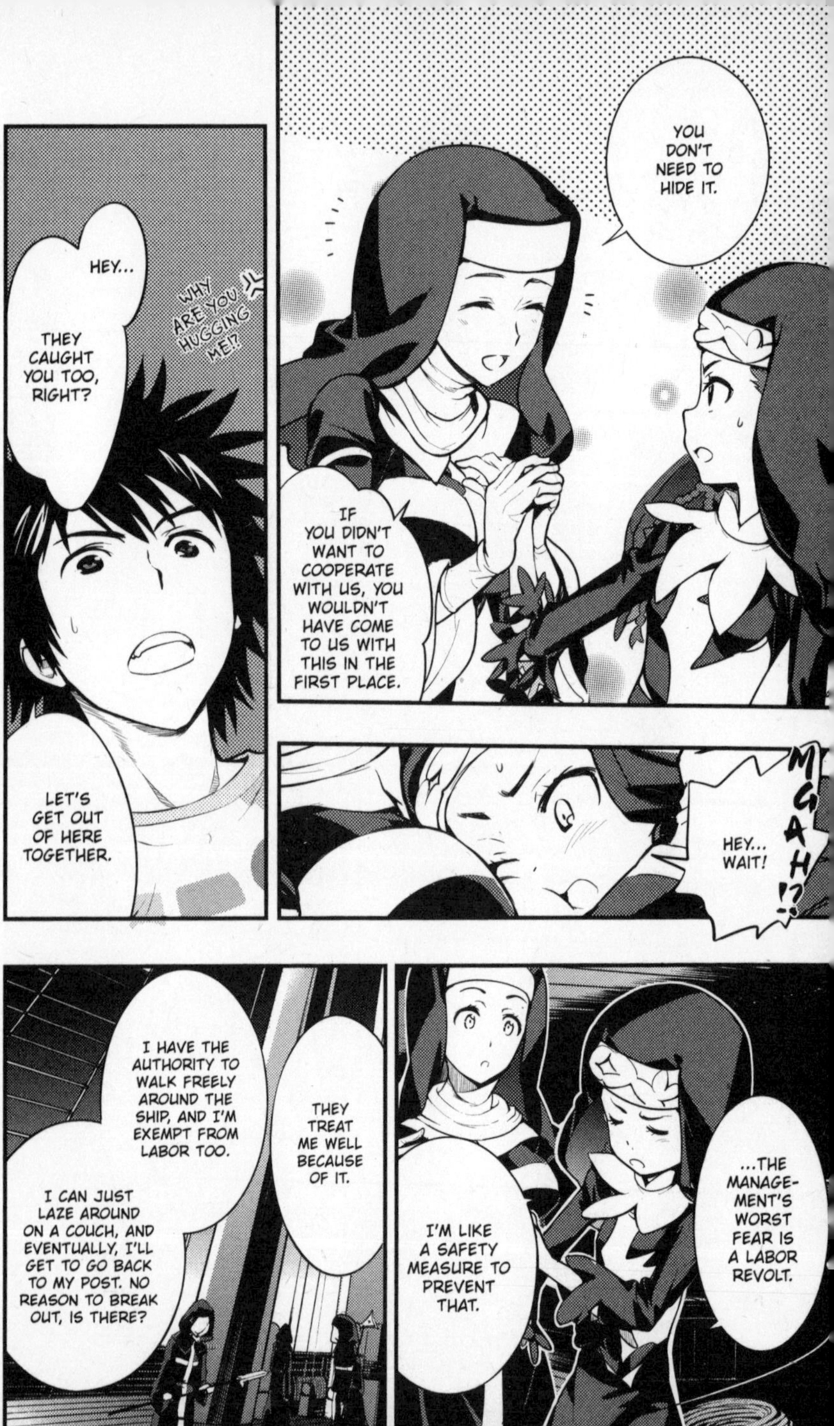
YOU DON'T NEED TO HIDE IT.
IF YOU DIDN'T WANT TO COOPERATE WITH US, YOU WOULDN'T HAVE COME TO US WITH THIS IN THE FIRST PLACE.
MGAH!?
HEY... WAIT!
WHY ARE YOU HUGGING ME!?
HEY...
THEY CAUGHT YOU TOO, RIGHT?
LET'S GET OUT OF HERE TOGETHER.
...THE MANAGEMENT'S WORST FEAR IS A LABOR REVOLT.
I'M LIKE A SAFETY MEASURE TO PREVENT THAT.
THEY TREAT ME WELL BECAUSE OF IT.
I HAVE THE AUTHORITY TO WALK FREELY AROUND THE SHIP, AND I'M EXEMPT FROM LABOR TOO.
I CAN JUST LAZE AROUND ON A COUCH, AND EVENTUALLY, I'LL GET TO GO BACK TO MY POST. NO REASON TO BREAK OUT, IS THERE?

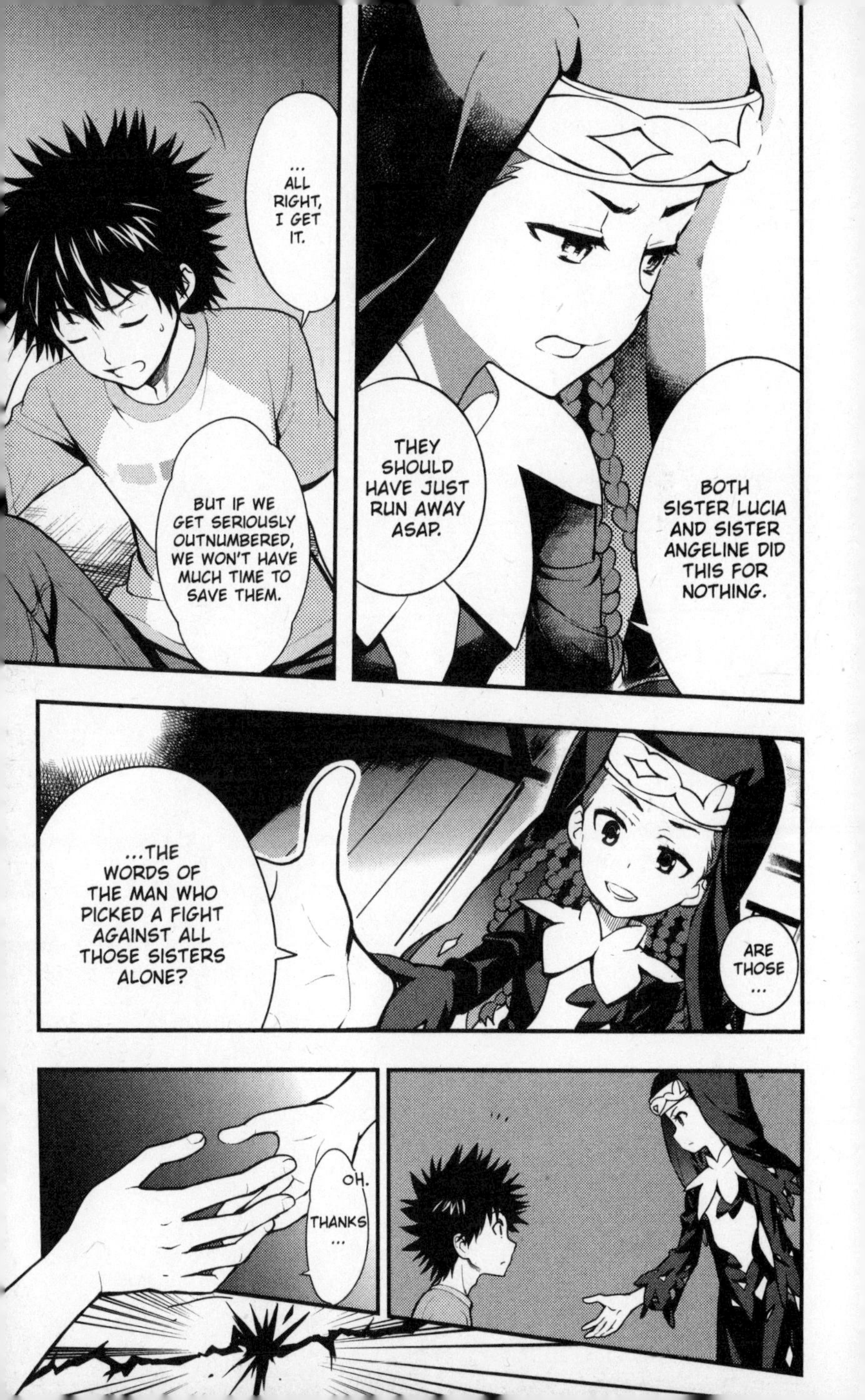
BOTH SISTER LUCIA AND SISTER ANGELINE DID THIS FOR NOTHING.
THEY SHOULD HAVE JUST RUN AWAY ASAP.
... ALL RIGHT, I GET IT.
BUT IF WE GET SERIOUSLY OUTNUMBERED, WE WON'T HAVE MUCH TIME TO SAVE THEM.
ARE THOSE ...
...THE WORDS OF THE MAN WHO PICKED A FIGHT AGAINST ALL THOSE SISTERS ALONE?
...
OH.
THANKS ...

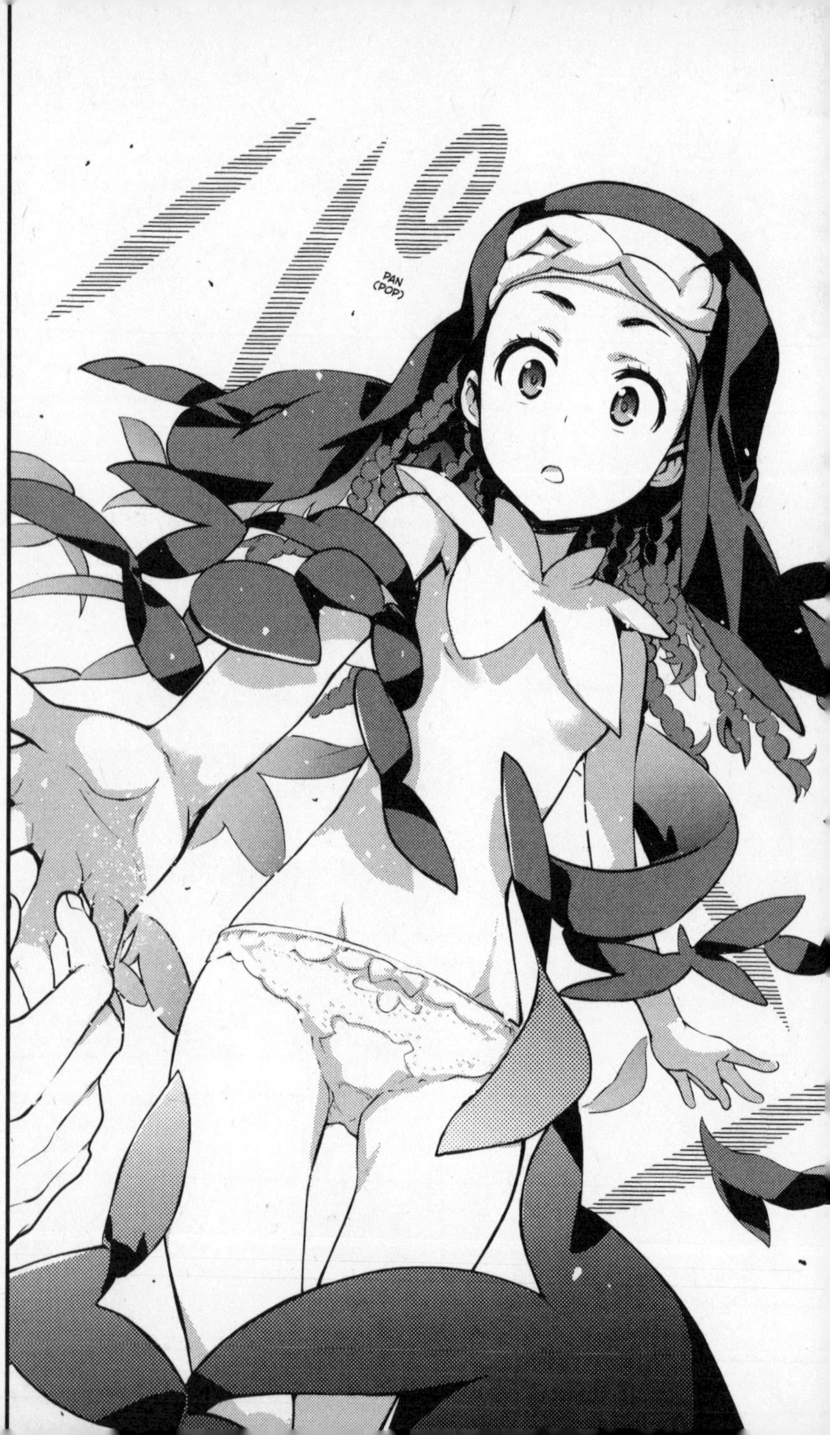
PAN
(POP)

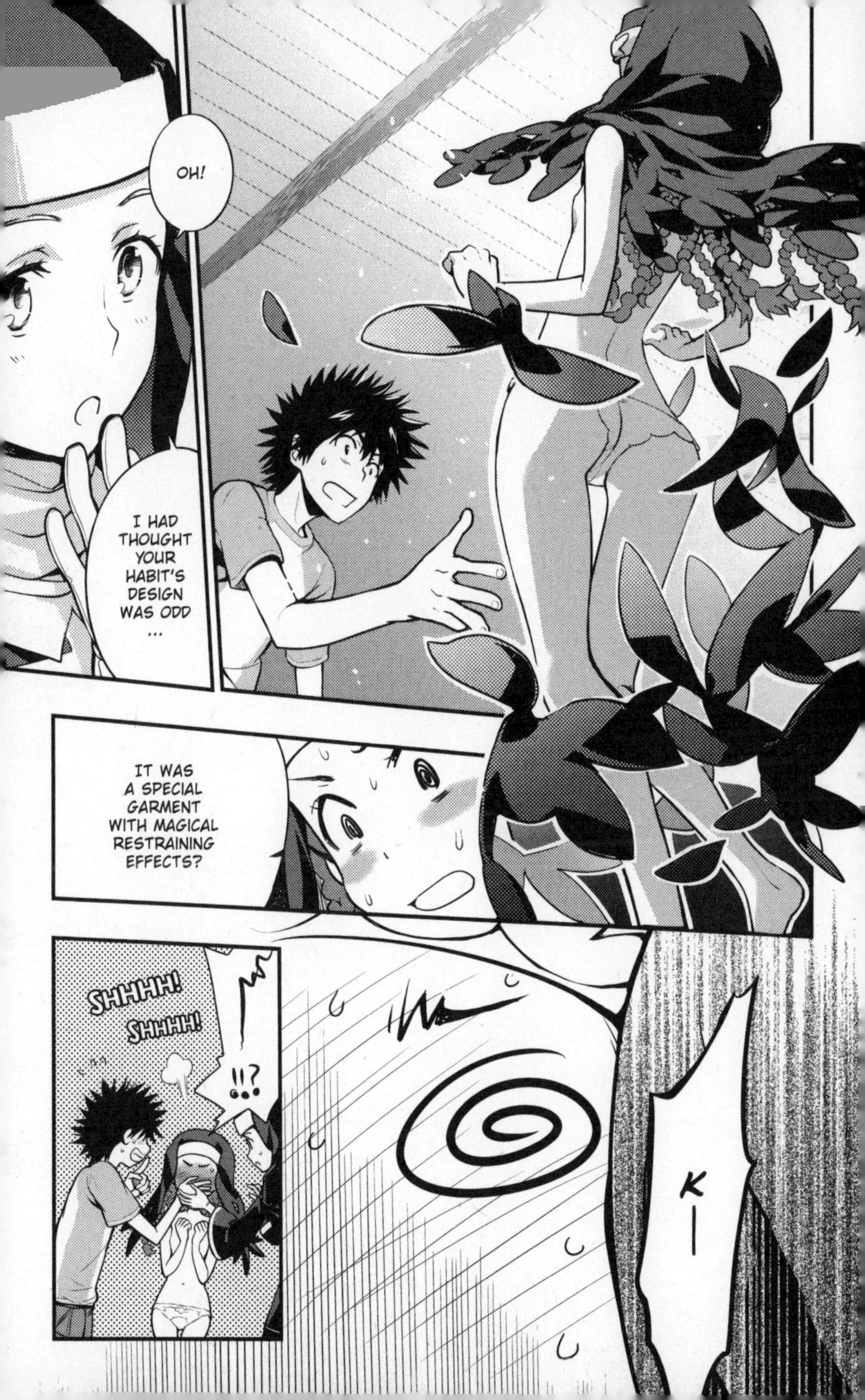
OH!
I HAD THOUGHT YOUR HABIT'S DESIGN WAS ODD ...
IT WAS A SPECIAL GARMENT WITH MAGICAL RESTRAINING EFFECTS?
KI-
SHHHH!
SHHHH!
!!?

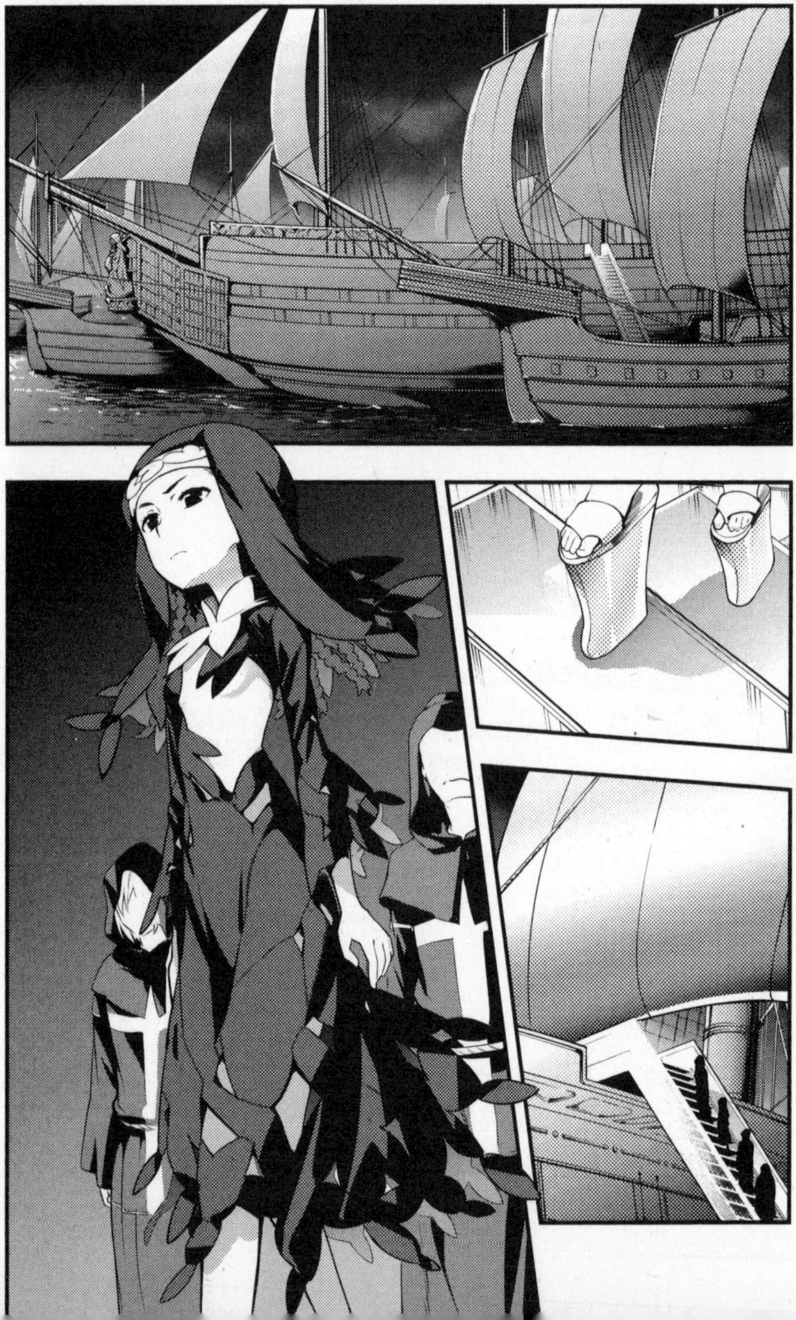

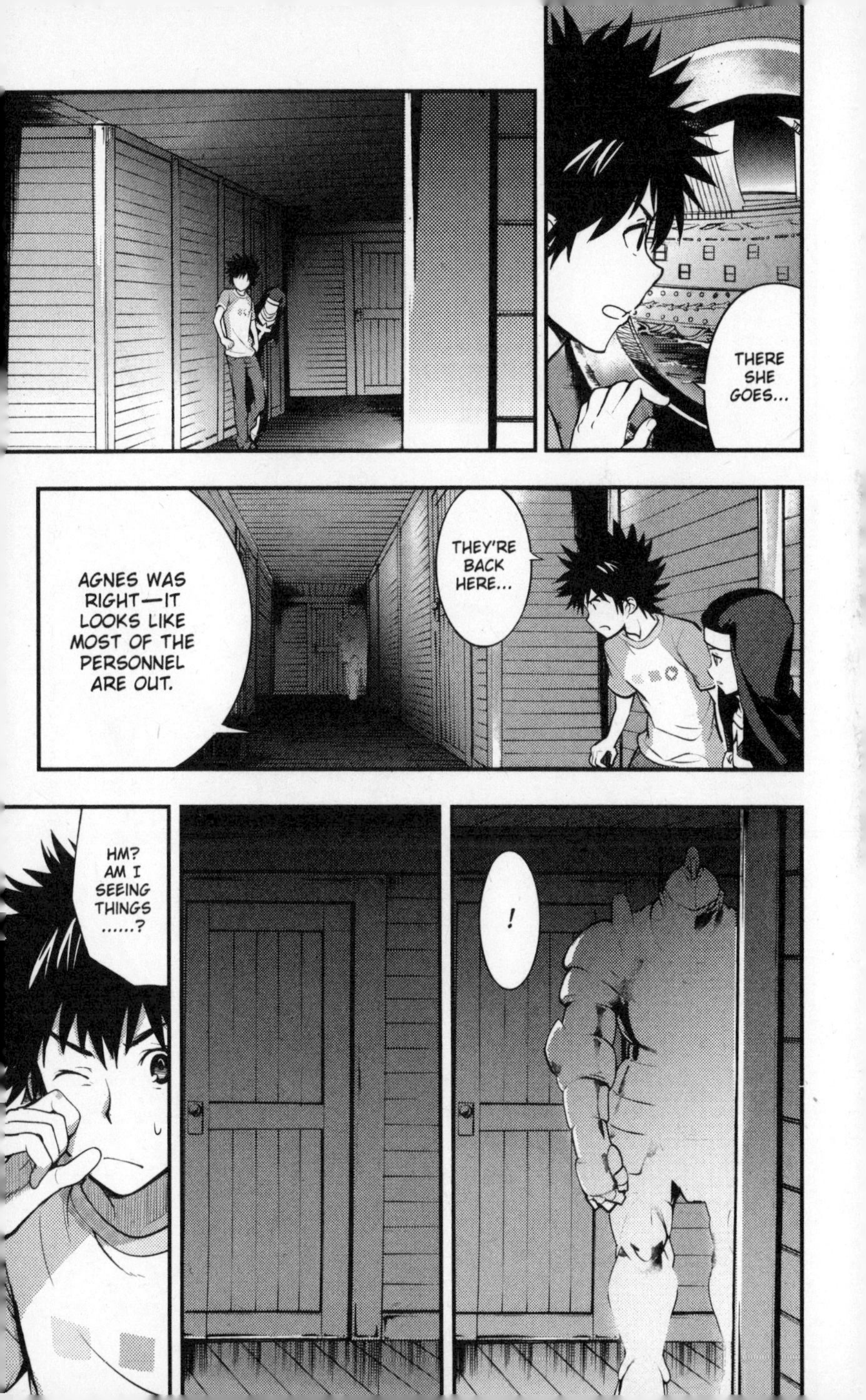
THERE SHE GOES...
THEY'RE BACK HERE...
AGNES WAS RIGHT—IT LOOKS LIKE MOST OF THE PERSONNEL ARE OUT.
!
HM? AM I SEEING THINGS ......?

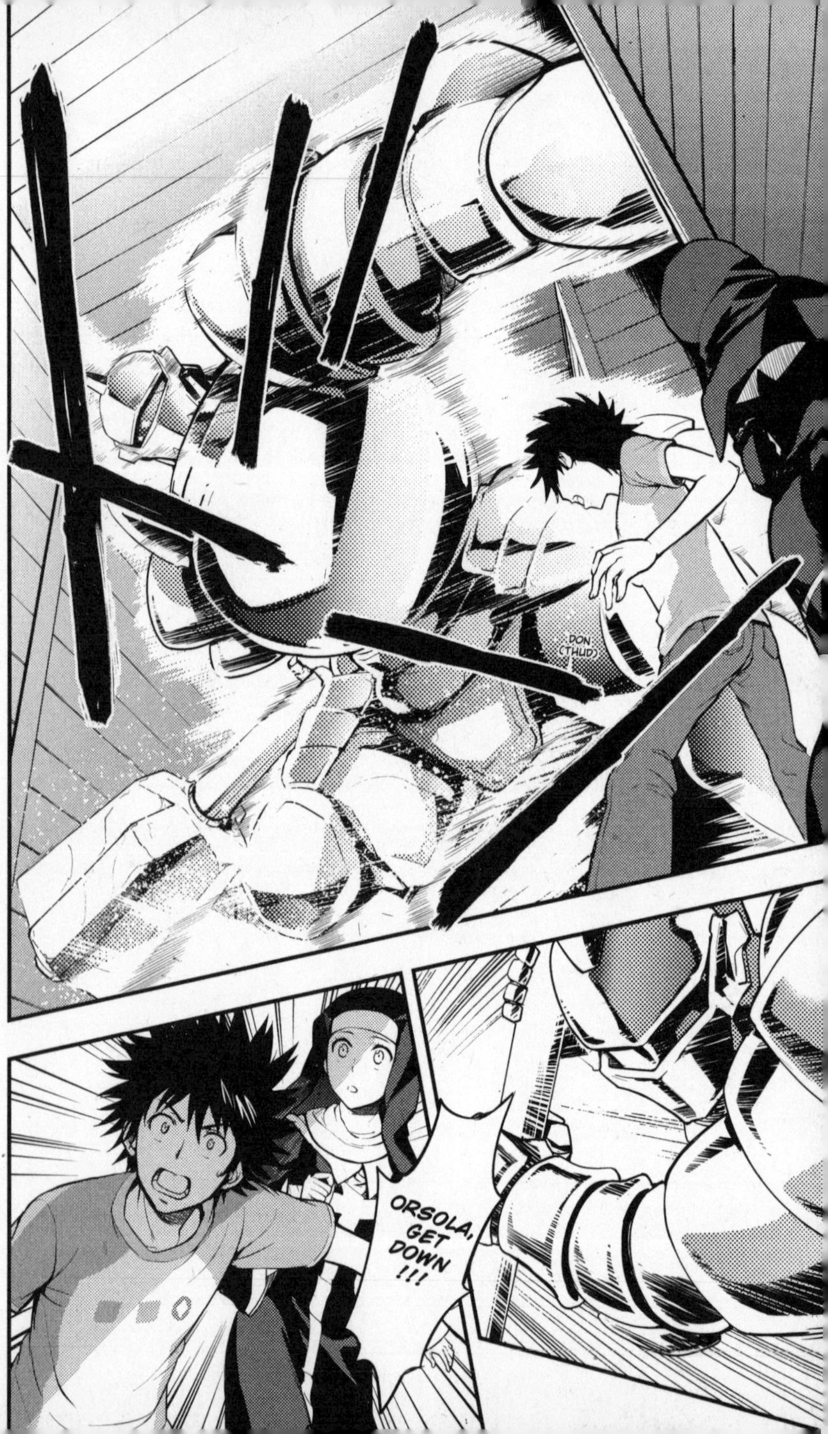
DON (THUD)
ORSOLA, GET DOWN!!!

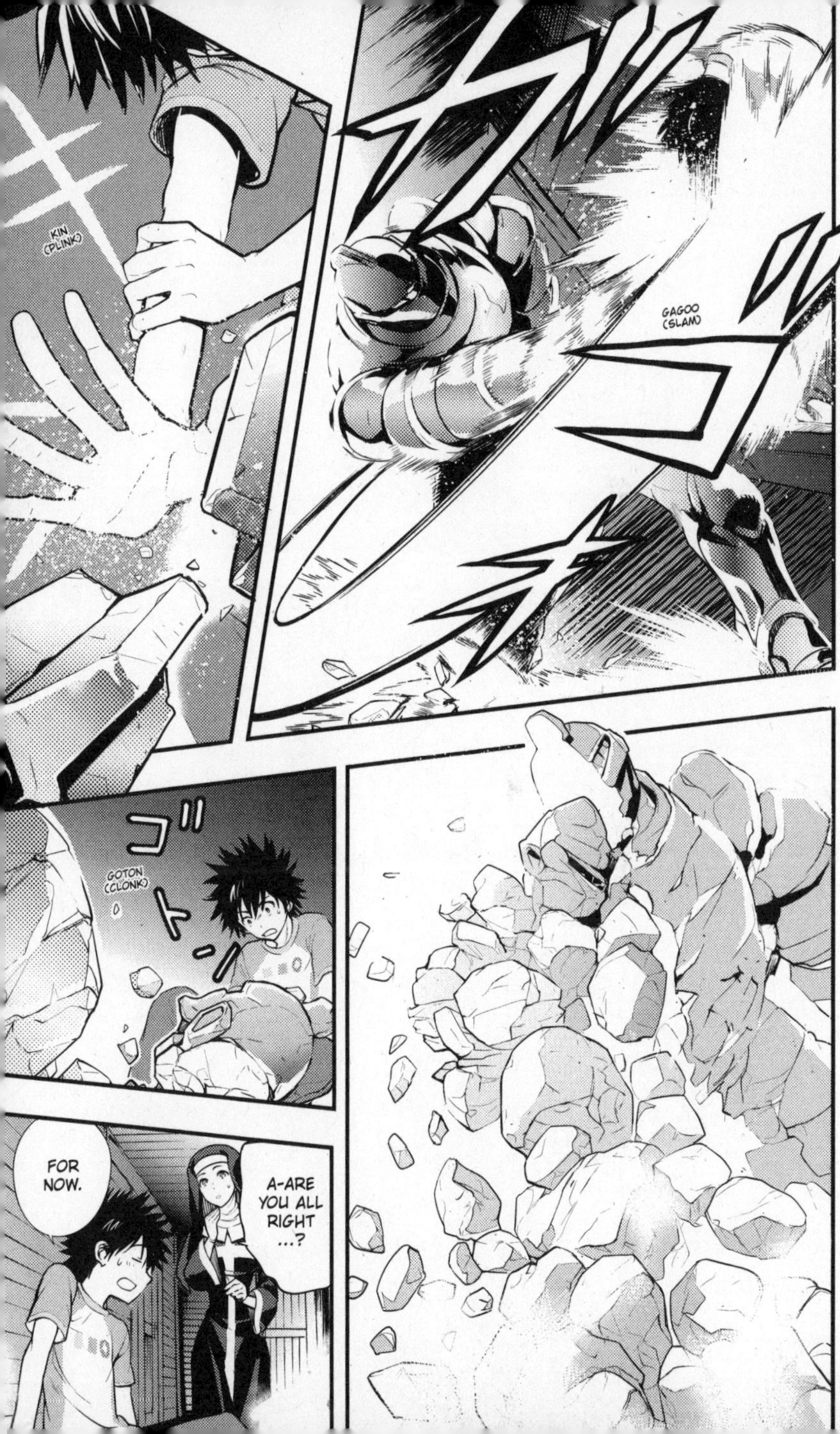
GAGOO
(SLAM)
KIN
(PLINK)
GOTON
(CLONK)
A-ARE YOU ALL RIGHT ...?
FOR NOW.

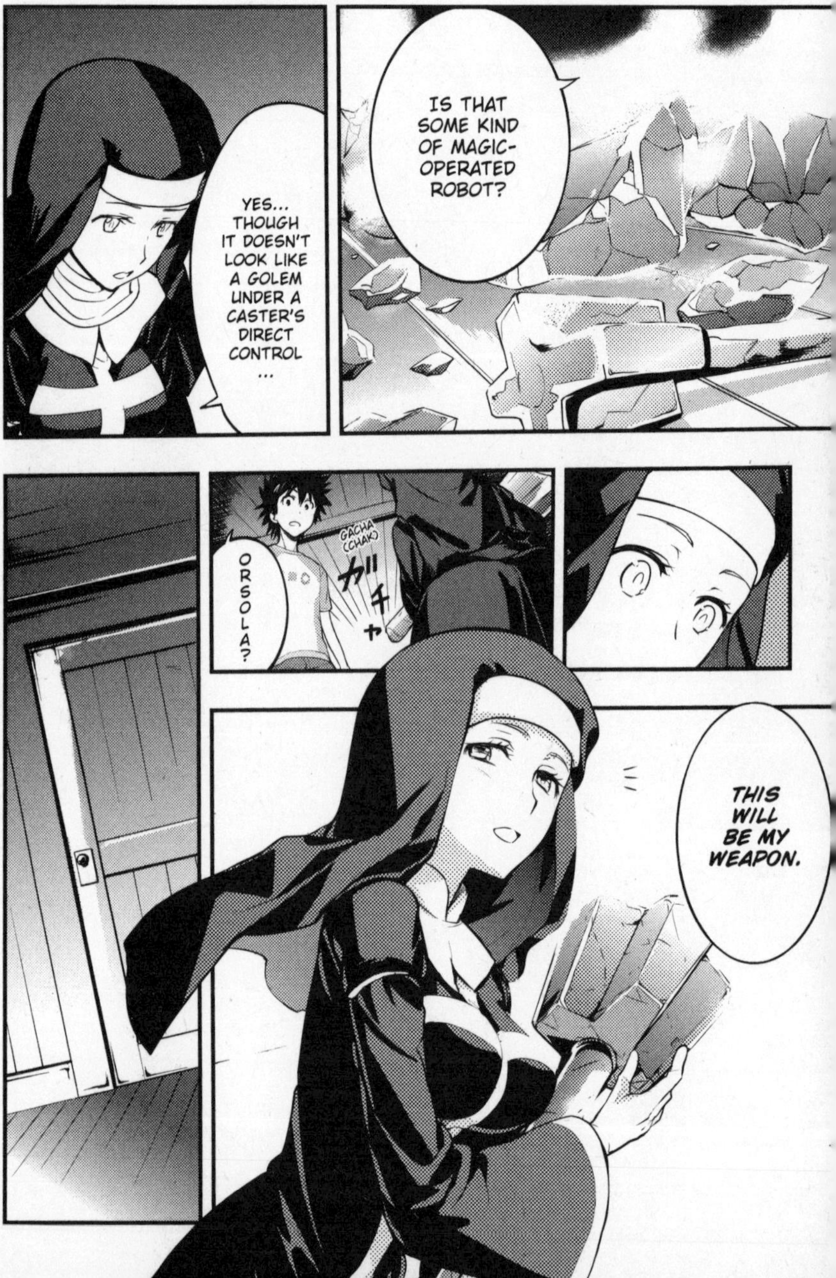
IS THAT SOME KIND OF MAGIC-OPERATED ROBOT?
YES... THOUGH IT DOESN'T LOOK LIKE A GOLEM UNDER A CASTER'S DIRECT CONTROL ...
GACHA (CHAK)
ガチャ
ORSOLA?
THIS WILL BE MY WEAPON.

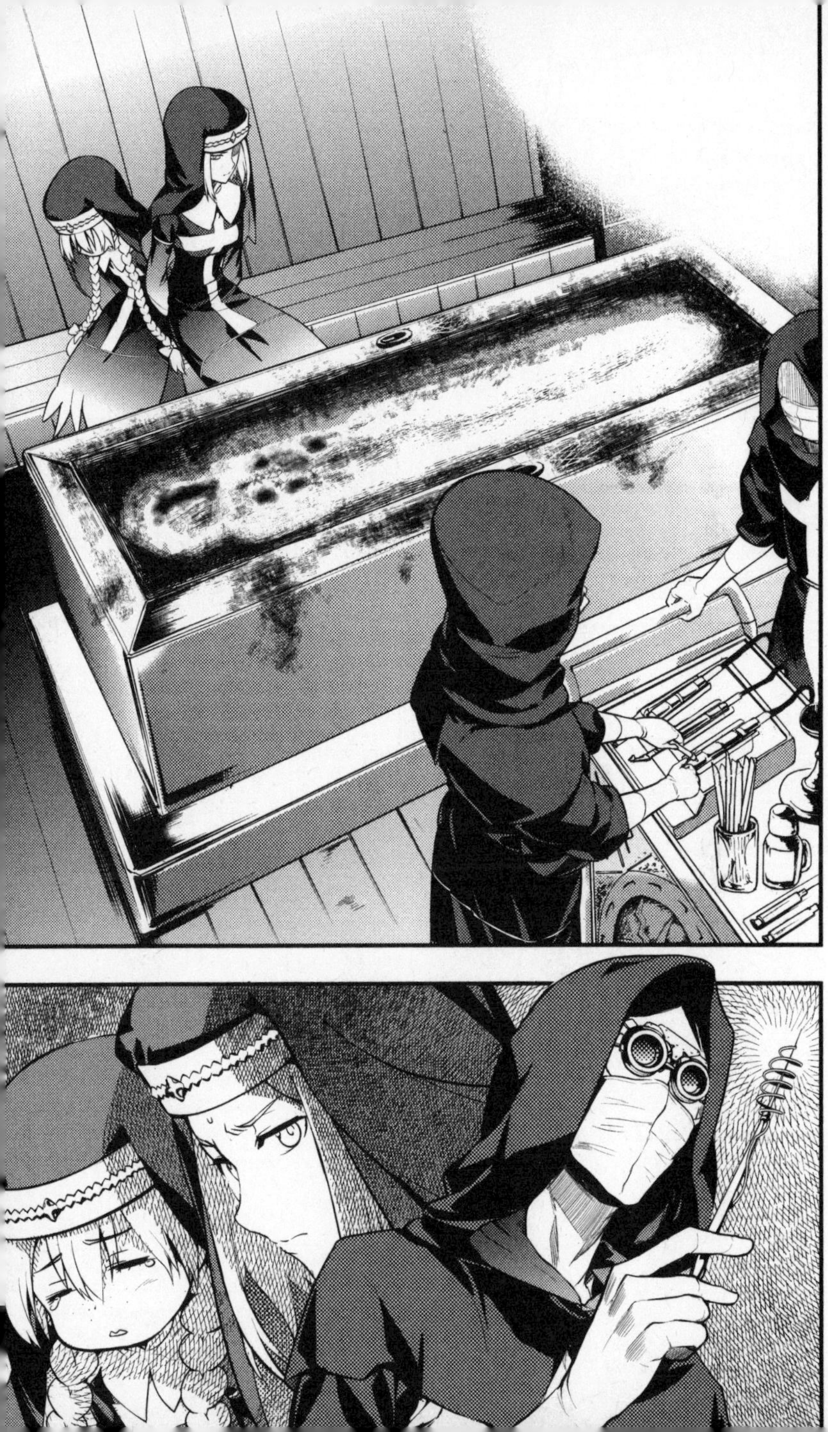

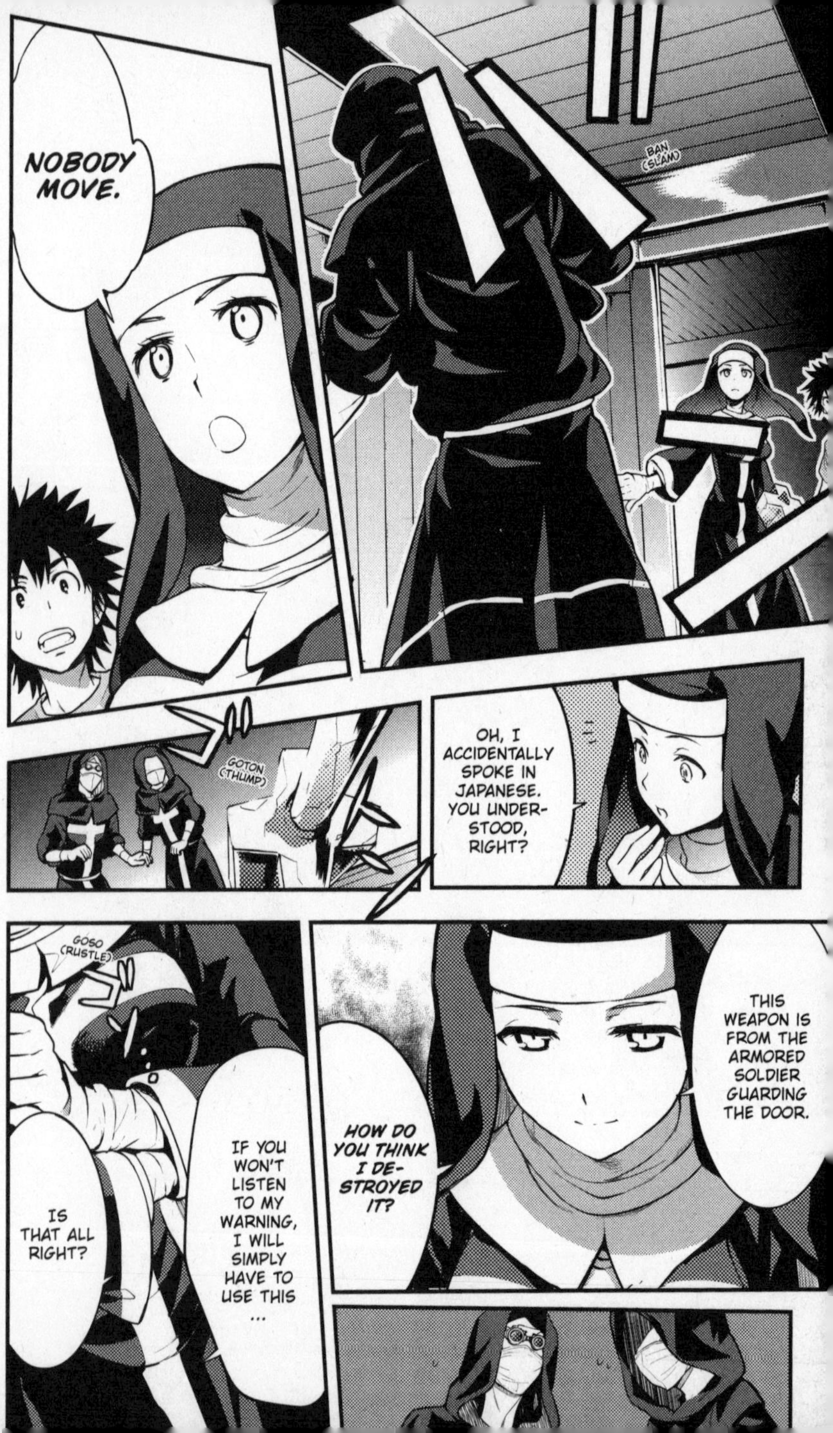
BAN (SLAM)
NOBODY MOVE.
OH, I ACCIDENTALLY SPOKE IN JAPANESE. YOU UNDER-STOOD, RIGHT?
GOTON (THUMP)
THIS WEAPON IS FROM THE ARMORED SOLDIER GUARDING THE DOOR.
HOW DO YOU THINK I DE-STROYED IT?
GOSO (RUSTLE)
IF YOU WON'T LISTEN TO MY WARNING, I WILL SIMPLY HAVE TO USE THIS ...
IS THAT ALL RIGHT?

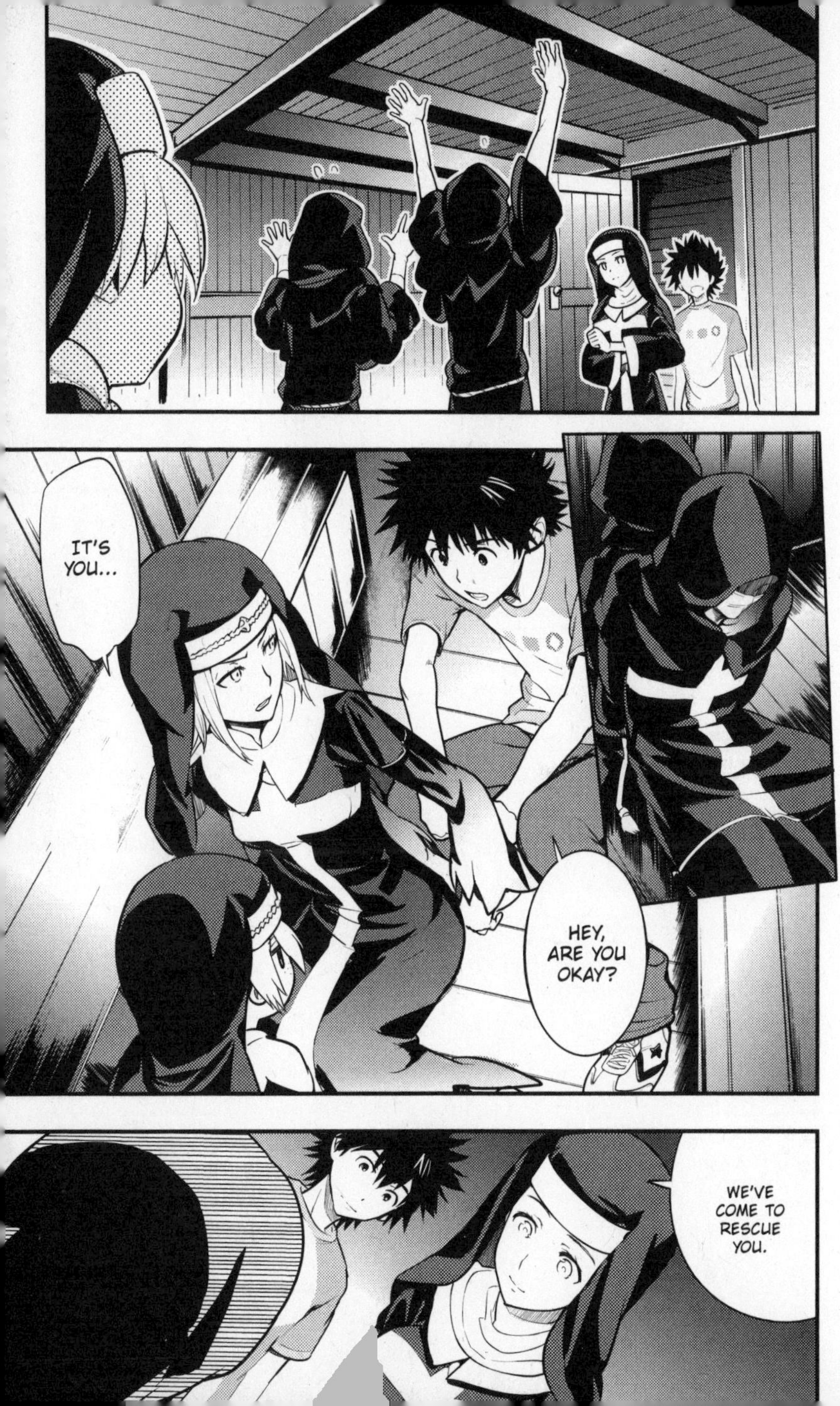
HEY, ARE YOU OKAY?
IT'S YOU...
WE'VE COME TO RESCUE YOU.

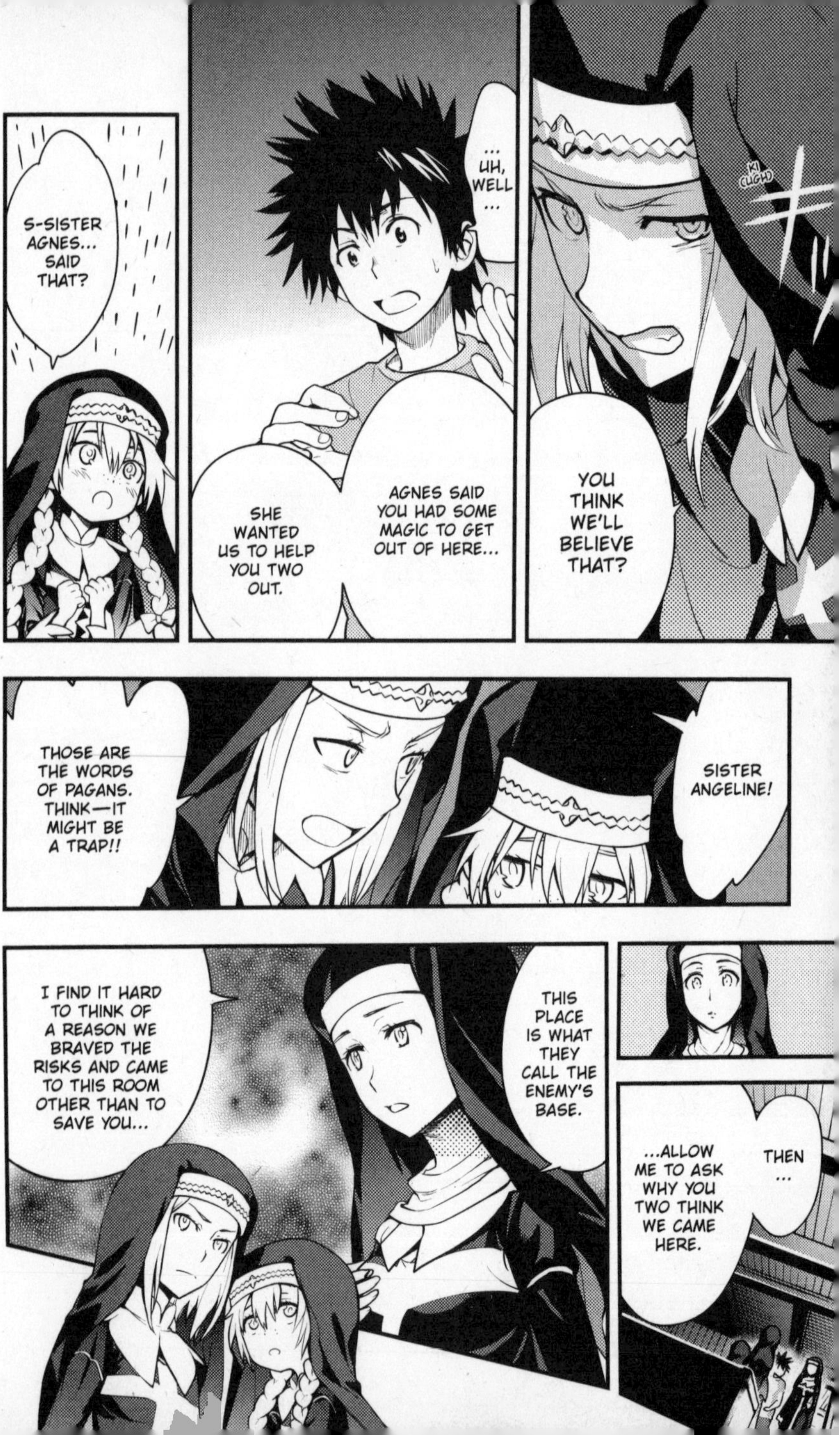
KI (UGH)
YOU THINK WE'LL BELIEVE THAT?
...UH, WELL...
AGNES SAID YOU HAD SOME MAGIC TO GET OUT OF HERE...
SHE WANTED US TO HELP YOU TWO OUT.
S-SISTER AGNES... SAID THAT?
SISTER ANGELINE!
THOSE ARE THE WORDS OF PAGANS. THINK—IT MIGHT BE A TRAP!!
THEN...
...ALLOW ME TO ASK WHY YOU TWO THINK WE CAME HERE.
THIS PLACE IS WHAT THEY CALL THE ENEMY'S BASE.
I FIND IT HARD TO THINK OF A REASON WE BRAVED THE RISKS AND CAME TO THIS ROOM OTHER THAN TO SAVE YOU...

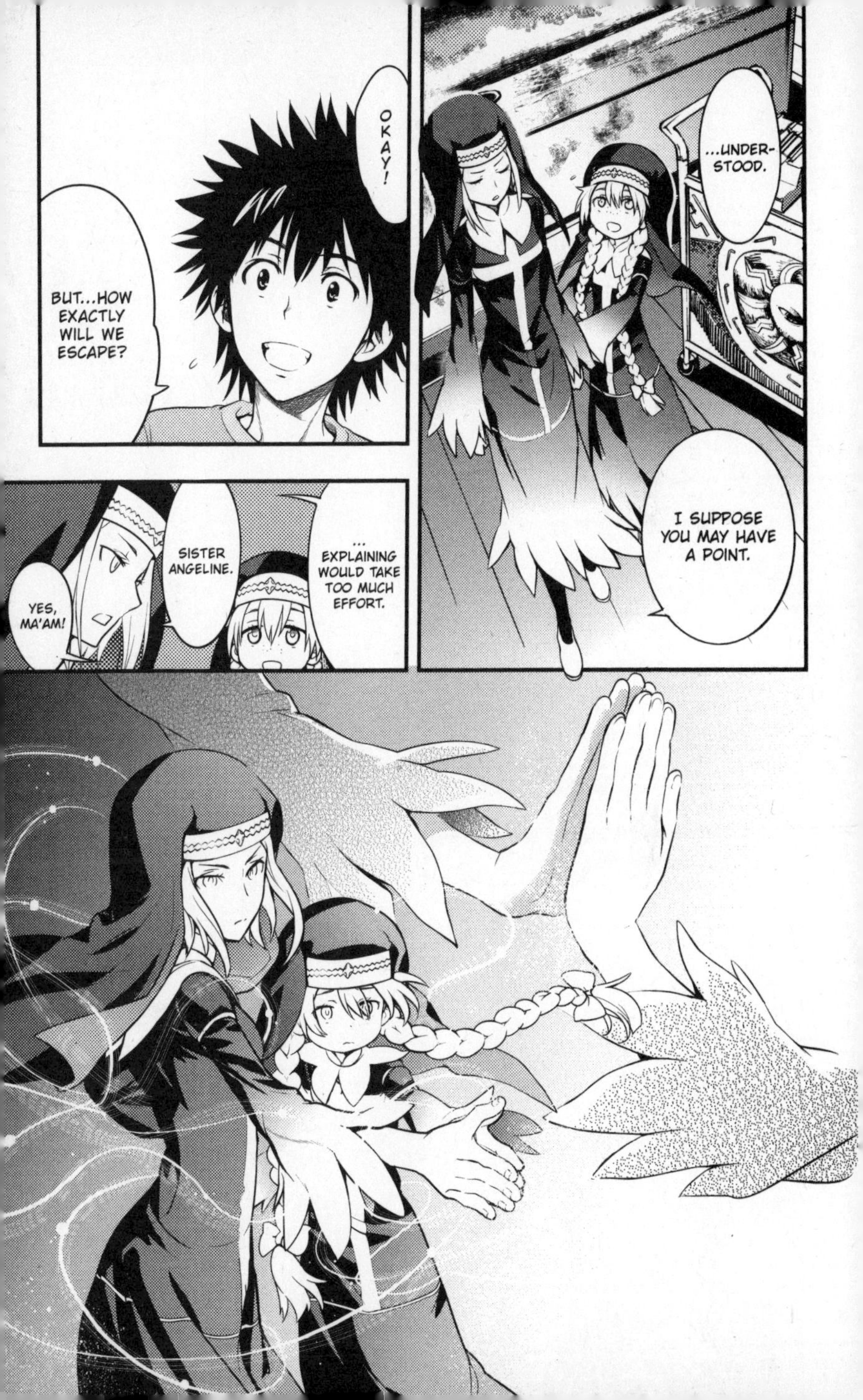
...UNDER-
STOOD.
I SUPPOSE YOU MAY HAVE A POINT.
OKAY!
BUT...HOW EXACTLY WILL WE ESCAPE?
... EXPLAINING WOULD TAKE TOO MUCH EFFORT.
SISTER ANGELINE.
YES, MA'AM!

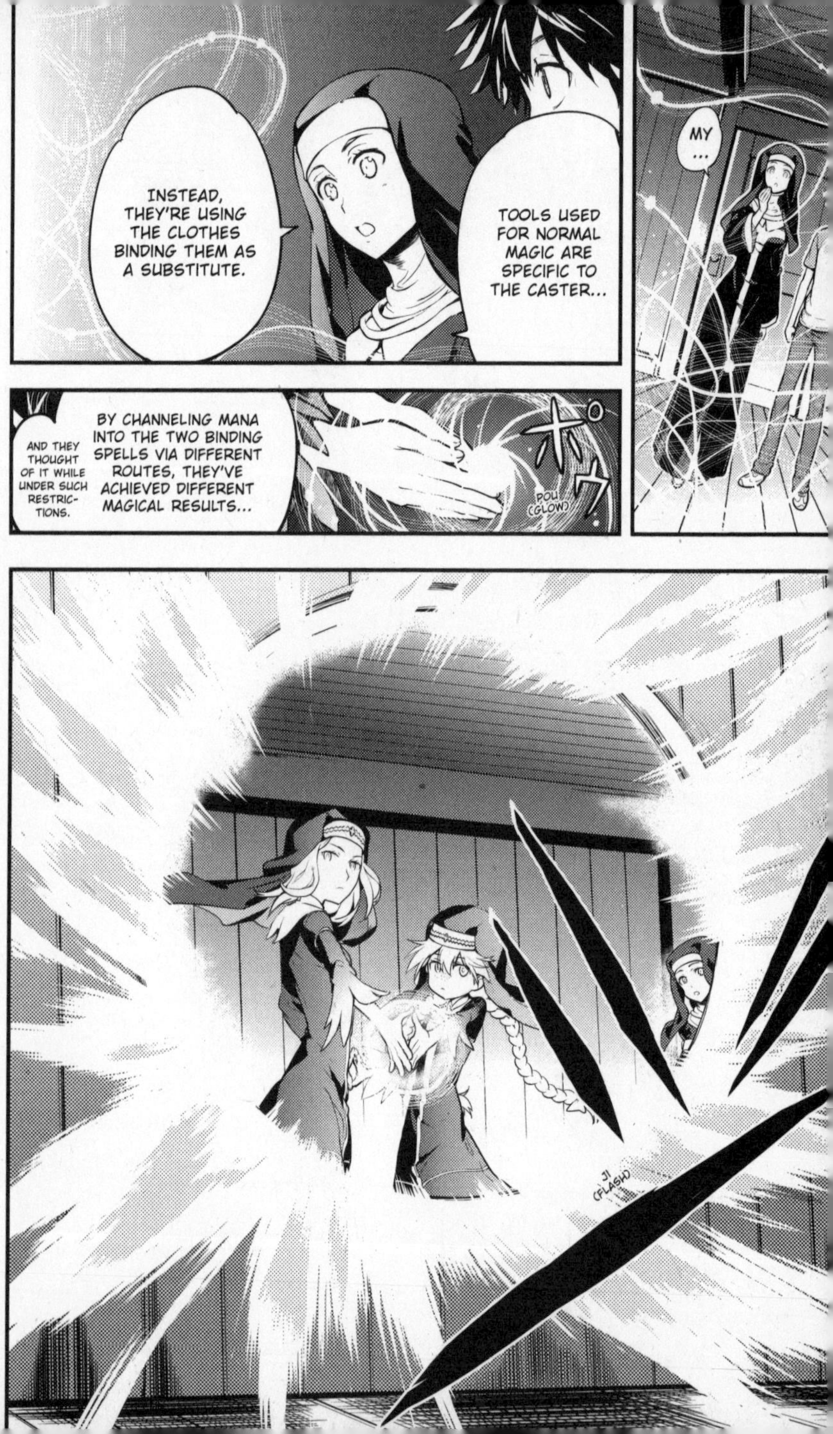
MY ...
TOOLS USED FOR NORMAL MAGIC ARE SPECIFIC TO THE CASTER...
INSTEAD, THEY'RE USING THE CLOTHES BINDING THEM AS A SUBSTITUTE.
POU (GLOW)
BY CHANNELING MANA INTO THE TWO BINDING SPELLS VIA DIFFERENT ROUTES, THEY'VE ACHIEVED DIFFERENT MAGICAL RESULTS...
AND THEY THOUGHT OF IT WHILE UNDER SUCH RESTRICTIONS.
JI (FLASH)

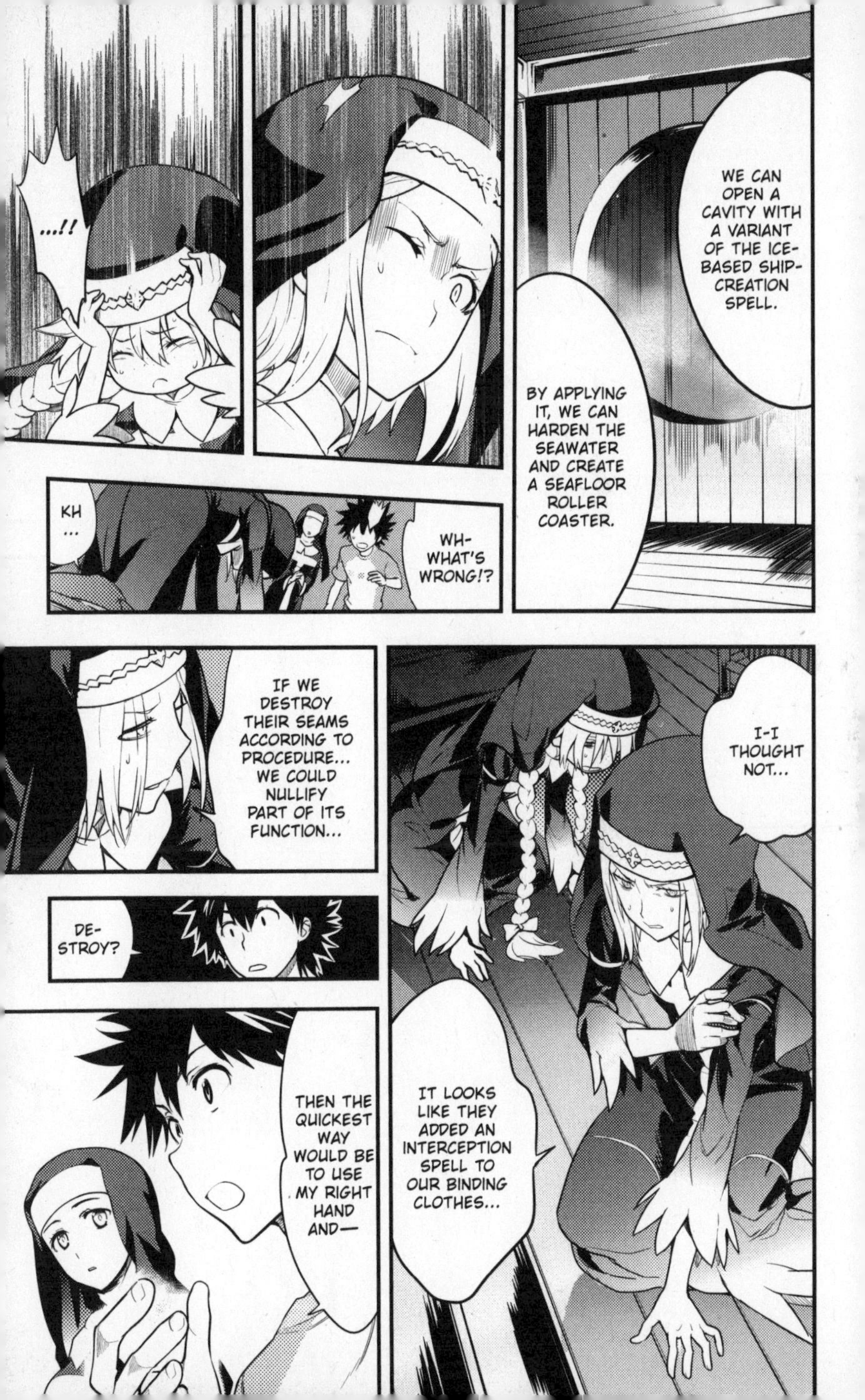
WE CAN OPEN A CAVITY WITH A VARIANT OF THE ICE-BASED SHIP-CREATION SPELL.
BY APPLYING IT, WE CAN HARDEN THE SEAWATER AND CREATE A SEAFLOOR ROLLER COASTER.
...!!
WH- WHAT'S WRONG!?
KH ...
I-I THOUGHT NOT...
IT LOOKS LIKE THEY ADDED AN INTERCEPTION SPELL TO OUR BINDING CLOTHES...
IF WE DESTROY THEIR SEAMS ACCORDING TO PROCEDURE... WE COULD NULLIFY PART OF ITS FUNCTION...
DE-STROY?
THEN THE QUICKEST WAY WOULD BE TO USE MY RIGHT HAND AND—

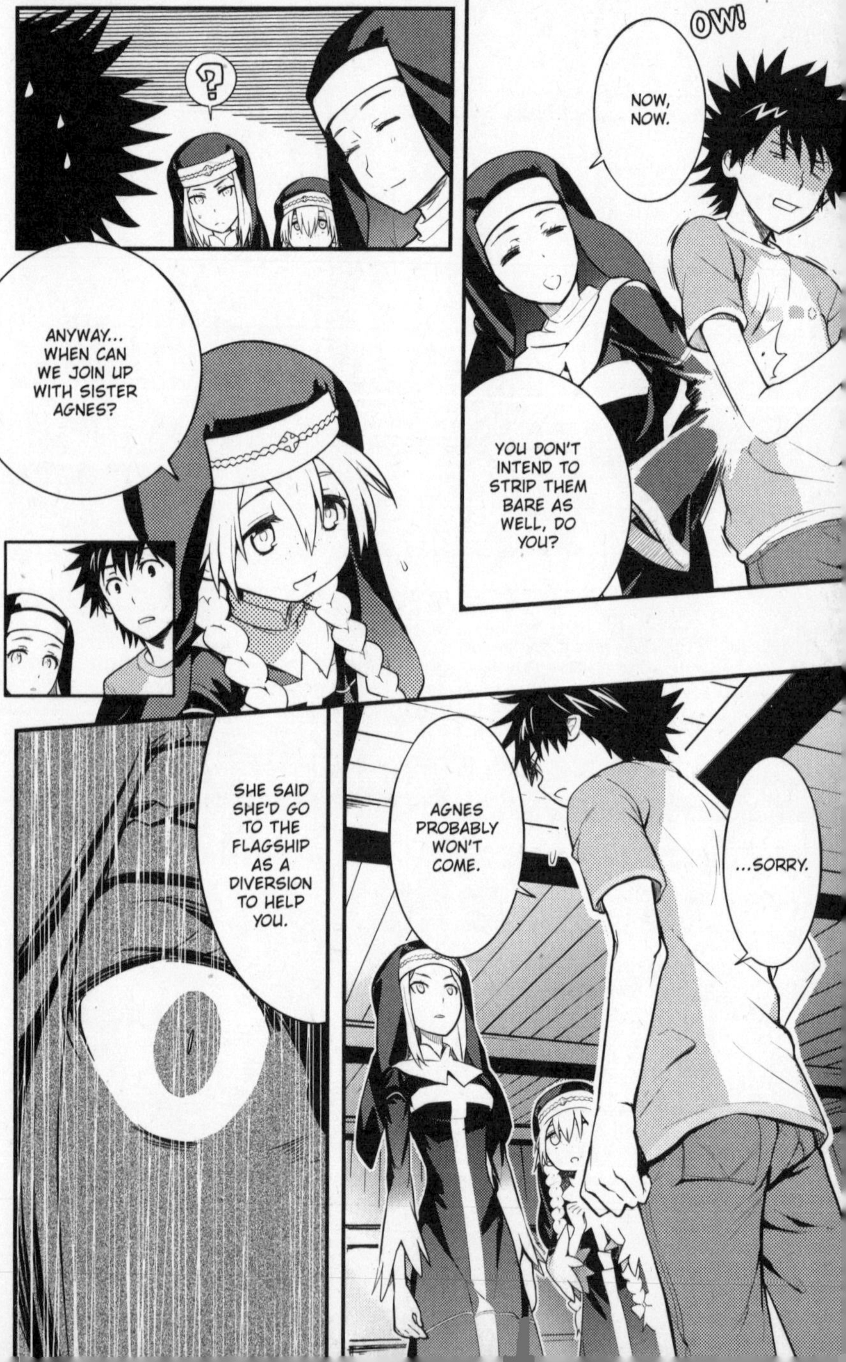
OW!
NOW, NOW.
YOU DON'T INTEND TO STRIP THEM BARE AS WELL, DO YOU?
?
ANYWAY... WHEN CAN WE JOIN UP WITH SISTER AGNES?
...SORRY.
AGNES PROBABLY WON'T COME.
SHE SAID SHE'D GO TO THE FLAGSHIP AS A DIVERSION TO HELP YOU.

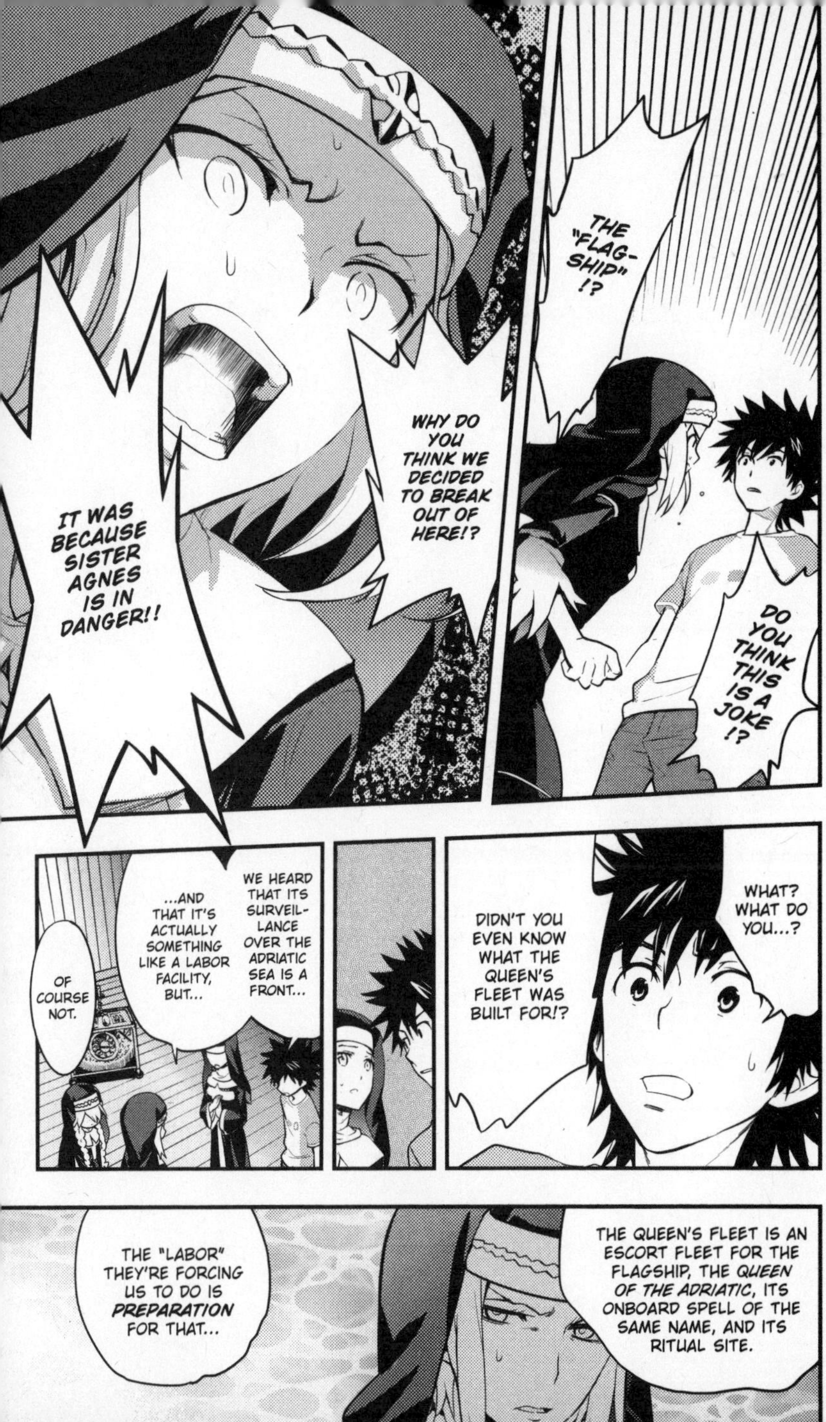
THE "FLAG-SHIP"!?
DO YOU THINK THIS IS A JOKE!?
WHY DO YOU THINK WE DECIDED TO BREAK OUT OF HERE!?
IT WAS BECAUSE SISTER AGNES IS IN DANGER!!
WHAT? WHAT DO YOU...?
DIDN'T YOU EVEN KNOW WHAT THE QUEEN'S FLEET WAS BUILT FOR!?
WE HEARD THAT ITS SURVEIL-LANCE OVER THE ADRIATIC SEA IS A FRONT...
...AND THAT IT'S ACTUALLY SOMETHING LIKE A LABOR FACILITY, BUT...
OF COURSE NOT.
THE QUEEN'S FLEET IS AN ESCORT FLEET FOR THE FLAGSHIP, THE *QUEEN OF THE ADRIATIC*, ITS ONBOARD SPELL OF THE SAME NAME, AND ITS RITUAL SITE.
THE "LABOR" THEY'RE FORCING US TO DO IS ***PREPARATION*** FOR THAT...

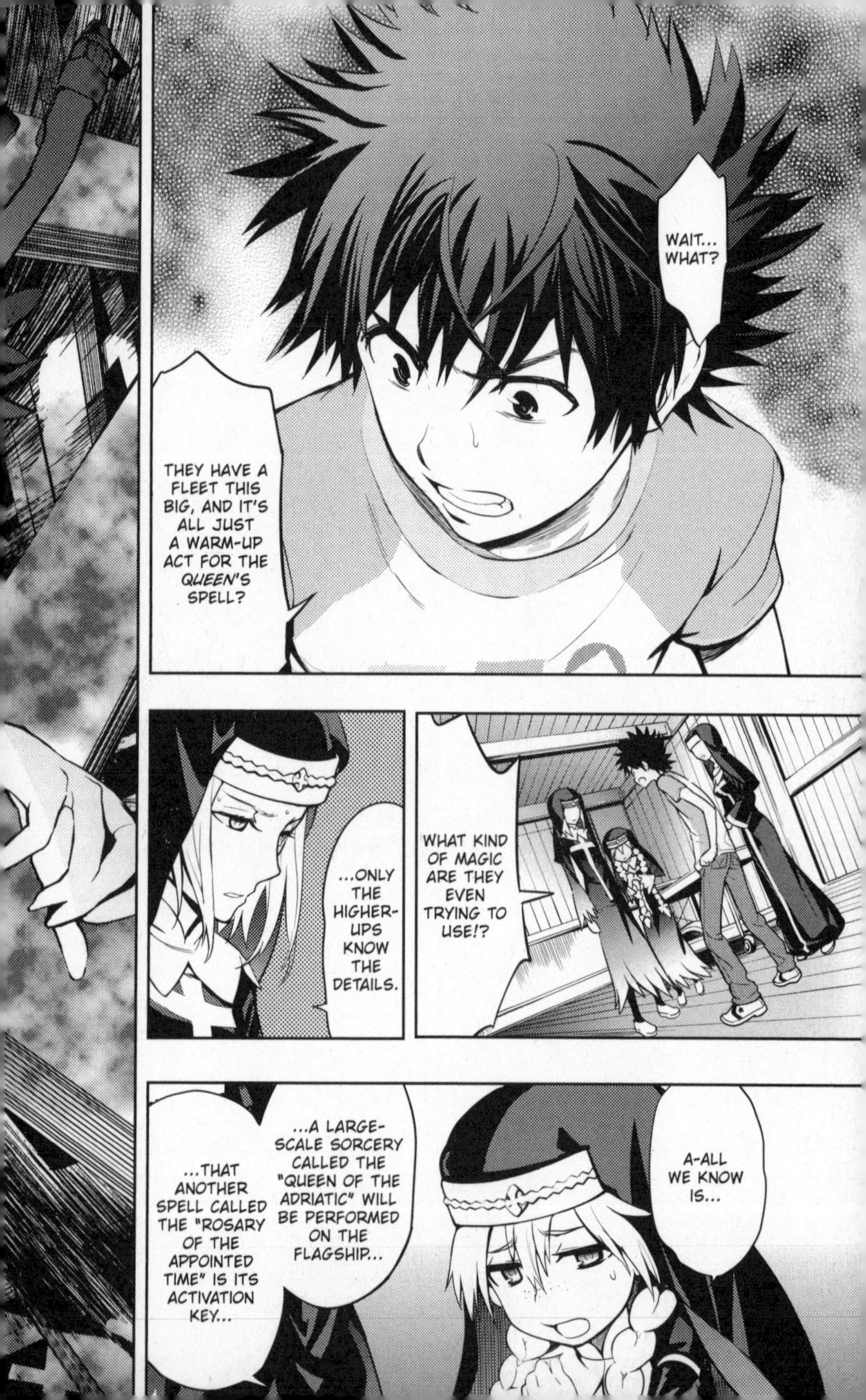
WAIT... WHAT?
THEY HAVE A FLEET THIS BIG, AND IT'S ALL JUST A WARM-UP ACT FOR THE *QUEEN*'S SPELL?
WHAT KIND OF MAGIC ARE THEY EVEN TRYING TO USE!?
...ONLY THE HIGHER-UPS KNOW THE DETAILS.
A-ALL WE KNOW IS...
...A LARGE-SCALE SORCERY CALLED THE "QUEEN OF THE ADRIATIC" WILL BE PERFORMED ON THE FLAGSHIP...
...THAT ANOTHER SPELL CALLED THE "ROSARY OF THE APPOINTED TIME" IS ITS ACTIVATION KEY...

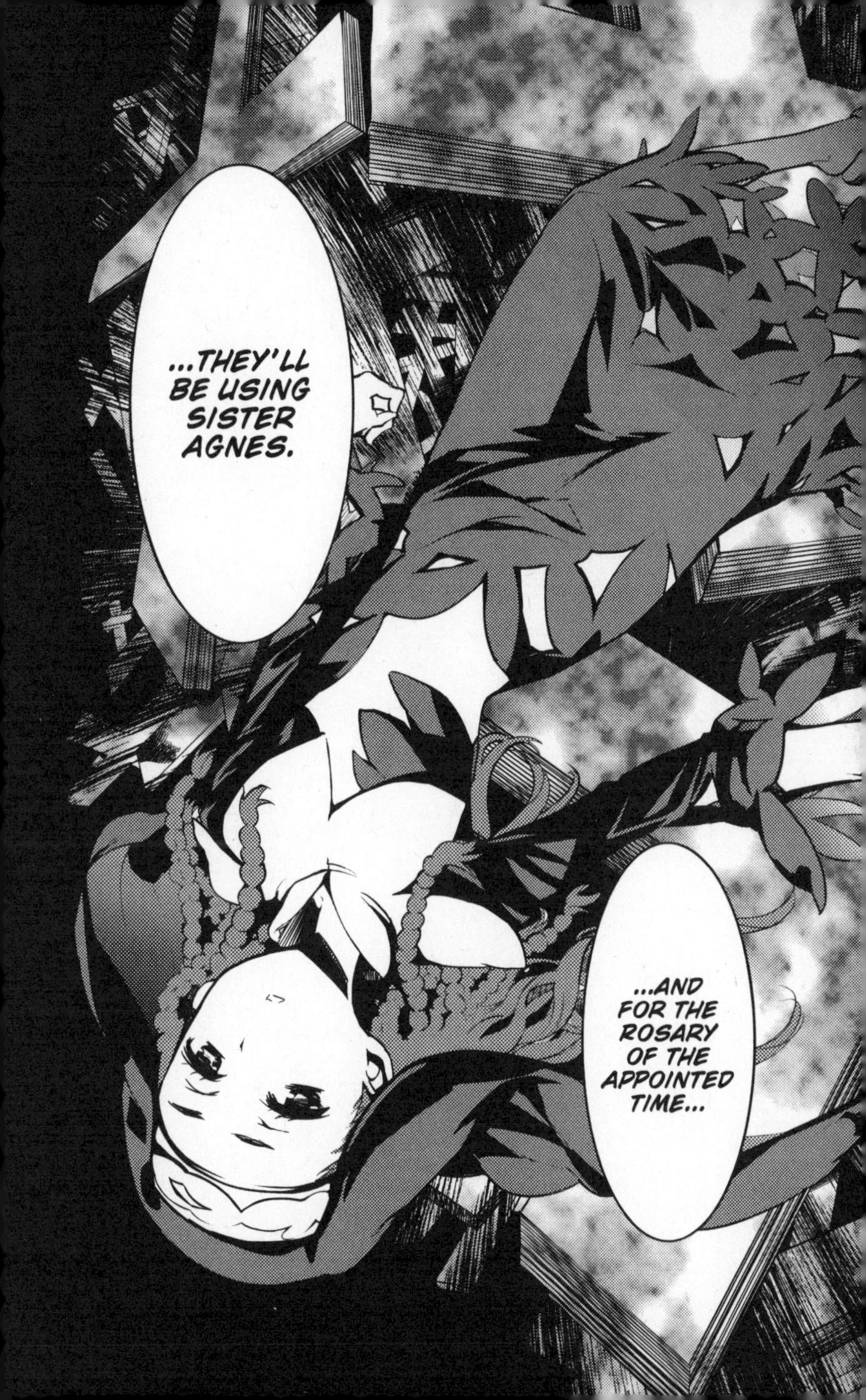
...THEY'LL BE USING SISTER AGNES.
...AND FOR THE ROSARY OF THE APPOINTED TIME...

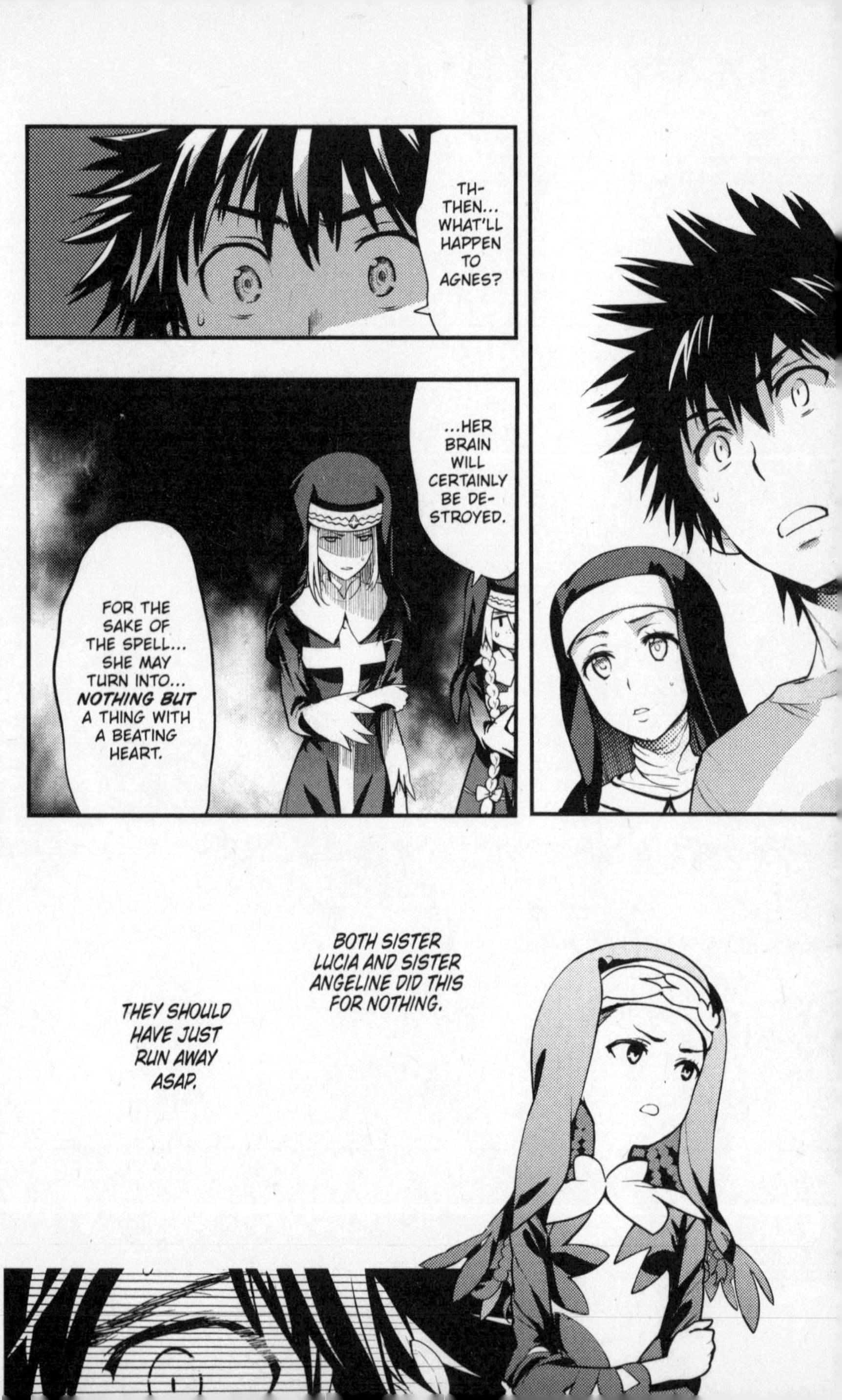
TH- THEN... WHAT'LL HAPPEN TO AGNES?
...HER BRAIN WILL CERTAINLY BE DE-STROYED.
FOR THE SAKE OF THE SPELL... SHE MAY TURN INTO... NOTHING BUT A THING WITH A BEATING HEART.
BOTH SISTER LUCIA AND SISTER ANGELINE DID THIS FOR NOTHING.
THEY SHOULD HAVE JUST RUN AWAY ASAP.

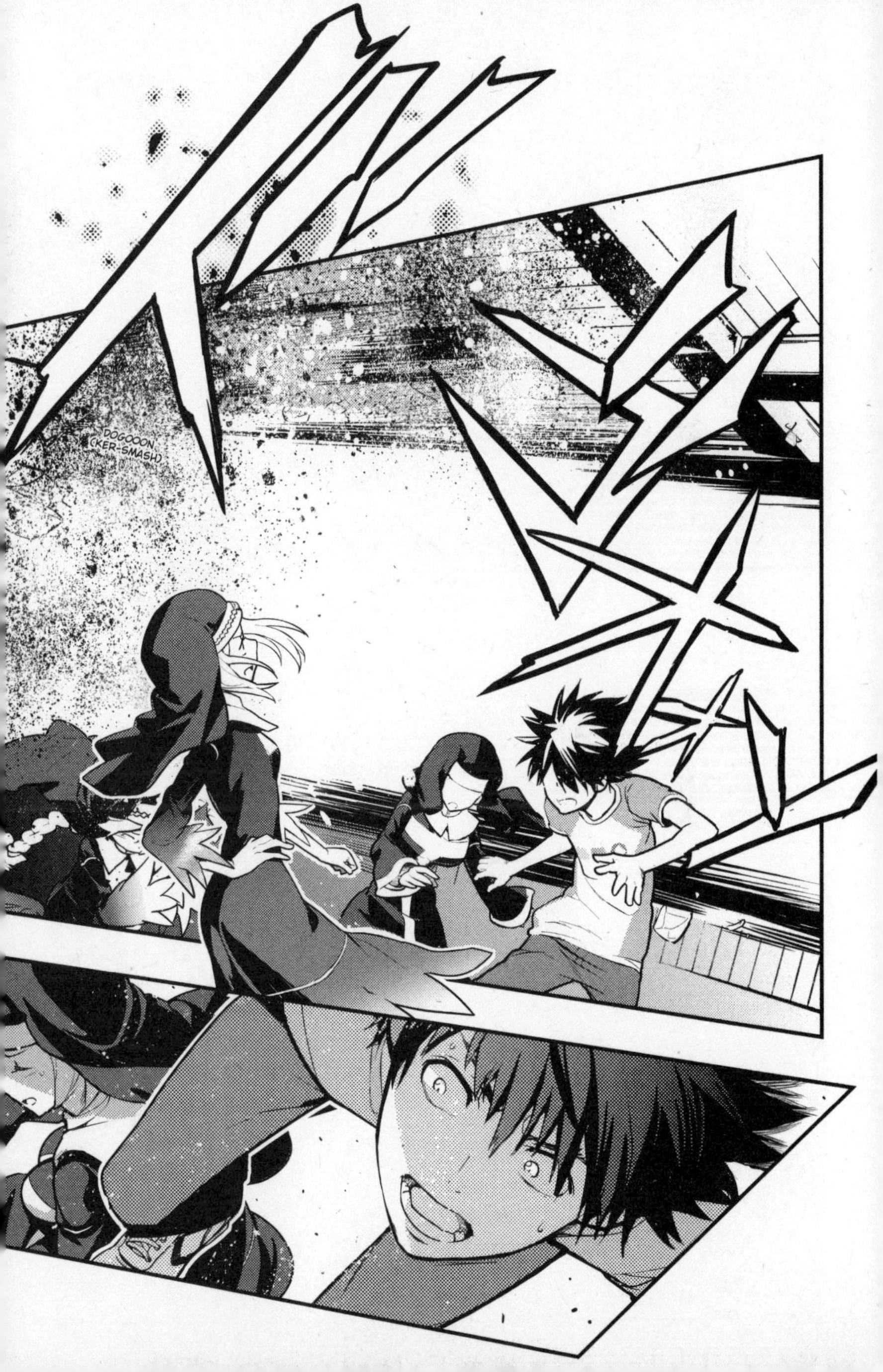
DOGOOON (KER-SMASH)

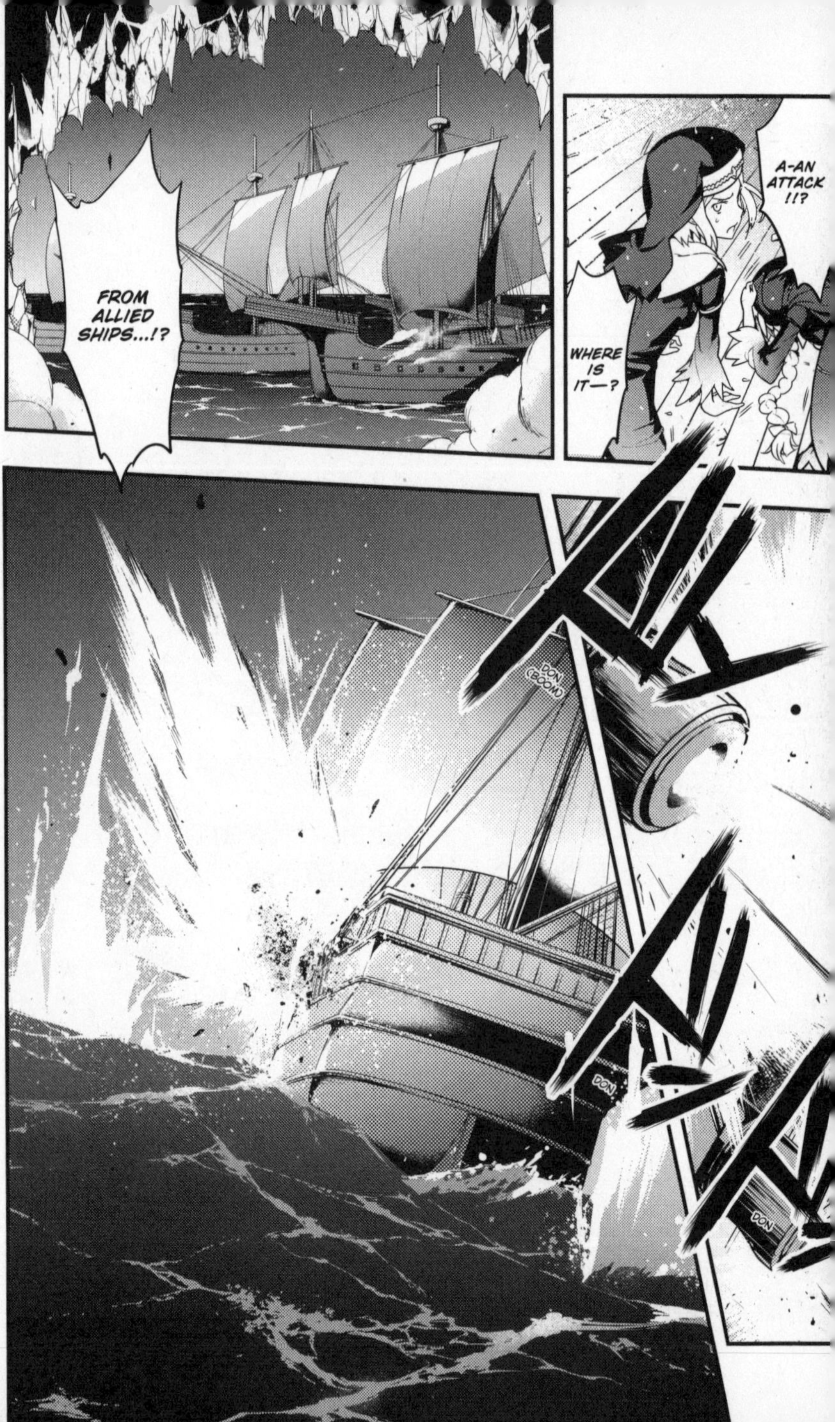
A-AN ATTACK !!?
WHERE IS IT—?
FROM ALLIED SHIPS...!?
DON (BOOM)
DON
DON

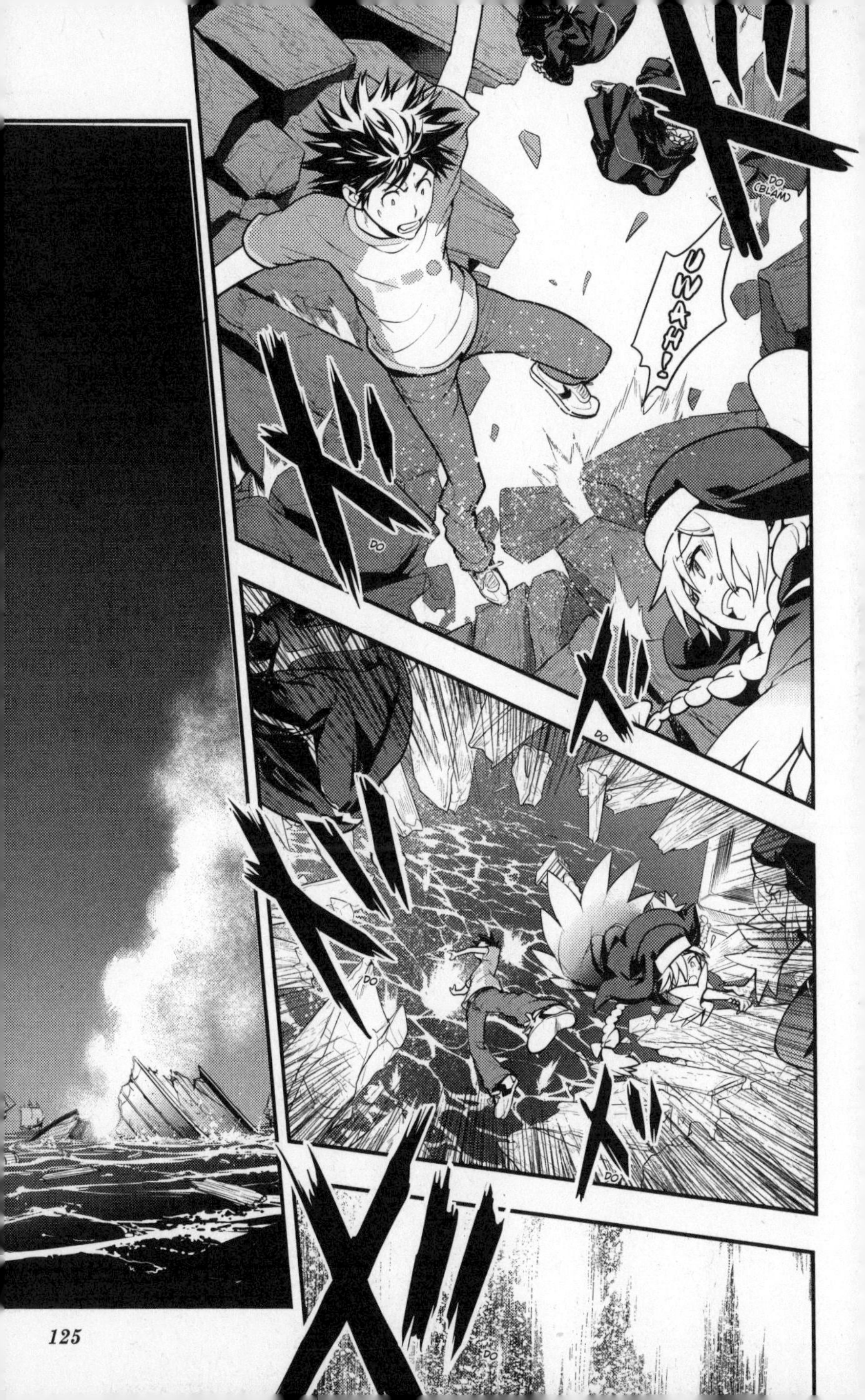
DO (BLAM)
UWAH...!
DO
DO
DO
DO
DO

A Certain Magical Index

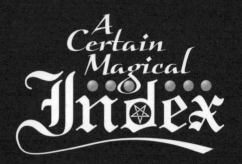

# #90 THE QUEEN'S FLEET ③

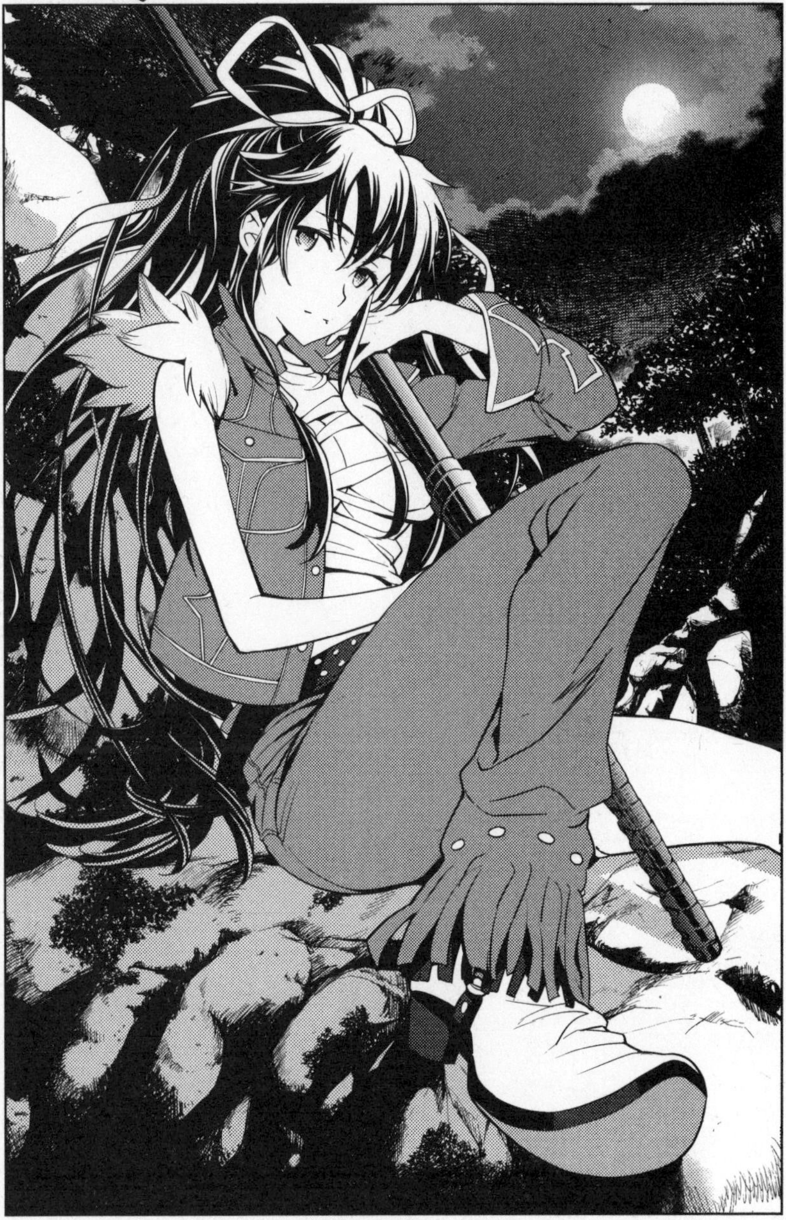

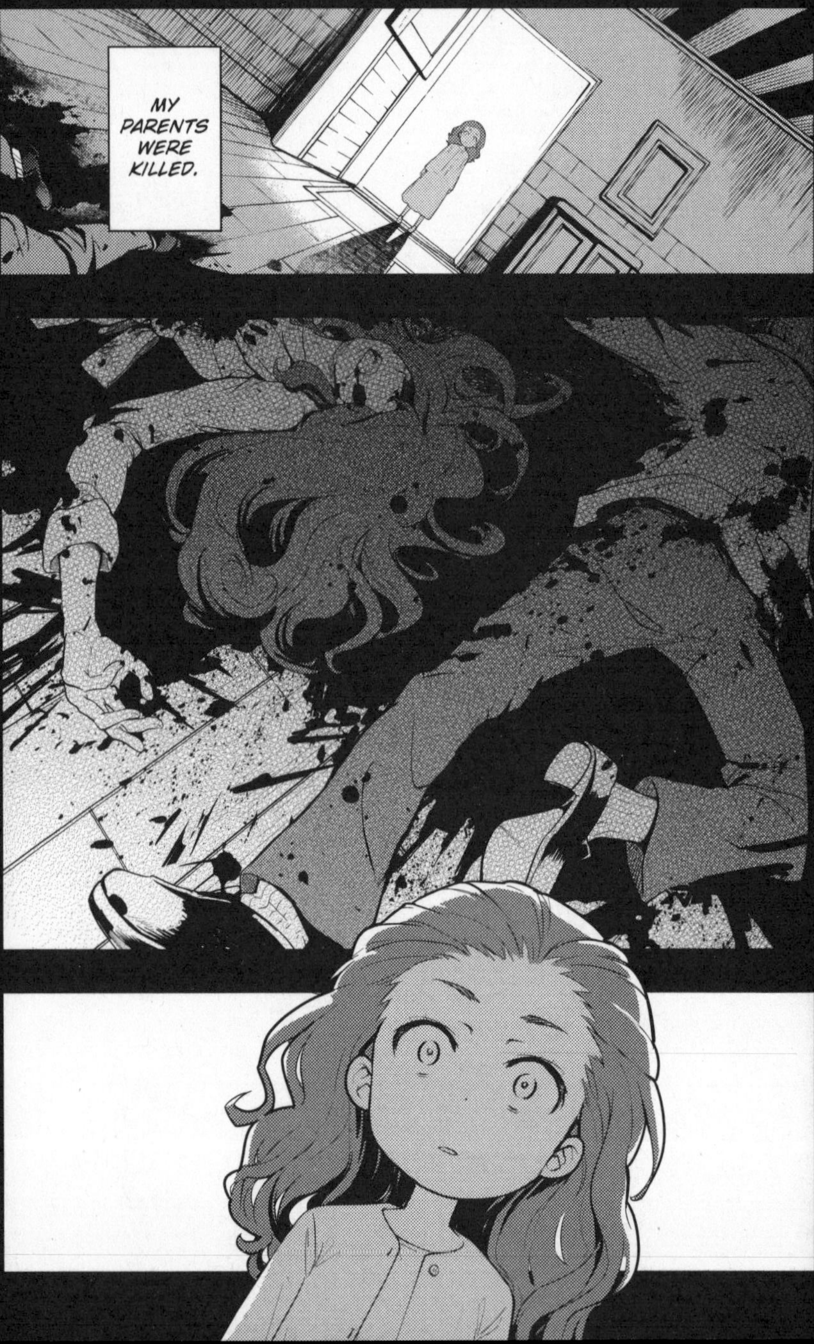
MY PARENTS WERE KILLED.

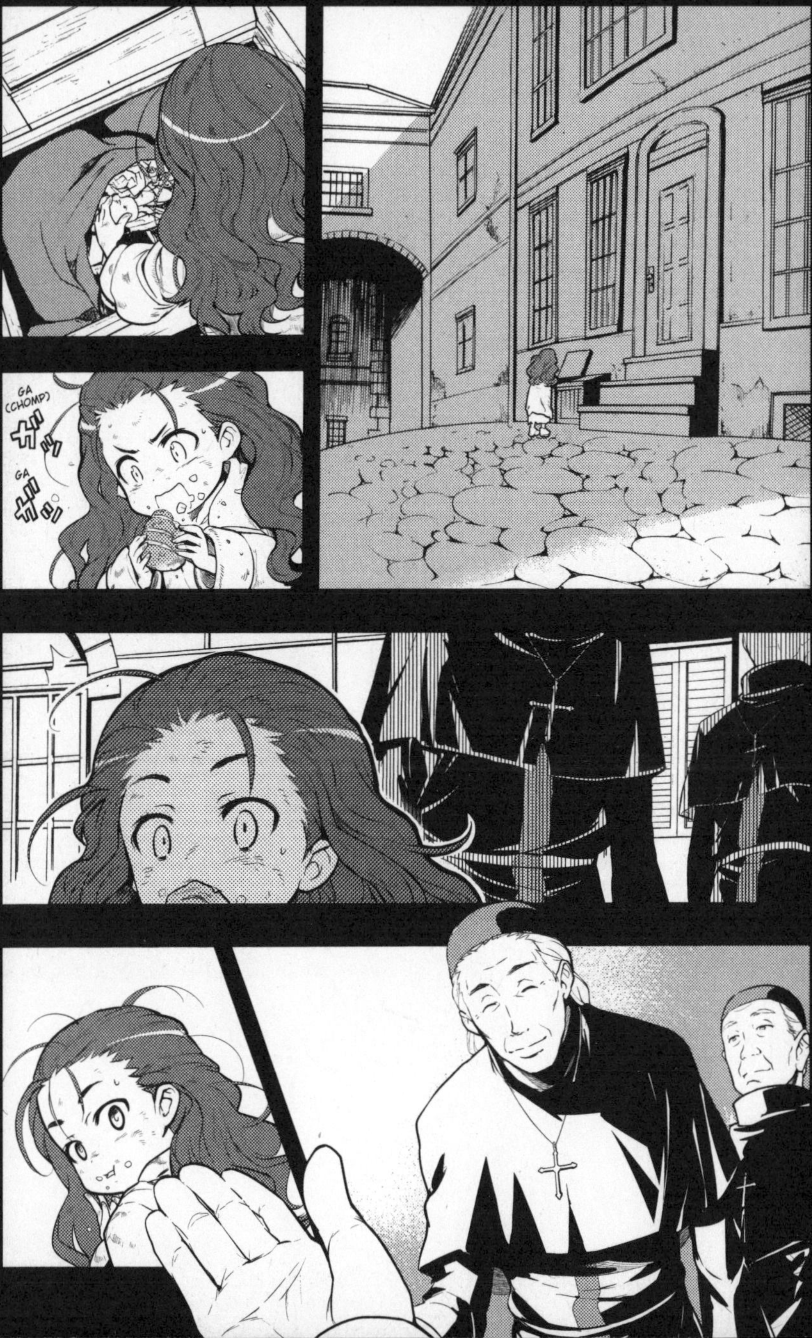
GA (CHOMP)
GA

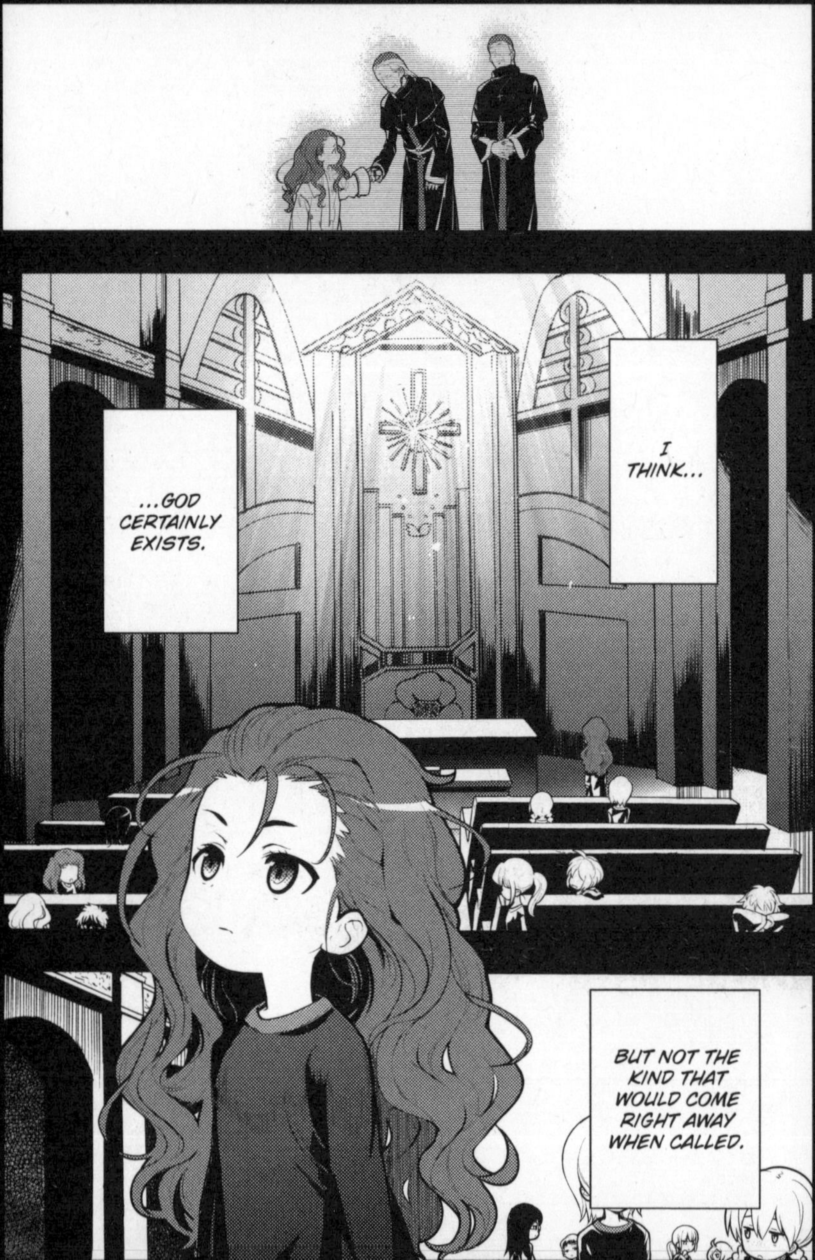
I THINK...
...GOD CERTAINLY EXISTS.
BUT NOT THE KIND THAT WOULD COME RIGHT AWAY WHEN CALLED.

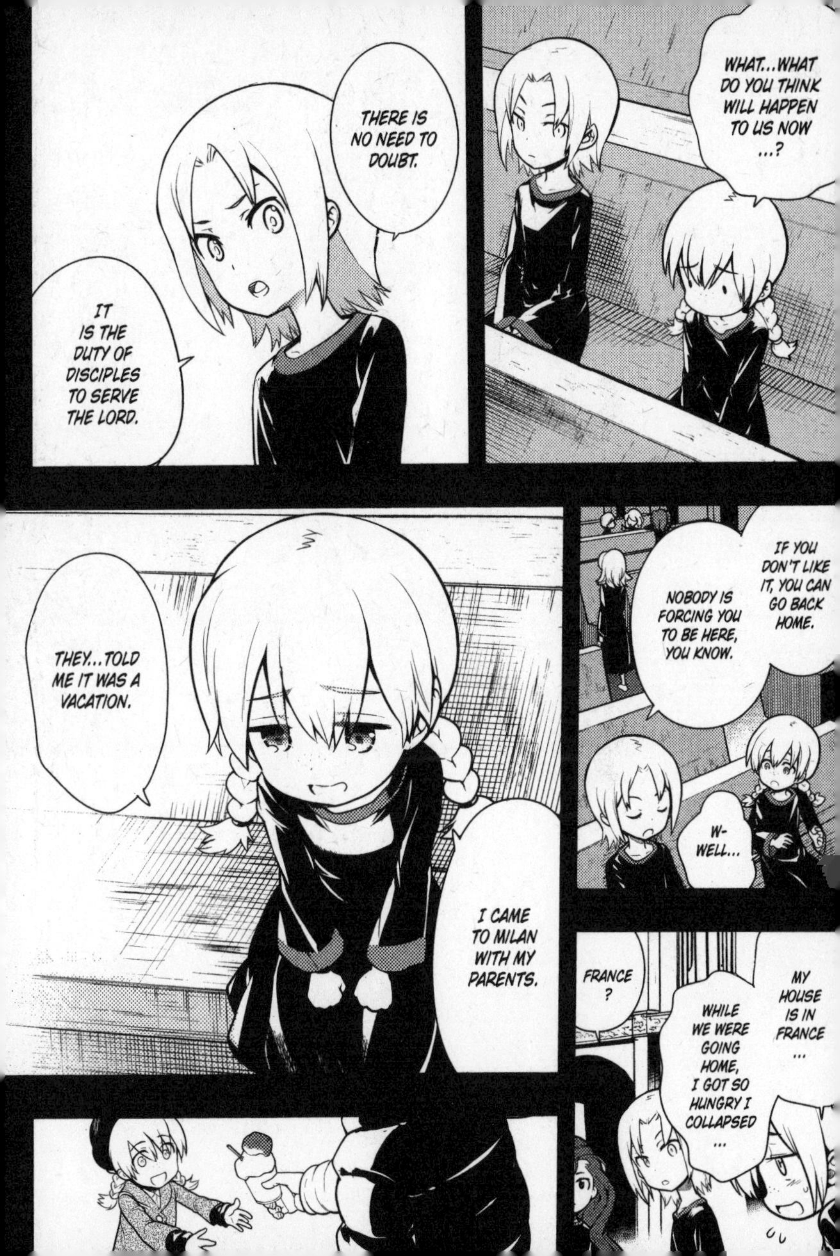
WHAT...WHAT DO YOU THINK WILL HAPPEN TO US NOW ...?
THERE IS NO NEED TO DOUBT.
IT IS THE DUTY OF DISCIPLES TO SERVE THE LORD.
IF YOU DON'T LIKE IT, YOU CAN GO BACK HOME.
NOBODY IS FORCING YOU TO BE HERE, YOU KNOW.
W-WELL...
MY HOUSE IS IN FRANCE ...
WHILE WE WERE GOING HOME, I GOT SO HUNGRY I COLLAPSED ...
FRANCE ?
THEY...TOLD ME IT WAS A VACATION.
I CAME TO MILAN WITH MY PARENTS.

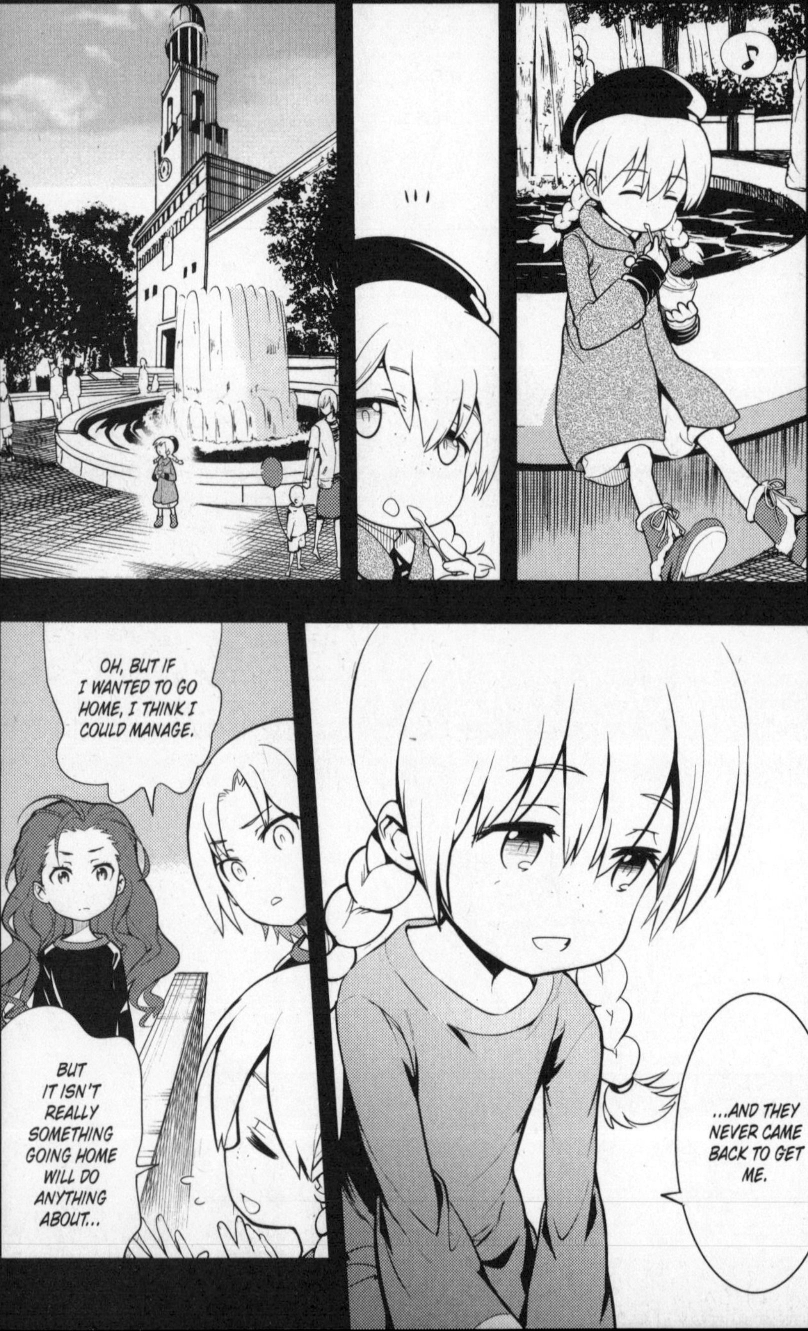
♪
...AND THEY NEVER CAME BACK TO GET ME.
OH, BUT IF I WANTED TO GO HOME, I THINK I COULD MANAGE.
BUT IT ISN'T REALLY SOMETHING GOING HOME WILL DO ANYTHING ABOUT...

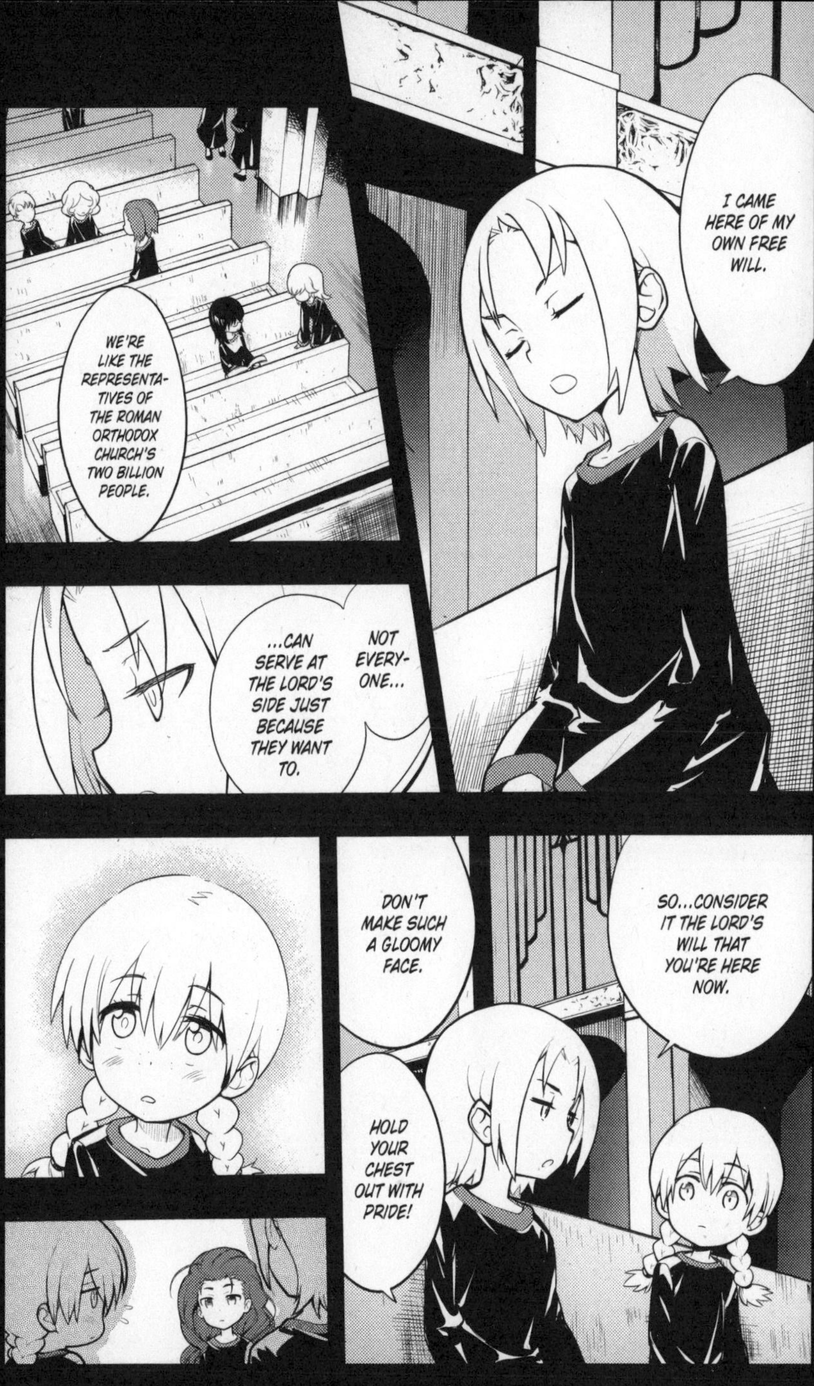
I CAME HERE OF MY OWN FREE WILL.
WE'RE LIKE THE REPRESENTATIVES OF THE ROMAN ORTHODOX CHURCH'S TWO BILLION PEOPLE.
NOT EVERYONE...
...CAN SERVE AT THE LORD'S SIDE JUST BECAUSE THEY WANT TO.
SO...CONSIDER IT THE LORD'S WILL THAT YOU'RE HERE NOW.
DON'T MAKE SUCH A GLOOMY FACE.
HOLD YOUR CHEST OUT WITH PRIDE!

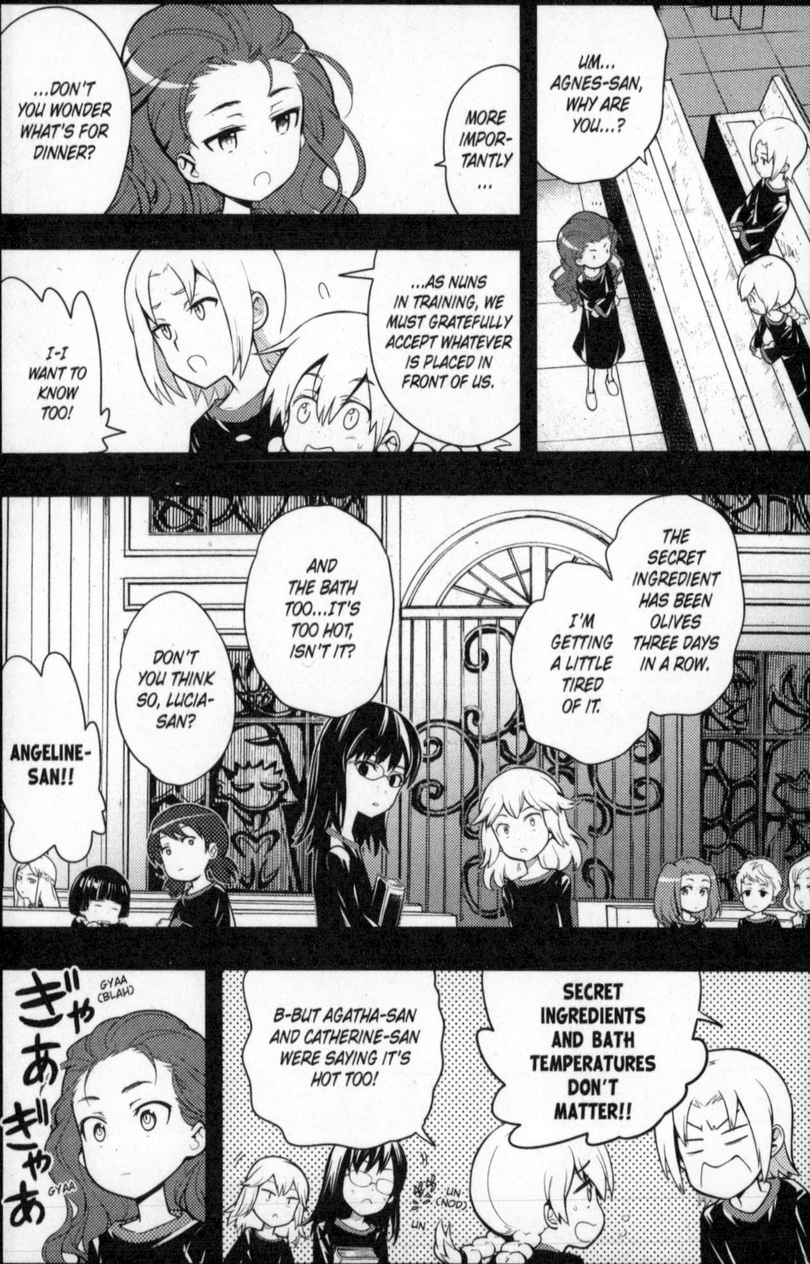
UM... AGNES-SAN, WHY ARE YOU...?
...
MORE IMPORTANTLY ...
...DON'T YOU WONDER WHAT'S FOR DINNER?
...AS NUNS IN TRAINING, WE MUST GRATEFULLY ACCEPT WHATEVER IS PLACED IN FRONT OF US.
I-I WANT TO KNOW TOO!
THE SECRET INGREDIENT HAS BEEN OLIVES THREE DAYS IN A ROW.
I'M GETTING A LITTLE TIRED OF IT.
AND THE BATH TOO...IT'S TOO HOT, ISN'T IT?
DON'T YOU THINK SO, LUCIA-SAN?
ANGELINE-SAN!!
SECRET INGREDIENTS AND BATH TEMPERATURES DON'T MATTER!!
B-BUT AGATHA-SAN AND CATHERINE-SAN WERE SAYING IT'S HOT TOO!
UN (NOD)
UN
ぎゃあ GYAA (BLAH)
ぎゃあ GYAA

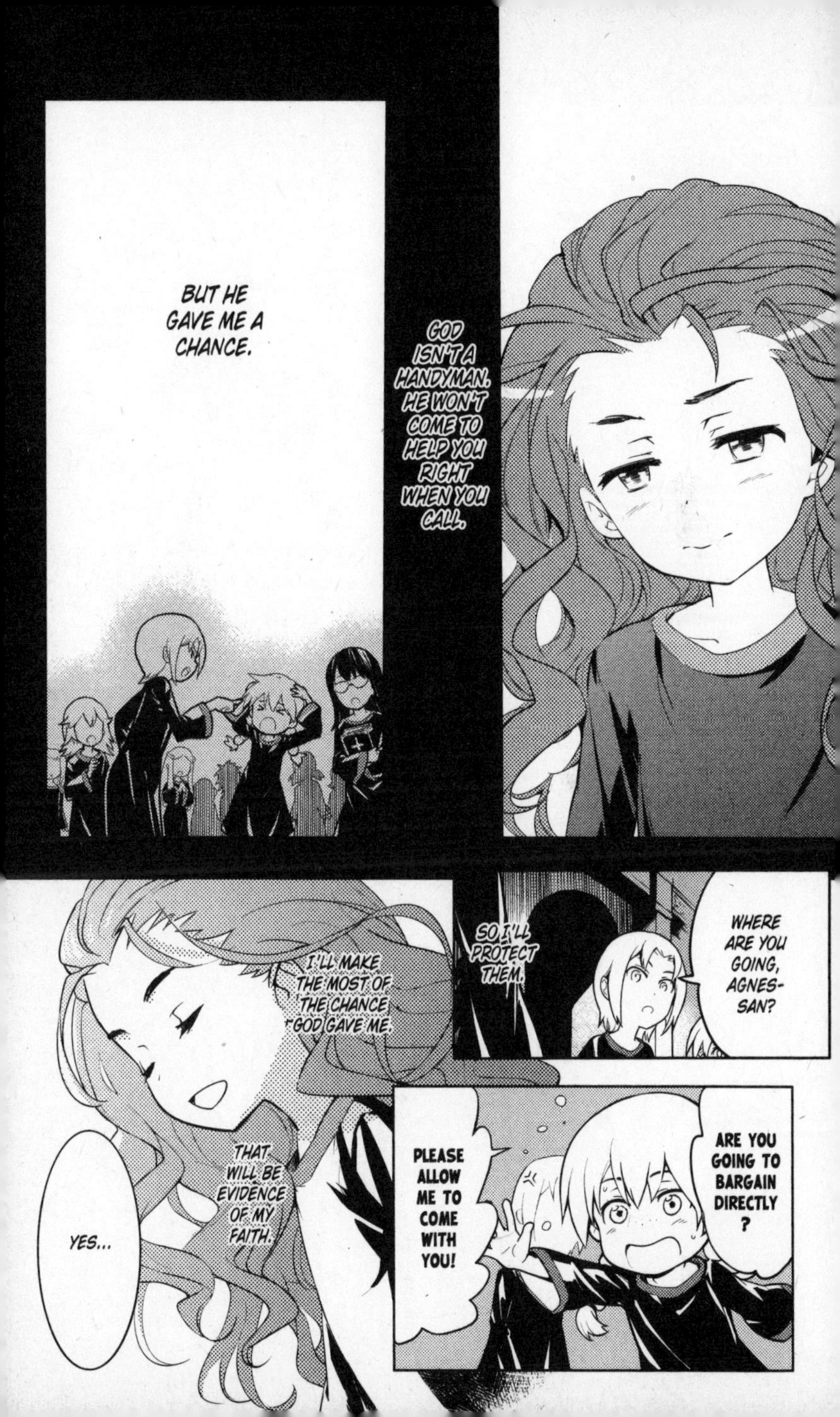
GOD ISN'T A HANDYMAN. HE WON'T COME TO HELP YOU RIGHT WHEN YOU CALL.
BUT HE GAVE ME A CHANCE.
WHERE ARE YOU GOING, AGNES-SAN?
SO I'LL PROTECT THEM.
ARE YOU GOING TO BARGAIN DIRECTLY?
PLEASE ALLOW ME TO COME WITH YOU!
I'LL MAKE THE MOST OF THE CHANCE GOD GAVE ME.
THAT WILL BE EVIDENCE OF MY FAITH.
YES...

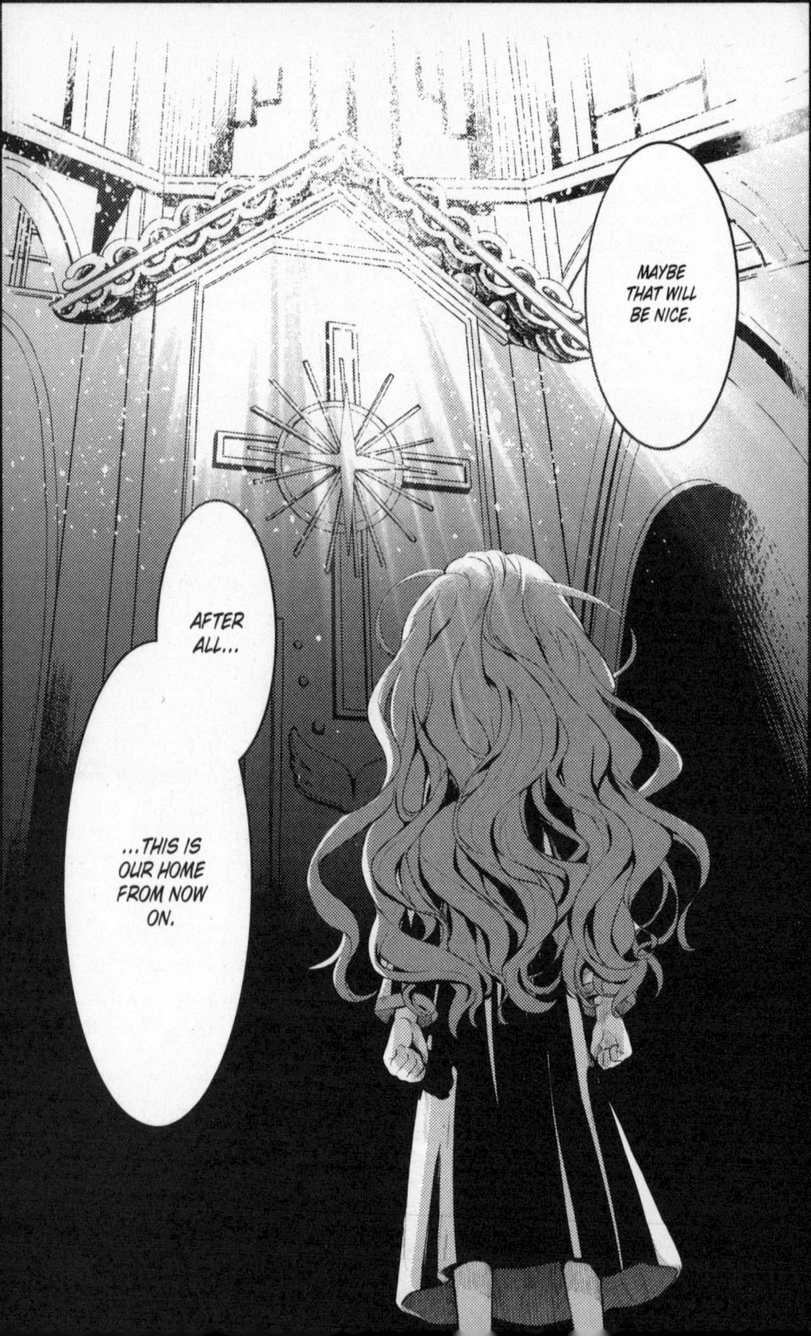
MAYBE THAT WILL BE NICE.
AFTER ALL...
...THIS IS OUR HOME FROM NOW ON.

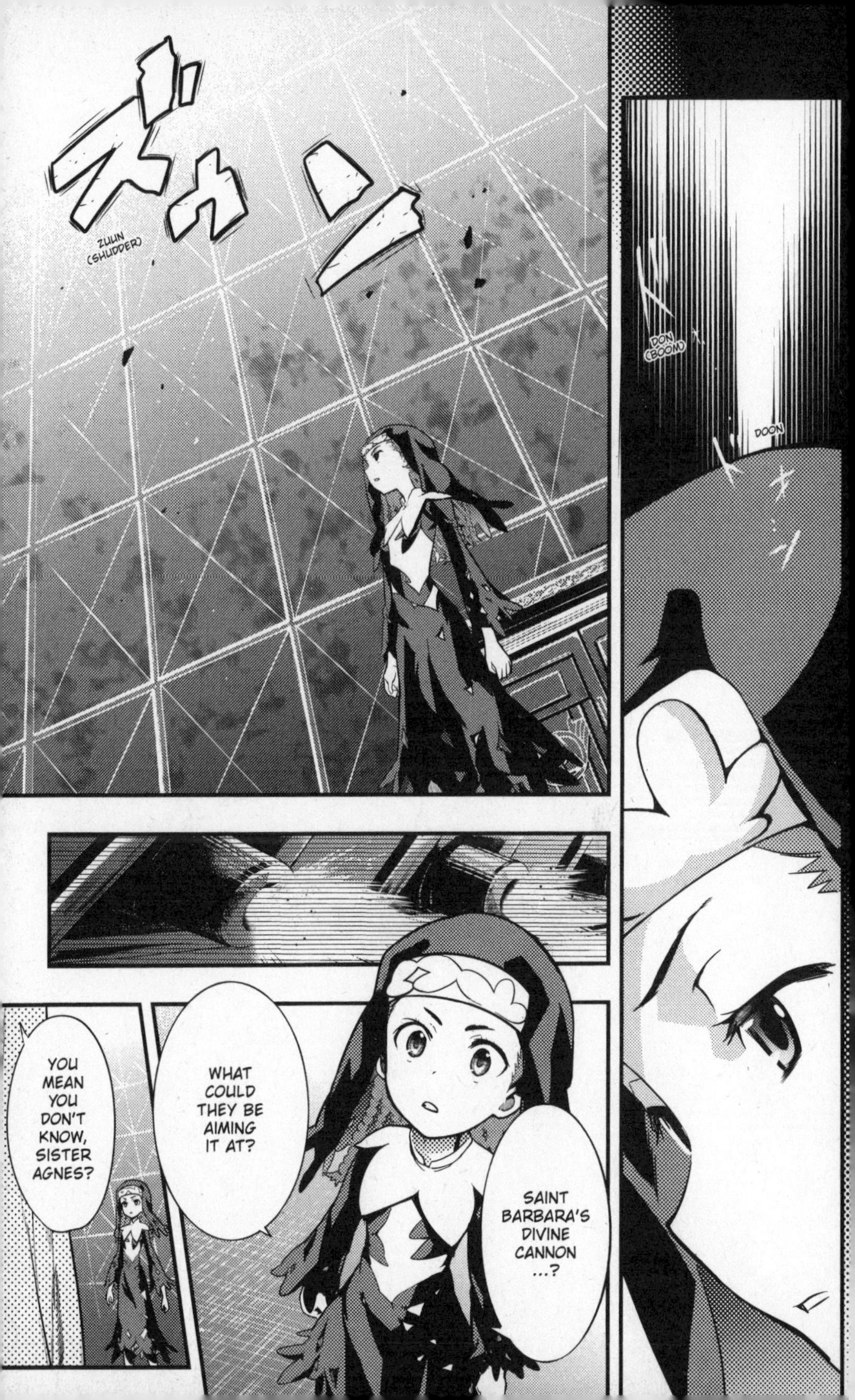
DON (BOOM)
DOON
ZUUN (SHUDDER)
SAINT BARBARA'S DIVINE CANNON ...?
WHAT COULD THEY BE AIMING IT AT?
YOU MEAN YOU DON'T KNOW, SISTER AGNES?

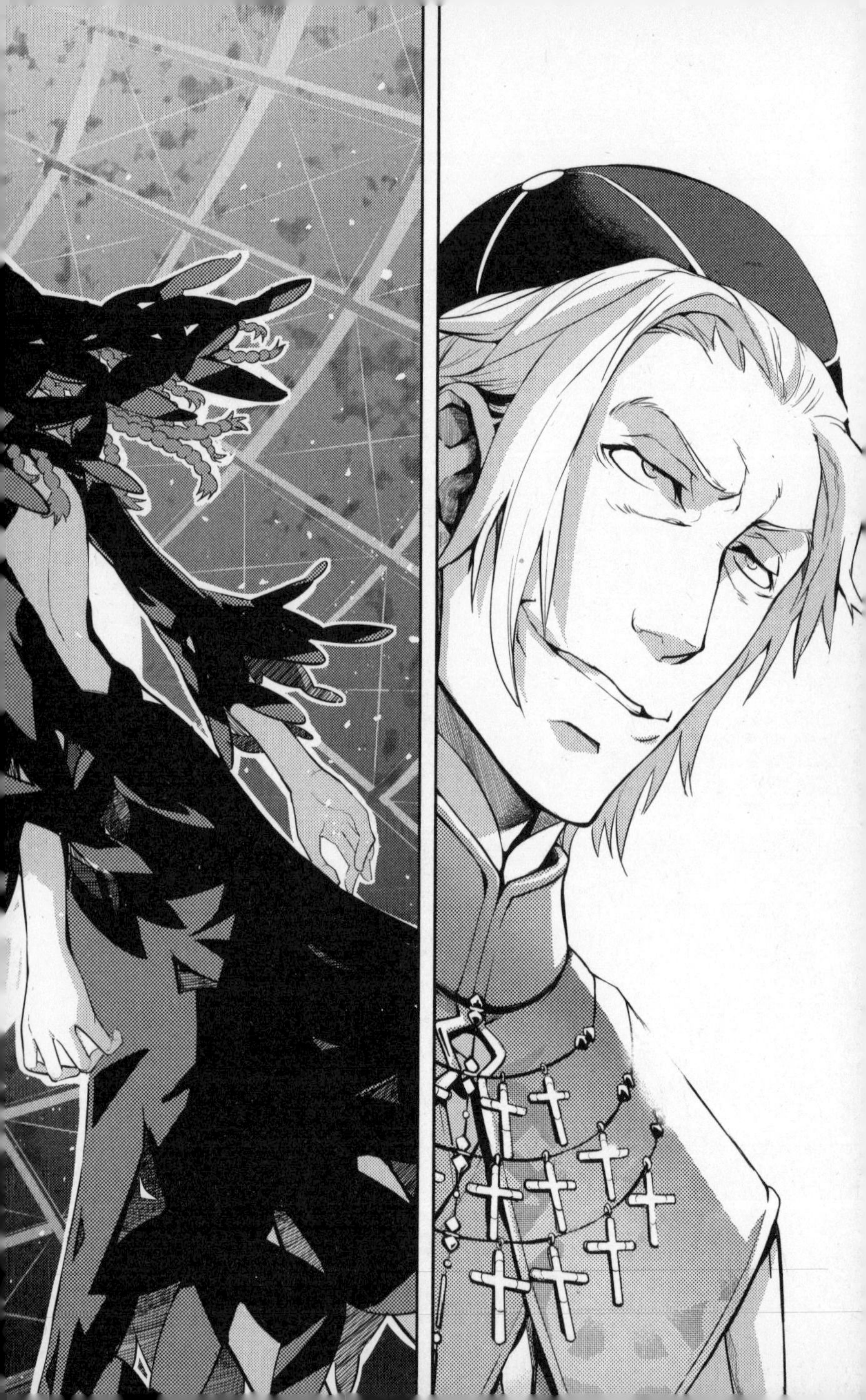

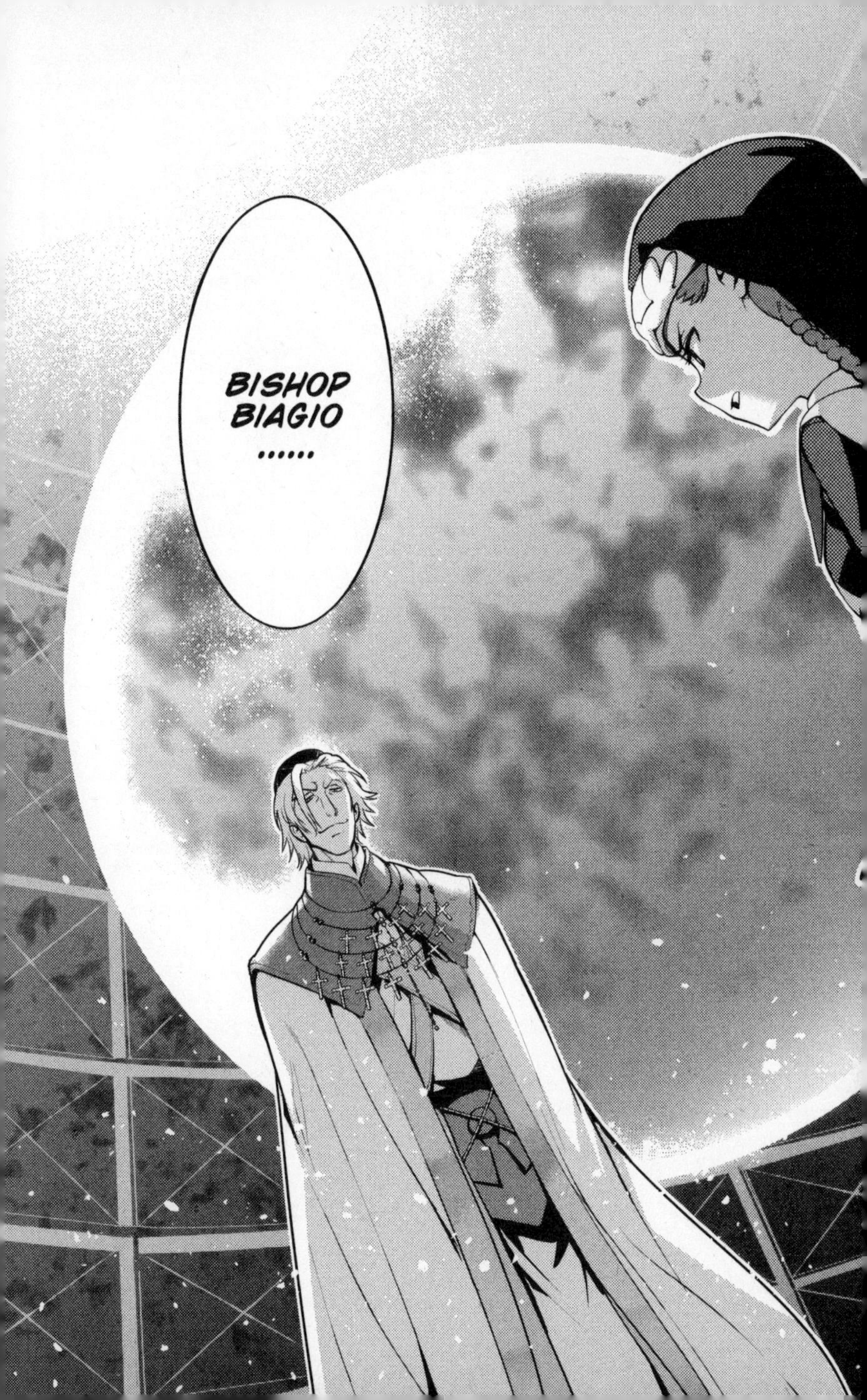
BISHOP BIAGIO ......

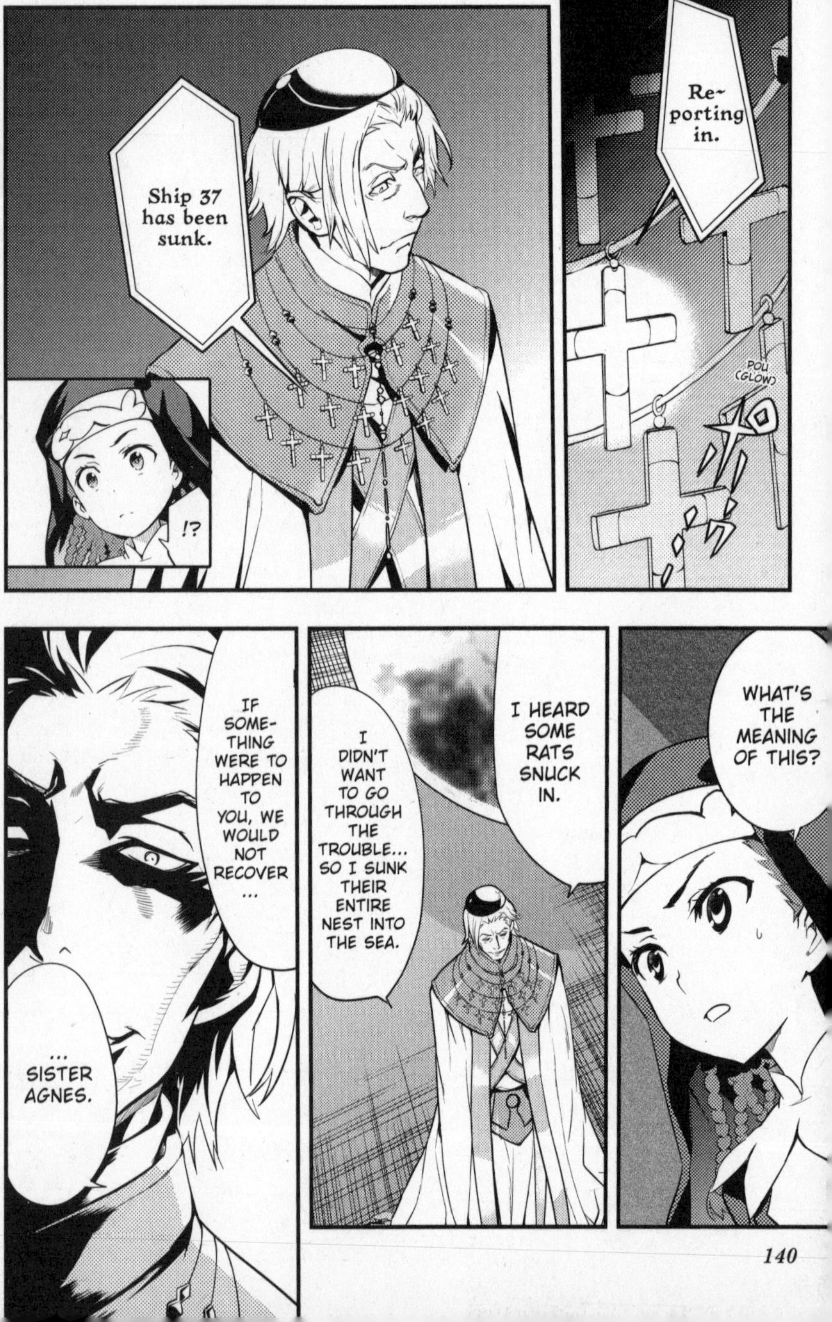
Re-porting in.
POU (GLOW)
Ship 37 has been sunk.
!?
WHAT'S THE MEANING OF THIS?
I HEARD SOME RATS SNUCK IN.
I DIDN'T WANT TO GO THROUGH THE TROUBLE... SO I SUNK THEIR ENTIRE NEST INTO THE SEA.
IF SOMETHING WERE TO HAPPEN TO YOU, WE WOULD NOT RECOVER...
...SISTER AGNES.

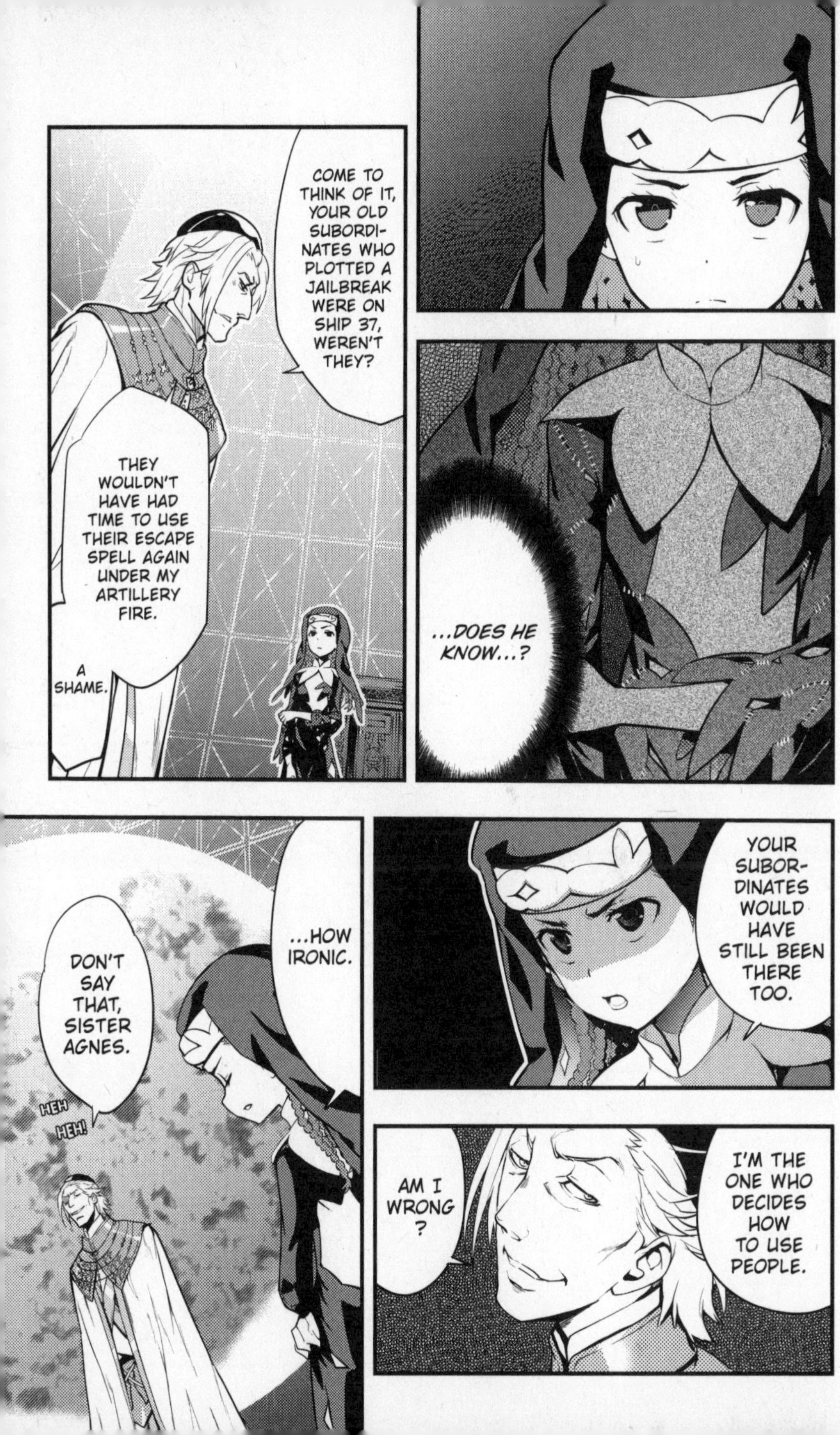
...DOES HE KNOW...?
COME TO THINK OF IT, YOUR OLD SUBORDINATES WHO PLOTTED A JAILBREAK WERE ON SHIP 37, WEREN'T THEY?
THEY WOULDN'T HAVE HAD TIME TO USE THEIR ESCAPE SPELL AGAIN UNDER MY ARTILLERY FIRE.
A SHAME.
YOUR SUBORDINATES WOULD HAVE STILL BEEN THERE TOO.
I'M THE ONE WHO DECIDES HOW TO USE PEOPLE.
AM I WRONG?
...HOW IRONIC.
DON'T SAY THAT, SISTER AGNES.
HEH HEH!

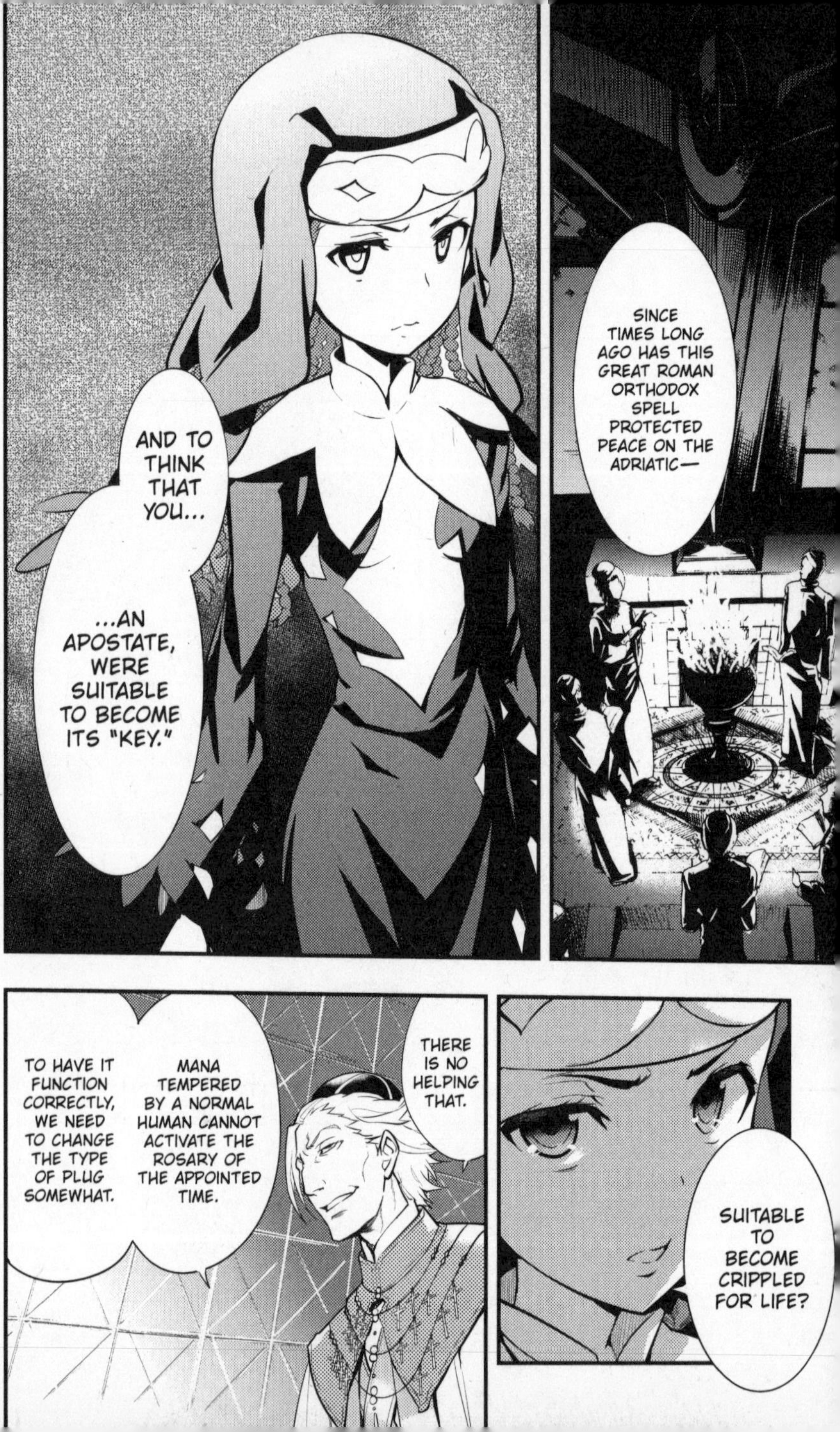
SINCE TIMES LONG AGO HAS THIS GREAT ROMAN ORTHODOX SPELL PROTECTED PEACE ON THE ADRIATIC—
AND TO THINK THAT YOU...
...AN APOSTATE, WERE SUITABLE TO BECOME ITS "KEY."
SUITABLE TO BECOME CRIPPLED FOR LIFE?
THERE IS NO HELPING THAT.
MANA TEMPERED BY A NORMAL HUMAN CANNOT ACTIVATE THE ROSARY OF THE APPOINTED TIME.
TO HAVE IT FUNCTION CORRECTLY, WE NEED TO CHANGE THE TYPE OF PLUG SOMEWHAT.

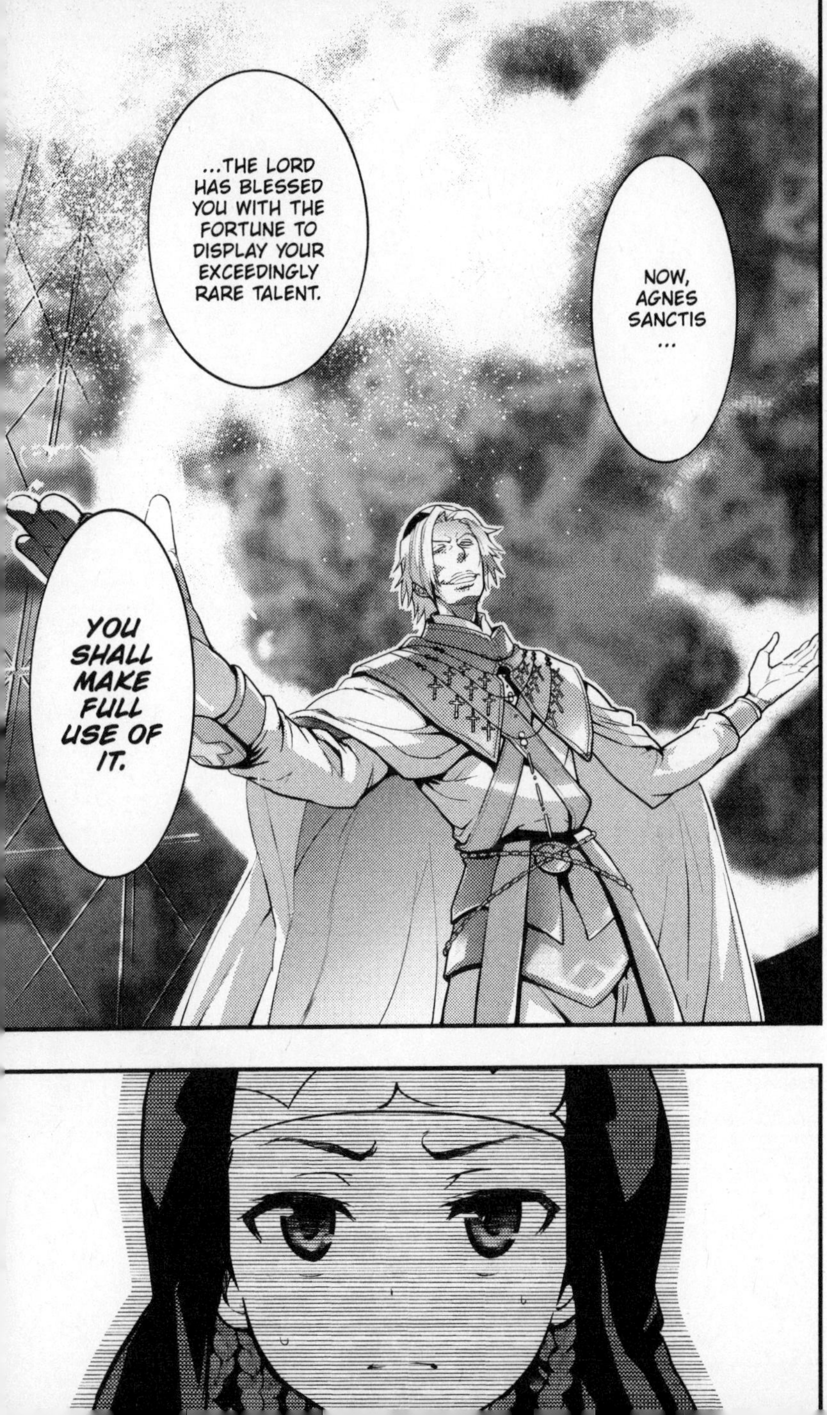
NOW, AGNES SANCTIS...
...THE LORD HAS BLESSED YOU WITH THE FORTUNE TO DISPLAY YOUR EXCEEDINGLY RARE TALENT.
YOU SHALL MAKE FULL USE OF IT.

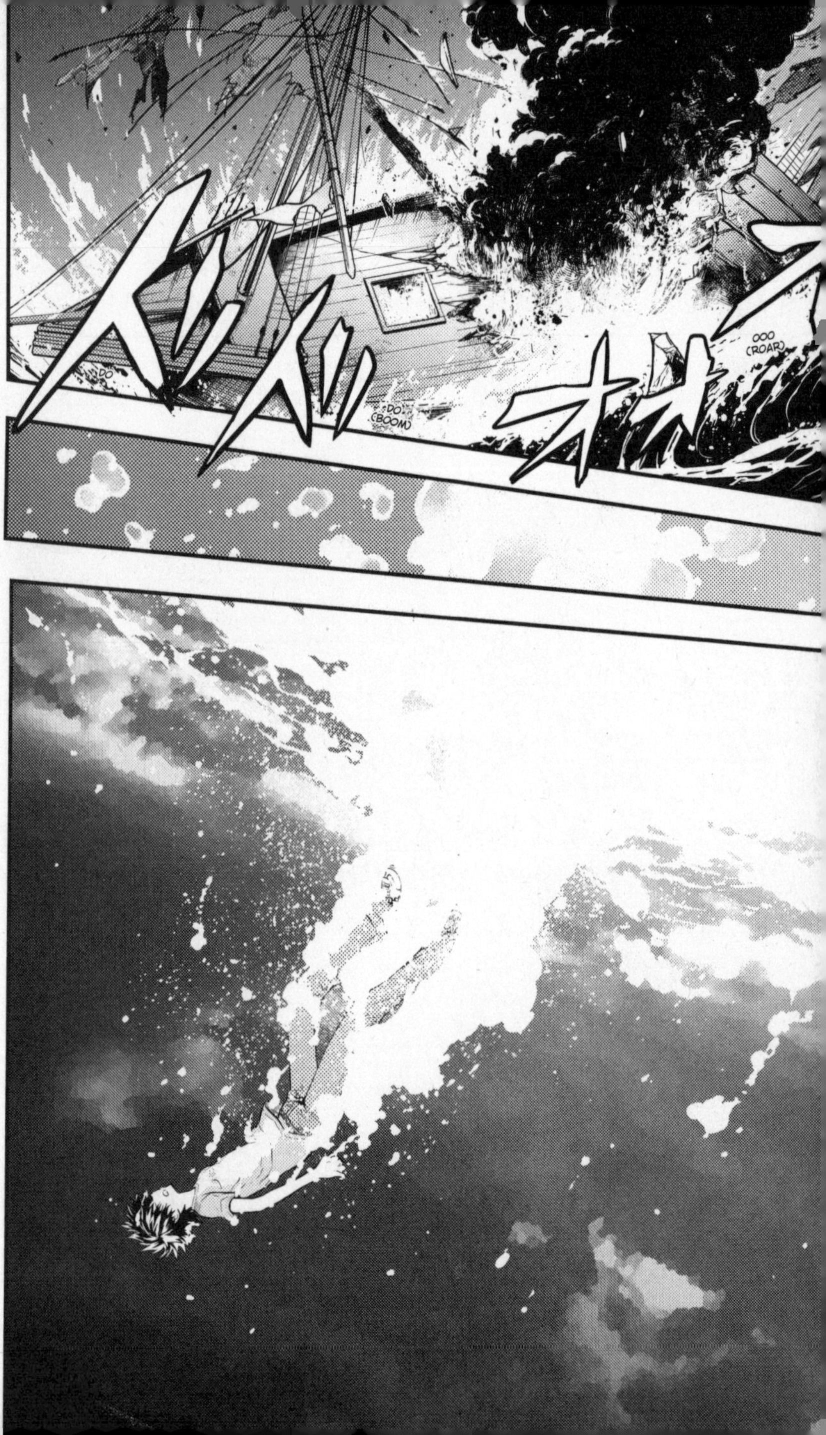
DO
DO (BOOM)
OOO (ROAR)

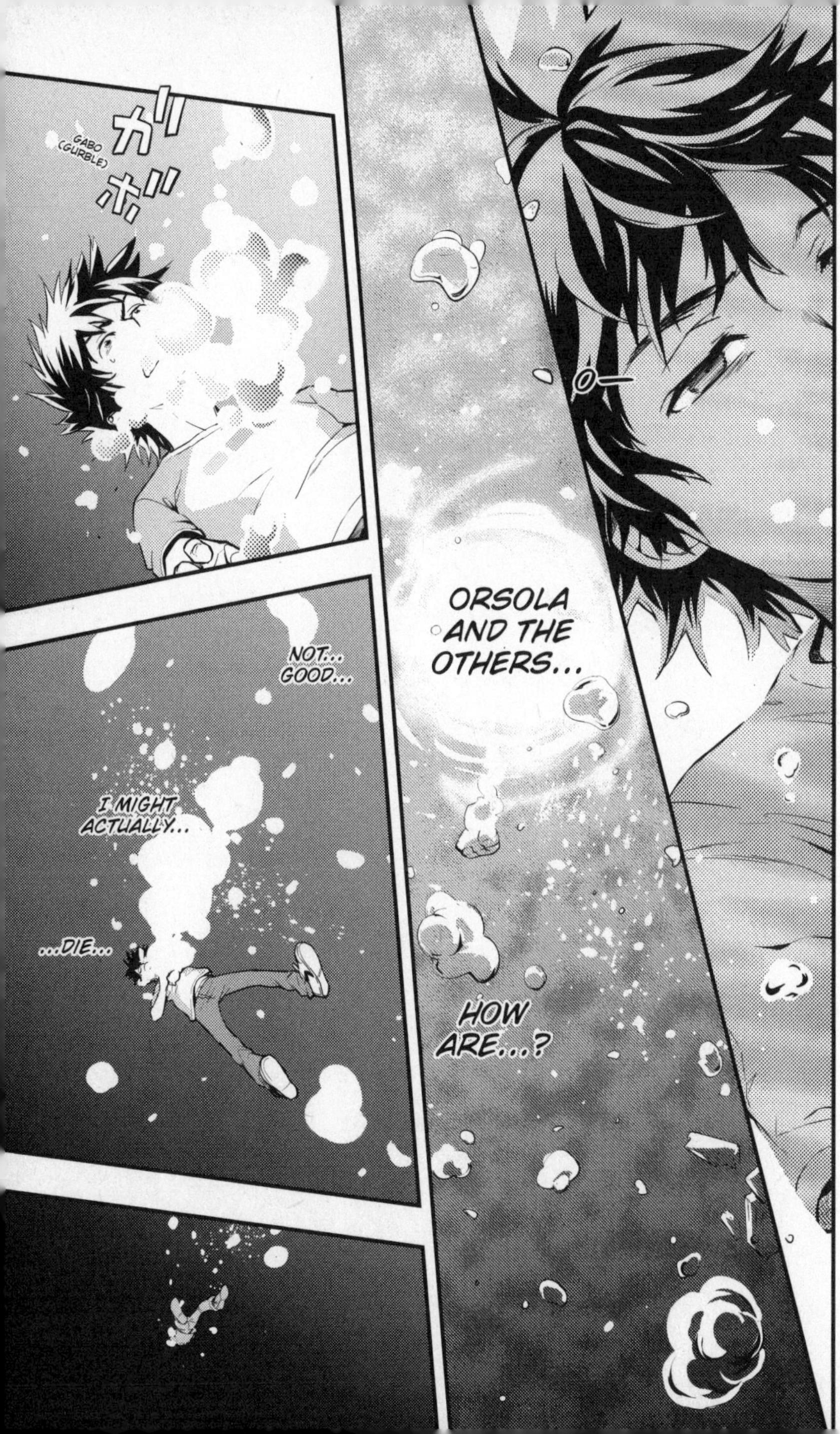
ORSOLA AND THE OTHERS...
HOW ARE...?
ガボ
GABO (GURBLE)
NOT... GOOD...
I MIGHT ACTUALLY...
...DIE...

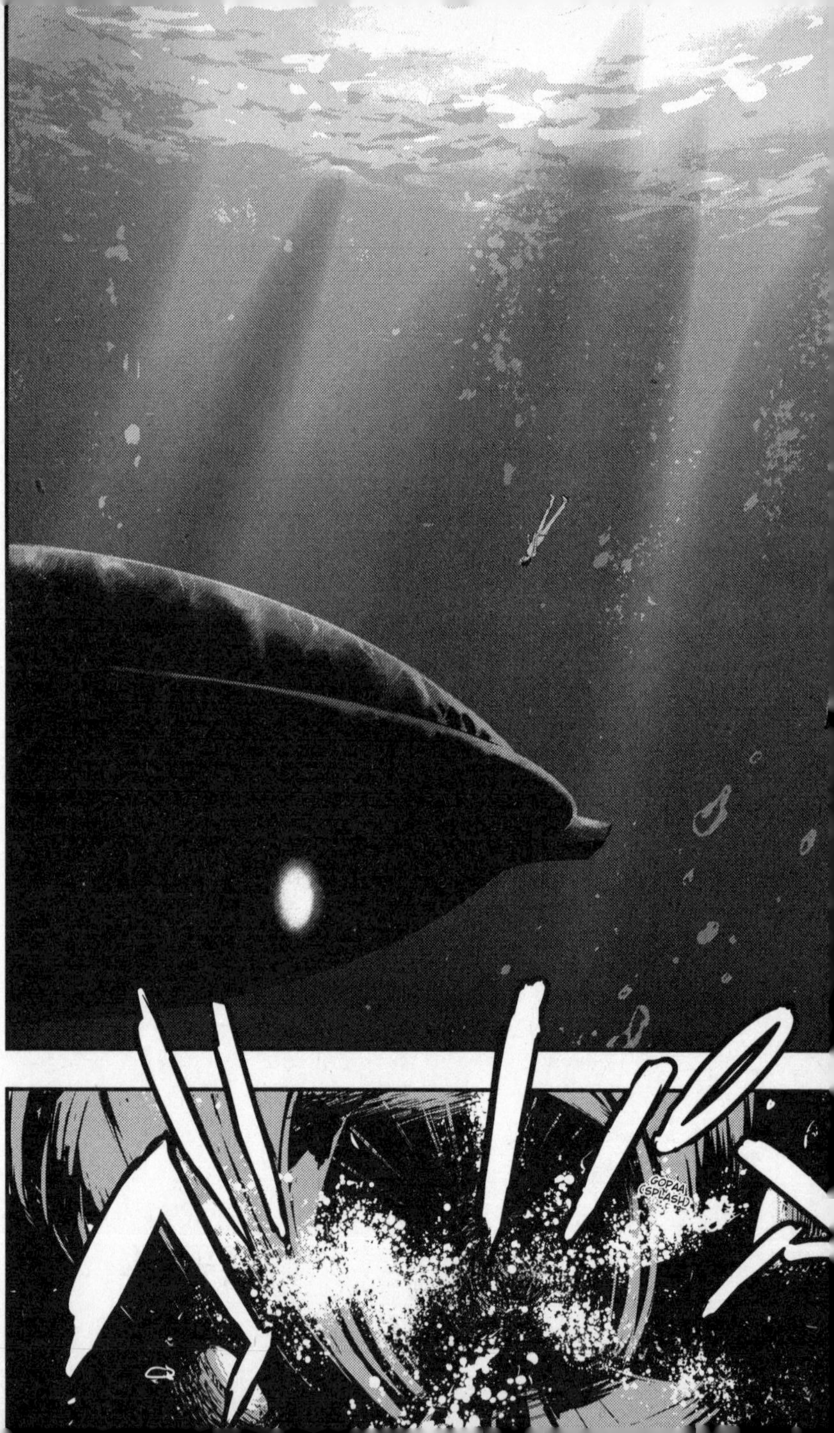
GOPAA
(SPLASH)

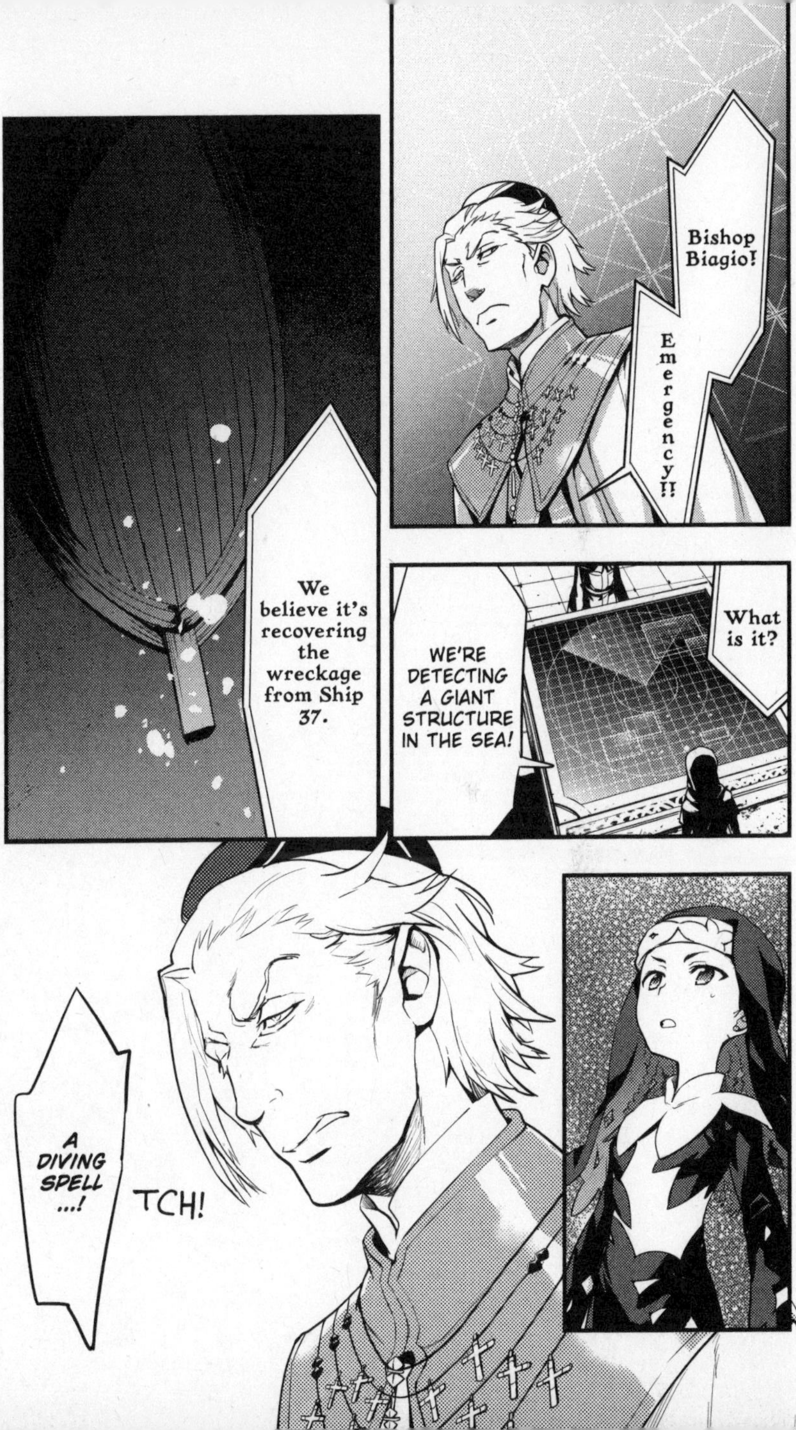
Bishop Biagio!
Emergency!!
What is it?
WE'RE DETECTING A GIANT STRUCTURE IN THE SEA!
We believe it's recovering the wreckage from Ship 37.
TCH!
A DIVING SPELL ...!

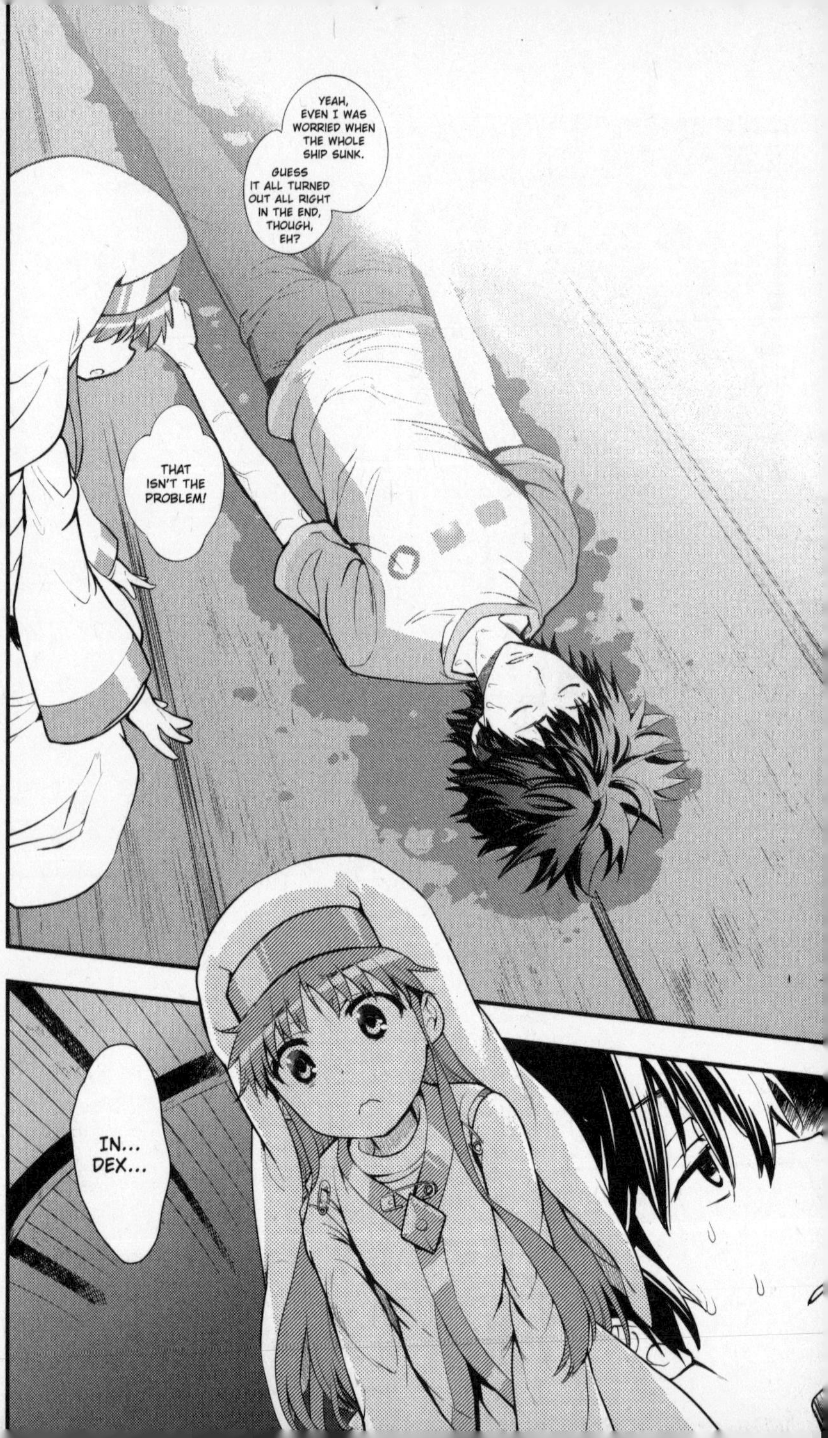
YEAH, EVEN I WAS WORRIED WHEN THE WHOLE SHIP SUNK.
GUESS IT ALL TURNED OUT ALL RIGHT IN THE END, THOUGH, EH?
THAT ISN'T THE PROBLEM!
IN... DEX...

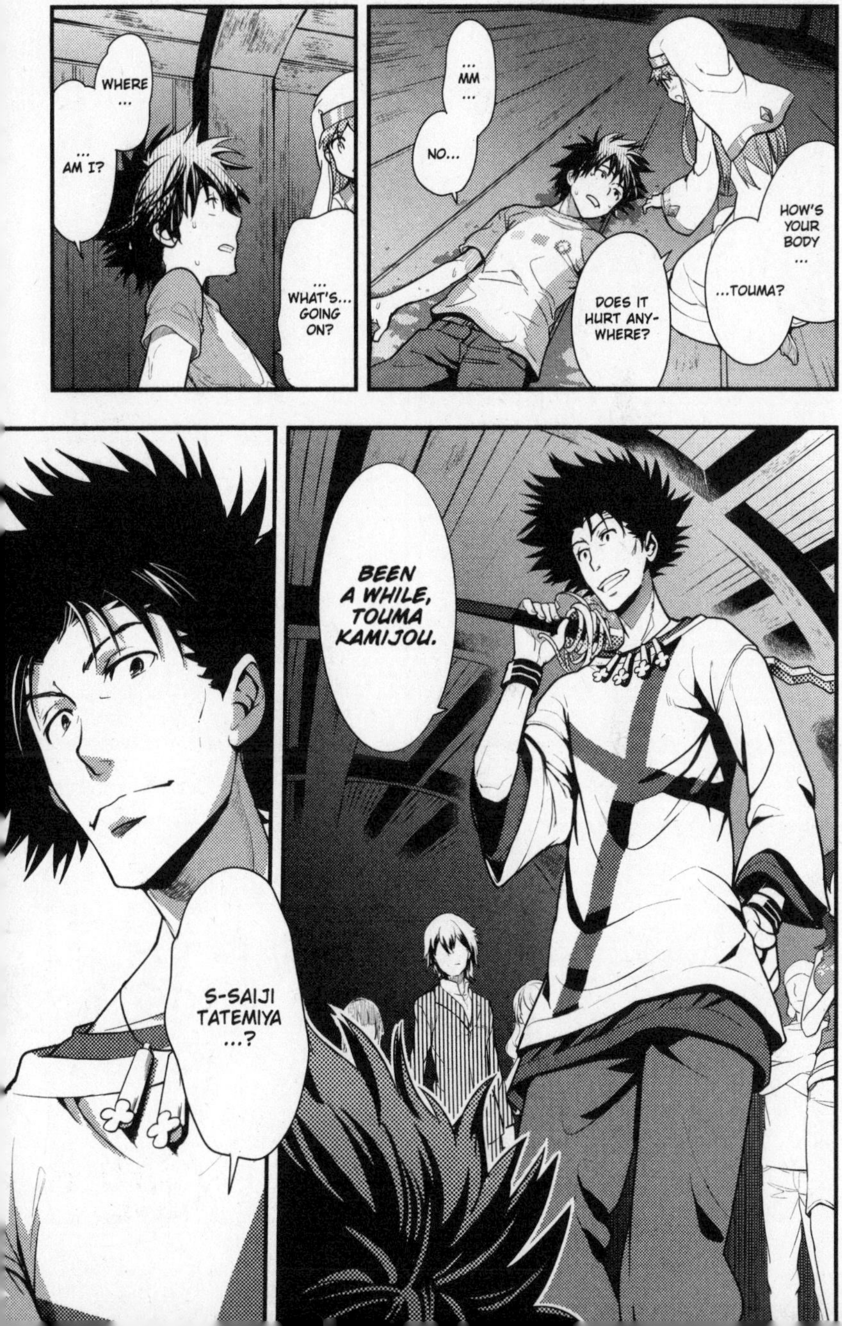
HOW'S YOUR BODY ...
...TOUMA?
DOES IT HURT ANY-WHERE?
... MM ...
NO...
WHERE ...
... AM I?
... WHAT'S... GOING ON?
BEEN A WHILE, TOUMA KAMIJOU.
S-SAIJI TATEMIYA ...?

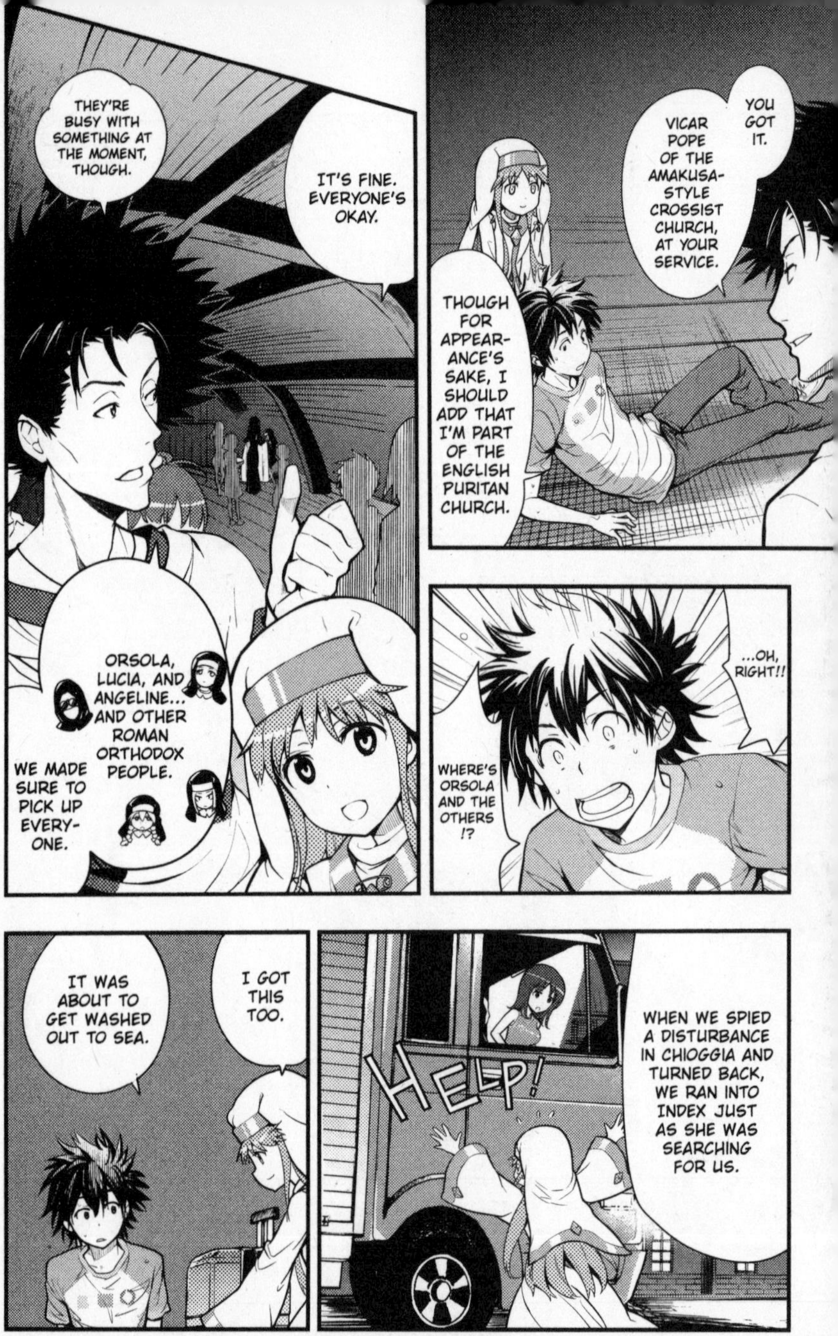
YOU GOT IT.
VICAR POPE OF THE AMAKUSA-STYLE CROSSIST CHURCH, AT YOUR SERVICE.
THOUGH FOR APPEARANCE'S SAKE, I SHOULD ADD THAT I'M PART OF THE ENGLISH PURITAN CHURCH.
...OH, RIGHT!!
WHERE'S ORSOLA AND THE OTHERS!?
IT'S FINE. EVERYONE'S OKAY.
THEY'RE BUSY WITH SOMETHING AT THE MOMENT, THOUGH.
ORSOLA, LUCIA, AND ANGELINE... AND OTHER ROMAN ORTHODOX PEOPLE.
WE MADE SURE TO PICK UP EVERYONE.
WHEN WE SPIED A DISTURBANCE IN CHIOGGIA AND TURNED BACK, WE RAN INTO INDEX JUST AS SHE WAS SEARCHING FOR US.
HELP!
I GOT THIS TOO.
IT WAS ABOUT TO GET WASHED OUT TO SEA.

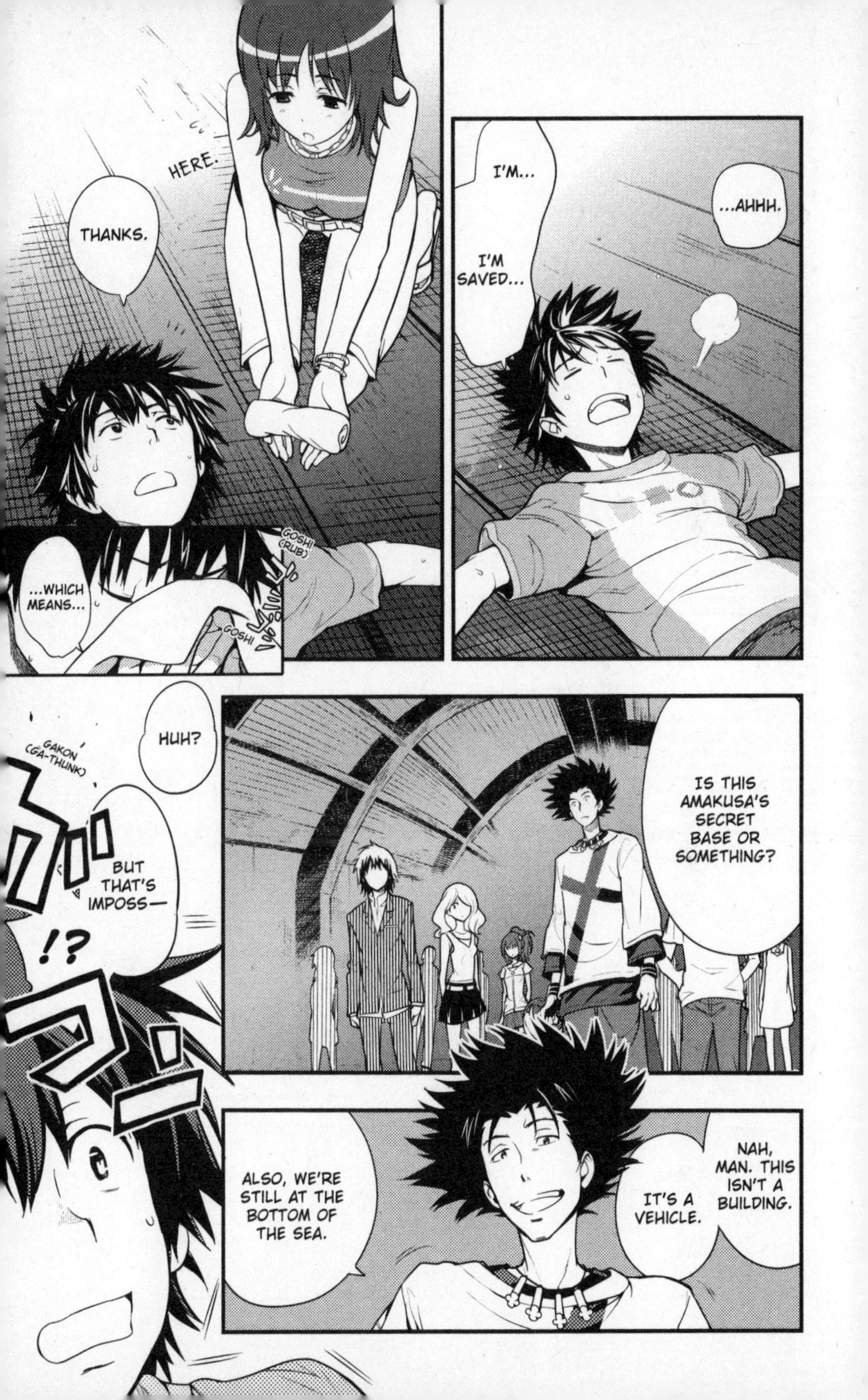
...AHHH.
I'M...
I'M SAVED...
HERE.
THANKS.
GOSHI (RUB)
...WHICH MEANS...
GOSHI
IS THIS AMAKUSA'S SECRET BASE OR SOMETHING?
NAH, MAN. THIS ISN'T A BUILDING.
IT'S A VEHICLE.
ALSO, WE'RE STILL AT THE BOTTOM OF THE SEA.
HUH?
GAKON (GA-THUNK)
BUT THAT'S IMPOSS—
!?

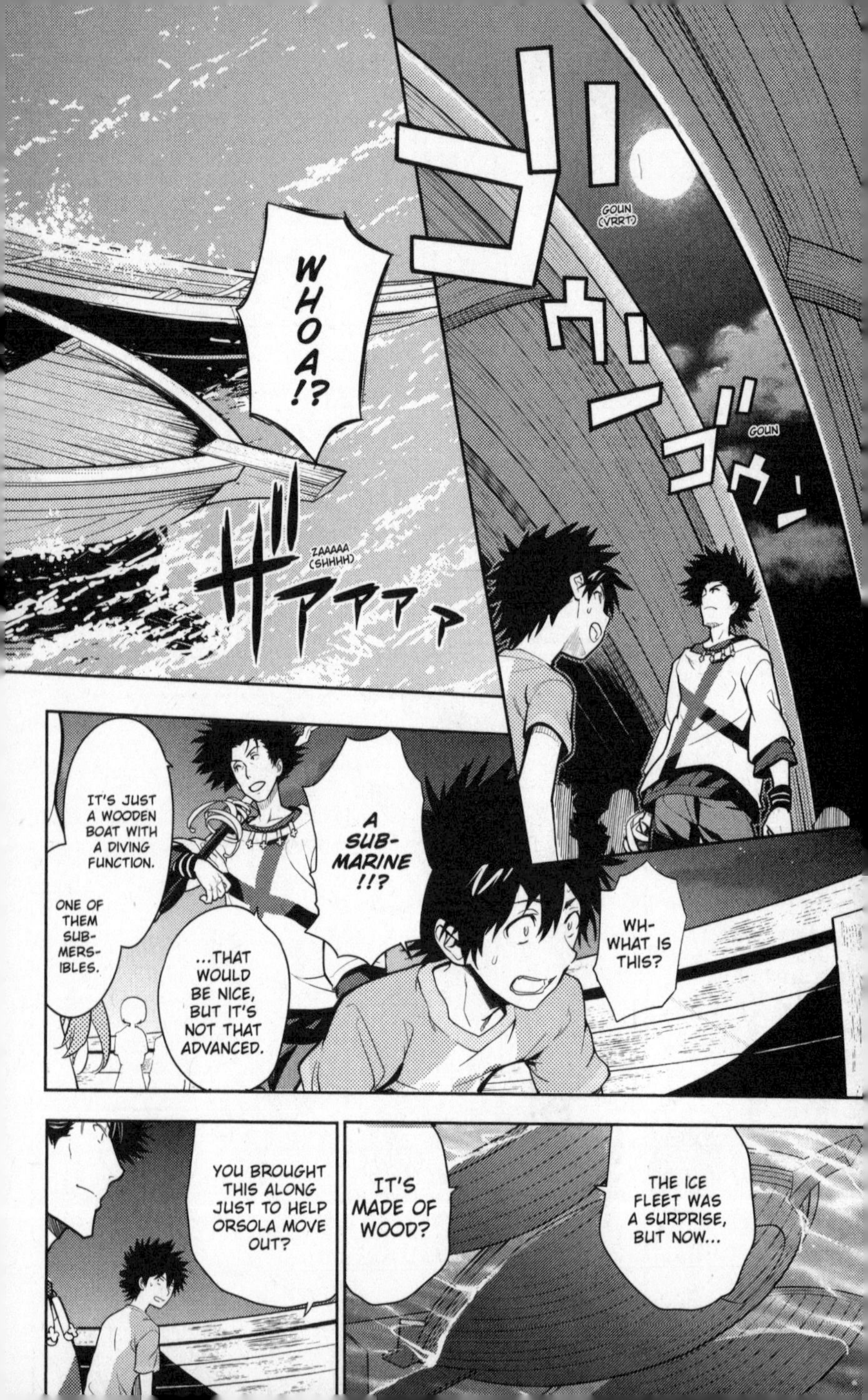
ゴウン
GOUN (VRRT)
ゴウン
GOUN
WHOA!?
ザァァァァ
ZAAAAA (SHHHH)
WH-WHAT IS THIS?
A SUB-MARINE!!?
...THAT WOULD BE NICE, BUT IT'S NOT THAT ADVANCED.
IT'S JUST A WOODEN BOAT WITH A DIVING FUNCTION.
ONE OF THEM SUB-MERS-IBLES.
THE ICE FLEET WAS A SURPRISE, BUT NOW...
IT'S MADE OF WOOD?
YOU BROUGHT THIS ALONG JUST TO HELP ORSOLA MOVE OUT?

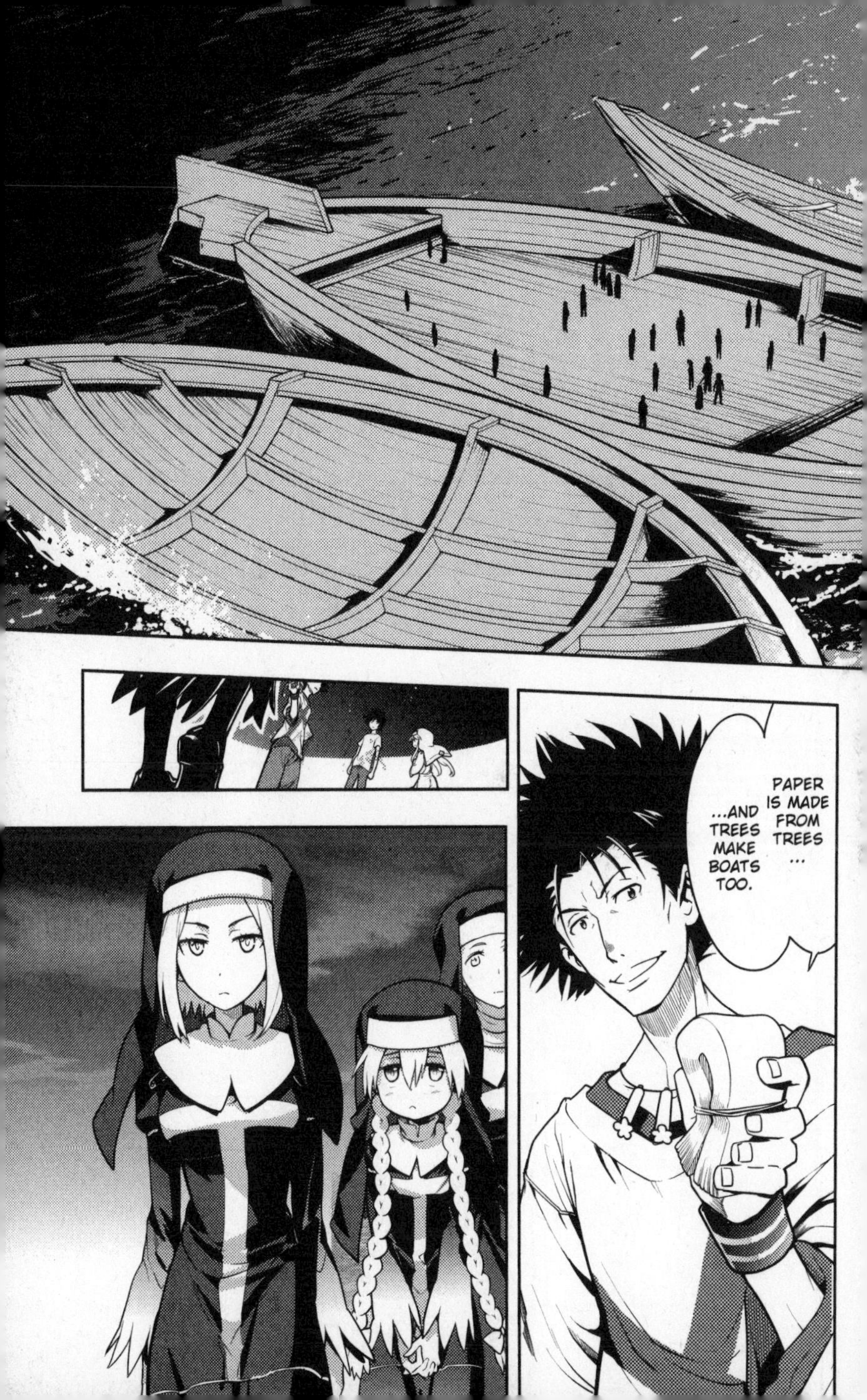
PAPER IS MADE FROM TREES ...
...AND TREES MAKE BOATS TOO.

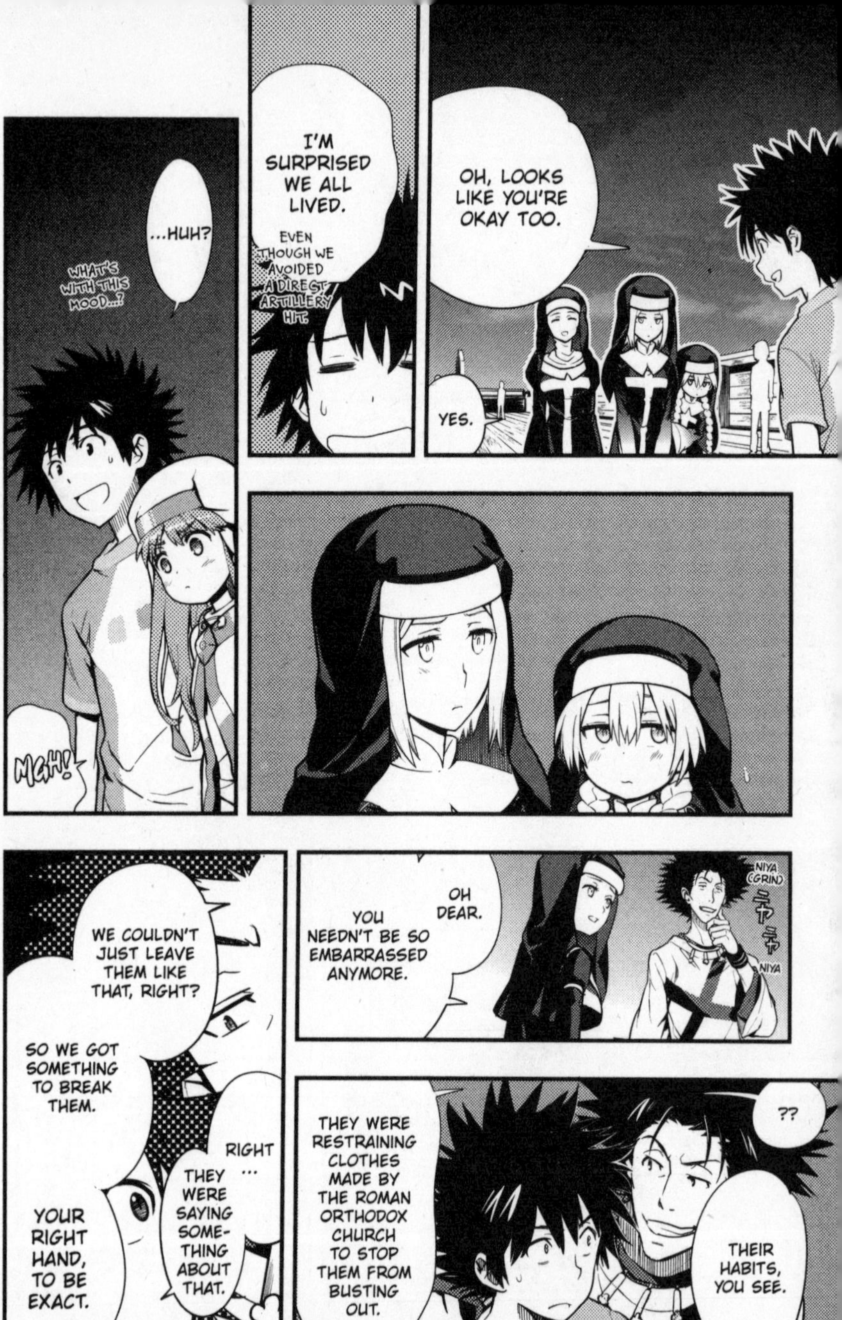
OH, LOOKS LIKE YOU'RE OKAY TOO.
YES.
I'M SURPRISED WE ALL LIVED.
EVEN THOUGH WE AVOIDED A DIRECT ARTILLERY HIT.
...HUH?
WHAT'S WITH THIS MOOD...?
MGH!
OH DEAR.
YOU NEEDN'T BE SO EMBARRASSED ANYMORE.
NIYA (GRIN)
NIYA
??
THEIR HABITS, YOU SEE.
THEY WERE RESTRAINING CLOTHES MADE BY THE ROMAN ORTHODOX CHURCH TO STOP THEM FROM BUSTING OUT.
WE COULDN'T JUST LEAVE THEM LIKE THAT, RIGHT?
SO WE GOT SOMETHING TO BREAK THEM.
RIGHT...
THEY WERE SAYING SOMETHING ABOUT THAT.
YOUR RIGHT HAND, TO BE EXACT.

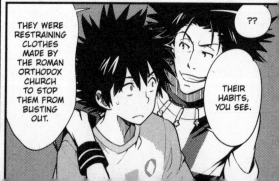

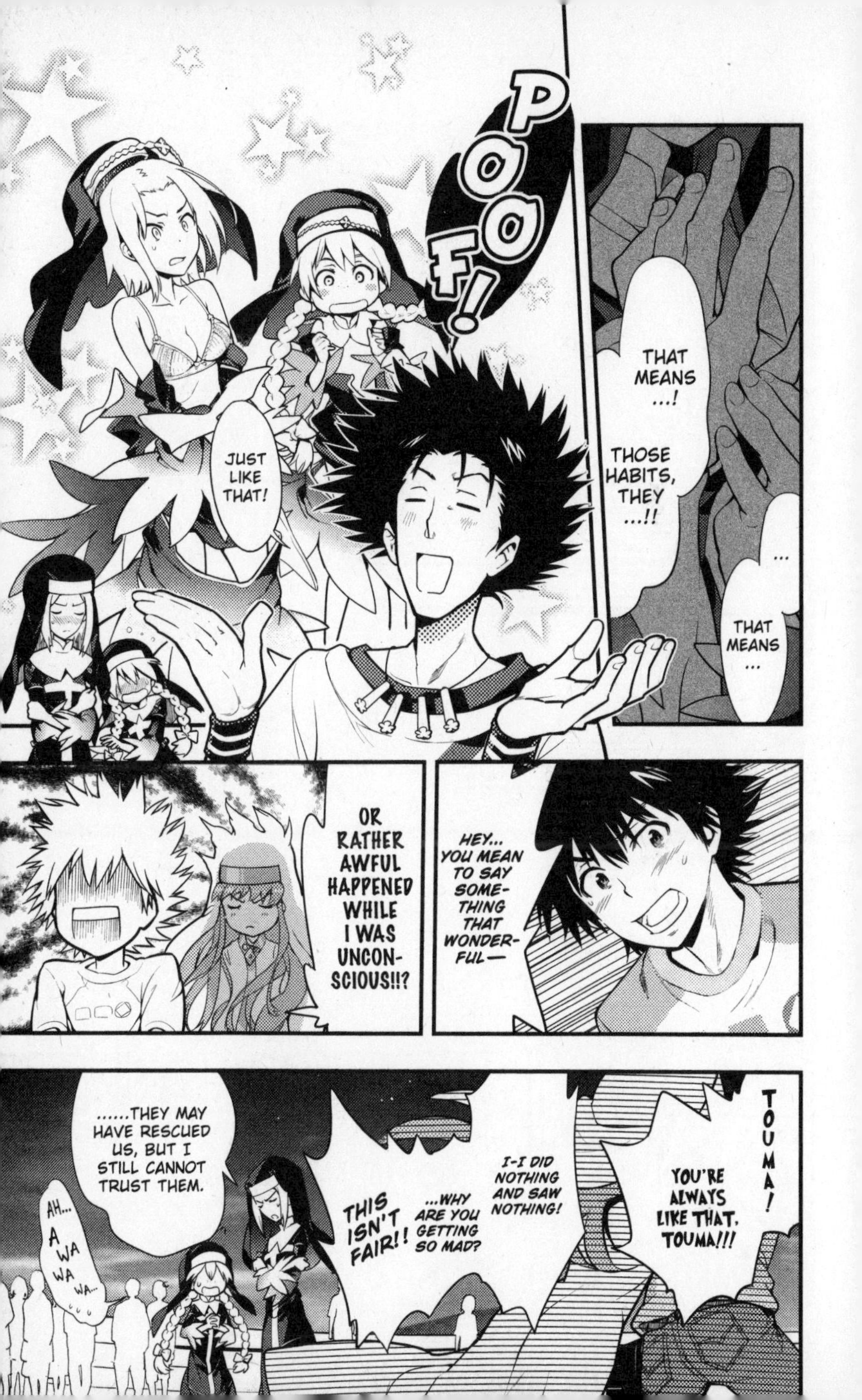
THAT MEANS ...!
THOSE HABITS, THEY ...!!
...
THAT MEANS ...
POOF!
JUST LIKE THAT!
HEY... YOU MEAN TO SAY SOMETHING THAT WONDERFUL—
OR RATHER AWFUL HAPPENED WHILE I WAS UNCONSCIOUS!!?
TOUMA!
YOU'RE ALWAYS LIKE THAT, TOUMA!!!
I-I DID NOTHING AND SAW NOTHING!
...WHY ARE YOU GETTING SO MAD?
THIS ISN'T FAIR!!
......THEY MAY HAVE RESCUED US, BUT I STILL CANNOT TRUST THEM.
AH... A WA WA WA...

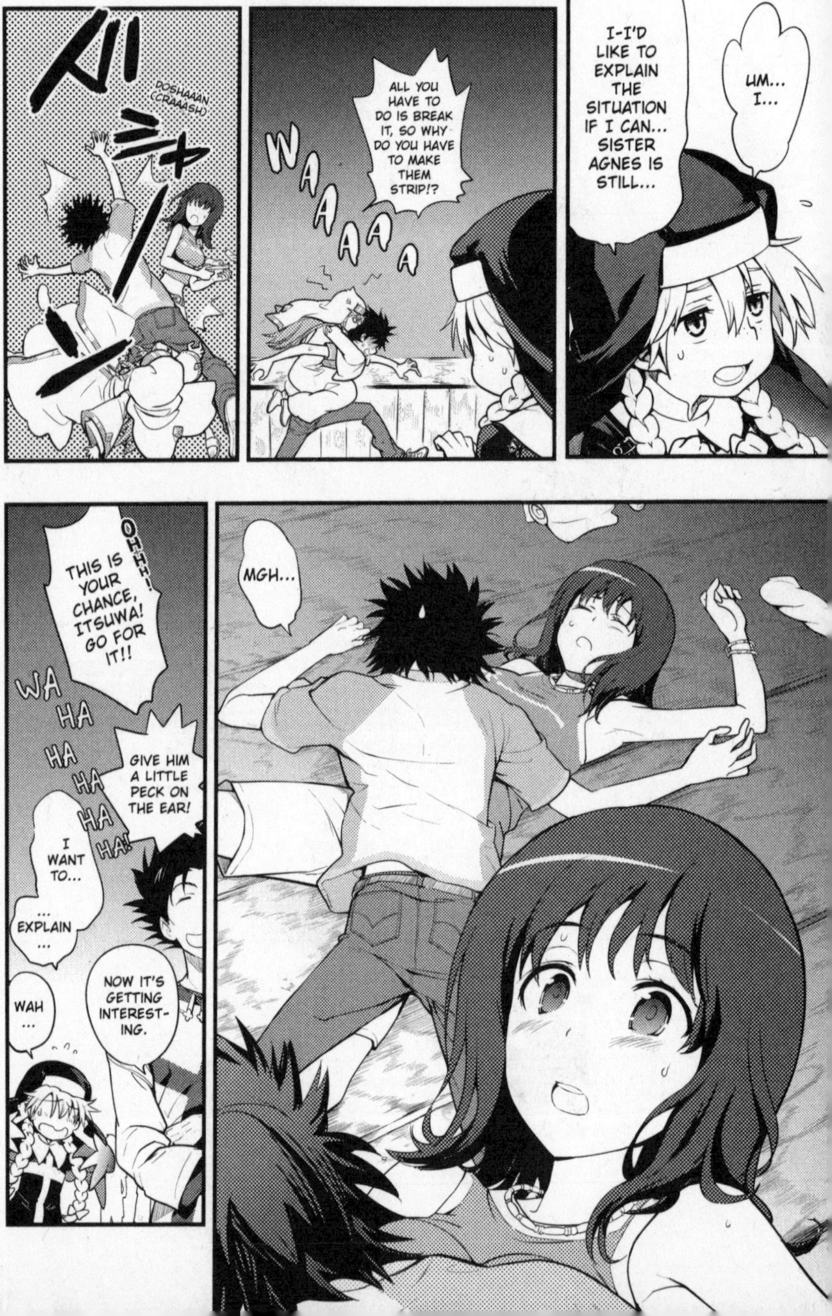
UM... I...
I-I'D LIKE TO EXPLAIN THE SITUATION IF I CAN... SISTER AGNES IS STILL...
ALL YOU HAVE TO DO IS BREAK IT, SO WHY DO YOU HAVE TO MAKE THEM STRIP!?
WAAAAAAA
DOSHAAAN (CRAAASH)
MGH...
OHHH!
THIS IS YOUR CHANCE, ITSUWA! GO FOR IT!!
WA HA HA HA HA HA HA!
GIVE HIM A LITTLE PECK ON THE EAR!
I WANT TO...
...EXPLAIN...
NOW IT'S GETTING INTERESTING.
WAH...

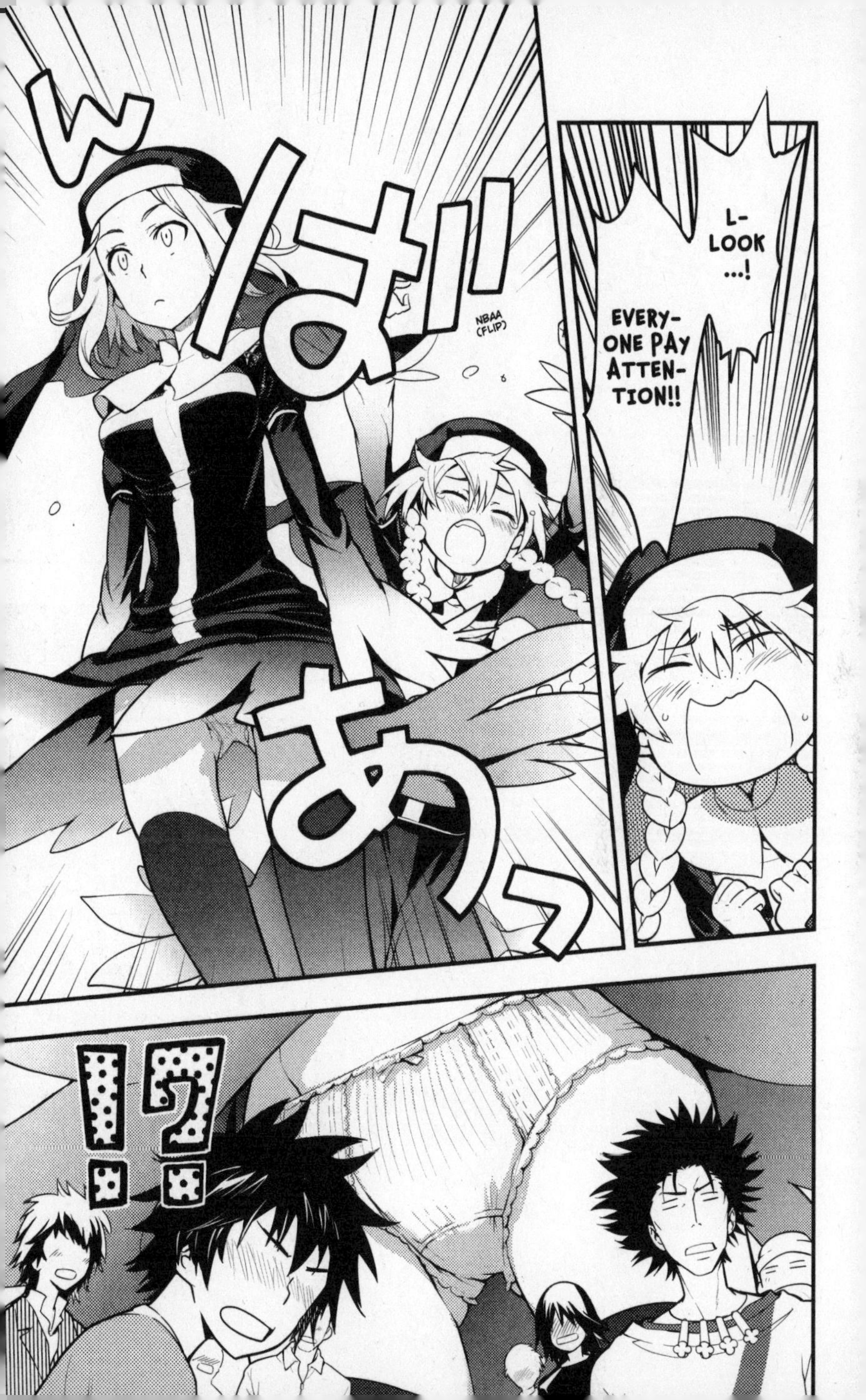
L-LOOK...!
EVERYONE PAY ATTENTION!!
NBAA (FLIP)
んばあっ
!?

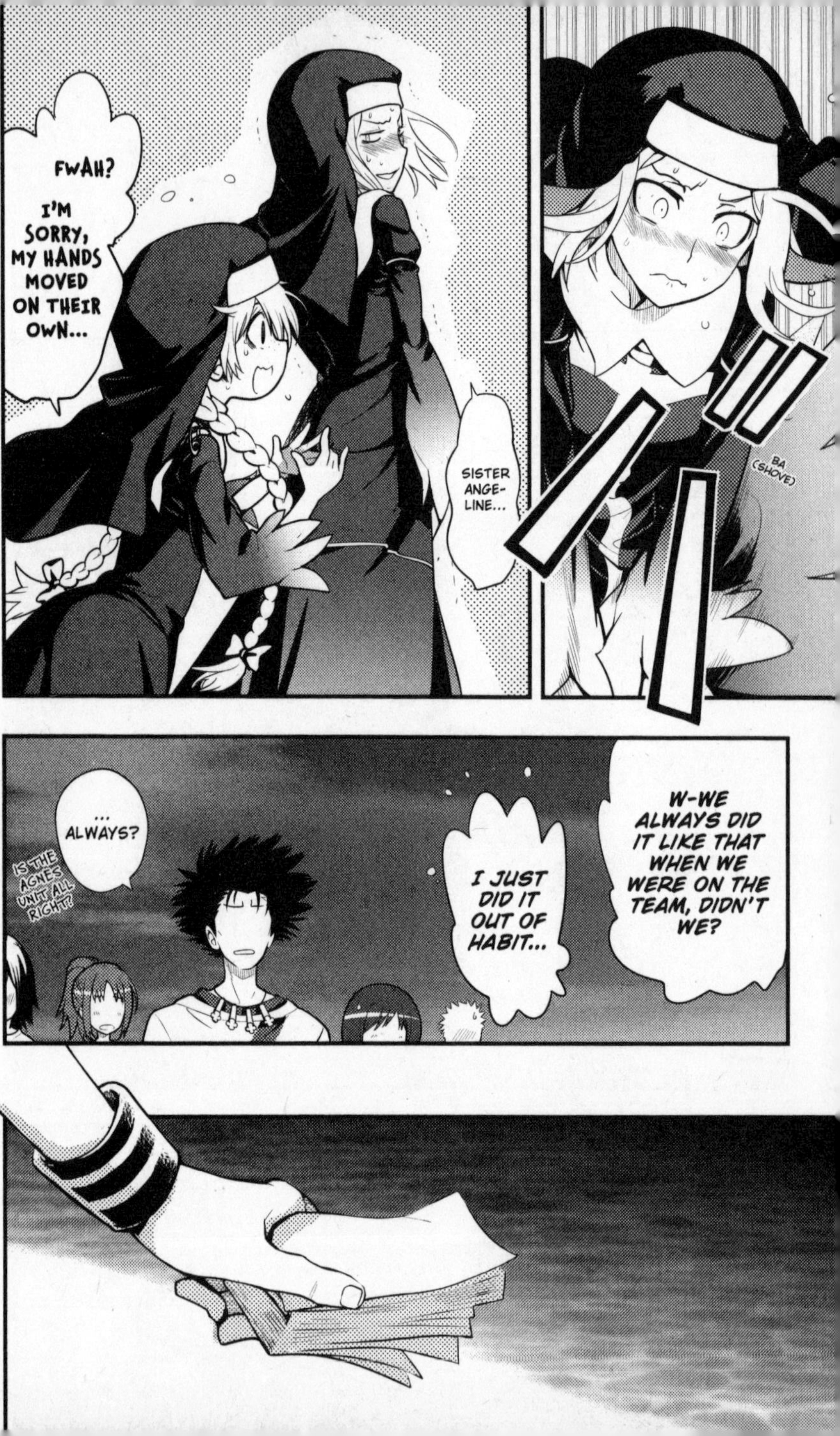
BA (SHOVE)
SISTER ANGE-LINE...
FWAH?
I'M SORRY, MY HANDS MOVED ON THEIR OWN...
W-WE ALWAYS DID IT LIKE THAT WHEN WE WERE ON THE TEAM, DIDN'T WE?
I JUST DID IT OUT OF HABIT...
... ALWAYS?
IS THE AGNES UNIT ALL RIGHT?

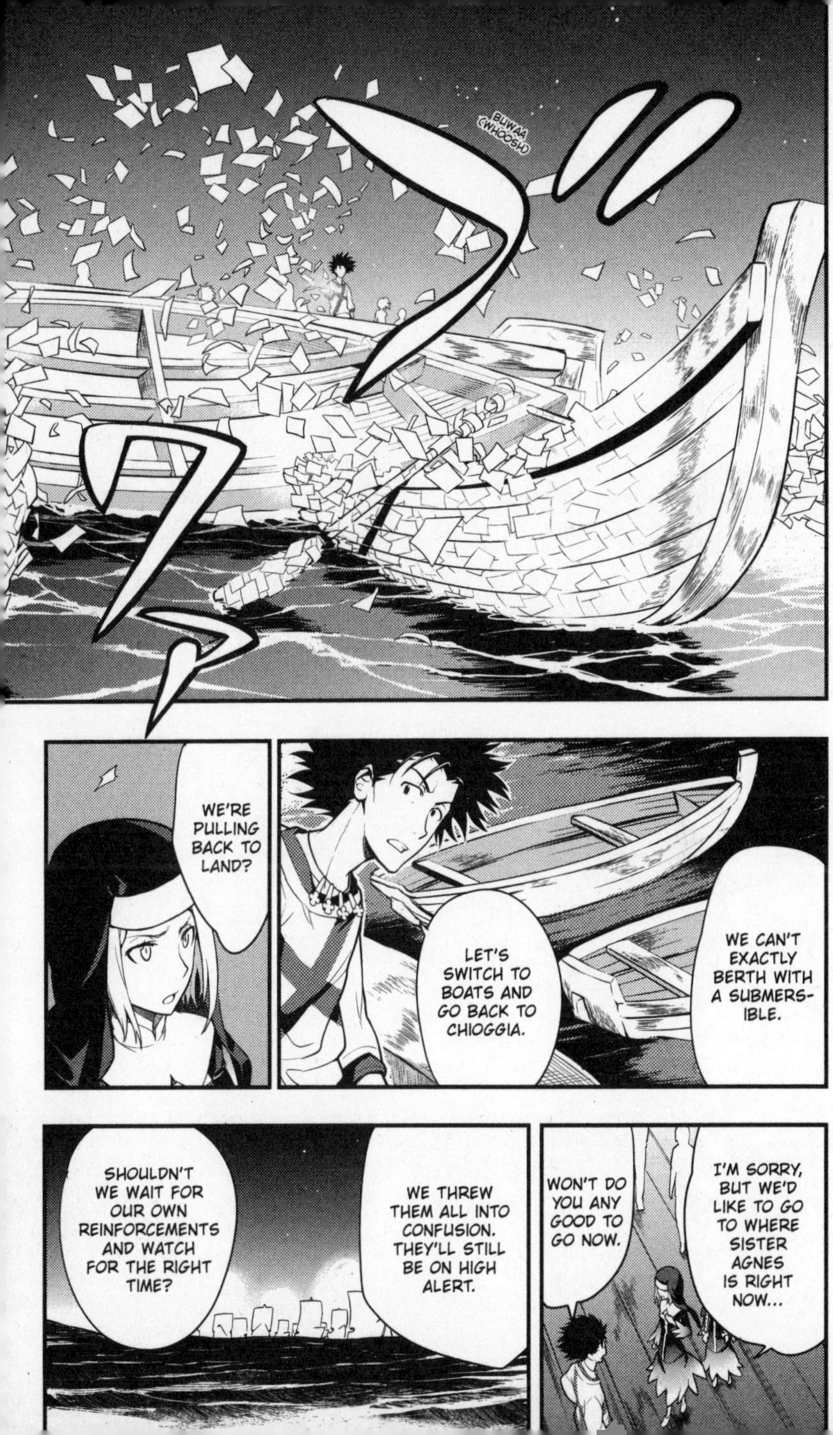
BUWAA (WHOOSH)
WE CAN'T EXACTLY BERTH WITH A SUBMERSIBLE.
LET'S SWITCH TO BOATS AND GO BACK TO CHIOGGIA.
WE'RE PULLING BACK TO LAND?
I'M SORRY, BUT WE'D LIKE TO GO TO WHERE SISTER AGNES IS RIGHT NOW...
WON'T DO YOU ANY GOOD TO GO NOW.
WE THREW THEM ALL INTO CONFUSION. THEY'LL STILL BE ON HIGH ALERT.
SHOULDN'T WE WAIT FOR OUR OWN REINFORCEMENTS AND WATCH FOR THE RIGHT TIME?

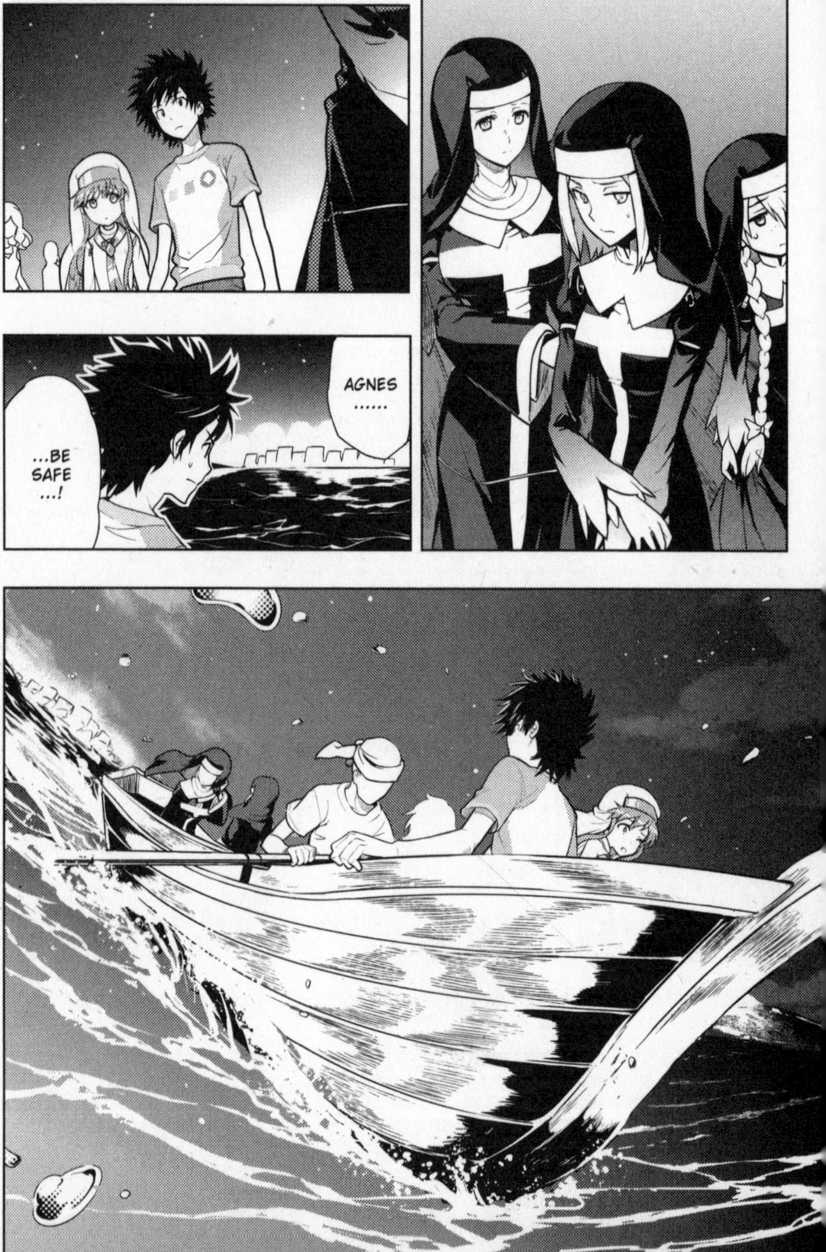
AGNES ......
...BE SAFE ...!

# #91 THE QUEEN'S FLEET ④

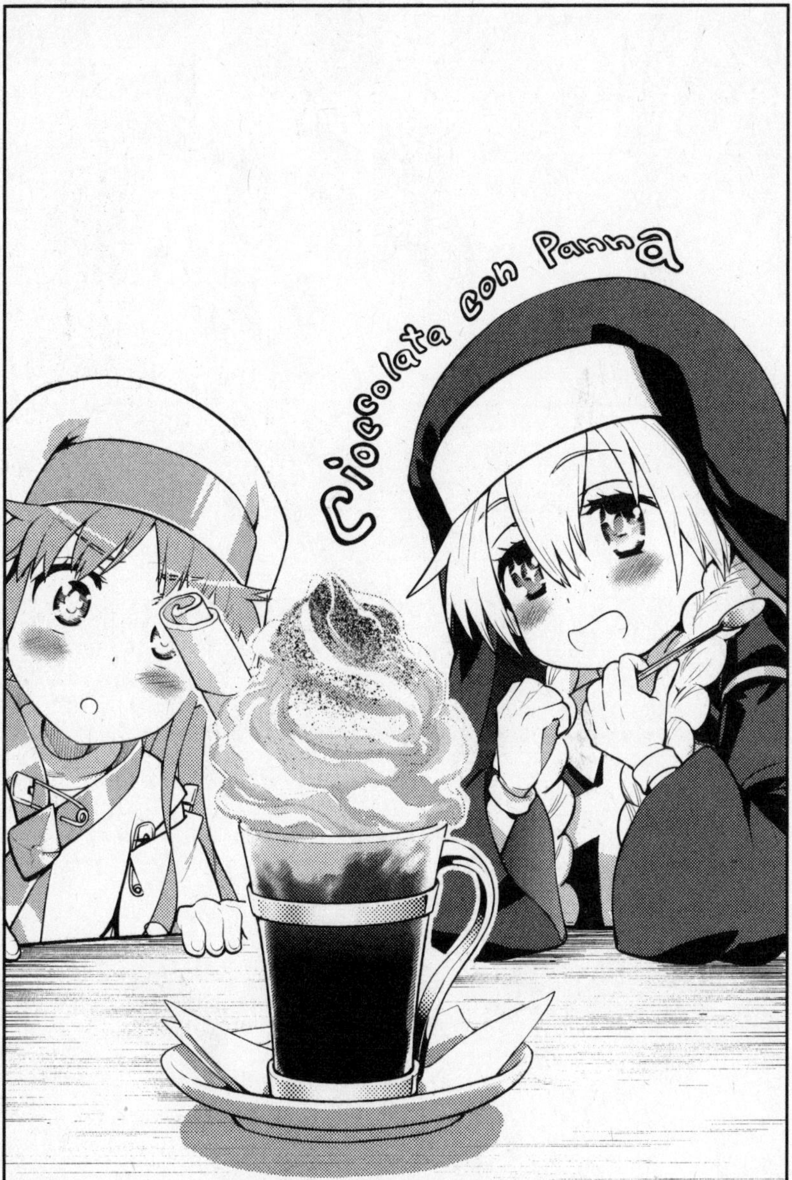
Cioccolata con Panna

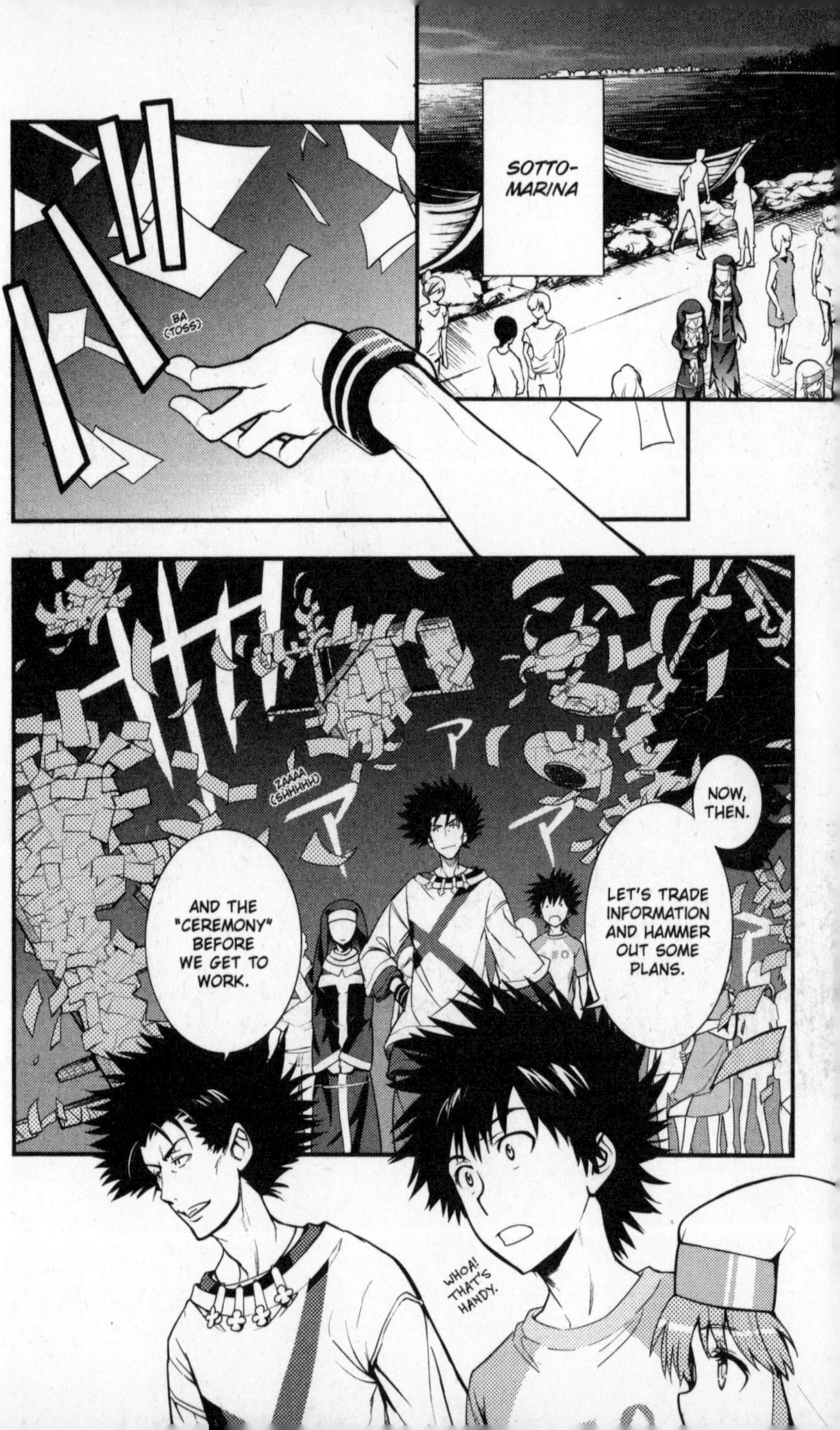
SOTTO-MARINA
BA (TOSS)
NOW, THEN.
LET'S TRADE INFORMATION AND HAMMER OUT SOME PLANS.
ZAAAA (SHHHHH)
AND THE "CEREMONY" BEFORE WE GET TO WORK.
WHOA! THAT'S HANDY.

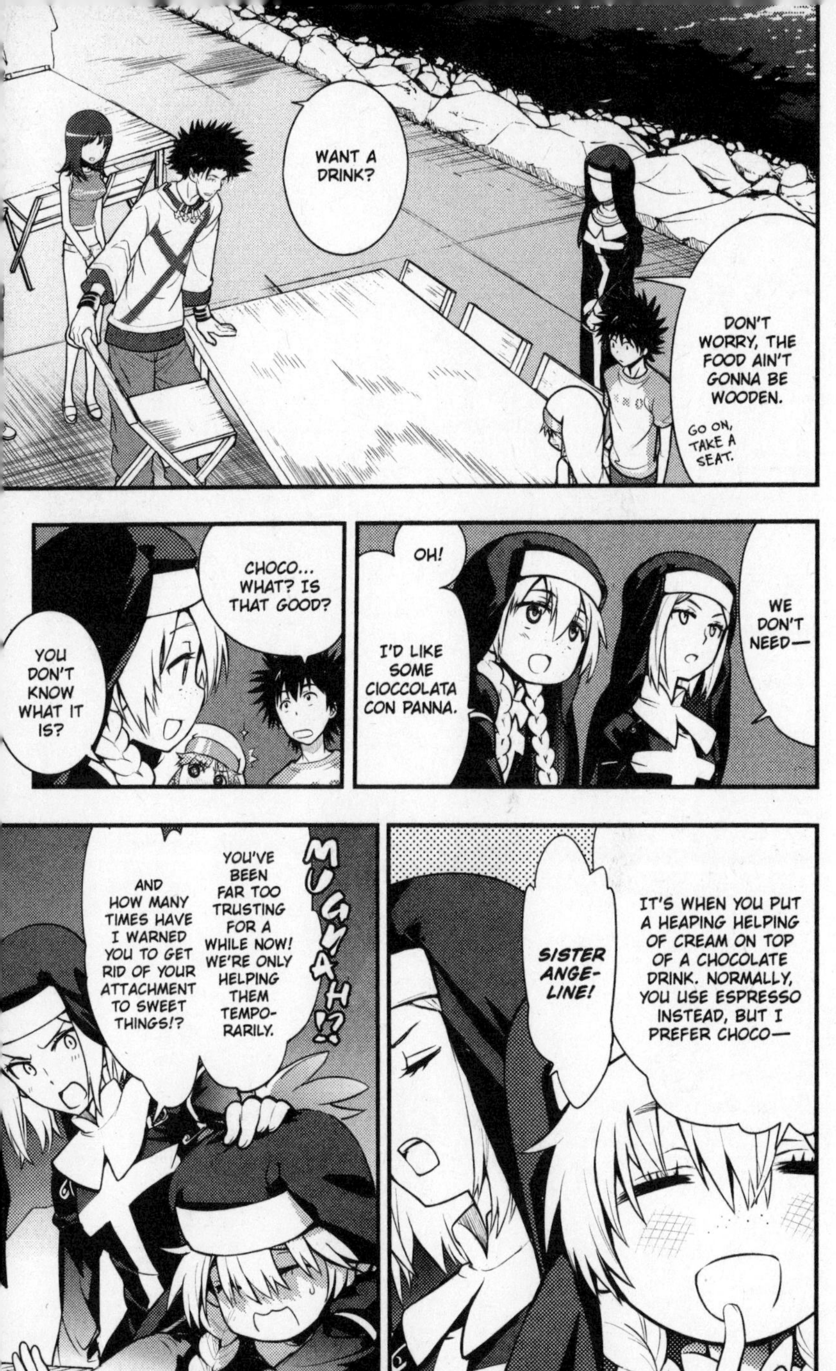
DON'T WORRY, THE FOOD AIN'T GONNA BE WOODEN.
GO ON, TAKE A SEAT.
WANT A DRINK?
WE DON'T NEED—
OH!
I'D LIKE SOME CIOCCOLATA CON PANNA.
CHOCO... WHAT? IS THAT GOOD?
YOU DON'T KNOW WHAT IT IS?
IT'S WHEN YOU PUT A HEAPING HELPING OF CREAM ON TOP OF A CHOCOLATE DRINK. NORMALLY, YOU USE ESPRESSO INSTEAD, BUT I PREFER CHOCO—
SISTER ANGE-LINE!
MUGYAH!?
YOU'VE BEEN FAR TOO TRUSTING FOR A WHILE NOW! WE'RE ONLY HELPING THEM TEMPO-RARILY.
AND HOW MANY TIMES HAVE I WARNED YOU TO GET RID OF YOUR ATTACHMENT TO SWEET THINGS!?

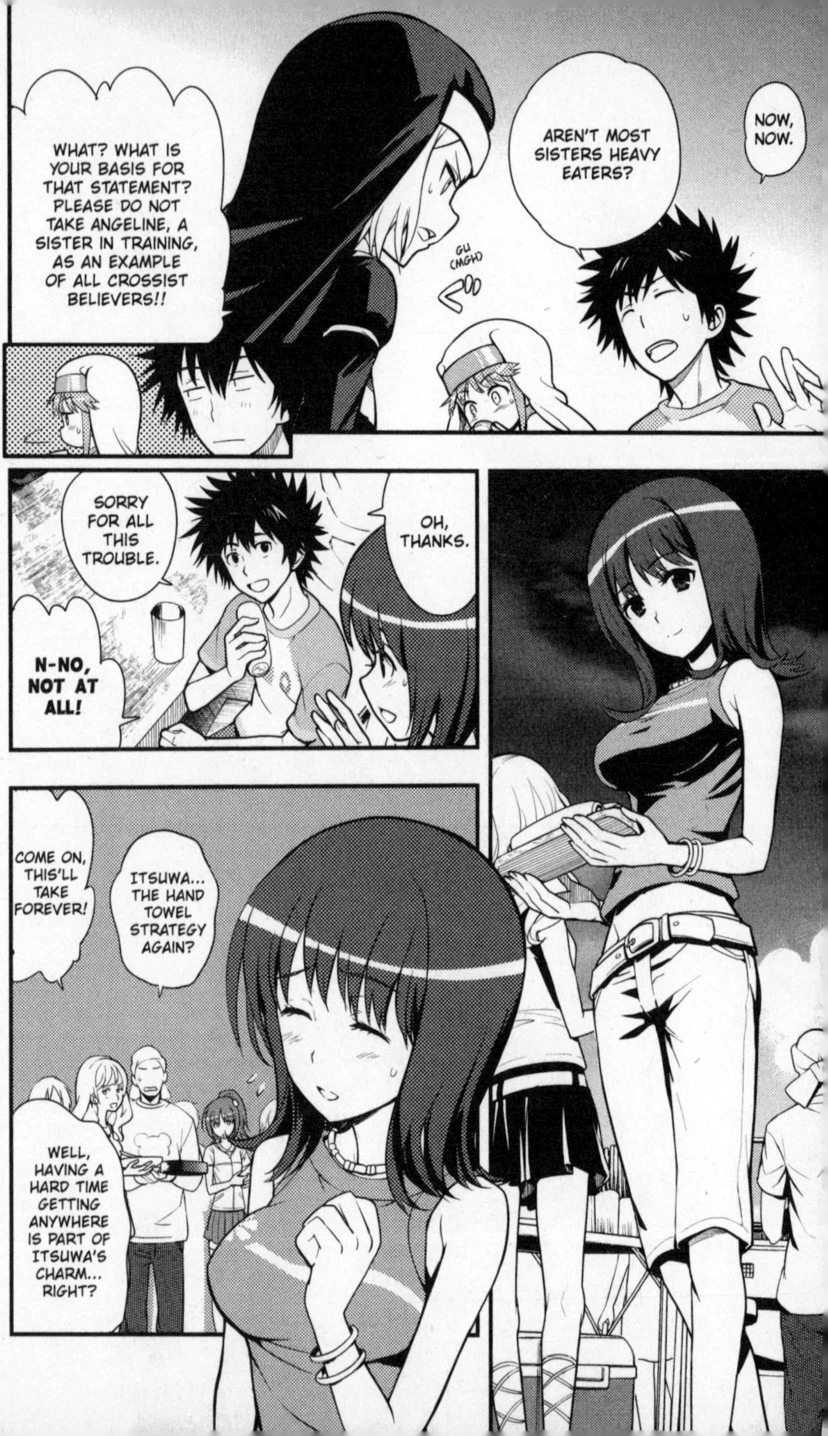
NOW, NOW.
AREN'T MOST SISTERS HEAVY EATERS?
GU (MGH)
WHAT? WHAT IS YOUR BASIS FOR THAT STATEMENT? PLEASE DO NOT TAKE ANGELINE, A SISTER IN TRAINING, AS AN EXAMPLE OF ALL CROSSIST BELIEVERS!!
OH, THANKS.
SORRY FOR ALL THIS TROUBLE.
N-NO, NOT AT ALL!
ITSUWA... THE HAND TOWEL STRATEGY AGAIN?
COME ON, THIS'LL TAKE FOREVER!
WELL, HAVING A HARD TIME GETTING ANYWHERE IS PART OF ITSUWA'S CHARM... RIGHT?

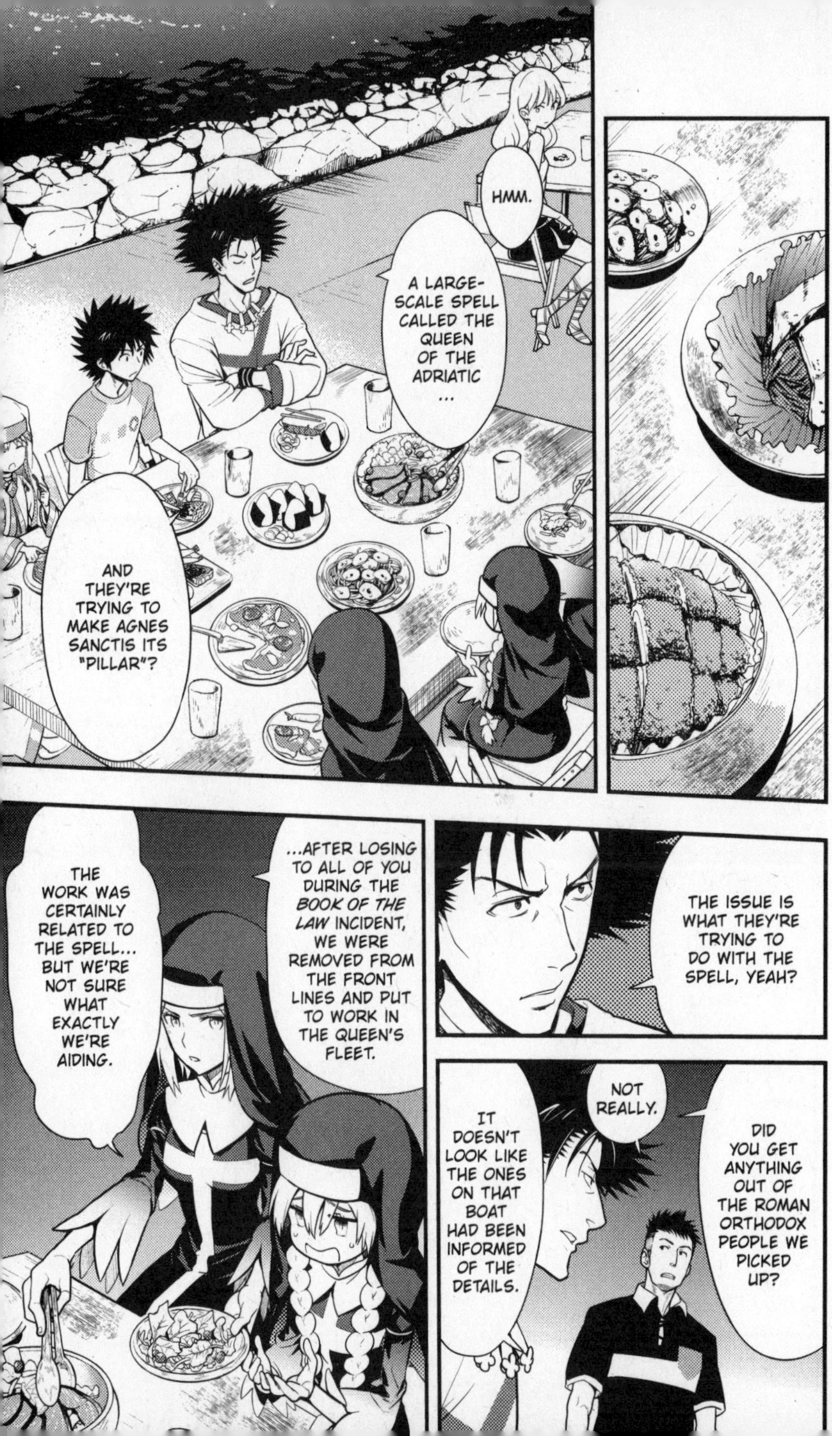
HMM.
A LARGE-SCALE SPELL CALLED THE QUEEN OF THE ADRIATIC ...
AND THEY'RE TRYING TO MAKE AGNES SANCTIS ITS "PILLAR"?
THE ISSUE IS WHAT THEY'RE TRYING TO DO WITH THE SPELL, YEAH?
DID YOU GET ANYTHING OUT OF THE ROMAN ORTHODOX PEOPLE WE PICKED UP?
NOT REALLY.
IT DOESN'T LOOK LIKE THE ONES ON THAT BOAT HAD BEEN INFORMED OF THE DETAILS.
...AFTER LOSING TO ALL OF YOU DURING THE *BOOK OF THE LAW* INCIDENT, WE WERE REMOVED FROM THE FRONT LINES AND PUT TO WORK IN THE QUEEN'S FLEET.
THE WORK WAS CERTAINLY RELATED TO THE SPELL... BUT WE'RE NOT SURE WHAT EXACTLY WE'RE AIDING.

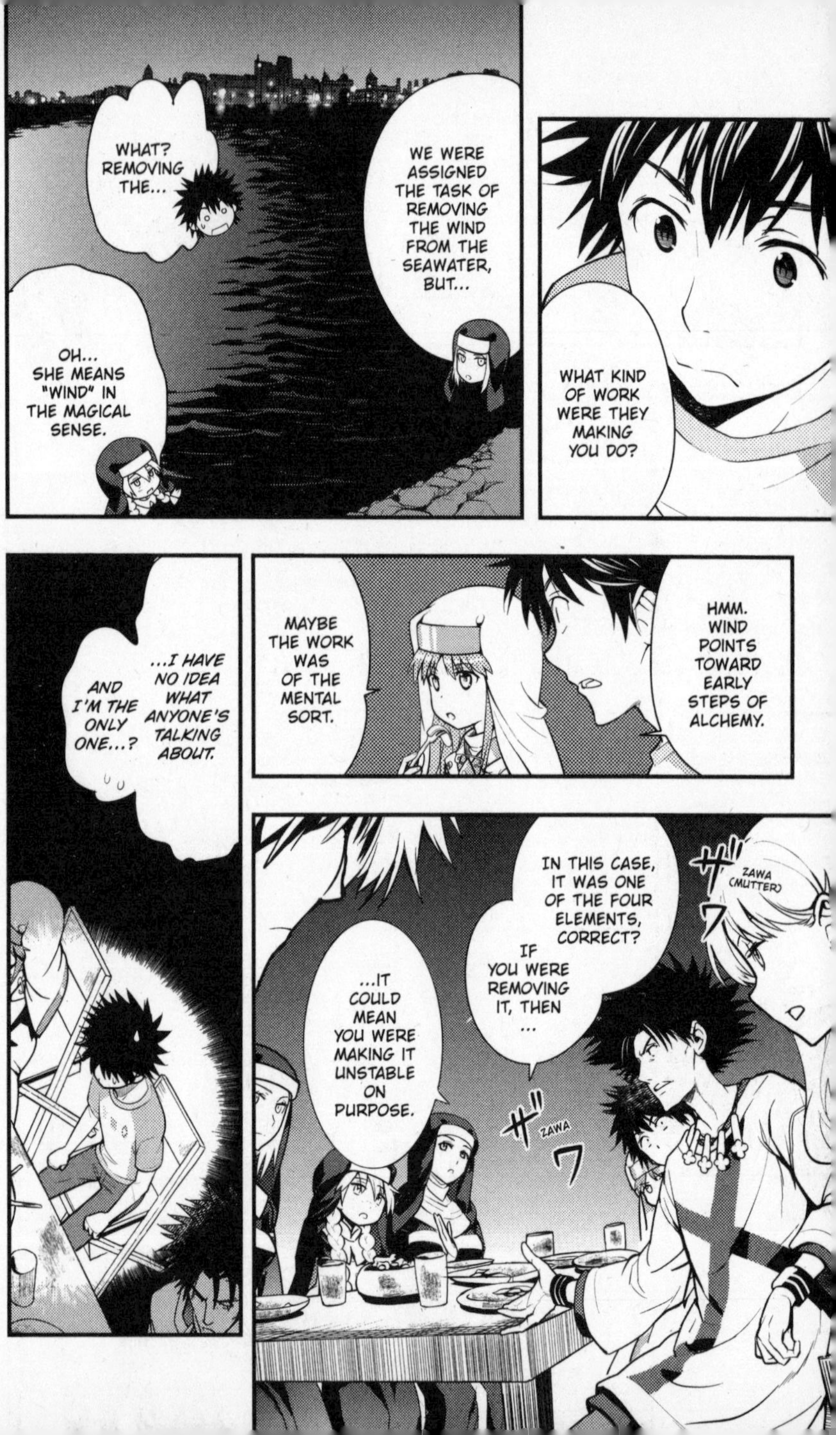
WHAT KIND OF WORK WERE THEY MAKING YOU DO?
WE WERE ASSIGNED THE TASK OF REMOVING THE WIND FROM THE SEAWATER, BUT...
WHAT? REMOVING THE...
OH... SHE MEANS "WIND" IN THE MAGICAL SENSE.
HMM. WIND POINTS TOWARD EARLY STEPS OF ALCHEMY.
MAYBE THE WORK WAS OF THE MENTAL SORT.
ZAWA (MUTTER)
IN THIS CASE, IT WAS ONE OF THE FOUR ELEMENTS, CORRECT?
IF YOU WERE REMOVING IT, THEN ...
...IT COULD MEAN YOU WERE MAKING IT UNSTABLE ON PURPOSE.
ZAWA
...I HAVE NO IDEA WHAT ANYONE'S TALKING ABOUT.
AND I'M THE ONLY ONE...?

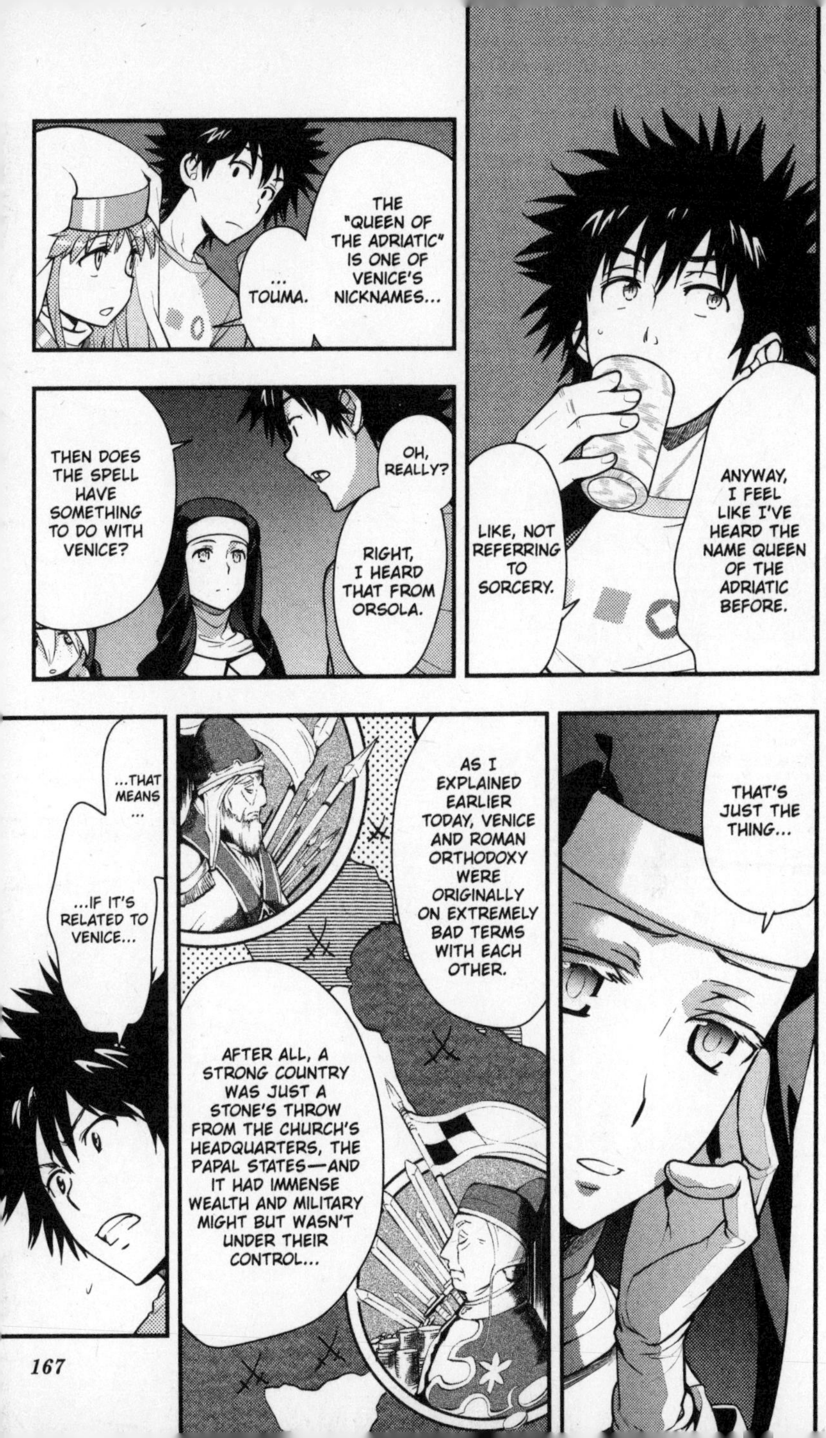
ANYWAY, I FEEL LIKE I'VE HEARD THE NAME QUEEN OF THE ADRIATIC BEFORE.
LIKE, NOT REFERRING TO SORCERY.
THE "QUEEN OF THE ADRIATIC" IS ONE OF VENICE'S NICKNAMES...
... TOUMA.
OH, REALLY?
RIGHT, I HEARD THAT FROM ORSOLA.
THEN DOES THE SPELL HAVE SOMETHING TO DO WITH VENICE?
THAT'S JUST THE THING...
AS I EXPLAINED EARLIER TODAY, VENICE AND ROMAN ORTHODOXY WERE ORIGINALLY ON EXTREMELY BAD TERMS WITH EACH OTHER.
AFTER ALL, A STRONG COUNTRY WAS JUST A STONE'S THROW FROM THE CHURCH'S HEADQUARTERS, THE PAPAL STATES—AND IT HAD IMMENSE WEALTH AND MILITARY MIGHT BUT WASN'T UNDER THEIR CONTROL...
...THAT MEANS ...
...IF IT'S RELATED TO VENICE...

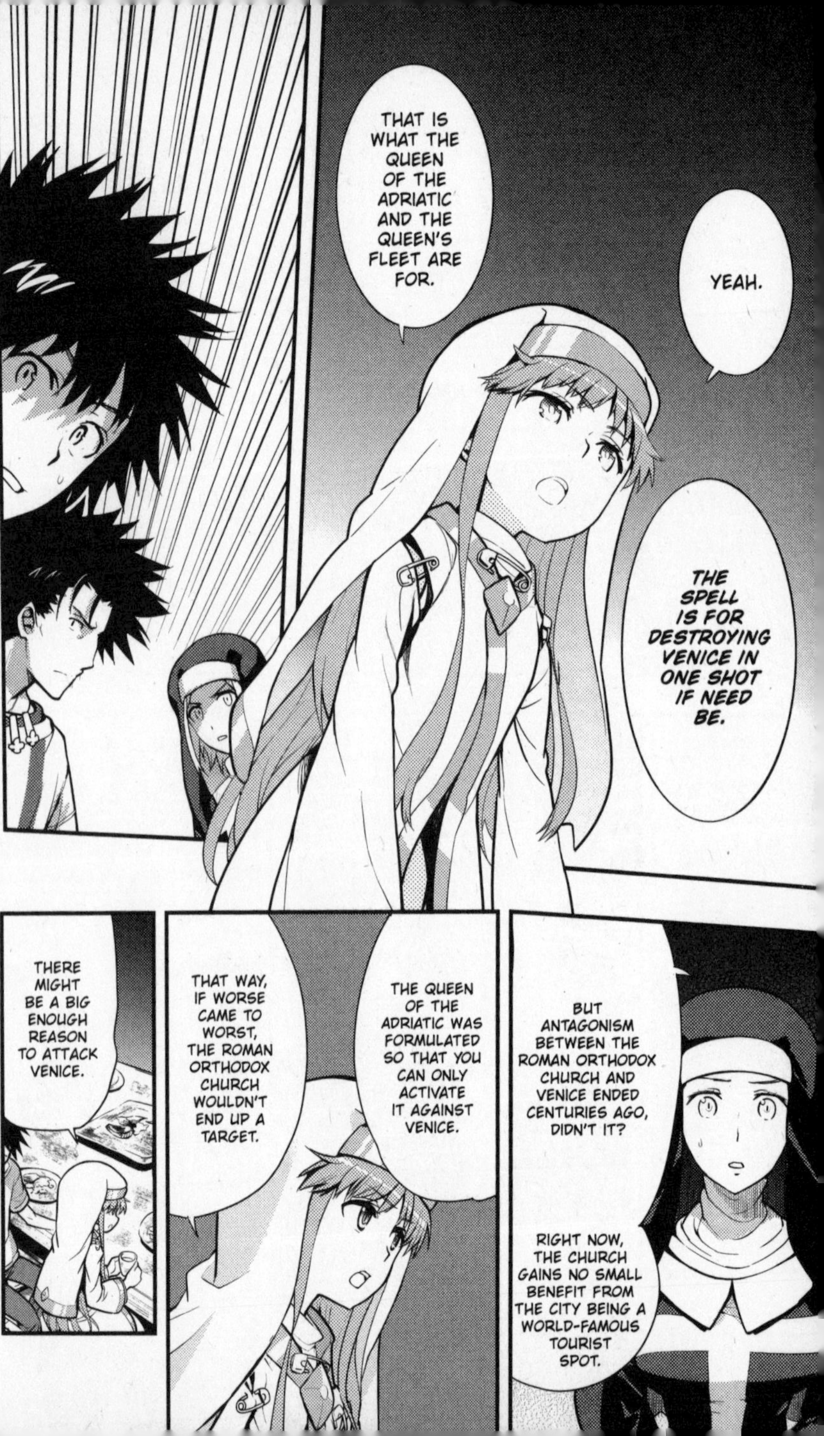
YEAH.
THAT IS WHAT THE QUEEN OF THE ADRIATIC AND THE QUEEN'S FLEET ARE FOR.
*THE SPELL IS FOR DESTROYING VENICE IN ONE SHOT IF NEED BE.*
BUT ANTAGONISM BETWEEN THE ROMAN ORTHODOX CHURCH AND VENICE ENDED CENTURIES AGO, DIDN'T IT?
RIGHT NOW, THE CHURCH GAINS NO SMALL BENEFIT FROM THE CITY BEING A WORLD-FAMOUS TOURIST SPOT.
THE QUEEN OF THE ADRIATIC WAS FORMULATED SO THAT YOU CAN ONLY ACTIVATE IT AGAINST VENICE.
THAT WAY, IF WORSE CAME TO WORST, THE ROMAN ORTHODOX CHURCH WOULDN'T END UP A TARGET.
THERE MIGHT BE A BIG ENOUGH REASON TO ATTACK VENICE.

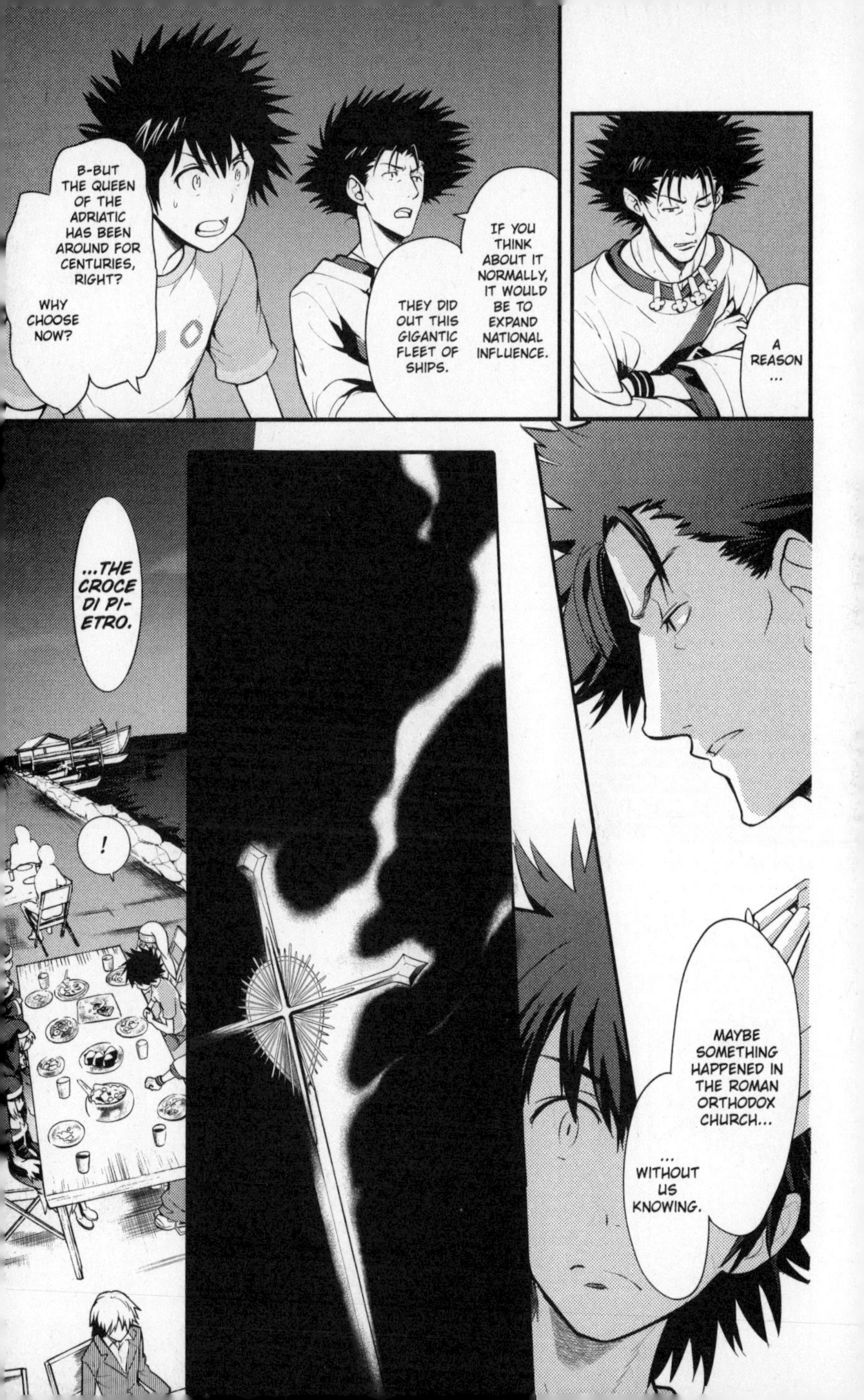
A REASON ...
IF YOU THINK ABOUT IT NORMALLY, IT WOULD BE TO EXPAND NATIONAL INFLUENCE.
THEY DID OUT THIS GIGANTIC FLEET OF SHIPS.
B-BUT THE QUEEN OF THE ADRIATIC HAS BEEN AROUND FOR CENTURIES, RIGHT?
WHY CHOOSE NOW?
MAYBE SOMETHING HAPPENED IN THE ROMAN ORTHODOX CHURCH...
... WITHOUT US KNOWING.
...THE CROCE DI PIETRO.
!

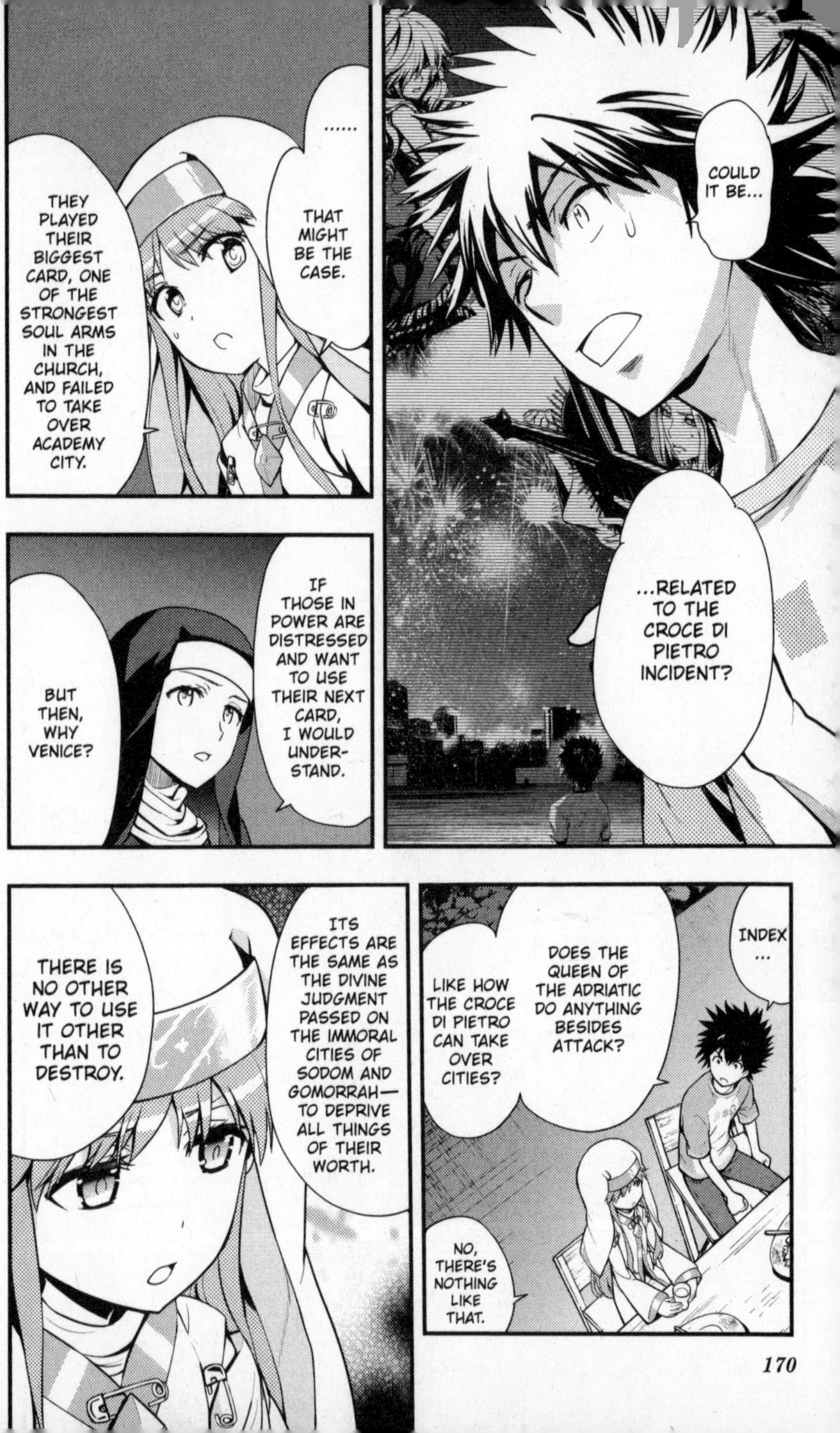
COULD IT BE...
...RELATED TO THE CROCE DI PIETRO INCIDENT?
......
THAT MIGHT BE THE CASE.
THEY PLAYED THEIR BIGGEST CARD, ONE OF THE STRONGEST SOUL ARMS IN THE CHURCH, AND FAILED TO TAKE OVER ACADEMY CITY.
IF THOSE IN POWER ARE DISTRESSED AND WANT TO USE THEIR NEXT CARD, I WOULD UNDER-STAND.
BUT THEN, WHY VENICE?
INDEX...
DOES THE QUEEN OF THE ADRIATIC DO ANYTHING BESIDES ATTACK?
LIKE HOW THE CROCE DI PIETRO CAN TAKE OVER CITIES?
NO, THERE'S NOTHING LIKE THAT.
ITS EFFECTS ARE THE SAME AS THE DIVINE JUDGMENT PASSED ON THE IMMORAL CITIES OF SODOM AND GOMORRAH— TO DEPRIVE ALL THINGS OF THEIR WORTH.
THERE IS NO OTHER WAY TO USE IT OTHER THAN TO DESTROY.

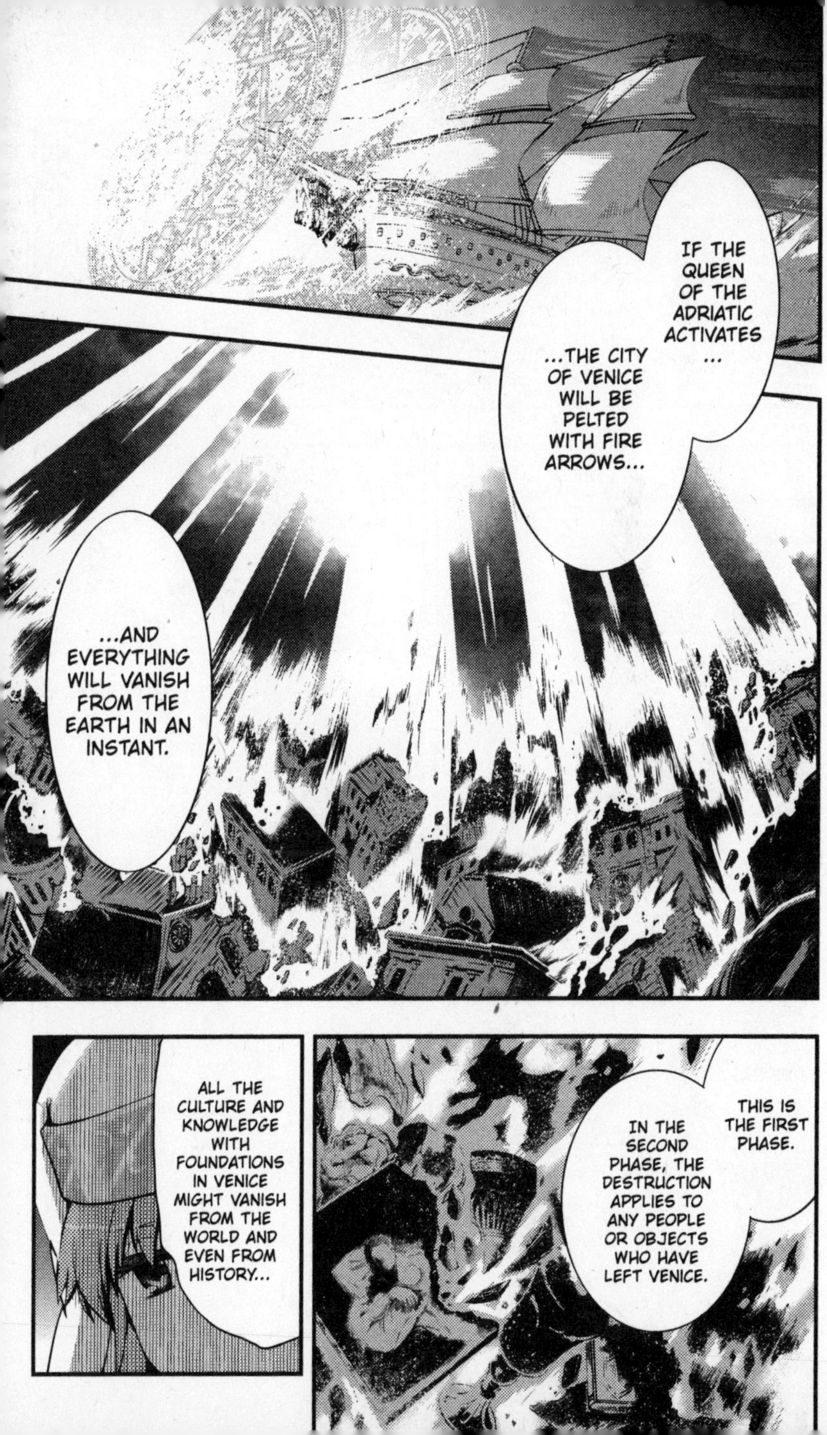
IF THE QUEEN OF THE ADRIATIC ACTIVATES ...
...THE CITY OF VENICE WILL BE PELTED WITH FIRE ARROWS...
...AND EVERYTHING WILL VANISH FROM THE EARTH IN AN INSTANT.
THIS IS THE FIRST PHASE.
IN THE SECOND PHASE, THE DESTRUCTION APPLIES TO ANY PEOPLE OR OBJECTS WHO HAVE LEFT VENICE.
ALL THE CULTURE AND KNOWLEDGE WITH FOUNDATIONS IN VENICE MIGHT VANISH FROM THE WORLD AND EVEN FROM HISTORY...

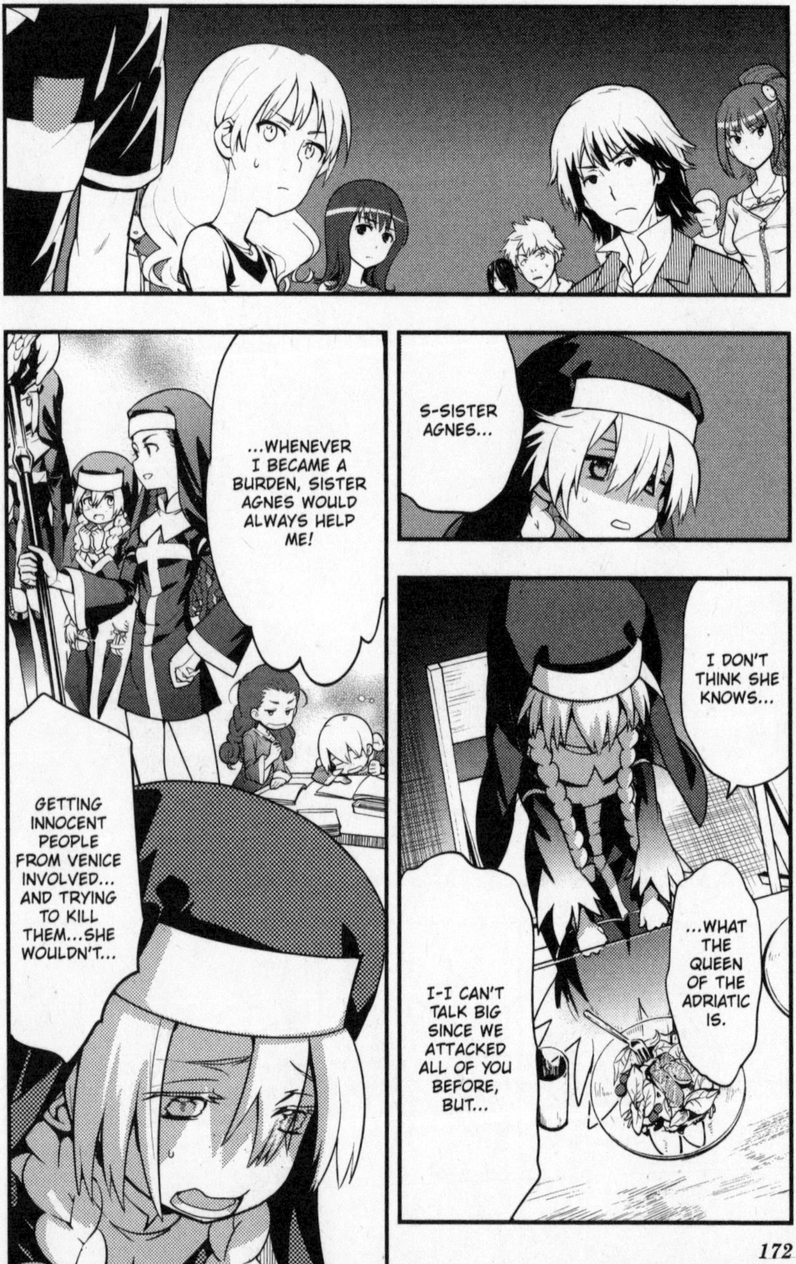
S-SISTER AGNES...
I DON'T THINK SHE KNOWS...
...WHAT THE QUEEN OF THE ADRIATIC IS.
I-I CAN'T TALK BIG SINCE WE ATTACKED ALL OF YOU BEFORE, BUT...
...WHENEVER I BECAME A BURDEN, SISTER AGNES WOULD ALWAYS HELP ME!
GETTING INNOCENT PEOPLE FROM VENICE INVOLVED... AND TRYING TO KILL THEM...SHE WOULDN'T...

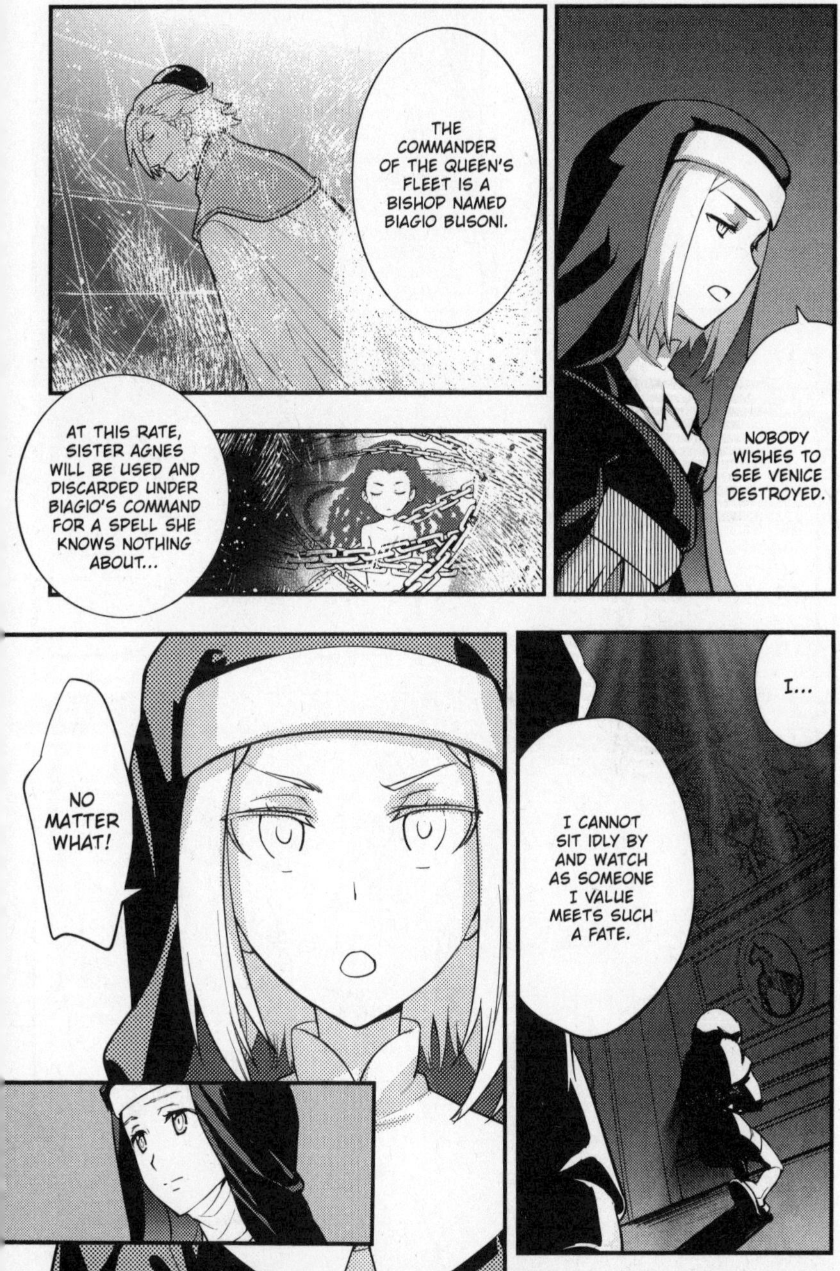
NOBODY WISHES TO SEE VENICE DESTROYED.
THE COMMANDER OF THE QUEEN'S FLEET IS A BISHOP NAMED BIAGIO BUSONI.
AT THIS RATE, SISTER AGNES WILL BE USED AND DISCARDED UNDER BIAGIO'S COMMAND FOR A SPELL SHE KNOWS NOTHING ABOUT...
I...
I CANNOT SIT IDLY BY AND WATCH AS SOMEONE I VALUE MEETS SUCH A FATE.
NO MATTER WHAT!

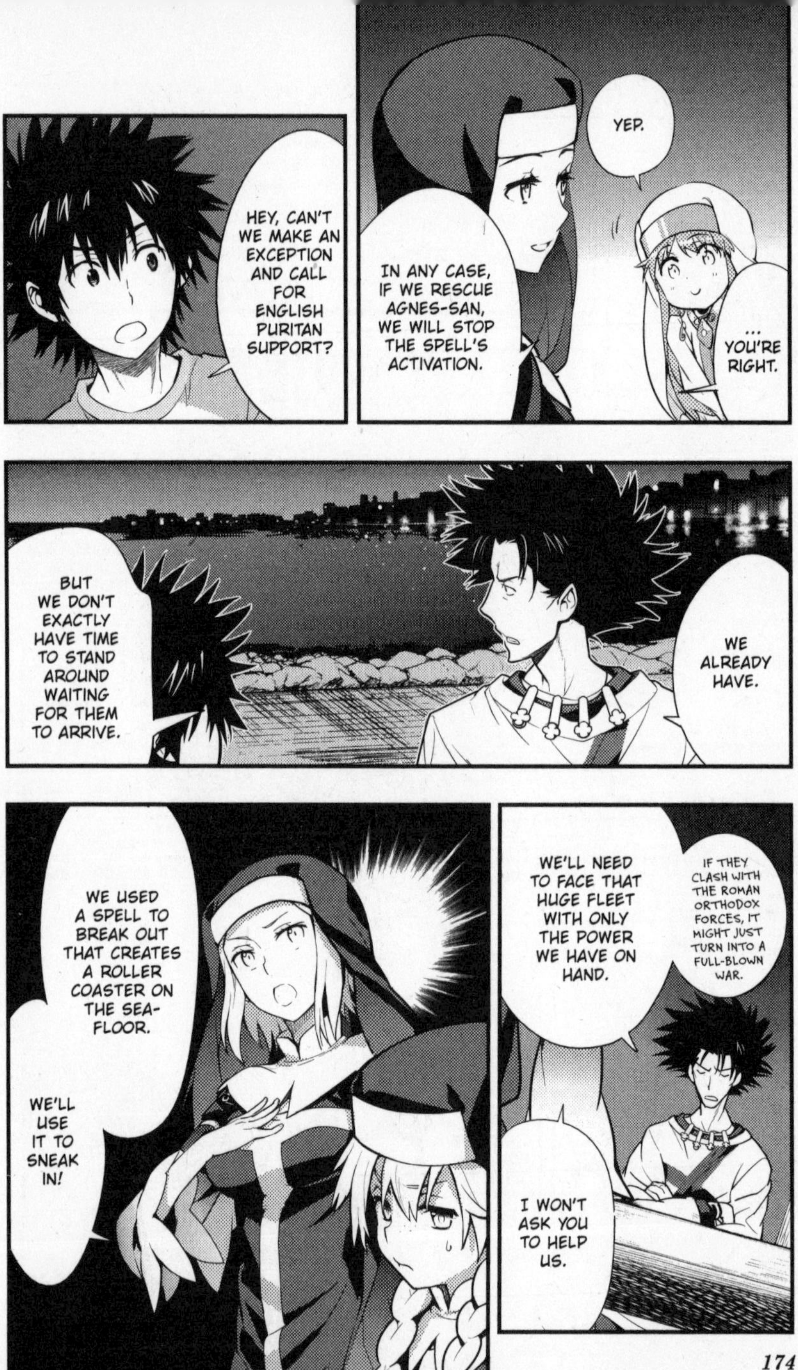
YEP.
IN ANY CASE, IF WE RESCUE AGNES-SAN, WE WILL STOP THE SPELL'S ACTIVATION.
... YOU'RE RIGHT.
HEY, CAN'T WE MAKE AN EXCEPTION AND CALL FOR ENGLISH PURITAN SUPPORT?
WE ALREADY HAVE.
BUT WE DON'T EXACTLY HAVE TIME TO STAND AROUND WAITING FOR THEM TO ARRIVE.
IF THEY CLASH WITH THE ROMAN ORTHODOX FORCES, IT MIGHT JUST TURN INTO A FULL-BLOWN WAR.
WE'LL NEED TO FACE THAT HUGE FLEET WITH ONLY THE POWER WE HAVE ON HAND.
I WON'T ASK YOU TO HELP US.
WE USED A SPELL TO BREAK OUT THAT CREATES A ROLLER COASTER ON THE SEA-FLOOR.
WE'LL USE IT TO SNEAK IN!

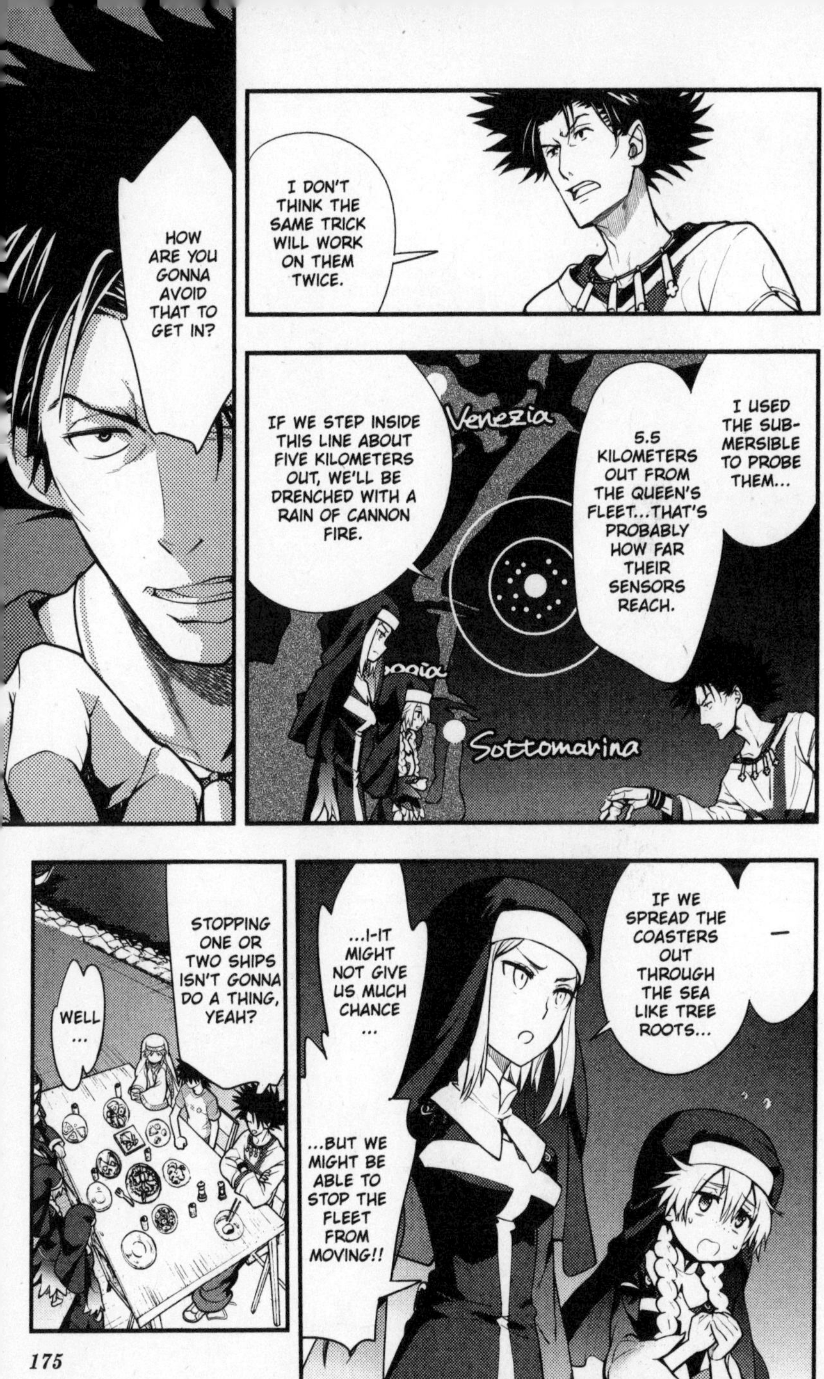
I DON'T THINK THE SAME TRICK WILL WORK ON THEM TWICE.
I USED THE SUBMERSIBLE TO PROBE THEM...
5.5 KILOMETERS OUT FROM THE QUEEN'S FLEET...THAT'S PROBABLY HOW FAR THEIR SENSORS REACH.
Venezia
IF WE STEP INSIDE THIS LINE ABOUT FIVE KILOMETERS OUT, WE'LL BE DRENCHED WITH A RAIN OF CANNON FIRE.
Sottomarina
HOW ARE YOU GONNA AVOID THAT TO GET IN?
—
IF WE SPREAD THE COASTERS OUT THROUGH THE SEA LIKE TREE ROOTS...
...I-IT MIGHT NOT GIVE US MUCH CHANCE...
...BUT WE MIGHT BE ABLE TO STOP THE FLEET FROM MOVING!!
STOPPING ONE OR TWO SHIPS ISN'T GONNA DO A THING, YEAH?
WELL...

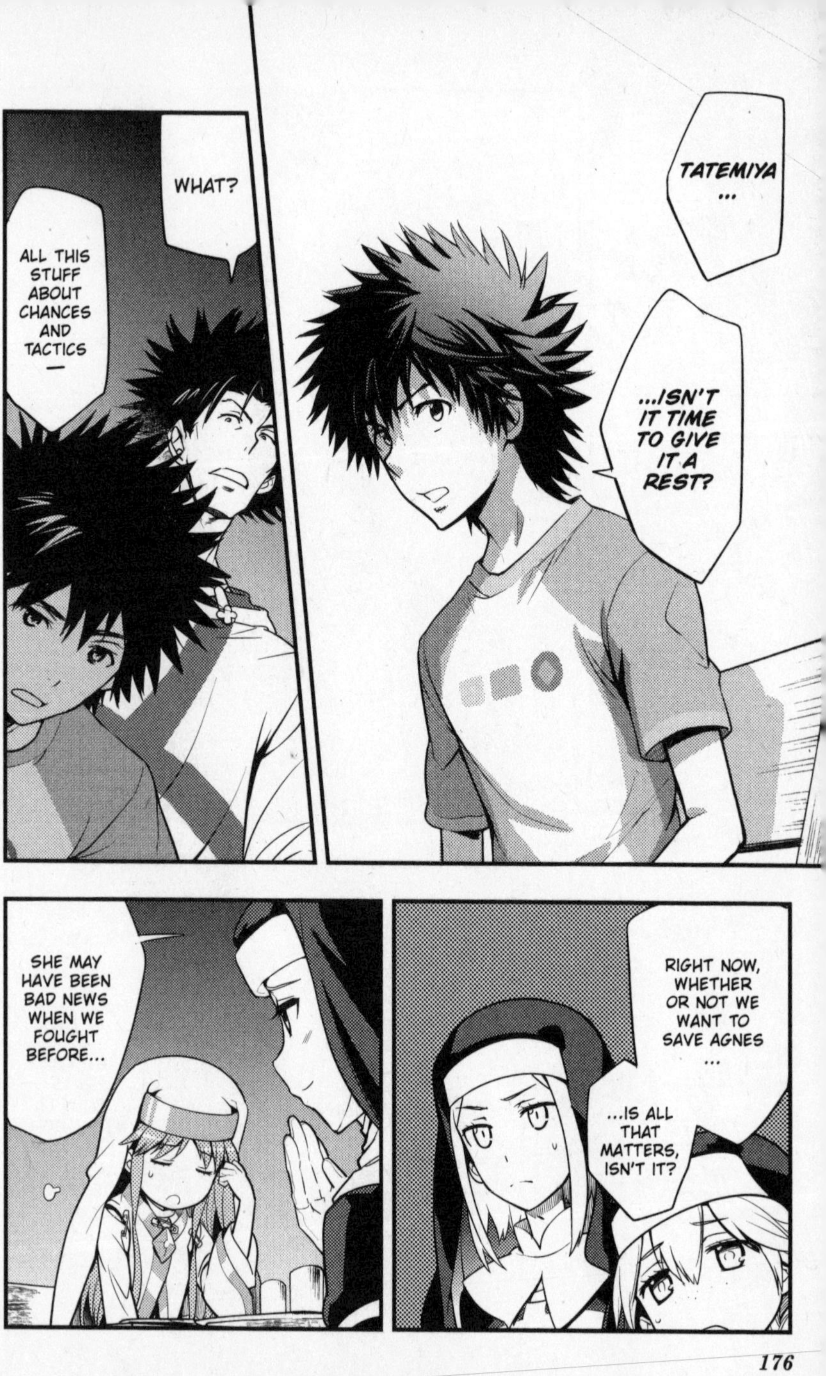
TATEMIYA ...
...ISN'T IT TIME TO GIVE IT A REST?
WHAT?
ALL THIS STUFF ABOUT CHANCES AND TACTICS —
RIGHT NOW, WHETHER OR NOT WE WANT TO SAVE AGNES ...
...IS ALL THAT MATTERS, ISN'T IT?
SHE MAY HAVE BEEN BAD NEWS WHEN WE FOUGHT BEFORE...

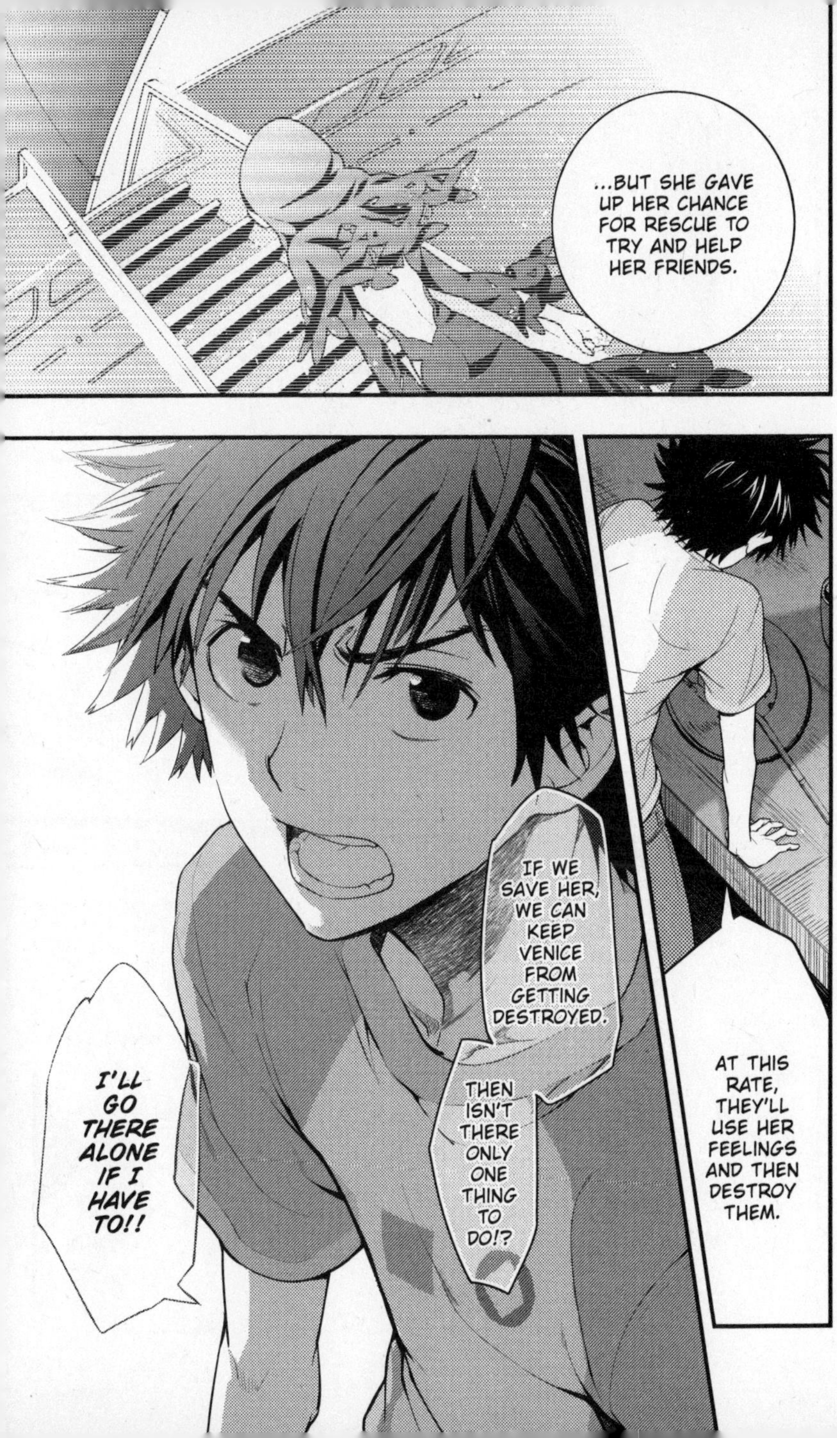
...BUT SHE GAVE UP HER CHANCE FOR RESCUE TO TRY AND HELP HER FRIENDS.
AT THIS RATE, THEY'LL USE HER FEELINGS AND THEN DESTROY THEM.
IF WE SAVE HER, WE CAN KEEP VENICE FROM GETTING DESTROYED.
THEN ISN'T THERE ONLY ONE THING TO DO!?
I'LL GO THERE ALONE IF I HAVE TO!!

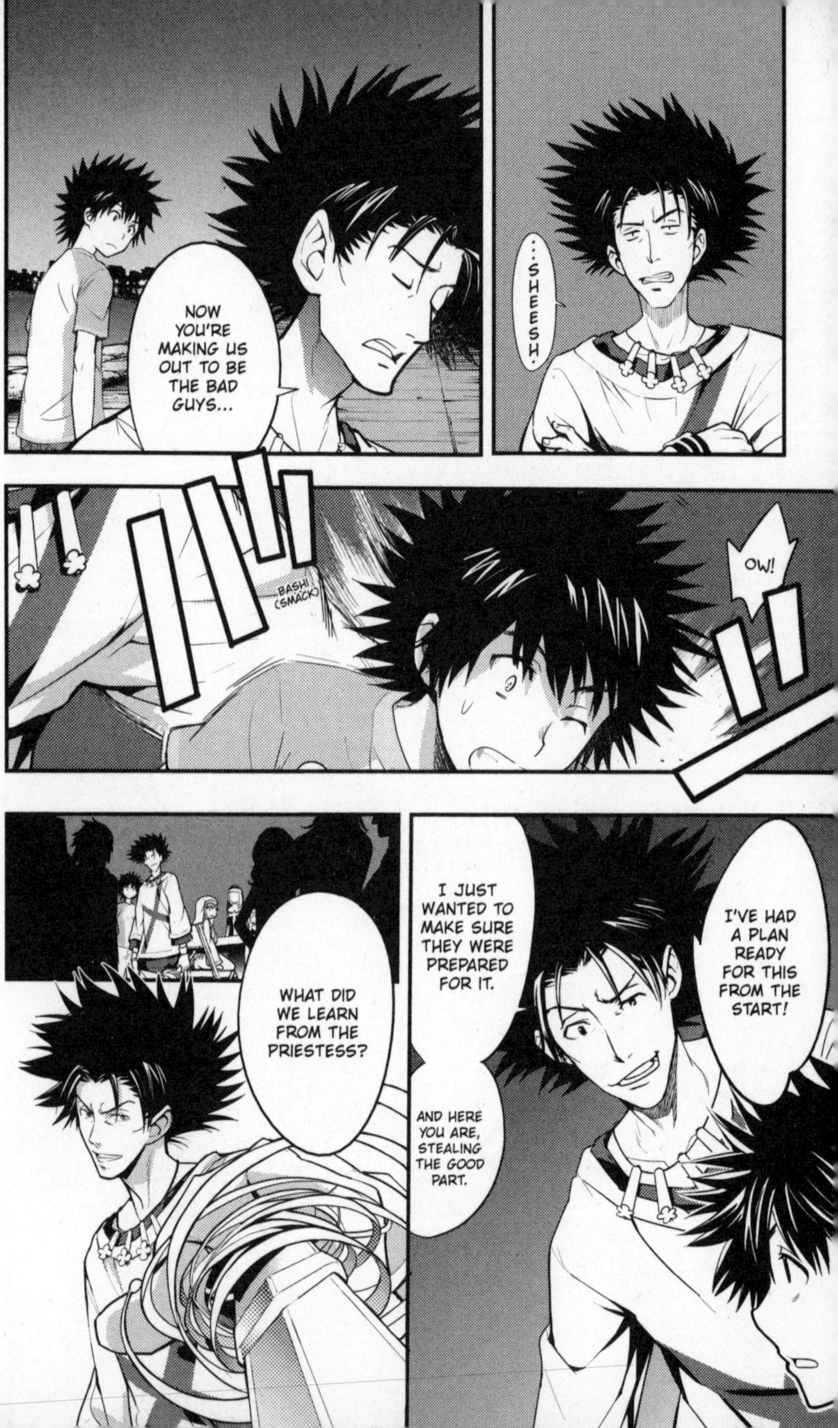
...SHEESH.
NOW YOU'RE MAKING US OUT TO BE THE BAD GUYS...
OW!
BASHI (SMACK)
I'VE HAD A PLAN READY FOR THIS FROM THE START!
I JUST WANTED TO MAKE SURE THEY WERE PREPARED FOR IT.
AND HERE YOU ARE, STEALING THE GOOD PART.
WHAT DID WE LEARN FROM THE PRIESTESS?

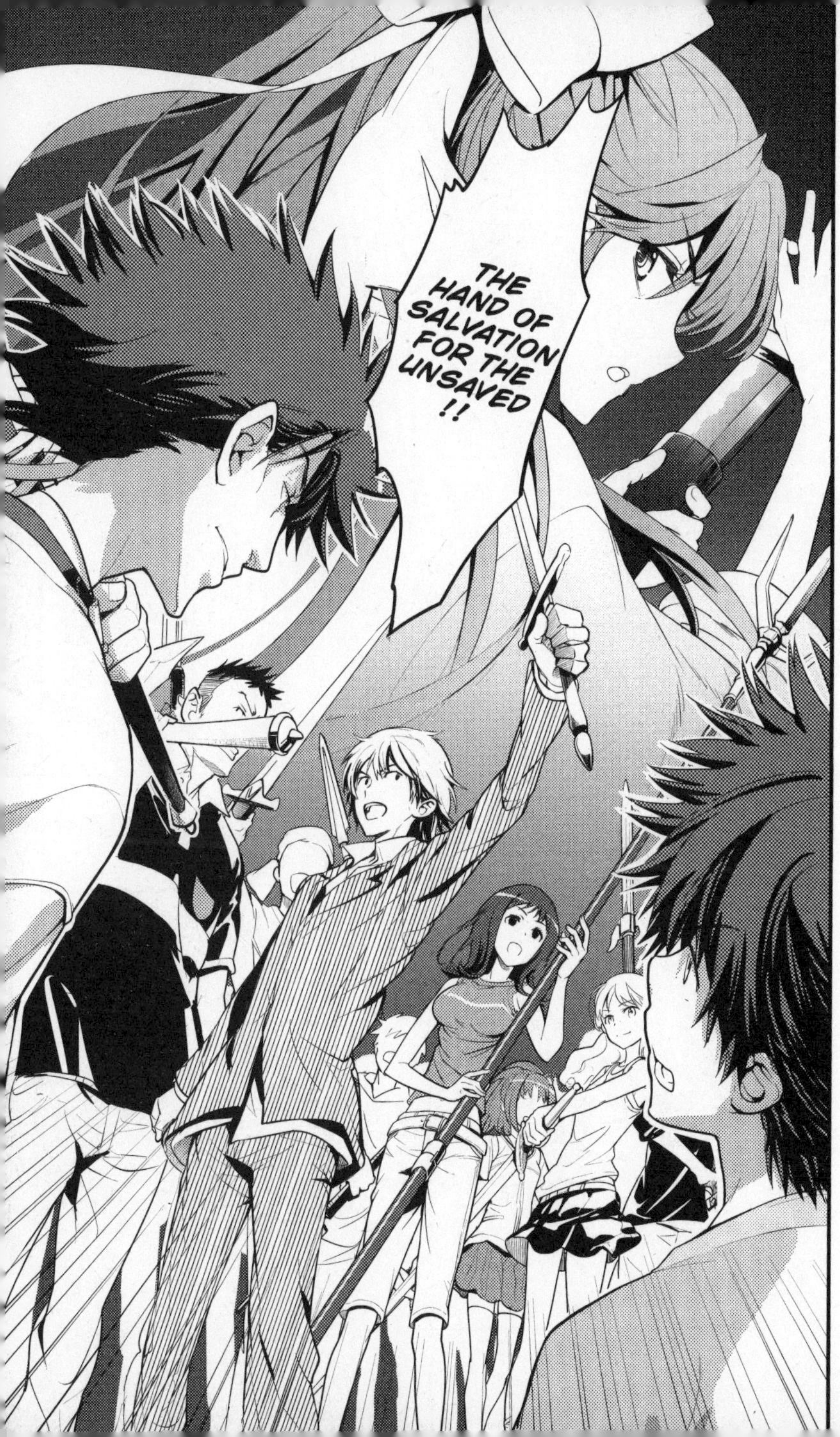
THE HAND OF SALVATION FOR THE UNSAVED !!

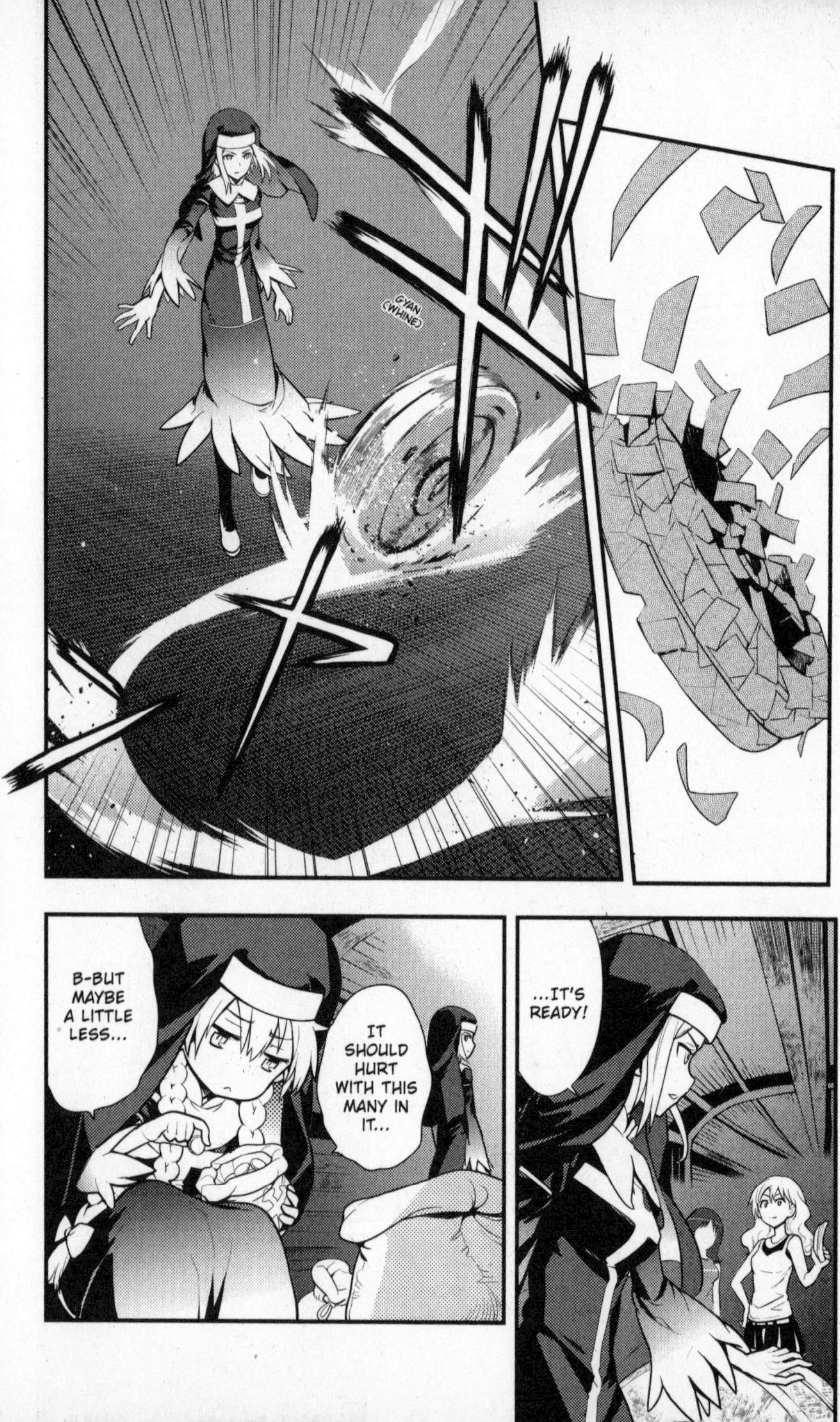
GYAN (WHINE)
...IT'S READY!
IT SHOULD HURT WITH THIS MANY IN IT...
B-BUT MAYBE A LITTLE LESS...

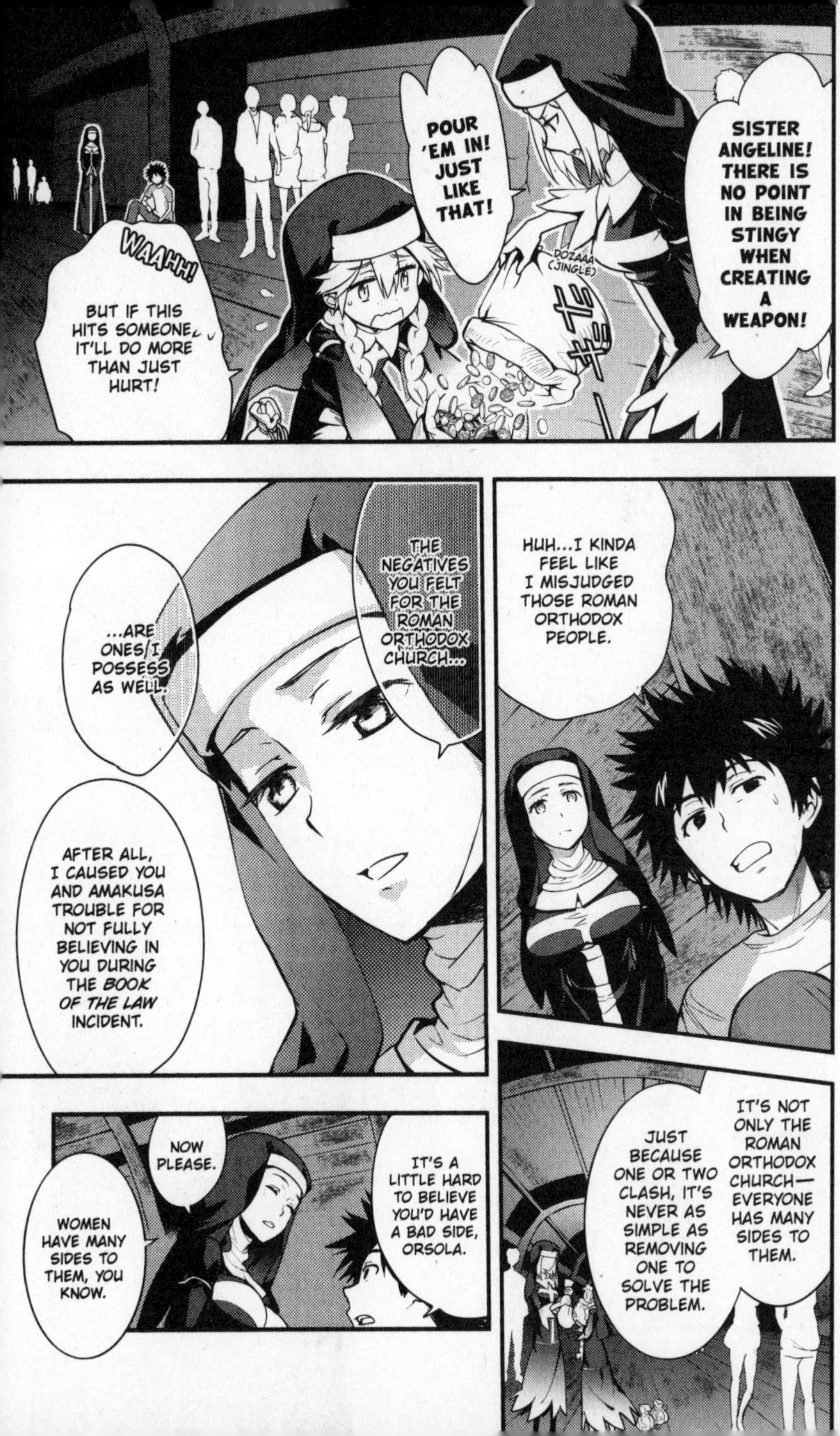
SISTER ANGELINE! THERE IS NO POINT IN BEING STINGY WHEN CREATING A WEAPON!
POUR 'EM IN! JUST LIKE THAT!
DOZAAA (JINGLE)
WAAHH!
BUT IF THIS HITS SOMEONE, IT'LL DO MORE THAN JUST HURT!
HUH...I KINDA FEEL LIKE I MISJUDGED THOSE ROMAN ORTHODOX PEOPLE.
THE NEGATIVES YOU FELT FOR THE ROMAN ORTHODOX CHURCH...
...ARE ONES I POSSESS AS WELL.
AFTER ALL, I CAUSED YOU AND AMAKUSA TROUBLE FOR NOT FULLY BELIEVING IN YOU DURING THE *BOOK OF THE LAW* INCIDENT.
IT'S NOT ONLY THE ROMAN ORTHODOX CHURCH—EVERYONE HAS MANY SIDES TO THEM.
JUST BECAUSE ONE OR TWO CLASH, IT'S NEVER AS SIMPLE AS REMOVING ONE TO SOLVE THE PROBLEM.
IT'S A LITTLE HARD TO BELIEVE YOU'D HAVE A BAD SIDE, ORSOLA.
NOW PLEASE.
WOMEN HAVE MANY SIDES TO THEM, YOU KNOW.

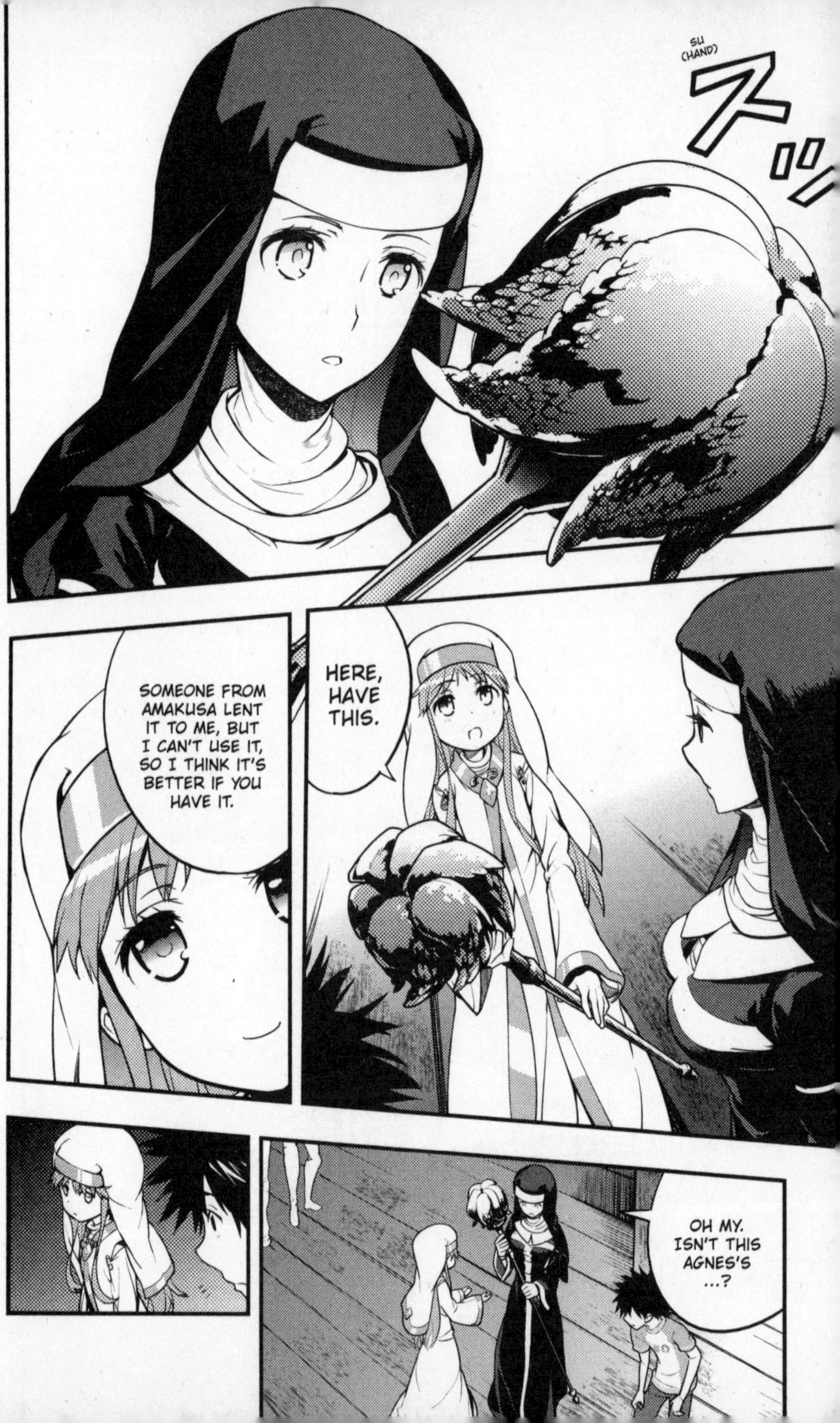
SU (HAND)
HERE, HAVE THIS.
SOMEONE FROM AMAKUSA LENT IT TO ME, BUT I CAN'T USE IT, SO I THINK IT'S BETTER IF YOU HAVE IT.
OH MY. ISN'T THIS AGNES'S ...?

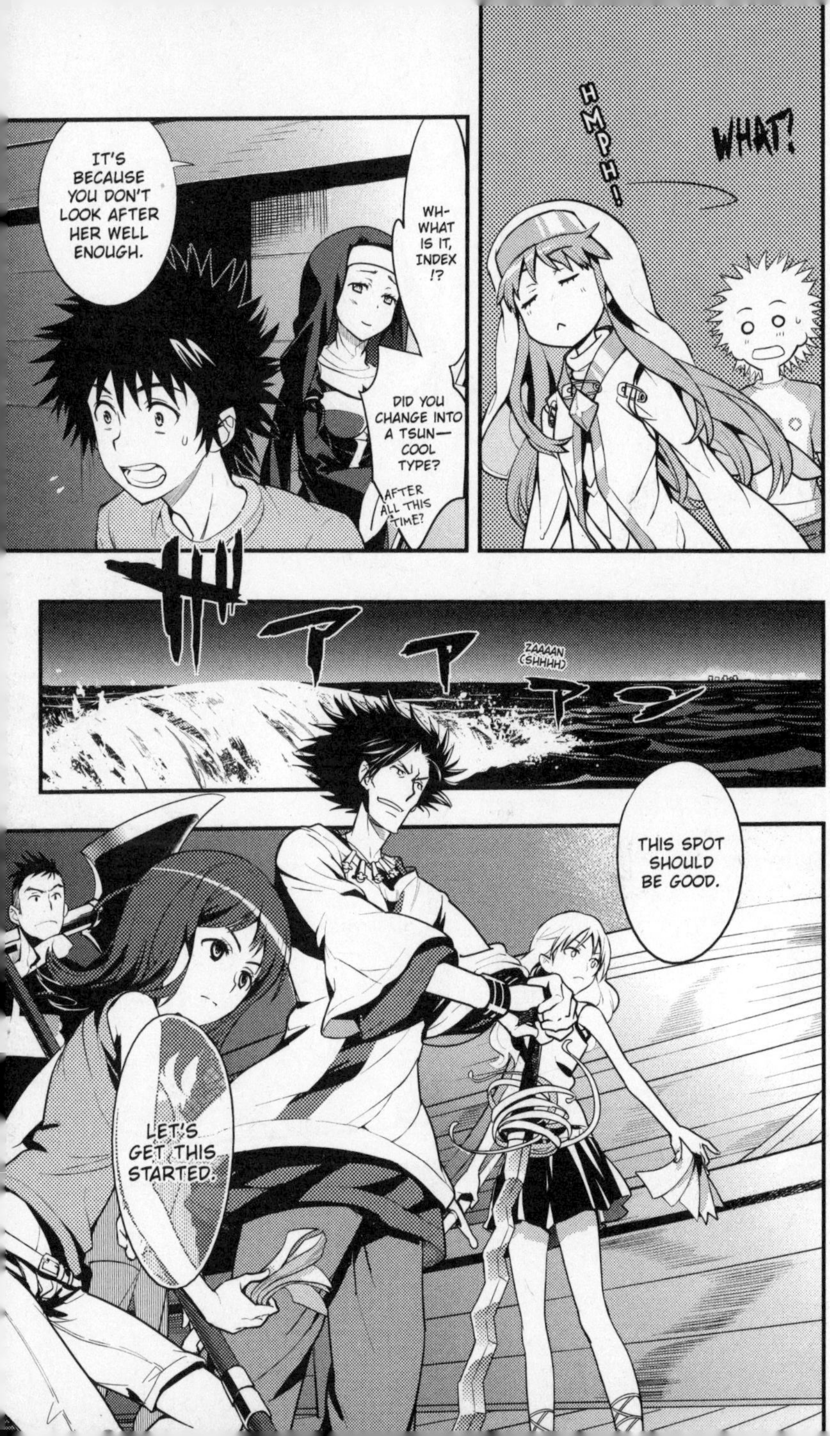
HMPH!
WHAT!
WH-WHAT IS IT, INDEX!?
DID YOU CHANGE INTO A TSUN—COOL TYPE?
AFTER ALL THIS TIME?
IT'S BECAUSE YOU DON'T LOOK AFTER HER WELL ENOUGH.
ZAAAAN (SHHHH)
THIS SPOT SHOULD BE GOOD.
LET'S GET THIS STARTED.

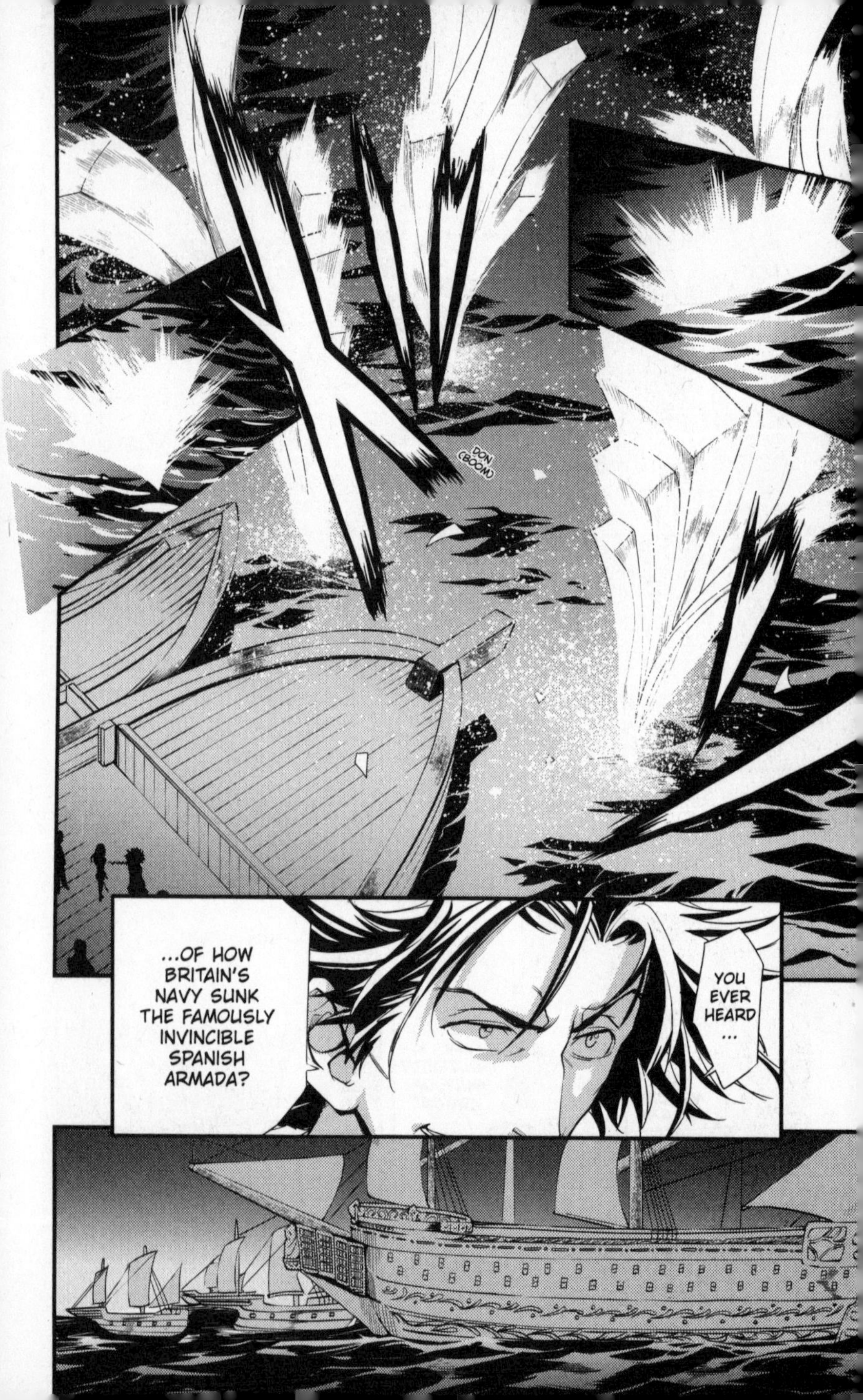
DON (BOOM)
YOU EVER HEARD ...
...OF HOW BRITAIN'S NAVY SUNK THE FAMOUSLY INVINCIBLE SPANISH ARMADA?

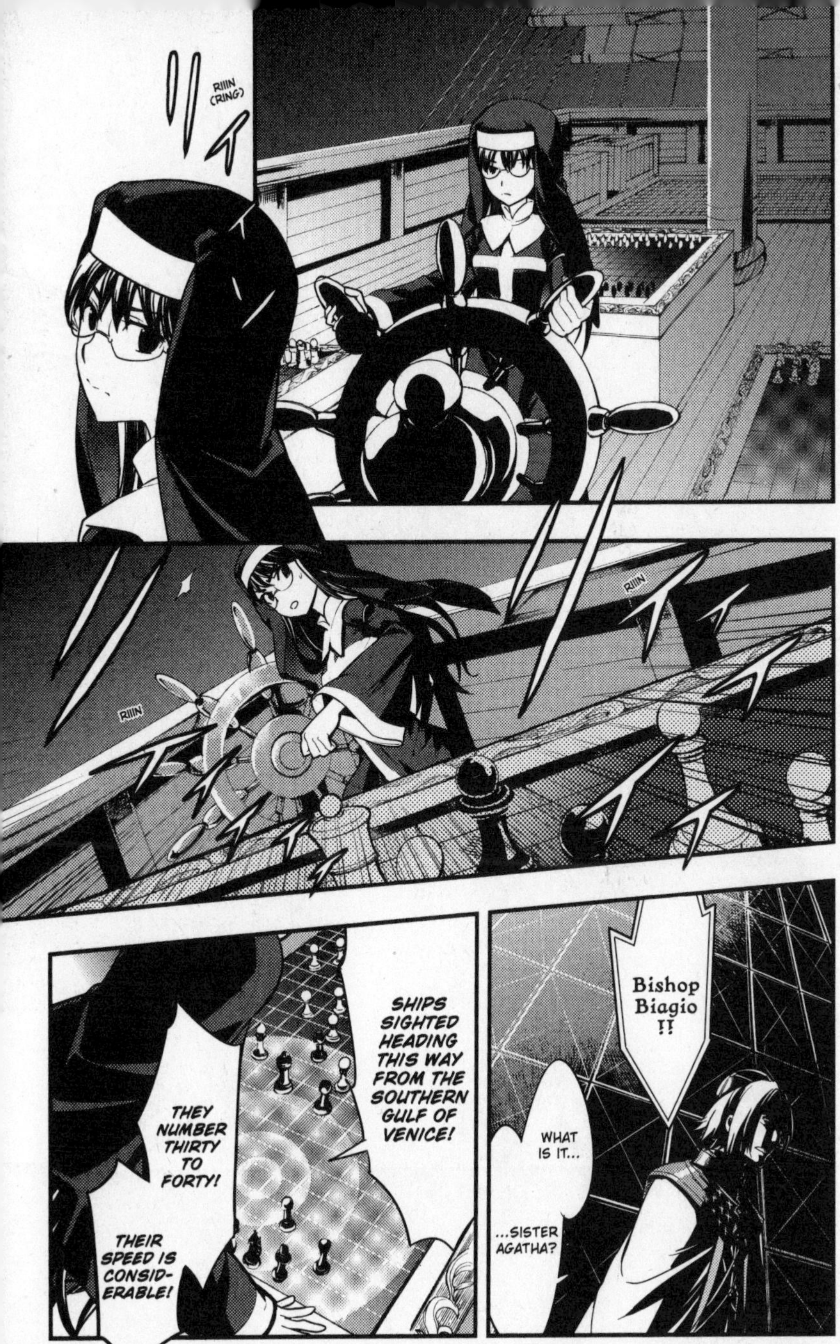
RIIIN (RING)
RIIIN
RIIIN
Bishop Biagio!!
WHAT IS IT...
...SISTER AGATHA?
SHIPS SIGHTED HEADING THIS WAY FROM THE SOUTHERN GULF OF VENICE!
THEY NUMBER THIRTY TO FORTY!
THEIR SPEED IS CONSIDERABLE!

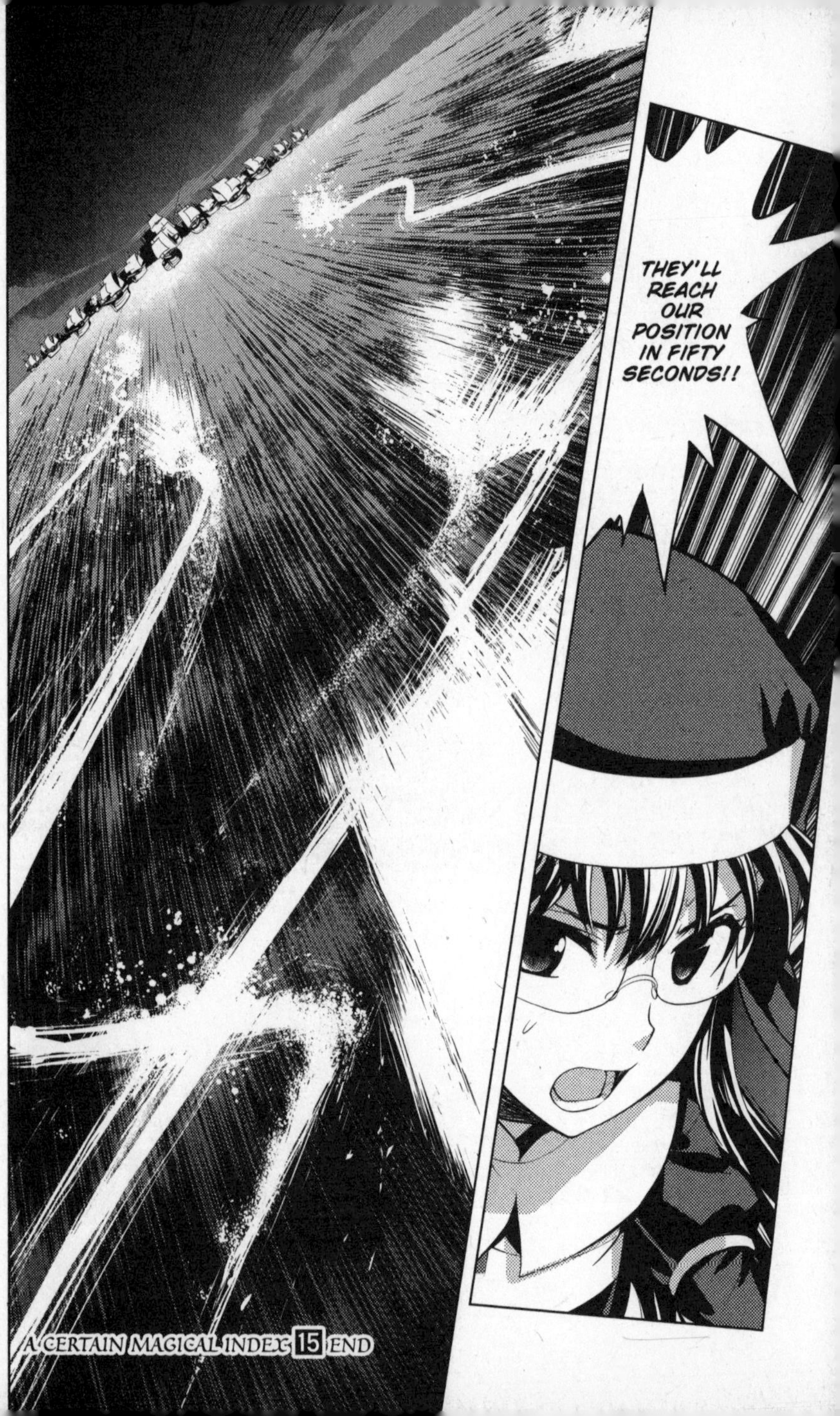
THEY'LL REACH OUR POSITION IN FIFTY SECONDS!!
A CERTAIN MAGICAL INDEX 15 END

A Certain Magical Index

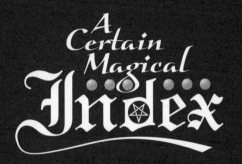

Dive into the latest light novels from *New York Times* bestselling author REKI KAWAHARA, creator of the fan favorite *SWORD ART ONLINE* and *ACCEL WORLD* series!

©REKI KAWAHARA    ILLUSTRATION: abec

**SWORD ART ONLINE Light Novels ▼**

©REKI KAWAHARA    ILLUSTRATION: abec

**SWORD ART ONLINE Manga ▼**

©REKI KAWAHARA/
TAMAKO NAKAMURA

©REKI KAWAHARA/TSUBASA HADUKI

©REKI KAWAHARA/NEKO NEKOBYOU

©REKI KAWAHARA/KISEKI HIMURA

©REKI KAWAHARA/CSY

©REKI KAWAHARA/TSUBASA HADUKI

©REKI KAWAHARA/KOUTAROU YAMADA

**abec Artworks ▶**

Featuring original, full color artwork from multiple *Sword Art Online* manga and light novels.
**A must for any *Sword Art Online* fan!**

©abec  ©REKI KAWAHARA

www.YenPress.com

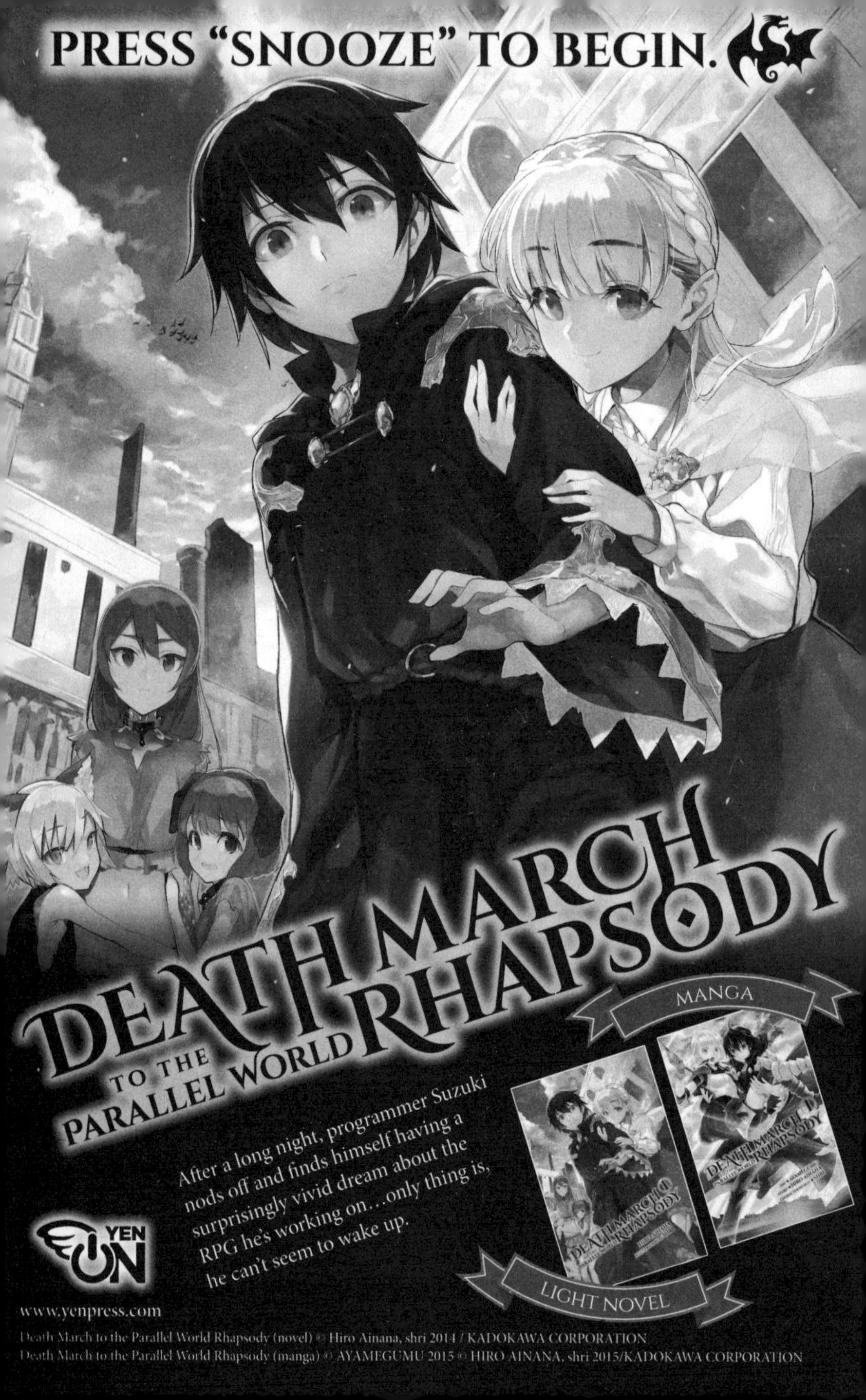
PRESS "SNOOZE" TO BEGIN.
DEATH MARCH
TO THE PARALLEL WORLD
RHAPSODY
MANGA
After a long night, programmer Suzuki nods off and finds himself having a surprisingly vivid dream about the RPG he's working on…only thing is, he can't seem to wake up.
LIGHT NOVEL
YEN ON
www.yenpress.com
Death March to the Parallel World Rhapsody (novel) © Hiro Ainana, shri 2014 / KADOKAWA CORPORATION
Death March to the Parallel World Rhapsody (manga) © AYAMEGUMU 2015 © HIRO AINANA, shri 2015/KADOKAWA CORPORATION

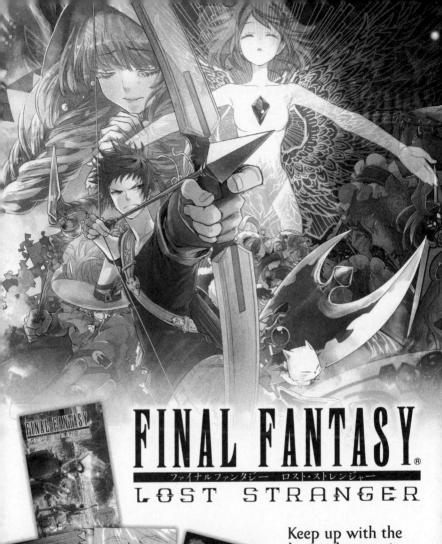

# FINAL FANTASY®
ファイナルファンタジー ロスト・ストレンジャー

## LOST STRANGER

Keep up with the latest chapters in the simul-pub version! Available now worldwide wherever e-books are sold!

For more information, visit www.yenpress.com

Yen Press

# A CERTAIN MAGICAL INDEX ⑮

Kazuma Kamachi
Kiyotaka Haimura
Chuya Kogino

## Translation: Andrew Prowse

## Lettering: Brndn Blakeslee

TOARU MAJYUTSU NO INDEX Vol. 15
© 2015 Kazuma Kamachi
© 2015 Chuya Kogino / SQUARE ENIX CO., LTD.
Licensed by KADOKAWA CORPORATION ASCII MEDIA WORKS
First published in Japan in 2015 by SQUARE ENIX CO., LTD.
English translation rights arranged with SQUARE ENIX CO., LTD.
and Yen Press, LLC through Tuttle-Mori Agency, Inc.

English translation © 2018 by SQUARE ENIX CO., LTD.

Yen Press
1290 Avenue of the Americas
New York, NY 10104

Visit us at yenpress.com
facebook.com/yenpress
twitter.com/yenpress
yenpress.tumblr.com
instagram.com/yenpress

First Yen Press Edition: October 2018

Yen Press is an imprint of Yen Press, LLC.
The Yen Press name and logo are trademarks of Yen Press, LLC.

Library of Congress Control Number: 2015373809

ISBN: 978-1-9753-5444-2 (paperback)

10 9 8 7 6 5 4 3 2 1

WOR

Printed in the United States of America